Leaders of the Opposition

Leaders of the Opposition

From Churchill to Cameron

Edited by

Timothy Heppell
Lecturer in British Politics, School of Politics and International Studies (POLIS), University of Leeds, UK

palgrave
macmillan

First published 2012 by
PALGRAVE MACMILLAN

Palgrave Macmillan in the UK is an imprint of Macmillan Publishers Limited, registered in England, company number 785998, of Houndmills, Basingstoke, Hampshire RG21 6XS.

Palgrave Macmillan in the US is a division of St Martin's Press LLC, 175 Fifth Avenue, New York, NY 10010.

Palgrave Macmillan is the global academic imprint of the above companies and has companies and representatives throughout the world.

Palgrave® and Macmillan® are registered trademarks in the United States, the United Kingdom, Europe and other countries.

ISBN 978–0–230–29647–3

This book is printed on paper suitable for recycling and made from fully managed and sustained forest sources. Logging, pulping and manufacturing processes are expected to conform to the environmental regulations of the country of origin.

A catalogue record for this book is available from the British Library.

A catalog record for this book is available from the Library of Congress.

10 9 8 7 6 5 4 3 2 1
21 20 19 18 17 16 15 14 13 12

Printed and bound in the United States of America
by Edwards Brothers Malloy, Inc.

Contents

Acknowledgements

I would like to thank the Centre for British Government within POLIS for providing funding for the opposition leadership event that took place at POLIS in July 2010. I would also like to thank the Political Studies Association (PSA) Specialist Group in Political Leadership for their backing and support for this project. Particular thanks must be given to the contributors, both for delivering their papers at the conference and for making my editorial role so straightforward. I would like to thank Amber Stone-Galilee and Liz Blackmore at Palgrave for their help and guidance throughout.

Dr Timothy Heppell,
Leeds, December 2011

Notes on Contributors

Tim Bale is Professor of Politics within the Department of Politics and Contemporary European Studies at the University of Sussex. He is the author of *The Conservative Party from Thatcher to Cameron* (Polity Press, 2010).

Peter Dorey is Reader in British Politics within the School of European Studies at the University of Cardiff. He is the author of *The Labour Party and Constitutional Reform: A History of Constitutional Conservatism* (Palgrave Macmillan, 2008) and editor of *The Labour Governments 1964–1970* (Routledge, 2006).

Nigel Fletcher is the founder and chairman of the Centre for Opposition Studies. He is currently researching a doctoral thesis on Parliamentary Opposition at Kings College London. He is the editor of *How to be in Opposition: Life in the Political Shadows* (Biteback, 2011).

Mark Garnett is Lecturer in British Politics within the Department of Politics and International Relations at the University of Lancaster. He has an extensive publishing record on Conservative Party politics, including co-authoring (with Andrew Denham) *Keith Joseph* (Acumen, 2001) and authoring *Splendid! Splendid! The Authorised Biography of William Whitelaw* (Jonathan Cape, 2002).

Ed Gouge is Senior Teaching Fellow within the School of Politics and International Studies (POLIS) at the University of Leeds. He co-authored *Life after Losing or Leaving* for the Association of Former Members of Parliament (2007) with Kevin Theakston and Victoria Honeyman.

Simon Griffiths is Lecturer in British Politics within the Department of Politics at Goldsmiths, University of London and a Senior Research Fellow at the Social Market Foundation. He is the co-editor (with Kevin Hickson) of *British Party Politics and Ideology after New Labour* (Palgrave Macmillan, 2009).

Richard Hayton is Senior Lecturer in Politics within the Division of Criminology, Politics and Sociology at the University of Huddersfield. He is the author of *Reconstructing Conservatism: The Conservatives in Opposition 1997–2010* (Manchester University Press, 2012).

Timothy Heppell is Lecturer in British Politics within the School of Politics and International Studies (POLIS) at the University of Leeds. He is the author of *Choosing the Tory Leader: From Heath to Cameron* (I. B. Tauris, 2008) and *Choosing the Labour Leader: From Wilson to Brown* (I. B. Tauris, 2010).

Michael Hill is Lecturer in British Politics within the Department of Education and Social Sciences at the University of Central Lancashire. He has published on Conservative Party politics and party leadership selection.

Victoria Honeyman is Lecturer in British Politics within the School of Politics and International Studies (POLIS) at the University of Leeds. She is the author of *Richard Crossman: A Reforming Radical of the Labour Party* (I. B. Tauris, 2007).

Stuart McAnulla is Lecturer in British Politics within the School of Politics and International Studies (POLIS) at the University of Leeds. He is the co-author of *Post War British Politics in Perspective* (Polity Press, 1999) and the author of *British Politics: A Critical Introduction* (Continuum, 2006).

Stephen Meredith is Principal Lecturer in British Politics within the Department of Education and Social Sciences at the University of Central Lancashire. He is the author of *Labours Old and New: The Parliamentary Right of the British Labour Party 1970–79 and the Roots of New Labour* (Manchester University Press, 2008).

Philip Norton (Lord Norton of Louth) is Professor of British Politics and Director of the Centre for Legislative Studies, within the Department of Politics and International Studies at the University of Hull. He is the author of 27 books covering British politics, the constitution, the Conservative Party and legislatures in comparative perspectives. He was elevated to the House of Lords in 1998. He has served as chairman to the House of Lords Select Committee on the Constitution.

Mark Stuart is a Research Fellow within the School of Politics and International Relations at the University of Nottingham. He is the author of *Douglas Hurd: The Public Servant* (Mainstream, 1998) and *John Smith: A Life* (Politicos, 2005).

Kevin Theakston is Professor of British Government within the School of Politics and International Studies (POLIS) at the University of Leeds. He has published ten books, including *Winston Churchill and the British Constitution* (Politicos, 2004) and *After Number Ten: Former Prime Ministers in British Politics* (Palgrave Macmillan, 2010).

1
Introduction

Timothy Heppell

There is a substantive body of academic work on British Prime Ministers, with regular chronologically organised and thematically driven books being published, including notable contributions from Peter Hennessy (2000), Richard Rose (2001), Michael Foley (2000) and Dick Leonard (2005). In recent years, academics working on British political leadership have developed new areas of focus in terms of the career trajectory of British Prime Ministers. Recognising the famous comment of Anthony King in the aftermath of the fall of Margaret Thatcher that the role of Prime Minister is 'a party job before it is a government job' (King, 1991: 25), there has been a growth in academic research on party leadership selection (see, for example, Denham and O'Hara, 2008; Heppell, 2008a, 2010a). In addition to the increasing emphasis on how they acquire access to the party leadership and thereby the opportunity to be Prime Minister, such research also places a considerable focus on the ejection process. With this in mind, an interesting addition to the Prime Ministerial studies literature has been the recent study by Kevin Theakston on how former Prime Ministers utilise their status and influence once they leave Downing Street (Theakston, 2010).

What is interesting to note within this emphasis on the career trajectory of Prime Ministers is the limited academic focus on their time as Leader of the Opposition. While many post-war Prime Ministers have entered Downing Street from within Government, those that do so are not in the upper echelons of Prime Ministerial rankings. Of the six in this category only Harold Macmillan (1957–63) represents a relative success, whereas Anthony Eden (1955–7), Alec Douglas-Home (1963–4), James Callaghan (1976–9), John Major (1990–7) and more recently Gordon Brown (2007–10) have fallen into the relegation zone of the Prime Ministerial league table (Theakston and Gill, 2006, 2011). Of the remaining post-war Prime Ministers, many were propelled into (or back into) Downing Street after a period as Leader of the Opposition – Winston Churchill (Prime Minister 1940–5 and 1951–5; Leader of the Opposition 1945–51), Harold Wilson

(Prime Minister 1964–70 and 1974–6; Leader of the Opposition 1963–4 and 1970–4), Edward Heath (Prime Minister 1970–4; Leader of the Opposition 1965–70 and 1974–5), Margaret Thatcher (Prime Minister 1979–90; Leader of the Opposition 1975–9), Tony Blair (Prime Minister 1997–2007; Leader of the Opposition 1994–7) and David Cameron (Prime Minister 2010–; Leader of the Opposition 2005–10). Clement Attlee served as Leader of the Opposition until 1955 after being Prime Minister (1945–51) but failed to regain office, as did Edward Heath in 1974–5. Douglas-Home (1963–4) and Callaghan (1979–80) endured brief spells as Leader of the Opposition after the ignominy of being rejected by the electorate, but unlike Attlee and Heath they never actually won a General Election in their own right. The humiliation of electoral rejection for Major prompted his resignation and a brief seven-week period carrying out the role of Leader of the Opposition with minimal enthusiasm and even less public notice. Brown resigned as Labour leader as soon as Labour lost office and thus avoided the role altogether.

With the exception of Eden, Macmillan, Major and Brown, most Prime Ministers have experienced being Leader of the Opposition, either en route to Downing Street or elder statesmanship. We also need to consider those who were Leader of the Opposition but failed to become Prime Minister. Hugh Gaitskell (1955–63) and John Smith (1992–4) were both thought to have been on the brink of becoming Prime Minister before their untimely deaths. The reputations of Michael Foot (1980–3), Neil Kinnock (1983–92), William Hague (1997–2001), Iain Duncan Smith (2001–3) and Michael Howard (2003–5) are undermined by their failure to make the transition from Leader of the Opposition to Prime Minister. Only time will tell if the recently elected Labour Party leader and current Leader of the Opposition Ed Miliband is the next Neil Kinnock or Tony Blair.

How important to Prime Ministerial tenures is the preparatory time spent as Leader of the Opposition? How difficult is it as a former Prime Minister to serve as Leader of the Opposition? Why is it that some Leaders of the Opposition fail to become Prime Minister – can that failure be in any way attributed to their political leadership limitations? This edited collection seeks to address such questions, and in doing so begin the process of addressing the previous neglect of Opposition leadership studies.

This edited collection is based on the fact that Opposition politics matters. It is a central feature of the British political system and intrinsic to British democratic society (Jennings, 1961: 16; N. Johnson, 1997: 236; Norton, 2008: 236). The contributors to this edited collection believe that studying Opposition politics, and the role of Leader of the Opposition specifically, is necessary for four clear reasons:

1. The Opposition plays a vital role of scrutiny and agenda-setting, holding the Government of the day to account, and how well they do this is a hugely important democratic issue.

2. Any political party entering Government will have spent a considerable time in Opposition, forming their policy programme and making preparations for assuming office.
3. How they conduct this process and how successful they are during this period will therefore have a major effect on them as a future Government.
4. There is the raw political issue of how Opposition parties win power, and, just as importantly, why some do not.

Opposition politics is institutionalised within and beyond Parliament. Within Parliament, the Leader of the Opposition, the Shadow Cabinet and shadow ministerial teams act as a Government and Prime Minister in waiting. The process of acting as the alternative Government makes a major contribution to their preparation for office (N. Johnson, 1997: 495). To the wider electorate political argument and debate is shaped by the Government – Opposition relationship (N. Johnson, 1997: 496). Oppositions need to take care in how they approach critiquing the Government – the electorate can become cynical about opportunistic conduct which is seen as partisan and self serving. The art of Opposition is to offer constructive criticism, which highlights the folly of Government policy and thinking, and the merits of their alternative approach (N. Johnson, 1997: 498).

On the more generalised role that Opposition politics plays within the British political system, and specifically how to be an effective party of Opposition, we can now benefit from the edited collection from the Centre for Opposition Studies edited by Nigel Fletcher (Fletcher, 2011; see also Punnett, 1973). By comparison, and to complement that study, this edited collection will explicitly focus on Leaders of the Opposition, considering both the circumstances, whether they be constraining or enhancing, and the performance of each of the Leaders of the Opposition, from Churchill to Cameron.

This involves case-study profiles of sixteen Leaders of the Opposition. Excluded from analysis are the following. As mentioned above, Major was briefly Leader of the Opposition from May to late June 1997 as the Conservative Party set about electing a new leader after Major announced his intention to leave the stage after the curtain came down at the General Election. Given the short time frame of seven weeks, and the knowledge throughout that this was temporary there was no need to include him in the study. The Labour Party has had three short-term temporary party leaders who have held the post briefly as they were the deputy leader of the party and were required to act as party leader before the formal election of a new party leader. Between January and February 1963 George Brown was acting Labour leader and thus briefly Leader of the Opposition in the time between the death of Gaitskell and the election of Wilson. Between May and July 1994 Margaret Beckett was in a similar position to Brown following the death of John Smith and the election of Tony Blair. Both Brown and Beckett were candidates for the leadership while also acting as party leader and performing the role of acting Leader of the Opposition.

The final temporary leader excluded is Harriet Harman. She held the position between May and September 2010, after the immediate resignation of Gordon Brown and before the election of Ed Miliband. Unlike George Brown and Beckett, Harman was not a candidate for the party leadership while acting as party leader and Leader of the Opposition.

In addition to the exclusion of Major, Brown, Beckett and Harman as temporary Leaders of the Opposition, we have also excluded Ed Miliband. This is for two reasons. First, at the time of our conference (July 2010) Labour was still in the process of selecting their new party leader, and second, it may be too early to make clearly defined judgements on Miliband's effectiveness in a role that he will presumably occupy until 2015.

To ensure a degree of overall coherence to our analysis of our selected sixteen case-studies, each Leader of the Opposition will be evaluated against the following criteria:

1. Their proficiency as a public communicator
   This relates to their ability to effectively communicate their views, policies and strategy both internally within their own party and externally to the electorate. It is concerned with how well they interact through various means – be that through Parliament, Party Conference or television – to establish a connection that enables them to gain an image of competence that will ultimately aid their chances of electoral success.
2. Their construction of a public policy platform
   This concerns their ability to construct a long-term policy agenda that shores up the support internally of parliamentarians and activists while reaching out to a sufficient section of the electorate to maximise the chances of electoral success. In balancing those competing interests, does the public policy platform that they construct sound feasible – that is, will it allow them to govern competently if they are elected?
3. Their abilities at party management
   Recognising the old maxim that the electorate will punish divided parties, it is essential that a party that aspires to government can demonstrate unity. Being in Opposition is evidence of political failure, either losing power or failing to regain it, and in these circumstances avoiding internal disputes about overall strategy and specific policy issues is one of the primary challenges for a Leader of the Opposition.
4. Their emotional intelligence
   Any politician with the ambition to acquire the position of Leader of the Opposition will find the position immensely frustrating. They want power to enable them to implement their policy agenda and their ideological vision. How do they cope emotionally with that exclusion from power and the criticism they are subjected to from those in power,

from those critical voices from within their own party, and from political commentators? Do they have the emotional intelligence to separate criticism that is constructive and worthy of recognition from that which should be dismissed? Failure to do so will diminish their effectiveness in the role and raise question marks about their suitability as a potential Prime Minister.

The criteria selected are partly influenced by a number of leadership personality traits that impact upon US Presidential performance, as outlined in the work of Fred Greenstein (Greenstein, 2001, 2009). Three of the criteria listed here relate to Greenstein's – public communication; public policy vision; and emotional intelligence. Three of his other criteria – organisational skill; political skills; and cognitive style – are not explicitly defined within our framework. Organisational skill is specifically orientated around the inner workings of the Presidency and is excluded, while our study blends together cognitive style with emotional intelligence. Rather than utilise the political skills criteria we prefer to utilise the term 'party management', which seems more in suiting to the demands of British party political leadership than the US Presidency.

Theakston has argued that the Greenstein criteria can be transferred and applied to the British Prime Minister, providing there is sufficient recognition of the altered contexts (Theakston, 2007, 2011). Embracing this argument on its transferability, this edited book utilises an amended version of the Greenstein model, on the basis that if it can be applied to the British Prime Minister, it can a useful analytical framework through which to examine those who seek to become Prime Minister – that is, Leaders of the Opposition. In making that case we are arguing that the Greenstein model has had wide appeal and influence because it is seen as accessible, coherent and offers a solid historical understanding, (in our case of the role of Leader of the Opposition), and in doing so it can offer clear insights into the qualities of those who have sought the highest office.

With Leaders of the Opposition aspiring to be Prime Minister then assessing them as individual political leaders against a framework that can be applied to Prime Ministerial leadership is a valid approach. Each contributor has therefore assessed their Leader of the Opposition against the criteria outlined above. To try and ensure a degree of coherence contributors were asked to orientate their analysis around the themes in an explicit manner, although editorially there was no attempt to impose a set order in which the criteria should be assessed. So the case-studies amount to thematically driven rather than chronologically organised accounts. There is, however, one exception to this and for good reasons. This is the case of Edward Heath. While Churchill and Wilson lost office, served as Leader of the Opposition, and then resumed office and later retired as Prime Minister, Heath's circumstances were different. Churchill had one period as Leader of the Opposition while Wilson had two, but what united them both was the ultimate success in reclaiming power. Heath had two periods as Leader of the Opposition. The first period between 1965 and 1970 was successful in that he won the General Election of 1970. The second period between March 1974 and February 1975 was unsuccessful in that he failed to reclaim power at the October 1974 General Election, and was then forcibly evicted from the Conservative Party leadership by rule changes that permitted a challenge to him. As the Heath circumstances are unique, the chapter by Mark Garnett on his experiences as Leader of the Opposition is chronologically organised. The criteria are incorporated into that analysis, but not in the explicit manner that is evident in the other chapters.

The accounts provided will give a clear insight into the constraints and opportunities offered to Leaders of the Opposition within British politics. The following sixteen case-studies will evaluate the context and skills of post-war Leaders of the Opposition, through which the Conclusion will be able to outline: (1) the changing role of Leader of the Opposition; and (2) the factors that make for a successful Leader of the Opposition. Before beginning, though, it might be worth reflecting on the recent comments of two former Leaders of the Opposition, one who was successful in pursuit of the keys to Downing Street, and one who was not. One year before becoming Prime Minister David Cameron commented upon the futility of Opposition: 'those who hold an opposition post tend of course to have one thing in common: they don't want to hold it much longer' (Cameron, 2009). Conversely, the longest-serving Leader of the Opposition in the post-war era, Neil Kinnock, made the following comment, which Ed Miliband should note: 'opposition can be hell ... but the lessons you learn whilst you're there are hugely important – if you learn them' (Kinnock, 2010). Hopefully, by reading the following case-studies the reader will get a sense of what those lessons are, who failed to learn from them, and who did and why.

2
Winston Churchill, 1945–51

Kevin Theakston

Even though there is no single historical pattern to which a Leader of the Opposition has been expected to conform, Winston Churchill was an unusual Leader of the Opposition for the six years he held that position, 1945–51. He did not enjoy opposition very much (Gilbert, 1988: 163), and he found it difficult to adapt himself to his new role (Macmillan, 1969: 41), which he performed in a distinctive, not to say idiosyncratic, way. Although the Conservatives subsequently returned to office, most accounts of their time in Opposition suggest that their recovery occurred despite Churchill rather than because of him (Ramsden, 1995b: 117). Churchill's performance, approach and leadership style as Leader of the Opposition has been criticised as ineffective (Rhodes James, quoted in Mayer, 1992: 1) and variously described as: 'olympian' (Ramsden, 1995a: 179), 'semi-detached' (Addison, 2005: 217), 'relaxed' (Robbins, 1992: 158), 'absentee' (Ball, 2001: 326), 'erratic' (K. Morgan, 1984: 286), 'loose-rein' (Ramsden, 1995a: 182), as a 'figurehead role' (Ramsden, 1995b: 109) and as 'negligent and often inept' (Carlton, 1981: 293). Only Mayer (1992: 162) and Ball (2001: 326, 330) really give him credit for the contribution he made to the party during the Opposition years and rate him as an effective Leader of the Opposition.

Prime Ministers who stay on as the Leader of the Opposition after an election defeat often do not last long in that new role or impress in it. Nine nineteenth-century Premiers had two or more non-consecutive terms in that office. But only four Premiers serving entirely in the twentieth century managed to hang on to the party leadership after losing a General Election and going into Opposition, before then coming back for another term in Downing Street, with only two of these cases since the Second World War: Churchill and Harold Wilson (Theakston, 2010: 3). And Churchill differed from Wilson in that the scale of his defeat in 1945 compared to 1970 was greater and the way back was longer, taking two General Elections and six years.

Churchill was different in another way too in that he was almost a part-time Leader of the Opposition for much of this period. He had 'plenty of other things to do' (Macmillan, 1969: 40): working with a team of assistants and researchers on his multi-volume and immensely lucrative war memoirs; painting pictures; undertaking a great deal of foreign travel. Despite his election defeat and being out of office, 'as a world statesmen he grew in stature after the war' (Addison, 1992: 386). He came to seem a figure almost 'above and beyond British politics' (Ramsden, 1977: 415). His memoirs and his headline-grabbing and agenda-setting speeches and interventions in the USA and in European politics helped to boost his world reputation, feed a personality cult and put him in different (and higher) league than other British politicians in a way unique for a Leader of the Opposition (Ramsden, 1995a: 180).

Public communication

Churchill is remembered for his famous speeches on the international stage during these Opposition years – at Fulton, Zurich and Strasbourg. Other Conservative politicians were often unhappy about his pronouncements about the 'Iron Curtain', the threat from Soviet expansionism and the need for European unity when he made these speeches, but as events moved on his warnings about Stalin could be seen as prescient and fitted into a narrative about his role in the 1930s (Ramsden, 1995b: 109–10). However, in all only about one in eight of his speeches in the 1945–51 period was delivered outside the UK (30 out of 252, with only two of these in 1950 and none in 1951). Of the rest, slightly more were made outside Parliament than in it (118 to 104), the majority of his speeches in the country being made in the last three years of Opposition, with very few in the first two years out of office (calculated from Rhodes James, 1974). But it is difficult to cite a speech on domestic political issues that had as much impact (then or later) as the ones on international issues (Ramsden, 1977: 414). It is striking that between 1945 and 1947 Churchill took part in none of the Parliamentary debates over the Labour Government's key nationalisation, social insurance or health service measures (Addison, 1992: 390).

'On a good day', says Addison (1992: 388), 'Churchill was still a great parliamentarian.' He could make powerful, fighting speeches that went down well on his own side at least, and always liked a good House of Commons ding-dong argument, though some Tories felt that he was liable to go over the top (Ball, 1999: 494, 498, 517, 528, 530, 535; Catterall, 2003: 26, 36, 52; Nicolson, 1968: 114). Hoffman put it well:

A brilliantly delivered harangue of the Government's policy by Winston Churchill might have – and often did have – the desired effect on the Press Gallery, but within the narrower parliamentary context, the speech might be regarded, even by some of his own party, as a wild, unreasonable, and perhaps embarrassing display, whose only contribution was to unite a divided government party.

(Hoffman, 1964: 222)

'Total war', commented Hoffman (1964: 222) 'is not always effective opposition'.

In any case, Churchill's set-piece Parliamentary speeches could sometimes be too ponderous, lengthy and stylised to be effective. The more pedestrian Attlee – dry, astringent, precise, unemotional, matter-of-fact – could often cut Churchill down to size and score tactical debating victories (Macmillan, 1969: 41–2, 50; Kilmuir, 1964: 141–2). Churchill's speeches were often better received outside Parliament, at big public meetings or Party Conferences where he could 'enliven the ... faithful' (Ramsden, 1995b: 110).

Churchill played a less prominent role in communicating the Tory message and in the party's campaigns during the 1950 and 1951 General Election campaigns than in 1945. 'He was careful not to repeat the personal barnstorming of 1945 ... and realised that he must be careful about his broadcasts' (Ramsden, 1995a: 215–16). Attlee made extensive election tours and addressed a large number of meetings, but not Churchill. In the 1951 election he actually spoke less than any other leading figure in the campaign, making only five important speeches outside his constituency and two in it (D. Butler, 1952: 99–100). In 1950 he made two of the party's eight radio broadcasts (Nicholas, 1951: 127) and in 1951 only one of the six (D. Butler, 1952: 63); in 1945 he had made four out of the ten Tory broadcasts. He got big audiences (bigger than Attlee's), and his 1951 broadcast was judged to be the best of the campaign and perhaps his 'finest personal effort since the war' (D. Butler, 1952: 66–7). The Shadow Cabinet overruled his wish in 1951 to give one of the Conservative broadcast slots to Violet Bonham-Carter, though Churchill went off and made a hustings speech for the redoubtable Liberal *grande dame* who was contesting Colne Valley (the local Conservatives, at his urging, not running a candidate against her – in the event she lost to Labour). Churchill was not an enthusiast for television, and it was Eden who made the first Conservative television election broadcast, a stilted and scripted interview during the 1951 campaign ('spontaneity was lacking', noted D. Butler [1952: 76–77]).

Public policy platform

Churchill was opposed to policy-making in Opposition. His view was that 'when an Opposition spells out its policy in detail ... the Government becomes the Opposition and attacks the Opposition which becomes the Government. So, having failed to win the sweets of office, it fails equally to enjoy the benefits of being out of office' (R. A. Butler, 1971: 135). The main task of the Opposition was 'criticising and correcting, so far as they can, any errors and shortcomings [in government measures]'. He argued that 'the Opposition are not responsible for proposing integrated and complicated measures of policy. Sometimes we do, but it is not our obligation' (HC Debates, 12/9/1950, col. 972). 'The job of the leader of the Opposition', he told Lord Moran, was 'to attack the Government – that and no more' (Moran, 1968: 354). This echoed the dictum of his father, Lord Randolph Churchill, that 'the constitutional function of an Opposition is to oppose and not support the Government' (Rhodes James, 1978: 72). 'It is danger-ous to prescribe until you are called in', Churchill insisted to the 1922 Committee in 1947 (Goodhart, 1973: 143). 'I do not believe in looking about for some panacea or cure-all on which we should stake our credit and our fortunes', he declared at the 1946 Party Conference, 'and which we should try to sell in a hurry like a patent medicine to all and sundry' (Ramsden, 1995a: 142). 'It would not be wise for us to bind ourselves to a rigid programme of exactly what we should do', he argued the following year (Addison, 1992: 395).

Having long experience of the ups and downs of politics, some of this was rooted in a feeling that it was Governments that lost elections rather than Oppositions that won them. Coming up with new policy ideas or pro-grammes would avail little until the Government began to make mistakes, lose its way, run out of steam, became unpopular or was hit by adverse events (Robbins, 1992: 158). He did not want to create possible hostages to fortune, pre-empt future choices or to tie his hands unnecessarily. 'More interested in politics than policy' (Addison, 1992: 397), he was a reactive and pragmatic leader who did not get very directly involved in Opposition policy-making himself, leaving the running to others, and doing little to shape in a positive way the direction the Tory Party took in Opposition (Ramsden, 1995b: 112). But this is not to say that he was irrelevant to the remaking of Conservative policy or had no influence; in some ways the role he played was a crucial one.

Churchill's frequent and strong attacks on 'socialism' and on bureaucracy, nationalisation, mismanagement, red tape, queues, shortages and ration-ing in these years may have distracted attention away from the point that he actually led the Conservative Party from a centre ground position. He did not personally oppose measures like Bank of England nationalisation, and parts of Labour's programme, he argued, derived from the work of his wartime coalition government or built on the pre-1914 welfare reforms he could claim association with (Ramsden, 1995a: 138). But as Stuart Ball puts it, Churchill was

a vital part of the equation in 1945–51 – not least because his role and contributions did not duplicate the style and activities of his colleagues. His known reluctance to move too far to the left was reassurance to the party mainstream, which was always dubious about the novel panaceas offered by bright young men. At the same time Churchill wanted to win, and was willing to make the compromises necessary to do so.

(Ball, 2001: 326)

He helped open the way for rethinking and for changes of policy while keeping the party broadly united (Ramsden, 1977: 415). And it is arguable that criticisms of austerity and attacks on Labour's failings, linked to Churchill's call to 'set the people free', did at least as much as reassurance on welfare and full employment to bring back voters (especially women) to the Conservatives in 1950, so vindicating his general strategy (Ball, 2001: 326; Zweiniger-Bargielowska, 1994).

The 'facilitator and impresario' of Opposition policy-making, and the person 'who really put drive and coherence into the policy exercise' was, of course, Rab Butler, who ran the key committees and was chairman of the reconstituted Research Department. Mayer (1992: 162–3) cites the selection of Butler to chart a new policy direction, and of Woolton to rebuild the party organisation, as evidence of Churchill's successful Opposition leadership, but in fact neither were his own first choices for those roles. Churchill had actually wanted to put his son-in-law Duncan Sandys in charge of the Research Department but had been stopped by the Shadow Cabinet (Ramsden, 1995a: 144–5).

In the first year of opposition, Churchill's only positive proposal was to change the name of the party from Conservative to the 'Union Party', a label under which would gather, he argued in 1946, 'Conservative Unionists, Liberal Unionists, Trade Unionists or Labour Unionists' (Ramsden, 1995a: 198). Woolton supported the idea (Woolton, 1959: 335), and Macmillan backed a change to the 'National Democratic Party', but there was widespread scepticism and opposition to a change of name within the Shadow Cabinet, the 1922 Committee and the wider party. The name change fitted with a wider Churchill strategy of trying to foster anti-socialist unity, something he returned to later when he pushed for an arrangement with the Liberals, again meeting opposition within his own party.

Policy renewal in the shape of the famous 'Industrial Charter' of 1947 owed little, if anything, to Churchill. He had in fact tried to resist pressure from within the party (from within the Shadow Cabinet and from activists, the party in the country and the Conference), building up through 1946, for a restatement of party policy. He gave the Industrial Policy Committee he was forced to set up, chaired by Butler, instructions to avoid detailed policy, and the Charter was more about principles than promises (Ball, 2001: 326) or what Butler called 'impressionism' (Ramsden, 1977: 422), but it marked the party's coming to terms with the mixed-economy welfare state and, crucially, sealed it off from its pre-war past (Howard, 1987: 156). Churchill did not display conspicuous enthusiasm for the initiative – as R. A. Butler (1971: 145) commented, 'his ultimate imprimatur was not so much obtained as divined'. Eden doubted that Churchill had even read the Charter (Rhodes James, 1986: 329). The Shadow Cabinet meeting that gave approval to it was chaired by Eden, not Churchill (Ramsden, 1995a: 155). When Reginald Maudling, from the Research Department, gave the leader a draft paragraph about it for his conference speech, Churchill is supposed to have said, 'but I do not agree with a word of this', only to sigh 'oh well, leave it in' when it was explained that that was what the conference had adopted, before going on to read it out with a studied coolness (Maudling, 1978: 45–6). The right complained about 'pink socialism' but its opposition had little effect. Churchill was detached from the whole process, but securing his formal endorsement of it as leader was crucial and, as Willetts (2005: 179) says, 'had the charter received a hostile response it could easily have been abandoned before ever becoming party policy'.

Churchill had not changed his basic stance on policy-making but further unrest, internal party criticism and a crisis of confidence in his leadership after the poor showing in the 1949 South Hammersmith by-election meant that he had to give way to renewed demands for a full and detailed state-ment of policy. It was necessary for him also to promise the 1922 Committee that henceforth he would 'clear his own personal decks' and throw his ener-gies into the coming election fight (Goodhart, 1973: 147). He was more involved in the production of 'The Right Road for Britain' than he had been in the 'Industrial Charter', but in terms of drafting and language rather than policy content. He then went on to have a major input into the writing of the manifesto for the 1950 election, 'This is the Road' (Ramsden, 1995a: 160–2). In 1951 he was, says Addison (1992: 405), still hoping 'to win the election with broad statements of principle and a bare minimum of detailed policy ... "We are seeking to build a lighthouse rather than dress a shop-window."' There was both a 2,600-word personal Churchill manifesto and a longer party policy statement, 'Britain Strong and Free'. Churchill said that he wanted to 'proclaim a theme rather than write a prospectus' (Hoffman, 1964: 206). But he did not intend to abandon or reverse the main thrust of the post-1947 policy rethink, and his aim was always more that of 'keep-ing options open on timing and priorities' (Ramsden, 1995a: 167). Specific detailed policy interventions by him were the exception rather than the rule, but included the insistence in 1951 on a war profits tax (Ramsden, 1995b: 114) and the ruling out of legislation affecting trade unions (Addison, 1992: 406). However, he was careful about making promises during the 1951 campaign, describing his cautious approach as 'housing, red meat and not getting scuppered' (Ramsden, 1995a: 228).

Party management

In terms of the Conservative Party front bench, the Parliamentary Party and the party organisation, Churchill had immense authority and prestige but was not himself much concerned with the details and practicalities of party management, which he left to others.

The Conservatives had a strong and capable front bench team, with heavyweight figures like Eden, Butler, Salisbury, Macmillan, Crookshank, Oliver Stanley, Oliver Lyttelton, David Maxwell-Fyfe, James Stuart and Lord Woolton as well as Churchill intimates like Bracken and Cherwell. The Shadow Cabinet – more properly, the Leader's Consultative Committee, and referred to by Churchill as 'the shadows' – seems to have had initially only eleven members but it soon grew and numbered twenty-two by 1948 (Ramsden, 1995a: 183, 198). There was no formalised and announced allocation of responsibilities to a long list of 'shadow ministers' and a rigidly organised opposition team, such as became the norm in later decades. Although some Conservatives concentrated on particular issues (for instance, Eden on foreign affairs, and Stanley, Macmillan, Lyttelton and Butler on financial and economic policy), there was 'no precise or exclusive designation' (Macmillan, 1969: 44), and frontbenchers would range over a number of subjects in dealing with bills and debates in parliament. 'Out of office let them wander free and unencumbered' was how Macmillan described Churchill's philosophy. Rather than preparing for power by specialising in one area, the effect was to give the leading and rising figures experience on a broader front. It meant also that Shadow Ministers would or could not expect a particular job when the party got back into office (Eden probably excepted). Churchill very much wanted to keep control and discretion over eventual Cabinet appointments, and did not feel that concentrating on a particular subject in Opposition should translate into the same post in Government (Seldon, 1981: 76).

The Shadow Cabinet generally met weekly on Wednesday evenings in the Leader of the Opposition's room in the Commons. But Churchill often did not attend (Punnett, 1973: 52), Eden then chairing the meetings. Churchill, says Ball (2004: 275), 'was determined that senior members of the party would continue to be defined by their relationship to him rather than as a corporate body in which he was merely first among equals'. Between the 1950 and 1951 General Elections, the Shadow Cabinet met only fortnightly, with an inner group (of eleven) meeting in the intervening weeks (Ramsden, 1995a: 183). More to Churchill's taste, perhaps, were the fortnightly lunches for the Tory high command at the Savoy – which he called his 'advance battle headquarters' – where large amounts of food and alcohol were consumed and there was as much social as political talk, with the Great Man indulging his love of monologues, afterwards having a nap (Kilmuir, 1964: 149–50). Much of the donkey work was handled by the Business Committee, composed of the officers of the 1922 Committee and the officers of the Tory backbench subject committees, meeting usually before the Shadow Cabinet with Eden (or Butler) in the chair to decide Parliamentary business and tactics and to allocate speakers.

'Winston wants to run the opposition himself, in his own way, and does not intend to allow anyone to interfere or oppose him', complained Salisbury (Ball, 2004: 275). Churchill's approach did not help the coordination of policy and – ever the individualist rather than the team-player – he would sometimes leave to the last moment a decision as to whether he would intervene and speak in a particular debate, without necessarily consulting his colleagues about the line he was going to take (Addison, 1992: 390; Howard, 1987: 15). In 1948 Macmillan wrote to Churchill proposing a more methodical and businesslike system, with a secretary, agenda, papers and minutes for the Shadow Cabinet and a 'small management committee – comparable to the War Cabinet' to pull together policy-making (composed of Churchill, Eden, Salisbury, the Leader in the Lords, and the Chief Whip). Eden and Woolton agreed with Macmillan but Churchill would have none of it. 'It would be a great mistake to formalise the loose and unsubstantial association which governs the work of an Opposition', he insisted. 'I propose to continue with the present system as long as I am in charge' (Ramdsen, 1995a: 184; Kandiah, 1992: 121–22).

As far as Conservative backbenchers (nearly half of whom were new to Parliament) were concerned, Churchill could seem pretty remote. Clementine Churchill eventually organised a series of lunches to which all Conservative MPs were invited, usually half a dozen at a time, as a gesture towards bridging the gap between leader and Parliamentary followers (Ramsden 1995a: 179; Ball, 1999: 608–9; Gilbert, 1988: 461). The Parliamentary Party was demoralised, unhappy and divided (over tactics and policy) in the aftermath of defeat; there was a damaging and embarrassing split in December 1945 in the vote on the American loan, when 118 MPs followed Churchill's orders to abstain, but 71 rebelled and voted against and eight actually voted with Labour in favour (Addison, 1992: 388–9). Backbenchers were sometimes 'restive' (Macmillan, 1969: 287) and critical of Churchill's lax attendance and the time he gave to his memoirs and international speeches rather than to politics at home. Headlam noted (in February 1949) an 'undercurrent of discontent in the party about Winston's leadership', adding that 'the truth is that he is not, and never has been, a party man. He has always been much too interested in himself to run a party' (Ball, 1999: 574). There were complaints and strong criticism directed at the leader from the 1922 Committee at the end of 1945 and again in 1949. But as Goodhart (1973: 148) put it: 'the 1922 Committee ... was prepared to bark at Mr Churchill in his presence, but the great majority of Members had no desire to bite or to seek to force an early retirement of their Leader'.

Although Churchill had always been wary of the Conservative Party machine and suspicious of Central Office – keeping it at arm's length when he became Prime Minister in 1940 – and had limited interest in organisational matters (Ramsden, 1995a: 110), he recognised that it would need rebuilding, reorganising and reinvigorating after the 1945 defeat (Kandiah,

1992: 49). The first steps had been taken under the chairmanship of Ralph Assheton, but Churchill wanted a more dynamic personality at the helm (Addison, 1992: 390). He hoped to shoehorn a friend or acolyte into control of the machine, but his plan to get Oliver Lyttelton to lead an organisational inquiry, and then to replace Assheton with Macmillan as Party Chairman, was blocked by Eden, though he vetoed Eden's own candidate, Jim Thomas, who remained Vice Chairman. Woolton, who became Party Chairman in 1946, was thus a compromise figure but turned out to be an inspired appointment, firing up the Tory activists and spearheading much-needed organisational and financial reforms and a big increase in party membership (Ramsden, 1995a: 96). The two were never very close (Kandiah, 1992: 247), and Woolton (1959: 328) felt that Churchill himself was 'vague' about what needed to be done, but he demanded, and got, a 'completely free hand' in the overhaul and running of the party organisation (Hoffman, 1964: 81), his success in that role making a major contribution to the Conservative's eventual return to office. Ramsden (1995b: 111) describes Woolton as 'a staunch defender of the party against the Leader, notably in negotiations with the Liberals'. Churchill's enthusiasm for 'galloping after the Liberals' was, says Kandiah (1992: 168) 'well-known and distrusted'. Churchill even threatened to resign at one point if he could not have his way, but Woolton and other leading Tories were adamant that his pursuit (between the 1950 and 1951 elections) of an alliance or pact in which the Liberals would be given a free run in a large number of seats and possibly electoral reform was a non-starter and could not be delivered at constituency level (Addison, 1993: 404; Kandiah, 1992: 200–4).

The mass party – the Tory rank-and-file activists in the constituency parties – 'idolised' Churchill (Addison, 1992: 397), and 'came during these years to love [him] with an adulation entirely devoid of political calculation' (Ramsden, 1995a: 180). Some of this was down to his status as the heroic wartime saviour but also because of 'the great skill with which he played his audience at mass rallies' and at the Party Conferences (Ramsden, 1995a: 181). Bounced into the commitment to set a target of building 300,000 houses a year at the 1950 Conference, he was careful to leave some wriggle room (talking of 'our first priority in time of peace') (Addison, 1992: 405–6).

The heat was not turned on Churchill's leadership in the same way as had happened when Balfour and then Baldwin had earlier led the Conservative Party into Opposition (Hoffman, 1964: 47–8). There was from time to time what Macmillan (1969: 286–7) described as 'murmurings' among disgruntled backbenchers and in the Shadow Cabinet (Crookshank and Salisbury foremost among the critics of Churchill's leadership). But the Chief Whip, James Stuart, was sent away with a flea in his ear when he went to see Churchill in July 1947, at the urging of a cabal of half a dozen frontbenchers, to tell him that the Shadow Cabinet felt that he should retire. Shortly afterwards, he made a public speech saying he intended to carry on until he had 'turned out the socialists', signalling that he would not be bundled out without a fight (Ramsden, 1995a: 179–80). As Cuthbert Headlam observed in 1948 from the backbenches, 'the Tory Party cannot give Winston his *congé* [notice of dismissal], especially at a time when he is the only really "big noise" it possesses. The only way of getting rid of Winston is for him to retire of his own accord and this he will never do' (Ball, 1999: 544–45). Butler and other frontbenchers had recognised in the first year of Opposition that 'the older man could not be "shoved" & that either he goes early if he wants to or we just see things through' (Ramsden, 1995b: 107). After dining with senior Tories, including Eden, in 1946 Harold Nicolson (in N. Nicolson, 1968: 63) noted that 'the Tory Party are much embarrassed by Winston's presence. They cannot edge him aside; they can only throw him out; and that they do not wish to do.'

The critical point was that Churchill's determination to retain the leadership was stronger than Eden's ambition for it. While Eden's supporters manoeuvred, plotted and fumed, Churchill was safe so long as the heir apparent shrank from openly leading a direct challenge or confrontation (Ball, 2004: 279–83). Macmillan, describing Churchill as 'a man impossible to frighten and equally difficult to dislodge', believed that an attempt to force out Churchill would not have been understood by the wider party and would have backfired with the public (Macmillan, 1969: 287). However, poll evidence suggests that if Eden had played Brutus there may have been an electoral premium: a confidential party poll in 1949 suggested the Tories would do better under Eden, and a 1951 poll indicated even a majority of Conservative voters would prefer Eden rather than Churchill as leader (Gilbert, 1988: 633; Ponting, 1994: 747).

Churchill was expert at 'stringing Eden along' by dropping hints that he would not go on forever and might soon bow out (Ramsden, 1995b: 107). He even talked of handing over leadership functions to him, with Eden becoming Leader in the House of Commons (the salary of Leader of the Opposition being passed on to him) while Churchill kept the leadership of the party in the country. This scheme would never have worked. They had policy disagreements, Eden resented being in Churchill's shadow, and he 'was by no means brought fully into [Churchill's] confidence before he made his pronouncements' (Robbins 1992: 157). Eden complained plaintively there was no place for a 'Deputy Leader of the Opposition' but that was what he effectively became, standing in for Churchill as acting Leader of the Opposition on the front bench and in the Shadow Cabinet and 'doing all the work' during Churchill's prolonged absences (Thorpe 2003: 337; Gilbert 1988: 227–8). Disillusioned and frustrated, at one point he contemplated quitting British politics altogether and becoming head of the United Nations (Churchill would not have tried to stop him). Churchill was not a quitter, but he would only do the job of Leader of the Opposition his own way, and his colleagues and supporters had to accept that – and they mostly did.

Emotional intelligence

Apart from Gladstone, Churchill is the oldest British politician ever to have served as Leader of the Opposition, being 70 years old when he assumed the role in 1945, and celebrating his 77th birthday a month after regaining power in 1951. On age grounds there was reason to think that he would or could not stay on for long after 1945. Clementine Churchill would have liked him to retire. He was stunned, shocked and depressed by his sudden and unexpected eviction from office in 1945, and exhausted after his gruelling wartime premiership. Moran reports him as saying in July 1945 that 'at his age there could be no question of a come-back' (Moran, 1968: 312). However, a year later (July 1946) Churchill was saying that 'a short time ago I was ready to retire and die gracefully. Now I'm going to stay and have them out. ... I'll tear their bleeding entrails out of them' (Moran, 1968: 339). He was determined to fight on, avenge his defeat and be elected in his own right as Prime Minister (Ramsden, 1995a: 101). He would stay on leading the party, wrote Bracken, 'until he becomes Prime Minister on earth or Minister of Defence in Heaven' (Gilbert, 1988: 278).

Although in his seventies as Leader of the Opposition, Churchill was fairly healthy and fit for his age (Pelling, 1984: 573–4), capable of hard work on his memoirs and able to impress his backbenchers (in 1947) with his 'amazing' 'vitality and physical endurance' (Ball, 1999: 526). He husbanded his energy and resources, taking plenty of holidays. He had a stroke in 1949, but it was hushed up and described in the press as a 'chill'. From about that time the looming General Election fight and the prospect of a return to office 'reinvigorated him to an extraordinary degree', and he became more actively involved in Opposition business, and 'more imperious, impetuous and impatient' (Robbins, 1992: 59). He enjoyed the fighting tactics and occasional Parliamentary guerrilla warfare of the 1950 Parliament, attending the Commons more regularly and making more speeches there – 'no extinct volcano he', noted one contemporary observer (Ramsden, 1995a: 219). Macmillan commented how, in June 1951, the 76-years-old Churchill showed that there was life in the old lion still during protracted sittings on the Finance Bill:

> Conscious that many people feel that he is too old to form a Government and that this will probably be used as a cry against him at the election, he has used these days to give a demonstration of energy and vitality. He has voted in every division; made a series of brilliant little speeches; shown all his qualities of humour and sarcasm; and crowned all by a remarkable breakfast (at 7.30 a.m.) of eggs, bacon, sausages and coffee, followed by a large whisky and soda and a huge cigar. This latter feat commanded general admiration.
>
> (Macmillan, 1969: 322)

His style of leadership – 'the celebrity virtuoso soloist who inspired by the brilliance of his individual performances (or alarmed by the occasional wrong notes), rather than the leader of the orchestra who gave a constant and sustained lead to his fellow players' – was, says, Robbins (1992: 156) very much a matter of 'temperament'. And he was his usual mercurial character in these Opposition years; as one Shadow Cabinet member put it: 'his moods alternated, and there was no attempt at concealment; at times he was benign, at others bleak and morose; he could be gentle or ferocious, wise or irresponsible, cautious or incorrigible, sombre or frivolous, wonderfully generous or woundingly unfair' (Kilmuir, 1964: 167).

Looking back, Kilmuir (Maxwell-Fyfe) recalled Churchill's 'fertile, questing mind ... [and] wonderful capacity for original thought', generating a stream of ideas – some impractical, some absurd, others shrewd and realistic – '[we] were appalled by some of his proposals and marvelled at others', saying it needed guts and a command of the issues to stand up to him (Kilmuir, 1964: 166–7). Macmillan, however, felt that on economic questions in particular he was 'uncreative and unimaginative, in marked contrast to his contributions on wider issues'. He was open to the proposals of colleagues but 'was not capable or desirous of initiating new concepts of financial, monetary or economic policy' (Macmillan, 1969: 45). Moreover he was not a man for the policy details but 'painted with a broad brush' (Mayer, 1992: 2). But this is not to say that he was not up to the job (as could be said after his serious stroke when he was Prime Minister in 1953), though it is doubtful whether anyone else would have done it in the way he did (or got away with it).

Conclusion

Even a Churchill supporter like Harold Macmillan privately thought that he was 'sadly miscast as a Leader of the Opposition in peacetime' (Horne, 1988: 292). Churchill was 'a poor leader of the Opposition', James Stuart, his Chief Whip up to 1948, once conceded (Ball, 2004: 283). Edenite Richard Law's verdict (in January 1950) was that the Tories had been 'a deplorable opposition'. 'It is Winston's fault', he went on. 'I mean largely because of his very qualities, he's hopeless as leader of an opposition. You can't have a Field Marshal leading an opposition: what you want is a company commander who is on the job every day. ... Of course Winston had to be leader; there was no alternative. But what a tragedy it has been' (Carlton, 1981: 293). Kilmuir's view that Churchill was 'our greatest ... asset' in Opposition was a retrospective public gloss (Kilmuir, 1964: 148). Tory insiders were privately more sceptical, doubtful and resigned to, rather than enthusiastic about, his continuing at the helm than they could admit at the time or later. Unhappiness about his performance in the role of Leader of the Opposition was never far below the surface and often bubbled over.

It was never going to be easy to come back from a big defeat such as 1945 had been, which had left the Conservatives with only 213 seats, 180 behind

Labour, which had a majority of 146 and an 8 per cent vote-lead (47.8 per cent to 39.8 per cent). For the first two years the Government, as Macmillan (1969: 48) put it, 'were triumphant and seemed unshakeable'. The Conservatives at first offered little effective resistance, and Churchill came in for a great deal of internal criticism that only subsided as Eden stepped into the breach and provided the practical day-to-day Parliamentary Opposition leadership that was needed. From 1947 onwards the Government started to run into difficulties but it was still problematic for the Opposition to make headway. There were Conservative opinion poll leads for most of the period from the second half of 1947 through to January 1950 (King, 2001: 2–3), and Tory advances at Labour's expense in local elections in 1947 and 1949, but the party made no gains in by-elections. Though the Conservatives' vote went up by 3.7 per cent and they gained 88 seats in the February 1950 General Election, Labour was left hanging on with an overall majority of six. Churchill pledged 'one more heave', but it is likely that had Labour retained a majority big enough for another full term then he would have had to step down probably pretty quickly (Robbins, 1992: 159). As it was, it took the collapse of the Liberal vote between the 1950 and 1951 elections, the exhaustion of the Labour Government and Cabinet splits and resignations, and the economic problems caused by the outbreak of the Korean War to put the Conservatives back in Downing Street. Even then, the Labour vote still held up and the Conservatives actually polled fewer votes than Labour, while their majority was just 17 seats.

The negative argument for Churchill's leadership of the Opposition is that things may not have been any better under an alternative leader – almost certainly Eden. Eden may have had a public appeal but he had many enemies in the party and carried little of Churchill's weight, as Addison has pointed out. 'This was important at a time when the Tory party was troubled by latent conflicts which might have got out of control under the leadership of a less commanding personality [than Churchill]' (Addison, 1992: 388). In judging how much party leaders matter to Opposition performance, Ball (2003) argues that Churchill's success in 1945–51 was 'due more to prestige and charisma than to action or substance', adding that in 1950 and 1951 he may not have been any more attractive than in 1945. Churchill was the leader but he did not, in many ways, actually do the leading (Ramsden, 1995b: 108). The major policy and organisational contributions came from others – notably Butler and Woolton – and while Churchill backed them, or at least did not veto them, his practical involvement was limited and haphazard. He took a lower profile in the 1950 and 1951 campaigns than he had in 1945, with the emphasis more on the strong Conservative team around him. The Conservatives were in the end a successful Opposition in the 1945–51 period in that they got back into office relatively quickly – but it is difficult to argue that Churchill personally ranks high in any league table of 'effective Leaders of the Opposition'. Conservative recovery happened under him rather than because of him.

3
Clement Attlee, 1951–5

Victoria Honeyman and Timothy Heppell

Clement Attlee is considered to be the most successful Prime Minister in post-war Britain to date (Theakston and Gill, 2006: 198; 2011: 70). He had become leader of the Labour Party in 1935, just four short years after the collapse of the second Labour Government and the betrayal of Ramsay MacDonald, an event that loomed large in Labour's history. While Attlee did not directly succeed MacDonald, he really can be considered the calm after the storm, remaining leader for twenty years, and providing much-needed stability and consistency. When MacDonald was expelled from the Labour Party following the creation of the National Government in 1931, he was initially succeeded by Arthur Henderson. Henderson was certainly a competent politician and a leading figure in the party, but his leadership was to be extremely brief. The 1931 General Election reduced the number of Labour MPs to 52, a bitter blow for a party that had been in power only a matter of months before, and most of the leading members of the party lost their seats, including Henderson (Thomas-Symonds, 2010: 62). Of the 52 remaining members (46 Labour Party MPs and 6 Independent Labour Party MPs), the only member who seemed to have the necessary standing and support to lead the party was George Lansbury, the former First Commissioner of Works. Lansbury was a very popular figure, and he led the party as part of a trio: Lansbury was leader, Attlee was his deputy and Stafford Cripps acted as an unofficial deputy to them both (Thomas-Symonds, 2010: 62). However, Lansbury faced a number of difficulties as leader. This was largely because his personal views on pacifism became contrary to the changing official policy of the party, driven as it was by the increasingly hostile international environment of the 1930s (Shepherd, 2002: 307–46). Lansbury continued as leader until 1935 when he insisted upon resigning as leader and Attlee was elected after defeating Herbert Morrison in the second round of voting by 88 to 48 (Thorpe, 2001: 80).

Despite his hard work and attributes, it has been often stated that Attlee was not seen as the most obvious candidate to become leader, and was dismissed as being 'too quiet' and 'colourless' (Donoughue and Jones, 1973: 234;

R. Jenkins, 1948: 166). It is also commonly asserted that one of the main reasons that Attlee won the leadership contest was that he was seen as a stopgap, the assumption being that in the near future there would be another contest when someone more charismatic would become leader. However, Beckett questions this by arguing that

> Clem was the man Labour wanted in 1935 – not as a substitute for some-one else, not as a stopgap, but as the man the party believed it could trust to turn its dreams into legislation. He has been described as an acciden-tal leader, but he was probably the least accidental leader in the party's history.
>
> (Beckett, 2007: 130)

Despite being leader of the party during some of the most difficult circum-stances ever faced by a leader, including the Second World War and the economic crisis that followed it, Attlee initially maintained unity in the party and remained a calming, yet responsive figure. He aimed to defuse tension and maintain order, while reflecting the will of the party. He also proved a formidable opponent to Stanley Baldwin, Neville Chamberlain and Winston Churchill.

Attlee remained leader of the party until 1955, when he was succeeded by Hugh Gaitskell, a man who did not enter Parliament until 1945, ten years after Attlee was elected leader. During this twenty-year period, in addition to his six-year tenure as Prime Minister (1945–51), Attlee also served as Deputy Prime Minister (1940–5) in the wartime coalition administration. Before and after those terms in office, Attlee served as Leader of the Opposition, first in the period between 1937 and 1940, when the role was more explicitly formalised, and second in the aftermath of office between 1951 and 1955. Given the parameters of this edited collection, and its focus on post-war Opposition leadership, this chapter will offer an explicit examination of the performance of Attlee in the 1951 to 1955 period.

Public policy platform

The Attlee years would constitute an era of considerable policy achievement. As such the 1945 to 1951 Government has tended to be regarded within the Labour movement as the high point of Labour. As a consequence it has been subject to considerable (and mostly sympathetic) academic appraisal (see, for example, Hennessy, 1992; Jefferys, 1992; K. Morgan, 1984; and Pelling, 1984). Attlee's administrations would shape the contours of policy for a generation, and would embed the pillars of what became defined as the post-war consensus (see, for example, Addison, 1975; Kavanagh, 1987, 1992). Domestic policy involved an extensive programme of nationalisation that placed one-fifth of the economy under public ownership, while the establishment of the National Health Service was the jewel in the crown of the new welfare state (Jefferys, 1993: 8–10). Foreign policy involved independence for India and Pakistan, which acted as a prelude to the transition from Empire to Commonwealth, while the establishment of the North Atlantic Treaty Organisation secured the alliance with the Americans within the defence of Western Europe. However, as economic constraints undermined their popularity and Labour lost office in 1951 so a heated internal debate within the party gathered pace regarding future policy development. From the left came the call for further nationalisation as a symbol of their continuing commitment to socialism. From the right came the argument that they should consolidate the accomplishments of the Attlee Government: that is, the objective of a future Labour Government was the effective administration of the new welfare state (Shaw, 1996: 50; Jefferys, 2006).

This broadly sympathetic academic view of Attlee when in government is not as prevalent when considering the Opposition years of 1951 to 1955. Jefferys describes Attlee as 'producing no coherent programme of policy revision' despite, according to Rubenstein, having effectively 'exhausted' the viable aspects of their 1945 programme (Jefferys, 2000: 83; Rubenstein, 2006: 100). Pugh argues that the defeat of 1955 was a consequence of the 'folly' of continuing to rely on the policy platform that had propelled Labour to victory ten years earlier, and that this was a reflection of a 'reluctance to adjust' (Pugh, 2010: 302, 308). Attlee's biographer J. H. Brookshire has attempted to put these difficulties in terms of policy development into some form of context. He argues that in the 1930s and 1940s Attlee had a clear idea of his policy objectives – the establishment of coherent social services within a mixed economy. This left Attlee with a conundrum – having largely achieved his central policy objectives, what was the next stage of policy development? On how Attlee sought to address this Brookshire concludes that he 'focused on the practical applicability of specific proposals rather than a conceptual re-evaluation of party goals' (Brookshire, 1995: 232). The most noteworthy attempt at strategic rethinking in the Opposition era post-1951 occurred in 1956 with the publication of *The Future of Socialism* (1956) by Anthony Crosland, after Attlee had ceased to be party leader. Crosland had earlier contributed a chapter, alongside Roy Jenkins and Denis Healey, in an edited collection titled *New Fabian Essays* (1952) to which Attlee had provided a brief preface (Crossman, 1952). However, despite this Brookshire concludes that Attlee did little to encourage such thinking. He observes that Attlee was sceptical about the activities of younger Labourites and their attempt to 'explore a revisionist redefinition of British socialism' (Brookshire, 1995: 232). Theakston suggests that not only did Attlee have 'little interest' in the necessary task of rethinking social democratic policy and doctrine but by this stage he 'lacked the inspirational and innovative powers to rally his forces' (Theakston, 2010: 150).

Pugh concludes that losing office in 1951 was a 'critical' defeat, which created huge complexities for Labour in policy and strategic terms (Pugh, 2010: 301). This is because recovering power is always contingent upon two factors. First, there has to be an electoral perception that a Government is incompetent and thus vulnerable. This constitutes the *necessary* precondition for a potential change of government. Second, the necessary aspect may not be *sufficient* – that is, just because a Government is vulnerable to the charge of incompetence does not mean that the Opposition is going to be automatically swept into power. The party of Opposition has to demonstrate that it is credible and worthy of replacing the incumbent administration (Ball, 2005: 1–28; Norton, 2009: 31–3). The difficulty for Labour in Opposition post-1951 was the general policy trajectory of the Conservative Governments (in both the 1951–5 and 1955–9 Parliaments) and their performance. The Conservatives inherited power in an era that was moving towards prosperity and consumerism, and thus were able to present themselves as a party of governing competence and a Government that was improving living standards. (Black and Pemberton, 2004) Conservative tactics intensified the policy dilemmas facing Labour, as Pugh observes:

It was in this period that Labour became the *victim* of the political consensus that had sustained it in 1945 ... [the Conservatives] ... had calculated that electoral survival required them to uphold the domestic consensus because they were vulnerable to Labour warnings that their return to office would see a higher cost of living, mass unemployment and attacks on the welfare state. Significantly, however, that nightmare vision failed to materialise ... the new government upheld the fundamentals of the consensus.

(Pugh, 2010: 305–6)

By choosing to operate within a mixed economy, sustaining the welfare state and by adopting a conciliatory approach to the trade unions the Churchill administration had minimised the scope of Labour's Opposition strategy. That combination of competence and moderation meant that the necessary condition for a change of Government referred to earlier was not in place by 1955. When Labour sought a return to Government at the May 1955 General Election, against the newly appointed Prime Minister, Anthony Eden, they had been critically undermined by the fact that it was

Hard for Labour to argue with any credibility that its achievements had been threatened, and as a result Labour candidates found it difficult to know what line to take at the election; even an internal party report of 1955 identified 'the absence of clearly defined differences between the parties' as a cause of Labour's defeat.

(Pugh, 2010: 307)

However, while the necessary condition for a party of Opposition to win did not exist, there is a need to acknowledge that Labour did not help their own cause between 1951 and 1955. Despite entering Opposition with a degree of pride in their political achievements in Government they became engulfed by ideologically motivated infighting (Jefferys, 2000: 81). Caught in the 'middle of the political crossfire and attempting to hold the ring and reconcile the warring factions' was Attlee (Haseler, 1969: 9).

Party management

As Prime Minister between 1945 and 1951 Attlee had displayed consummate party management skills. In his seminal study of the revisionism in the Labour Party Haseler praised Attlee's ability to 'hold together a group of talented and rumbustuous politicians for six years' (Haseler, 1969: 10). Of his party management methods, Haseler noted that Attlee 'rarely gave a lead politically and seemed uninterested in aims. The unity of the party was his primary consideration and he was loath to alienate sections of it for fear that this unity would snap' (Haseler, 1969: 10). However, despite his well-regarded party management skills the 'divisions multiplied despite [his] efforts at conciliation' (Jefferys, 2000: 81).

The fracturing open of ideological factions was tied to both policy and personal issues – that is, it was a battle for the future policy direction of the party *and* the succession to Attlee. Crowcroft acknowledges this by arguing that while it has been 'seen as the high point of ideologically driven factionalism', the fact that the Attlee tenure was due to end soon meant that the 'actions of the involved politicians were consistently guided by the objective of securing for the factional leader the opportunity to succeed Attlee by extending their influence on the party and weakening that of their opponents' (Crowcroft, 2008: 679–80).

The battle was also partly aligned to competing interpretations of the reasons for their removal from office. To those of the socialist left, who coalesced around the charismatic leadership of Aneurin Bevan, defeat was a consequence of having been insufficiently socialist. Extending public ownership was thus essential, while in foreign and defence policy they were concerned about the reliance on nuclear weapons (Pugh, 2010: 302). Opposing that view were the social democratic right consolidators (or revisionists) who wanted to downscale the emphasis on public ownership as the defining policy objective of a future Labour Government, and were comfortable with a multilateralist rather than an unilateralist approach to foreign and defence policy. Over time this feuding became aligned to the individual 'leaders' and the terms Bevanites and Gaitskellites would become dominant labels within Labour politics in the 1950s (Laybourn, 2000: 102–3).

The Bevanites evolved from the Keep Left group, which had been given impetus by the resignations of Bevan and Harold Wilson from the Cabinet in the tail end of the Attlee administration (April 1951). As a faction it has been estimated that they represented at most 20 per cent of the Parliamentary Labour Party (PLP) and although small in quantity they comprised some influential figures including Barbara Castle, Tom Driberg, Ian Mikardo, Fenner Brockway, Jennie Lee and Richard Crossman. They could not be 'ignored by the party leadership' (Laybourn, 2000: 102).

The difficulties that the Bevanites caused for Attlee manifested themselves in two ways in terms of party management. First, there was their behaviour within Parliament and their increasing propensity to rebel. Second was their campaign to secure elections to the party's National Executive Committee (NEC) as a means of showcasing their support and broadening their influence. In March 1952, 57 Labour MPs disobeyed the party whip by voting against the Government's support for German rearmament, which the Attlee leadership had decided to support. This constituted the 'first major public act of defiance by the Bevanites' (Jefferys, 2000: 81). This acted as a prelude to a 'bad tempered' Annual Party Conference that autumn. Bevan and Wilson were elected to the NEC at the expense of Morrison and Hugh Dalton. Douglas Jay recalled the atmosphere at the conference as 'hideous', while the defeated Dalton recorded in his diaries that there was 'more hatred, and more love of hatred, in our party than I can ever remember' (Jay, 1980: 223; Pimlott, 1986: 601).

The Bevanites' influence within the 1952 to 1954 period became slightly less pronounced as Bevan decided to stand for the Parliamentary Committee (Shadow Cabinet) elections. He came in 12th (1952) and 9th (1953), having refused to stand in 1951 and then refused to stand again in 1954 (Sibley, 1978: 80). During those two years Attlee found Bevan 'less troublesome on the frontbench than behind it' (Sibley, 1978: 80), as he was 'subject to collective responsibility towards the policies of the party which prevented him from too obviously leading the left opposition within the Labour Party' (Laybourn, 2000: 103). However, Bevan was still able to generate attention for himself by disputing the deputy leadership by challenging Morrison in 1952 and 1953, and, having then resigned from the Shadow Cabinet, he challenged Gaitskell for the position of party treasurer (M. Foot, 1975: 383, 407; Sibley, 1978: 80).

Attlee was once again undermined by Bevan in his efforts to project the party as unified in 1955. Now outside of the Shadow Cabinet, Bevan lambasted Attlee in Parliament over American policy in South-East Asia, after Attlee had supported the position of the Government on this. When a subsequent Parliamentary division on the Government's decision on the hydrogen bomb took place, the Attlee leadership issued an instruction to the PLP to support the government. Bevan mobilised a group of 63 Labour parliamentarians to abstain, and as a consequence the PLP voted 141 to 112 to remove the whip from him (Pugh, 2010: 303). However, the NEC decided by one not to expel him (J. Morgan, 1981: 402–5, 411–12). The dilemma of how to deal with Bevan certainly dominated the party management thinking of Attlee in the 1951 to 1955 period. So problematic was Bevan that Gaitskell would claim that Attlee was contemplating making Bevan's expulsion a resignation issue (Williams, 1978: 383, 385–94). However, Richard Crossman disputed this assertion, and his diaries suggest that Attlee would have been reluctant to see Bevan expelled from the party, as Attlee was about to retire and he 'was too intent upon keeping the Labour party united' (J. Morgan, 1981: 396).

How should we assess the contribution of Attlee to the ideological feuding of the 1951 to 1955 period? Despite his reputation for party management his ability to project to the wider electorate an image of a unified party was undermined by the faction fighting between the Bevanites and the Gaitskellites. Attlee was unable to impose discipline and unity upon the party but he did intervene in critical ways to try and facilitate unity. After the controversial 1952 Conference Attlee attempted to 'get a grip' by carrying a resolution banning all unofficial groupings inside the party (Jefferys, 2000: 82). His denouncement of such unofficial groupings went hand in hand with a plea to the PLP to end the 'personal attacks on colleagues' (Brookshire, 1995: 232). This reflected Attlee's view that much of the disputation was being fuelled by factional identities as much as substantive policy disagreements. This was a view endorsed by Douglas Jay, who described Labour at the time as suffering from 'stasis' – that is, 'faction for faction's sake in which the protagonists know which side they are on, but usually cannot remember why it all started' (Jay, 1980: 221). In this context Attlee was not a factional protagonist but a 'centralist'. Attlee centralists 'tended to abdicate from the ideological debate' and preferred to 'concentrate instead upon finding formulae around which the party could unite' (Haseler, 1969: 9).

Therefore, between 1951 and 1955 rather than presenting himself to the electorate as an alternative Prime Minister of an alternative party of government, Attlee had become consumed by party management issues. In this context he would be left open to the accusation that he was 'following rather than leading his party' (Theakston, 2010: 150). This had significant implications as the divisions were 'so deep that party unity was an overriding consideration ... returning Labour to power at the next general election became secondary' (Thomas-Symonds, 2010: 252). In this time period Attlee thus gave the impression that he was vacillating, but if his aim was simply to keep the party together then his conduct in the 1951 to 1955 period was a qualified success, as the Bevanites were not expelled and their impact would dissipate over the next few decades (Thomas-Symonds, 2010: 252). An attempt to provide a more assertive and domineering leadership could have been counter-productive and may have intensified divisions, as Gaitskell was to experience in the 1959 to 1961 period.

Public communication

While Attlee warrants some qualified recognition as a party manager, albeit more pre-1951 than post, he is less well known for his communication skills.

Few historical appraisals of Labour history have references to his platform oratory, his Parliamentary debating skills or his performance as a television communicator. In this context it is worth reflecting on how often Attlee was mentioned in the 2010 General Election, which witnessed the introduction of the Prime Ministerial debates. For those who were sceptical of their value the memory of Attlee became a useful tool in support of their argument. Here the central point was that Attlee was recognised as a successful Prime Minister but a poor public communicator. Applying this logic, it could be argued that an excessive reliance on communicative style could prevent the emergence of politicians of substance like Attlee. In making that argument Allen, Bara and Bartle argued that Alistair Darling could not be considered as a possible Labour Party leader in 2010 even though he 'might have been a good [potential] Prime Minister in the Clement Attlee mould' (Allen, Bara and Bartle, 2011: 199).

Therefore, it is widely acknowledged that Attlee was not renowned as a great orator. Indeed, he had a reputation as being a 'laconic' communicator (Burridge, 1985: 90). However, although it is justifiable to say that Attlee was without charisma and unexciting as a platform orator and Parliamentary performer that does not necessarily equate to him being ineffective (Radice, 2008). He was capable and competent but he was operating in an era of memorable orators. His primary political opponent across the Parliamentary benches for ten years was Churchill after 1945, who had a worldwide reputation for his oratory. Within the Labour movement itself Attlee was not an inspirational or passionate communicator in the style of Bevan, but nor was he divisive in the way that Bevan was (Lawrence, 2009: 11). His quiet demeanour meant that he could be underestimated – for example, while Dalton initially described him as a 'quiet little mouse', he came to admire the understated and reflective way in which Attlee communicated to both the electorate and within the party (Dalton, 1957: 82).

When assessing his public communication in the period of Opposition between 1951 and 1955 we can argue that three key issues emerge. First, Attlee's communicative method involved projecting the party and its agreed policy and not himself. He saw himself as the 'mouthpiece' of the party. For example, he informed the 1953 Labour Party Annual Conference, 'I am only here to carry out your will'. As such Thomas-Symonds concludes that 'his public speeches were designed not to persuade reluctant colleagues to accept his point of view, but to speak for the agreed policy or strategy' (Thomas-Symonds, 2010: 257).

Second, despite his laconic reputation Attlee could still deliver the occasionally memorable line. For example, at the height of the internal wrangling flowing from the 1952 Conference, he famously pleaded with the party to remember the importance of unity and loyalty. Of the factionalism increasingly associated with the Bevanites on the left he complained: 'what is quite intolerable is the existence of a *party within a party*' (Pugh, 2010: 303, italics in original). However, Opposition leaders have to be careful about the language that they deploy when referring to their own party. An image of internal party division is something that can impede electoral recovery. Attlee's memorable line confirmed to the electorate what was already assumed – Labour was badly divided.

Third, Attlee was a politician ill suited to the emerging television age of electioneering. Through the increasing emphasis on party political broadcasts and television appearances Attlee was increasingly seen as 'too old, too tired and too weak' (Jefferys, 1997: 39). Of his electioneering in the 1955 campaign, Pugh describes his television performances as 'detached and defensive' (Pugh, 2010: 308). However, in Attlee's defence it has to be acknowledged that he was operating in an era that pre-dated the awareness of the possibilities for party advancement through professionalised political marketing (Wring, 2005).

Emotional intelligence

That Attlee was best described as a competent rather than a memorable public communicator is partly a reflection of his temperament. He once acknowledged that he was a 'diffident man', and surprisingly given the social dimension to political leadership he found it 'hard to carry on a conversation'. He was also subjected to humiliating putdowns, such as the one by Churchill when he caustically commented that Attlee was a 'modest little man, with much to be modest about' (Arnstein, 2000: 363). This reinforced a generally acknowledged impression, which was encapsulated by Beckett when he said: 'many people thought Clem dull: efficient and hard-working, certainly; intelligent, no doubt; sincere, probably; sometimes witty, in a dry way; but there was no getting away from it, dull' (Beckett, 2007: 122).

However, such observations have to seen alongside his evident personal strengths, which would be tested greatly in the 1951 to 1955 period. First, leadership places many complex and competing demands on the time of the individual. The ability to prioritise and compartmentalise is critical. Emotionally and intellectually Attlee was capable of dealing with these demands 'without fuss' and 'quickly', and after serving as Prime Minister these skills were well honed and served him well in the four years in Opposition (Thomas-Symonds, 2010: 270). Second, in a party with a propensity towards factionalism Attlee was still, even at the tail end of his leadership tenure, temperamentally well suited to the business of compromise. One of his attractions – 'his independence of cliques, social and political' – had been crucial in the years shortly after MacDonald and still applied nearly two decades later, and meant that he may well have been better placed than others to try and 'facilitate party cohesion' (Howell, 2006: 43). Third, Attlee placed a considerable emphasis on loyalty both personally and politically. As one of his biographers noted, 'he could be relied upon absolutely. His unassuming and tolerant nature was widely recognized to be genuine and not a façade' (Burridge, 1985: 317).

Attlee was therefore a man who had many skills, making him a capable political operator, if not exactly a charismatic leader. Throughout his two decades-long tenure as Labour Party leader he was surrounded by talented individuals, many of whom were extremely loyal to him, and he had the ability to delegate and operate in a collegiate manner. Rather than make key decisions himself, which Attlee as leader almost certainly could have attempted to do by simply interpreting the views of the party and forwarding his preferred option, he did not. He consulted widely within the party, recognising the importance of this and communicating the views he heard, although it could be argued that Attlee was communicating views that were very similar to his own – i.e. that he was representative of his party, rather than dragging it to conclusions that suited his purposes. Obviously, this approach has to be seen in light of what had occurred under MacDonald, which created a fear of disloyalty by the party leadership and a desire to prevent future leaders from becoming too powerful (McKenzie, 1963: 17–24).

MacDonald was thus a huge influence upon the Attlee approach to leadership. It would have been understandable if Attlee, having worked so closely with MacDonald as his Parliamentary Private Secretary from 1922 to 1924, and then in his Government in 1924 and 1930–1, had followed MacDonald out of the party and into the National Government. However, there is no suggestion that he ever considered the possibility. Indeed, Attlee's opinion of MacDonald seems to have already soured by 1930. As Attlee later wrote in 1956:

> In the old days, I had looked up to him as a great leader. He had a fine presence and great oratorical power. ... Despite his mishandling of the red letter episode, I had not appreciated his defects until he took office a second time. I then realised his reluctance to take positive action and noted with dismay his increasing vanity and snobbery, while his habit of telling me, a junior minister, the poor opinion he had of all his cabinet colleagues made an unpleasant impression.
>
> (Attlee, 1956: 90)

Therefore, by both political calculation and temperament Attlee was keen to negotiate within his party (whether that be within the confines of the PLP or the NEC) in order to reach consensus, and if that were not possible, to gain at least grudging agreement (Thomas-Symonds, 2010: 81). He allowed his colleagues to express their opinions and work independently, while trying to maintain a united party (Burridge, 1985: 271). Attlee was thus a collective leader who wanted to ensure that the whole party was committed to its aims, rather than the party's policies simply being the product of his own personal brand of socialism. Thomas-Symonds argues that Attlee was not obsessed with power for himself, and as such he was very careful to ensure his style was appropriate to the party. Thomas-Symonds concludes that 'Attlee had no *intention* of creating a personal style of leadership'; rather he 'saw himself as a spokesman for the settled policy of the party and his leadership style was a consensual one, seeking a common position to advocate' (Thomas-Symonds, 2010: 81).

Conclusion

The desire to retain party unity and imbue within a historically fractious party the merits of loyalty was a demanding task. Given those demands and the fact that Attlee was 68 when he became Leader of the Opposition in 1951, and would suffer from ill-health during the four-year period after 1951, one has to ask why he did not resign when Labour lost office. He would have been willing to retire immediately, but there was no clamour to remove him and he was re-elected unopposed (F. Williams, 1961: 255). Pearce noted the irony that while the party had previously regarded him as a 'transient' figure in the 1930s it had now decided that he 'could stay as long as he liked' (Pearce, 1997: 176). Thus Attlee continued and his justification for doing so was unity, rather than his ability to renew the party through the promotion of ideas, energy or enthusiasm (Pugh, 2010: 308). In 1951 Attlee feared that the unity of the party would be severely damaged if either of the two main rivals to succeed him – Bevan on the left or Morrison on the right – were elected. In the 1951–3 period Morrison seemed the most likely option, and Attlee was concerned that Morrison's 'inflexible dislike of the Bevanites' would makes things worse (Jefferys, 2000: 81). By prolonging his leadership tenure Attlee enabled Gaitskell to emerge as a candidate of the right who was capable of defeating both Morrison and Bevan (Pearce, 1997: 177–81).

However, owing to the longevity of Attlee's leadership tenure and his age (he entered his seventies during Labour's first term in Opposition), there was constant speculation about the succession for the duration of his time as Leader of the Opposition. During that period of factionalism and leadership debate, it could be argued (thus countering the earlier assumption by Howell) that Attlee displayed a degree of arrogance in assuming that only he could unite the party. Moreover, the idea that his continuation was an act of personal self-sacrifice in the interests of the party is only part of the explanation. He was also desperate for personal reasons to avoid Morrison being his successor, with memoirs revealing that he deeply disliked Morrison (H. Williams, 1978: 300). Attlee delayed his resignation until December 1955 after leading Labour into defeat in the General Election earlier in that year. In the interim period, the probability of Morrison defeating Bevan had faded as the factions became configured more around the personality cults of Bevan and Gaitskell. It was under Attlee, (although he was not the cause), that their factional warfare escalated, with implications for Labour that were cataclysmic:

> Between them, Nye Bevan and Hugh Gaitskell not only dominated the party: they threatened to destroy it as a serious contender for power. In fighting for its soul, they fought each other to a standstill. Two dissimilar but magnetic figures, they repelled each other and attracted eponymous bands of supporters who vilified each other more effectively than either of them hurt the Tories.
>
> (Clarke, 1999: 236)

Given the turbulence of the preceding four years, and the fact that they were challenging a relatively competent and moderate administration, Labour's performance at the 1955 General Election was not disastrous. The Conservatives' Parliamentary majority increased from 17 to 59. The Labour share of the vote fell from 48.8 per cent to 46.4 per cent, and numerically came down from 13.9 million to 12.4 million (Dorey, 1995: 339–40). As Jefferys notes, 'rising living standards and Labour disunity' made the outcome a formality, which confirmed that neither the necessary nor sufficient conditions for a change of government were in place (Jefferys, 2000: 82).

This was a huge disappointment, however, when placed within the context of expectations when leaving Government four years earlier. The NEC minutes of autumn 1951 identified that the 'party was in good fettle', and there was a widespread view within the party that Labour would return to office soon – indeed, given the small Parliamentary majority that Churchill had (of 17) when entering power, some within Labour were prone to calling it a 'stopgap administration' (Pugh, 2010: 301). A resolution put forward to the 1952 Conference arguing that defeat in 1951 had been due to 'failures in education and propaganda' was dismissed by the leadership as 'unfairly critical' (Pugh, 2010: 302). Opinion poll leads in the 1951 to 1953 period reinforced party confidence and complacency. It was that complacency that permitted the space for self-indulgent faction fighting to gain momentum – the energies that the party devoted to their internal feuds would have been better spent in policy renewal and party reorganisation (Pugh, 2010: 301–3).

When the Conservatives entered Opposition in 1945 they recognised that the causes of defeat could be partly attributed to their policy positions and organisational failings. Considerable efforts were made in terms of policy renewal and organisational reform – all of which were geared towards aiding voter mobilisation (Willetts, 2005: 169–91). In terms of intellectual renewal the Attlee Opposition tenure was 'dull and uninspiring and lacking in drive if compared to the work put in by the Conservative Party from 1947 to 1950' (Pugh, 2010: 307). Furthermore, Attlee's failure to look at the party organisation once in Opposition needs to be acknowledged. By 1955 they were felt to be 'pathetically inferior' to the Conservatives in organisational terms

(Jefferys, 1997: 39). Once Attlee was succeeded by Gaitskell an investigation into the organisational apparatus of the party was set up in an effort to enhance the electioneering capability of the party. It was chaired by Harold Wilson. It emphasised the need to increase the membership and for greater constituency-level activism; there was a need for more professional agents; and the party should focus more efforts (and resources) on marginal constituencies. In arguing that greater efficiency was needed at Party Headquarters, Wilson concluded that 'thirty five seats could have been won with improved organisation'. Attlee has to share some burden of responsibility for the investigation's conclusion of the 1955 campaign – 'our surprise is not that the General Election was lost but that we won as many seats as we did' (Pugh, 2010: 310–11).

Despite such assertions by the time Attlee finally did resign as party leader and Leader of the Opposition he could rightly claim that he left the party in far better condition than when he became leader – the 12 million supporters in the defeat of 1955 was 4 million more than in the 1935 General Election. This, alongside his policy legacy in Government, has ensured that Attlee is held in high regard within the Labour movement. After all, it was under his leadership that Labour had come of age as a political party, and his leadership style had indeed provided an important period of calm after the storms of the MacDonald era. However, his tenure as Leader of the Opposition between 1951 and 1955 did little to enhance his overall reputation (Theakston, 2010: 149). As Jefferys concludes:

> In Opposition after 1951 Attlee proved a far from inspiring figure. He may have hoped for unity but he had no strategy for achieving it [and] he failed to respond to an increasingly confident Tory government. Instead the party became mired ever deeper in squabbling, and it was a measure of how far things had been allowed to drift that Bevan should be on verge of expulsion shortly before the 1955 election. By insisting on remaining as leader until he was over seventy, Attlee damaged both his own reputation and the party's prospects.
>
> (Jefferys, 2000: 83–4)

4
Hugh Gaitskell, 1955–63

Timothy Heppell

Shortly after the Labour Party lost office in 1979, the BBC *Reputations* series ran a documentary on the late Hugh Gaitskell, entitled *The Lost Prime Minister*. Presented by the acclaimed political journalist Anthony Howard, it assumed that had ill-health not struck Gaitskell down in January 1963, it would have been him and not Harold Wilson, who would have stood outside Downing Street in October 1964 (BBC, 1979). It is this assumption that permeates the academic literature on Gaitskell, with the personal and wider political tragedy for the Gaitskellite social democratic right a central theme of the biographical work on his political career (see McDermott, 1972; P. Williams, 1978; Brivati, 1996). In retrospect the timing of the documentary did seem tragically appropriate. As Labour entered Opposition under James Callaghan, after governing for eleven of the previous fifteen years and having won four elections out of five between October 1964 and October 1974, the social democratic right was seen as discredited and in decline. Their cohesion had eroded, most notably over the Common Market, and they had lost their main heirs to Gaitskell. Anthony Crosland, like Gaitskell, suffered a premature death in 1977, while Roy Jenkins had departed to the European Commission. Notwithstanding the differences over the Common Market, many of those who defected to form the Social Democratic Party (SDP) within eighteen months of the BBC documentary saw themselves in the mould of Gaitskell (Marquand, 1999: 123–4).

Although Philip Williams, writing in 1978, claimed that Gaitskell had 'remained an inspiration' to the social democratic right in the fifteen years following his death, Brian Brivati observed in 1996 that Gaitskell had been 'largely disowned' by his own party in the 1980s (P. Williams, 1978: 767). Although Neil Kinnock modernised the Labour Party, and displayed some methods that seemed Gaitskellite, he 'hated the comparison' with Gaitskell (Brivati, 1996: 440). Therefore, as a political figure, Brivati concluded that Gaitskell had 'descended into political obscurity' as an influence within Labour politics, with the SDP 'claiming his mantle' (Brivati, 1996: 445). Nor did New Labour seek to suggest that Gaitskell was an influence upon them. When examining the relationship between revisionism and New Labour, Matt Beech emphasised how revisionism represented the 'old right', as compared to the modernised 'new right' of the Third Way (Beech, 2004: 89). The way in which Gaitskell has been utilised within the context of New Labour has been within comparative evaluations of how and why the 'effective' Tony Blair addressed the Clause IV conundrum in 1995, and why the 'ineffective' Gaitskell failed to in 1959 (T. Jones, 1996: 41–64, 139–47).

That Gaitskell has faded, relative to other Leaders of the Opposition within this study, is due to the fact that he did not become Prime Minister, and had not previously been Prime Minister. Nine of the post-war Leaders of the Opposition, have had (or will have in the case of David Cameron), their political reputations defined by their performance as Prime Minister. Of the seven who failed to reach Downing Street none, however, could claim the same influence upon the narrative of post-war British political history that Gaitskell had. Gaitskell was the standard bearer of the Attlee post-war settlement, and while the consensus thesis is widely disputed, a central theme or misinterpretation within this has been 'Butskellism' – the supposed continuity between the policy objectives of Chancellor R. A. Butler (post-1951) and Gaitskell as Chancellor pre-1951 (Marquand, 1999: 124).

Moreover, others who failed to make the transition from Leader of the Opposition to Prime Minister, notably Michael Foot, William Hague, Iain Duncan Smith and Michael Howard, never looked remotely likely to succeed in their objective. Like Kinnock in 1992, Gaitskell suffered the trauma of losing a General Election that he, and many others, thought he could win in 1959; and like John Smith in 1994, he was riding high in the opinion polls when his death denied him the chance of becoming Prime Minister. However, when one considers the events that defined his tenure as Leader of the Opposition between December 1955 and January 1963, that he was considered a Prime Minister in waiting at the time of his death was a remarkable achievement. This is because his conduct and record as Leader of the Opposition is open to a clear critique. He led his party to a 'serious' defeat in 1959; whereupon he was 'for all practical purposes defeated' over Clause IV and then entered a 'furious battle' over unilateralism (Marquand, 1999: 126). Marquand admits the verdict on Gaitskell was that he was a 'rather unsuccessful Leader of the Opposition' and his record as party leader was 'by no means dazzlingly successful' (Marquand, 1999: 124–6). By analysing Gaitskell against the four criteria identified for this collection – policy development; party management; public communication; and personal characteristics – we can come to some kind of conclusion as to whether the Marquand criticisms are justifiable.

Public policy platform

Any attempt to analyse policy development under Gaitskell is inextricably linked to matters of party management. This is because as Labour leader he would preside over a Labour movement that was fundamentally divided over nationalisation, unilateralism and the Common Market (Jefferys, 2004: 74–5). Moreover, those policy divides were mapped onto alternative narratives or strategies for Labour. To the socialist left was the demand for 'expansion' of the Attlee policy agenda. To the social democratic right was the commitment to 'consolidate' the Attlee settlement through revisionist thinking (Jefferys, 2006: 11). However, to complicate matters further, there was to be a cross-cutting nature to these groupings. Aneurin Bevan irritated the left by accepting the multilateralist leadership position, while Gaitskell's position on the Common Market put him at odds with many on the right.

With regard to all three of the aforementioned policy issues, Gaitskell was motivated by the drive for electoral appeal: in his eyes nationalisation and unilateralism constituted electoral liabilities, while advancing a critical position on the Common Market created electoral opportunities to exploit against a Conservative administration destined to see their application vetoed (T. Jones, 1996: 60). What we can say is that in moderate and relatively conciliatory terms during his first term, and by aggressive and confrontational methods for much of his second term, Gaitskell wanted to use policy development as a way to challenge negative assumptions about the party. He wanted to reconfigure the party policy platform around revisionist 'catch-all' electoral thinking (Fielding, 2007: 311). For Gaitskellites, revisionist thinking would aim to transcend the old-style corporate socialism associated with the Attlee era and allow the party to apply their policy agenda to take account of social change in 1950s Britain (Jefferys, 2006: 11).

In domestic terms, revisionism would seek to reconfigure policy thinking through the ends–means distinction. The policy aims should be clearly understood as social justice and greater equality, and the pursuit of a socially classless society. The focus on a more equal distribution of wealth would require a forthcoming Labour Government to be committed to economic planning; full employment; progressive taxation; comprehensive education; and improvements in health and housing (Jefferys, 2006: 11). Gaitskell possessed a commitment to planning as a means of retaining a degree of public control within an economy that would be dominated by private enterprise. Within this context, Gaitskell was seeking to persuade the Labour movement to end the obsession with nationalisation as the means of socialising society but to focus explicitly on the ends (Kenny and Smith, 1997: 110–15).

The primary intellectual influence on revisionist thinking was Tony Crosland. In his seminal publication, *The Future of Socialism*, published in 1956, Crosland argued that post-war management by the state and industry appeared to have addressed the central economic dilemma of delivering economic growth with full employment. The Crosland argument implied that economic growth within a capitalist framework could lead to a more socialist-orientated social order. This would justify and explain the need for Labour to redefine their policy objectives along the lines identified above. That downplaying of the centrality of nationalisation was evident in the 1957 policy document *Industry and Society*, which placed the primary focus on the pursuit of social justice, which was to be the precursor to the great Clause IV debates of 1959–60 (Jefferys, 2006: 13).

Running parallel to revisionist thinking in domestic policy was 'new thinking' in terms of foreign policy. This questioned the validity that 'foreign policy decisions could and should always be firmly based around socialist principles' (Haseler, 1969: 112). Rejecting the left's position as 'the last refuge of utopianism', the revisionists promoted the 'power-political' approach, which rejected the notion that 'ideology' should be a primary influence in foreign policy development (Black, 2001: 28, 34). Recognising the diminished standing of Britain on the world stage, revisionists argued that retaining influence required a strong relationship with America, which in part explained Gaitskell's strong condemnation of Eden's approach to Suez. Tied to this was their condemnation of unilateralism in matters of defence, which was to cause such damage to the credibility of Labour in Opposition as unilateralism was foisted upon the leadership at the 1960 Annual Conference; whereupon the Gaitskellites waged a successful campaign for its reversal at 1961 Annual Conference, when a multilateralist *Policy for Peace* platform was accepted (Black, 2001: 27–35).

The other foreign policy dimension to the Gaitskellite platform was more complex. On the matter of the Common Market, Gaitskell attempted to avoid committing himself publicly to a distinct policy position, partly because he did not view it as an important electoral issue (P. Williams, 1978: 703–4). This ambiguity on the matter was sustainable until the Macmillan Government sought entry, whereupon Gaitskell's eventual critical positioning was determined by a combination of important factors: first, his strong emotional commitment to the Commonwealth; second, his belief that the application would be vetoed and thereby opposition would have electoral advantages given its increasing saliency; and, third, out of a desire to retain party unity. For it was on this latter matter of party management that Gaitskell has been subject to significant criticism.

Party management

Assessing Gaitskell in terms of party management is complicated by the conflicting methods that he deployed in dealing with his fractious party. In acknowledging this it is important to recognise that any analysis of Gaitskell as Leader of the Opposition needs to consider the differing Gaitskell 'leadership types' that existed.

The first Gaitskell type, between 1955 and 1959, placed a tremendous emphasis on unity. He engaged in a series of 'strategic moves' that were designed to 'keep internal opposition quiet' (Brivati, 1996: 227). In an attempt to 'promote party unity' he made Wilson Shadow Chancellor, and then appointed Bevan as Shadow Foreign Secretary. He did so despite the 'distrust' that he had for both men (Pimlott, 1992: 220). He worked tirelessly to construct what was known as the Gaitskell–Bevan axis, calculating that if they could form an accommodation with each other then relative unity would follow. Binding Bevan to a more multilateralist position was central to diluting the cohesion and impact of the left. However, despite their efforts and the emergence of 'relative calm', Gaitskell could never escape the existence of factional blocs on the left critiquing his leadership, from the Campaign for Nuclear Disarmament to the new Victory for Socialism (Brivati, 1996: 227; Pugh, 2010: 314).

The second Gaitskell emerged after the defeat of 1959. Prior to then Gaitskell made such accommodations out of a conviction that the disunity created by the Bevanite left had been the primary reason for electoral defeat in 1955. Defeat prompted Gaitskell to argue that 'if there is anything that the 1959 General Election shows it is that unity is not enough' (P. Williams, 1978: 444). Thereafter the conciliatory approaches of 1955 to 1959 would be replaced with confrontation, and inevitably conflict (Brivati, 1996: 227). Between 1959 and 1961 Gaitskell would advance a 'concept of leadership' that did not try 'to reconcile the opposing sides' but attempted 'to educate the party by force of argument' (Brivati, 1999: 105). He demanded the party understand the need for change, in order to appeal to the interests of well-off younger workers, women and white-collar employees (Fielding, 2007: 310). In his effort to educate his party on the need for change, he sacrificed unity and ensured that between 1959 and early 1962 there was a 'consistent assault on his leadership of the party' (Brivati, 1996: 345). It is during this period that the behaviour of Gaitskell demonstrated that he was, in the eyes of Pugh, 'miscast as a party manager and a party leader' (Pugh, 2010: 299).

Gaitskell utilised defeat in 1959 to advance the revisionist policy argument. The scapegoat for defeat would be Labour theology and Clause IV of the Party Constitution, which committed the party to public ownership, and thereby nationalisation. Gaitskell believed that Clause IV was politically irrelevant and electorally unattractive. It was not an accurate expression of the policy goals of a forthcoming administration that he would lead. By maintaining its privileged position within the constitution of the party, he argued that it enabled the Conservatives to exploit it and engender fears surrounding the implications of Labour occupying power. The left put up a fierce defence of Clause IV, and in doing so compelled Gaitskell into a humiliating climb-down, although Clause IV would now be supplemented by a supporting statement of principles, which concluded that nationalisation could only be applied 'according to circumstances' (Fielding, 2007: 313).

For his assault on Clause IV, Gaitskell has been subjected to massive criticism for his weak tactical sense, both by his contemporaries and by political historians, as he had managed to deepen the divisions within the Parliamentary Labour Party (PLP), without securing his policy objectives (T. Jones, 1996: 58). Natural allies on the social democratic right, such as Jenkins and Crosland, felt that his move was 'tactically unwise' (Pugh, 2010: 319). Wilson felt that it was 'misconceived both tactically and strategically' (T. Jones, 1996: 58). Wilson simply could not relate to the policy objective or the method of seeking change. Wilson believed that Clause IV was inconsequential electorally, but massively important to the psyche of the Labour movement. By his approach, Gaitskell pitted the left and the right of the movement against each other. In doing so, he deprived the party of the time and space to focus their wrath on their real enemy. It was the worst misjudgement that Gaitskell made in terms of party management, as it produced 'tensions' among his own supporters and reinforced the latent 'suspicions' that the left had towards him (Howell, 1980: 224). Robert McKenzie described it as 'one of the most maladroit operations in the modern history of party politics' (McKenzie, 1963: 156). As an exercise in party (mis-)management, Jones has argued that Gaitskell made a series of critical miscalculations (T. Jones, 1996: 58; T. Jones, 1997: 16).

First, Gaitskell was foolish to allow his Clause IV reforms to be aligned to the wider discussions for change constructed by the 'clique' of intellectuals who surrounded him, and of whom the left were so deeply distrustful. Douglas Jay was advocating changing the name of the party, re-evaluating the link with the trade unions and hinting at the opportunities presented by closer co-operation with the Liberals, all of which the left strongly opposed. Although Gaitskell rejected these options, his weak planning and communications allowed his name to become associated with such radical proposals. This meant that when he launched his proposed Clause IV reform, many on the left regarded it as a Trojan horse to further reforms along the lines that Jay was advocating (T. Jones, 1996: 58). Second, attacking Clause IV head on might, if successful, reap electoral dividends in the longer term. Gaitskell feared that their economic credibility and ability to broaden their electoral appeal was constrained by the commitment to nationalisation; reform was to him a 'vote winner' (T. Jones, 1996: 59). However, in 'defeat' Gaitskell was open to the criticism that he had drawn further attention to an issue that he needed to reduce electoral awareness of (Pugh, 2010: 319). Third, part of the reason why Gaitskell was unsuccessful related to his 'misunderstanding' of how the trade union base would react. He assumed that he had sufficient support to ensure success, as they had been 'hitherto loyal' to him, but 'unaware that Trade Union leaders were about to desert him, [he] embraced a fight that he was unable to win' (Jefferys, 2004: 74–5). In addition to losing his traditional 'power base' by 'antagonising' natural trade union allies, he was also to lack his 'accustomed majority on the party's ruling

National Executive Committee (Fielding, 2007: 313). Fourth, the primary reason for his failure was that he underestimated the 'symbolic' importance of Clause IV to the Labour movement. His failure to appreciate that his proposals amounted to 'taking down the signpost to the promised land' (P. Williams, 1978: 570), indicated that he was 'simply not on the same wavelength as the majority of active Labour Party members' (Shore, 1993: 60).

Ultimately, the miscalculation that Gaitskell made was reflective of his poor political sense, which raised doubts about his judgement and decision-making. Gaitskell had allowed his sense of 'rationality' to triumph over 'common sense' (K. Morgan, 1987: 228). As Jones concluded, by raising the issue and unleashing such opposition and effectively being forced to retreat Gaitskell had:

> precluded the possibility of any discreet demotion of further nationalisation in Labour policy-making. As a consequence he found himself under fire not just from the left but also from pragmatists from the centre. The latter took the view that any squabble over 'theology' should have been avoided by silence in opposition until the same ends could be attained, still silently, in practice after coming into power. They were thus committed to submitting the party to a process of adaptation by stealth.
>
> (T. Jones, 1997: 18)

The Clause IV debacle was a 'prelude' to further conflict between 1959 and 1961, and the difficulties that Gaitskell experienced during this period undermined his credibility, as attention turned from nationalisation to unilateralism (Pugh, 2010: 319). In June 1960, Victory for Socialism condemned his leadership as a 'source of weakness, confusion and disunity' and demanded that he resign in the 'interests of the party' (Brivati, 1996: 336). Given that his mandate to lead was derived from the Parliamentary Labour Party, which was right-wing-dominated, and only they could formally replace him, such a demand in essence amounted to posturing. Nonetheless the Chief Whip called for a confidence motion to express support for Gaitskell; to condemn 'all attacks from whatever quarter'; and demanded 'all members to show by their actions and words their unity and loyalty to the party' (Brivati, 1996: 367). Although Gaitskell secured 179 votes to 7 against, a further 18 abstained and more importantly 53 members were 'absent', implying a 179–78 split (Brivati, 1996: 367).

The uncompromising reaction of Gaitskell, when Conference passed a resolution endorsing unilateralism, and his insinuation that the view of Conference was intolerable to him as leader and that he would seek to overturn it, created apoplexy on the left. Immediately prior to Conference, Wilson had stipulated that regardless of the verdict of Conference it was essential that the leadership acknowledge the sanctity of Conference decisions. Wilson was thus arguing that the Labour movement must then unify around the position taken – that is, acceptance of the process was critical (Pimlott, 1992: 238). Running simultaneously to the alternative approach that Wilson could offer was widespread criticism of the party management methods of Gaitskell within left-wing periodicals. The *New Statesman* ran an editorial entitled 'Wanted: A New Leader', within which their rationale for removing Gaitskell mirrored the unity appeal of Wilson. They said of Gaitskell that 'neither his method of leadership nor his view of socialism is compatible with a united party' (*New Statesman* Editorial, 24.10.1960). Similarly, writing in *Tribune*, Michael Foot commented that Gaitskell could 'neither unite the party, nor lead it to victory' (Foot, 1960).

Gaitskell would not resign, so his removal would require a formal challenge. Challenges to incumbent Labour Party leaders are actually very rare. There have been only three formal challenges in the post-war period: Tony Benn challenged Neil Kinnock in 1988, and Gaitskell was challenged twice – once by Wilson in 1960 and once again by Anthony Greenwood in 1961. Wilson was defeated 166–81 and Greenwood lost by 171–59 when the latter challenged in the aftermath of the Gaitskellites' successful reversal of the unilateralist platform (mobilised by the factional Campaign for Democratic Socialism group) from the 1960 Annual Conference. Gaitskell had survived the onslaught from the Greenwood-inspired unilateralist left and the Wilson faction who questioned his party management methods. However, as Kenneth Morgan concludes, it may have been victory but 'much blood was left along the way' (K. Morgan, 1987: 221).

The levels of internal party factionalism in the 1959 to 1961 period were 'bitter experiences' for Gaitskell, and influenced his party management thinking when the Common Market moved to the top of the political agenda in late 1961 (P. Williams, 1978: 707). Gaitskell feared that another bout of internal left–right warfare would consign Labour to another five years of Opposition; as such he was keener to manufacture unity on this issue than he had been over the previous two years (Brivati, 1996: 405). David Howell concludes that in his final months the 'great confrontationist' Gaitskell would use the Common Market to 'ironically' blur those 'factional divisions' (Howell, 1980: 235). Gaitskell was also influenced by the alternative dynamics surrounding the Common Market. During the Defence conflict, Gaitskell was secure in the knowledge that the majority of the PLP were multilateralists and thus supportive of his stance. Attitudes towards the Common Market differed. Stephen Haseler calculates that around 25 per cent of the PLP were pro-Common Market and around 75 per cent were in the anti-faction. Trade unionists and constituency Labour parties were also overwhelmingly hostile towards the Common Market (Haseler, 1969: 228). If Gaitskell came out pro-Common Market it would put him on a collision course with all three – the PLP, trade unions and constituency Labour parties – whereas coming out anti-Common Market was the best way of unifying the party, albeit marginalising the minority pro-Common Market revisionists, many of whom had been his principal allies in the battles of the previous two years (Brivati, 1996: 408). In alienating his traditional revisionist friends, and 'siding with the left' on a major policy issue, Gaitskell had brought the party together and secured a level of unity not previously seen during his leadership tenure (Brivati, 1996: 418; Haseler, 1969). That he did so, however, indicated a fracturing of the revisionist wing that he himself had been so associated with. Haseler, writing in 1969, noted that pro-Common Market revisionists, such as Jenkins and Bill Rodgers, were reported to feel Gaitskell's position had 'reinforced the impression that a real break was imminent' (Haseler, 1969: 238).

Public communication

The divisions identified above did tremendous damage to the effectiveness of the Opposition. Gaitskell had been determined that through Parliament, Conference and public speeches, Labour should 'attack vigorously' the record of the Conservative Government. At an international conference held in Washington, DC in 1961 to examine Opposition politics, Gaitskell argued that he saw that it was his duty to 'oppose, along the line' (McDermott, 1972: 190). While Geoffrey McDermott concluded that Gaitskell 'certainly satisfied that need, through and through' he is less complimentary about how effective Gaitskell was at holding the Government to account (McDermott, 1972: 190). He notes it 'was only natural that the Government could afford to laugh off criticisms from a party which seemed to be looking in about four different directions at once' (McDermott, 1972: 206).

In this context, Gaitskell suffered from comparisons with Macmillan, especially in the 1957 to 1960 period, when the 'Super Mac' imagery of Macmillan resonated in the age of affluence. Macmillan's 'great gifts, not just as a manipulator of mood', but also as a user of what Peter Hennessy called the 'subtle terrorism of words', demonstrated the difficulties that Gaitskell experienced against him (Hennessy, 2000: 249). Gaitskell's emotionalism and dislike of opponents was sometimes evident in Parliament; for example, exasperated by the conduct of Macmillan, he berated him for being 'rude and arrogant' (McDermott, 1972: 143).

Until the Macmillan administration began to degenerate from 1961 onwards, there was genuine concern that Macmillan was 'tactically superior', which was damaging to the morale of the PLP (P. Williams, 1978: 474). Gaitskell was to 'suffer from persistent and bitter interruptions every time he spoke and although he became more effective over time', Williams noted that his Parliamentary performance in the first two years was so poor that there was speculation that 'his effectiveness as Leader of the Opposition might have been permanently impaired' (P. Williams, 1978: 439).

Gaitskell was at his most effective in Parliamentary terms when critiquing the appointment of Lord Douglas-Home to the Foreign Office in 1961. He made Macmillan uncomfortable by questioning whether Douglas-Home was the 'best available' candidate. He suggested that Macmillan had selected Douglas-Home for his political compliance and that Macmillan would effectively perform the role himself. If 'puppets' were to be used, he concluded, they should be in the House of Commons, concluding with the comment, 'why bother with the monkey when the organ grinder is here'. Gaitskell had 'used satire, ridicule, and straight crushing argument' (McDermott, 1972: 194) to such devastating Parliamentary effect that Macmillan later described it as 'the cleverest and most effective speech I have heard him make' (Macmillan, 1972: 232). However, while effective at critiquing the appointment of Douglas-Home and raising morale within the PLP then, there was considerable disappointment at how Gaitskell failed to fully exploit 'the Night of the Long Knives' when Macmillan dismissed six members of his own Cabinet in July 1962 (Alderman, 1992: 243–65). Of his Parliamentary questioning of Macmillan, Gaitskell was less effective and failed to make the impact that the Opposition would have anticipated (P. Williams, 1978: 700). Critically he failed to match the 'much remembered words' of Liberal MP, Jeremy Thorpe, who said: 'greater love hath no man than this, than he lay down his friends for his life' (Douglas, 2005: 267).

If one made a list of great political quotes, Gaitskell's greatest were used when discussing his own party and not dissecting his Conservative opponents. His Conference speech in 1960 on the Defence debate saw him provocatively argue:

> Supposing all of us, like well behaved sheep, were to follow the policies of unilateralism, what kind of an impression would that make upon the minds of the British people? ... What sort of people do they think we are? Do they think that we can really accept a decision of this kind? Do they think we can become overnight the pacifists, unilateralists and fellow travellers that other people are? I say this to you: we may lose the vote today and the result may deal this party a grave blow. It may not be possible to prevent it, but I think there are many of us who will not accept that this blow need to be mortal, who will not believe that such an end is inevitable. There are some of us, Mr Chairman, who will fight and fight again to bring back sanity and honesty and dignity, so that our party with its great past may retain its glory and its greatness.
>
> (Brivati, 1996: 374)

David Marquand described it as 'great speech', and the term 'fight and fight again' resonated to such an extent that it was included on the cover of Stephen Haseler's 1969 book, *The Gaitskellites* (Marquand, 1999: 124; Haseler, 1969). Such rhetoric was potentially offensive to the unilateralist left of the movement, and yet two years later it was the pro-Common

Market right who were to find Conference was being used by Gaitskell to condemn their position. Gaitskell emotionally argued:

> We must be clear about this: it does mean, if this is the idea, the end of Britain as an independent European state. I make no apology for repeating it. It means the end of a thousand years of history. You may say 'let it end', but my goodness, it is a decision that needs a little care and thought. And it does mean the end of Commonwealth. How can one seriously suppose that if the mother country, the centre of the Commonwealth, is a province of Europe (which is what Federation means) it could continue to exist as the mother country of a series of independent nations? It is sheer nonsense.
>
> (Brivati, 1996: 414)

When Gaitskell concluded his 'hall ovation was unparalleled', although Gaitskell's wife commented that 'all the wrong people are clapping' (Brivati, 1996: 414). Jay, who was one of the few on the right hostile to the Common Market, was lavish in his praise of Gaitskell, describing the speech as 'unique', an 'intellectual massacre' and the 'finest' speech he ever heard (Jay, 1980: 286).

Brivati concluded that 'the speech delighted those who wanted to see the party united to take on the Tories', and that need for unity after the bruising battles of 1959–61 was a factor in Gaitskell's thinking (Brivati, 1996: 415). This was reflective of how Gaitskell was highly focused on the electioneering aspect of his leadership role and the party's public presentation. Gaitskell encouraged the party to pay greater attention to how it presented 'itself and its policies to the public, to the tone and content of its propaganda, and generally to the impression which it makes on the voters' (Fielding, 2007: 315). Recognising the decline in the importance of public meetings as a means for party projection, he encouraged the party that the best means of reaching out to, and appealing to, affluent voters was through the press and television (Fielding, 2007: 315). To aid this he welcomed the advice of advertising specialists and sought to utilise public opinion research more extensively (Haseler, 1969: 143–4). He paid particular attention to image projection through television. Williams noted that 'he saw that mastering television technique was now indispensable for a politician and patiently spent many weary hours in rehearsal' (P. Williams, 1978: 382).

Ultimately, however, while Gaitskell was a competent public communicator he lacked the televisual appeal and Parliamentary savvy of his successor, Wilson, or his main political opponent, Macmillan. Critically, Gaitskell found the multidimensional aspects of public image projection to be a 'strain'. He admitted that the pressure of Parliamentary, Conference and television performing was never-ending: 'if you do badly everybody notices it – though if you do well they forget it quickly. One keeps running in order to stand still' (P. Williams, 1978: 473).

Emotional intelligence

That Gaitskell placed such importance on trying to make the Labour Party more electorally appealing made the impact of the defeat in 1959 more profound (Haseler, 1969: 155). Gaitskell had strong expectations, based on competitive opinion polls, that Labour could win the election despite disputing power against an incumbent Conservative administration presiding over affluence (Fielding, 2007: 311). However, Gaitskell was deemed to be 'responsible for the worst gaffe' of the campaign (Brivati, 1999: 107). He announced that there would no increase in income tax under a Labour Government, 'but when Macmillan challenged him as to whether this promise could be extended to indirect tax, Labour began to lose credibility' (Pugh, 2010: 315). The Conservatives questioned the viability of such a commitment and sought to present Gaitskell as irresponsible and engaging in electoral bribes, whereupon greater scepticism was evident among voters and Labour lost their 'momentum' (Fielding, 2007: 311). For Gaitskell, the surprise at the scale of defeat, and the insinuation that his blunder had been a contributing factor, had an impact, according to Richard Crossman. In the aftermath of defeat, Crossman commented that Gaitskell looked 'dead tired and on the edge of an emotional collapse' (J. Morgan, 1981: 788).

The impact of defeat upon how Gaitskell behaved was profound. Marquand argues that Gaitskell's personality combined a 'rationalist' identity and that of a 'passionate turbulent political romantic' (Marquand, 1999: 135). Between 1955 and 1959 the rationalist personality was predominant, but after 1959 gradually 'the emotional aspect ... seeped through into his public persona' (Brivati, 1996: 371). Defeat in 1959 had created an environment in which, according to Marquand, Gaitskell felt he 'had nothing to lose' and the 'romantic broke free', and 'he *would* now pursue truth ... [and] ... putting his faith in the power of reason, he *would* try to persuade his party to see the light' (Marquand, 1999: 135). However, by doing so 'he breathed new life into the internal schism which had begun in the closing years of the Attlee Government' (Marquand, 1999: 135).

Such an attitude would fuel the collisions that Gaitskell would have with his own party over nationalisation, unilateralism and the Common Market. His behaviour over these issues would shape perceptions of his character. All forms of literature on Gaitskell have similar assertions. To critics on the left he is accused of 'arrogance', 'rigidity', 'intolerance', 'stubbornness', and of being 'blunt', 'insensitive' and 'uncompromising', although his admirers on the right emphasised his 'courage' and 'determination' (Brivati, 1996: 425; Marquand, 1999: 136). Being on the pro-Common Market right, Roy Jenkins had experience of being both with and against Gaitskell on these divisive issues, and admitted of 1962: 'I inevitably felt a little more sympathy with those who had differed from him in the past! Courage can be interpreted as inflexibility and an aggressive respect for rationality as a tendency to equate little points with big ones' (cited in J. Campbell, 1983: 72).

Gaitskell's desire to be 'in control' would lead to a 'recurrent pedantry that could be infuriating'; whereupon Brivati concludes that the 'Labour Party was the wrong party for someone so attached to control' (Brivati, 1996: 424). Drawing together these themes, Martin Pugh concludes that Gaitskell was 'hampered by defects of temperament' (Pugh, 2010: 299). This was most evident in his handling of Clause IV, where his 'outsider' status contributed to his failure to understand the 'history and ethos of the movement' that he had 'joined' (Marquand, 1999: 123). In a sense, though, Clause IV demonstrated that 'once he was committed to a course of action, his relentless application of intellectual honesty forced him on to take events to their logical conclusion, even if this was unpalatable, or damaging to his own interests' (Brivati, 1996: 421).

While acknowledging the critiques of Gaitskell's temperament and decision-making, there is also a need to consider the impact upon him of leading such a fractious movement and managing such prickly and egotistical political elites. He became 'fed up' with the unilateralists, for what he considered their 'perverse, disruptive stupidity' (McDermott, 1972: 197). The challenge made to him by Wilson in 1960 saw his 'mood fluctuate'. Jenkins admitted that 'he could still have dark moments – not least because of the sheer toil of the fight', even after defeating Wilson (Brivati, 1996: 378).

Gaitskell was also forced to devote considerable amounts of time receiving and responding to critical correspondence from Wilson supporters such as Crossman and Tony Benn. Crossman wrote to Gaitskell in March 1960 saying that 'I certainly have had the impression since the election that you would like to see me defeated in the present controversies'; and Crossman had earlier written to Gaitskell complaining of his 'personal attitude' and the way in which he treated Crossman with 'dislike and suspicion' (Gaitskell Papers, 26.02.1960 and 09.03.1960). In late 1960, Benn wrote to Gaitskell complaining about his leadership style, lamenting that 'I have tried to get through to you what I was thinking and what a lot of other people were thinking. But it seemed to make no difference to what you decided to do' (Gaitskell Papers, 28.10.1960).

Gaitskell was subject to widespread criticism outside the PLP. After 1960, he attracted 'crowds and controversy' whenever he made a speech (Brivati, 1996: 379). Jay was shocked by 'the sheer hatred directed towards him ... people would spit and shout abuse, and on some occasions there was a real threat of physical violence' (Brivati, 1996: 379). He became used to being 'heckled', but he was often angered by the 'boorishness of the demonstrators' and their 'arrant refusal to consider any logic or reasoning'. For example, in 1961 hundreds of students demonstrating at the University of Leeds chanted at him: 'in with socialism, out with Gaitskell' (McDermott, 1972: 237). Brivati observes that 'giving speech after speech in such circumstances must have been soul destroying and exhausting' (Brivati, 1996: 379).

Gaitskell's known hostility among the left, and his intolerance towards them at times, combined with the sense that he operated within a 'clique' of social democratic intellectuals, made his Common Market speech in 1962 particularly intriguing. As Brivati comments: 'he repaid his loyal supporters by turning on them' (Brivati, 1996: 420). His social democratic allies on the right of a pro-Common Market mentality felt that he was 'unfairly exploiting their loyalty, knowing that they would not retaliate', given that should they abandon their 'ties' to Gaitskell they would be completely isolated within the movement (Brivati, 1996: 415; P. Williams, 1978: 738).

There is an irony that a political leader, whose tenure was characterised by an apparent tribalism and accusations of being overly influenced by a small group of social democrats, and the pursuit of intellectual honesty, should see his final significant act portrayed as a cynical act of betrayal. That cynicism or calculation had enabled Gaitskell to exploit the (eventual) failure of the Macmillan Government to secure Common Market entry; unify the party; and demonstrate that he was 'independent of the right', having already demonstrated that the 'left could not overthrow him' (P. Williams, 1978: 757). It suggested that he was learning from the tactical and strategic mistakes of the 1959 to 1961 period, and he was now not only the predominant figure with the Labour Party, but destined to become Prime Minister. With a more unified party to lead he was better positioned to exploit the degeneration of a third-term Macmillan administration, for whom the image of affluence was replaced with the evidence of decline (P. Williams, 1978: 759).

Conclusion

How effective was Gaitskell as Leader of the Opposition? It is a role that involves a balance. On the one hand, there was a need to scrutinise Government policy; and on the other, there was the need to offer alternative policy solutions. However, the above analysis suggests that Gaitskell undermined his capacity to present the electorate with a viable alternative party of Government. He was as well-known for the struggles managing a fractious Labour movement as he was for critiquing Government policy and presenting himself as the leader of an alternative administration. Under Gaitskell there was a danger he was opposing the left of his own party as much as he opposed Macmillan. As Williams notes, so consumed was he by the internal issues of Labour politics that 'he gave too little weight to the Opposition leader's role as a national as well as a party spokesman' (P. Williams, 1978: 404).

It is the dominance of party management difficulties in the Gaitskell narrative that explains the Marquand critique identified at the beginning of the chapter. Given his political inheritance, party management was his primary political concern, but it was also his primary political failure (Brivati, 1996: 424). His policy platform and political/electoral strategy involved him attempting to educate, cajole or force his own party to change, and yet Brivati concludes 'he failed to teach his party the lesson' (Brivati, 1999: 97). His whole approach to leadership was to contrast sharply with that of his successor Wilson, who was to broadly sustain Gaitskell's policy positions (washed down with some selected left-wing rhetoric); but critically Wilson 'went out of his way to adopt a non- (even an anti-) Gaitskellite leadership style' (Marquand, 1999: 123). Therefore, much of the Marquand critique seems justified. That the Labour Party stood on the brink of claiming power under Gaitskell's leadership was primarily down to the degeneration of the third-term Macmillan Government, as much as the effective Opposition leadership of Gaitskell.

5
Harold Wilson, 1963–4 and 1970–4

Peter Dorey

> All along I have believed my duty was to be the custodian of
> party unity. ... I am determined to avoid the splits of 1959.
> (Wilson to Barbara Castle, quoted in Perkins, 2003: 259)

Harold Wilson died in 1995 but still remains an enigma, much maligned
and much misunderstood. His thirteen years as Labour Party leader still leave
many political historians perplexed about what exactly Wilson believed in
and stood for ideologically, and whether his undoubted pragmatism reflected
astute political intelligence and Machiavellian cunning or was little more
than the triumph of opportunism over principle, and short-term tactics over
longer-term strategy. Thus did Andrew Roth (1977: 77, 311) assert that: 'Few
politicians ... have so confused observers at where they stand as Sir Harold
Wilson', who evinced 'consistent inconsistency', while from the left, Ken
Coates wryly observed that Wilson's leadership was characterised by 'a developed lack of principle so systematic as almost to amount to a principle in
itself' (Coates, 1972: 240). More recently, Dominic Sandbrook (2006: 20) characterised Harold Wilson as: 'Ambiguous, contradictory, even unfathomable ...
a brilliant opportunist'.

The ambiguities concerning Wilson's ideological stance, coupled both
with various policy initiatives propounded in Opposition and aspects of his
leadership style, were therefore both a strength and a weakness. On the one
hand, the main ideological tendencies in the Labour Party could, at various
junctures, believe that Wilson was 'one of them', not only because of the
type of policy initiatives that he advanced or supported, but also because of
the ideological gloss with which he painted them, and which could then be
interpreted favourably by different sections of the PLP. In fact, to the extent
that Wilson's ideological position has been discerned, he has been characterised as: 'Collectivist, technocratic, meritocratic ... a pragmatic centrist
and a reconciler' (T. Jones, 1996: 78, 86) and as 'centrist, even corporatist'
(K. Morgan, 1992: 259). Another commentator has argued that, ideologically, Wilson was 'neither Left nor Right, but a Bevanite revisionist ... his

instincts were centrist' (Clarke, 1999: 258), while Warde deployed the term 'technocratic-collectivism' to signify an approach that bore strong similarities to 'classical Fabianism' owing to its largely top-down 'technicist notion ... of expert direction' of decision-taking and policy-making (Warde, 1982: 94, 95).

If Wilson's ideological outlook is understood in these terms, his frequently denigrated and derided political manoeuvrings and machinations become more explicable, and perhaps appear less condemnatory or contemptible. Certainly, the public policy platform developed by Harold Wilson during his leadership of the Labour Party in Opposition, particularly the 1963–4 period, was inextricably linked to his proficiency both as a public communicator and his abilities at party management, the latter aspect especially reflected and reinforced by his ideologically centrist stance and political pragmatism, with the pursuit of balance and party unity often seeming to constitute his primary objective. As such, while this chapter treats these three themes as analytically separate, they were, in practice, inextricably linked.

It must be emphasised, though, that Wilson's leadership of the Labour Party in Opposition was marked by notable differences between 1963–4 and 1970–4, for in the latter period, his reputation had been badly damaged by the vicissitudes and disappointments of governmental office between 1964 and 1970, when various decisions and policies were attacked by Labour's left and right alike, as well as the trade unions. It was largely during his second [1966–70] premiership that Wilson acquired his reputation for being 'shifty' and opportunistic, but this perception subsequently shaped many people's perception of Wilson thereafter, and was reinforced by various political positions he adopted during 1970–4.

A charitable interpretation of Wilson's Opposition leadership during the latter period (and previously as Prime Minister) was that he was in a no-win situation and in something of a vicious circle, for the more he adopted compromises or policy shifts in the interests of party unity, the more vulnerable he became to criticisms of opportunism, lack of principles or even betrayal. This, in turn, often exacerbated divisions within the PLP, often (but not always or solely) between left and right, whereupon Wilson was obliged to adopt even more contorted positions in order to manage or minimise intra-party schisms. His increasing exasperation and irascibility in these circumstances was thus not entirely surprising, such as the occasion when, having sought a compromise between Labour's left and right in determining the PLP's response to the 1970–4 Heath Government's application to join the (then) European Economic Community (EEC), Wilson tartly announced in a Shadow Cabinet meeting that 'I've been wading in shit for three months to allow others to indulge their consciences' (quoted in Healey, 1990: 360). External developments, intra-party divisions and his own ceaseless search for compromises to maintain the unity of PLP meant that throughout his leadership Wilson often found himself mired in *merde*.

Public communication

During his first (1963–4) period as Leader of the Labour Opposition, Harold Wilson acquired a reputation as a highly proficient public communicator, yet the two features that strongly characterised his public perorations and persona were an almost contradictory pairing: on the one hand, a strong emphasis on science and technology as the basis of social progress, and even socialism itself, yet on the other, Wilson's persona was often viewed or portrayed as down-to-earth and provincial, and lacking in 'airs-and-graces'. Kenneth Morgan depicted him as a 'no-nonsense Northerner' who could express himself and his ideas with 'a kind of Coronation Street folksiness' and endearing 'lack of pomposity' (K. Morgan, 1992: 251–2, 260; see also M. Williams, 1972: 119–20). As such, although Wilson was grammar school- and Oxbridge-educated, he never sought to portray himself as a Labour Party intellectual *à la* Anthony Crosland and Richard Crossman.

These characteristics did much to underpin Wilson's seemingly classless public image, a personification of the meritocratic society that he purported to want to establish for Britain in the latter third of the twentieth century, and in so doing, broaden his – and *inter alia* the Labour Party's – electoral appeal. One small example of how Wilson sought to cultivate an intelligent yet down-to-earth, man-of-the-people image was his penchant for appearing in public or on television with his famous pipe, even though, in private, he smoked cigars (A. Morgan, 1992: 253).

According to Peter Shore, for example, having secured victory over George Brown and James Callaghan in Labour's 1963 leadership contest, Wilson delivered 'a series of speeches and initiatives that were to hearten the PLP, send Labour's morale soaring in the country, rock the [Conservative] Government and spellbind the press'. So impressed was Shore that, writing in 1993, he averred that 'no leader of the Opposition, before or since, has equalled in sustained brilliance and effectiveness Wilson's campaign' from February 1963 until the October 1964 General Election victory (Shore, 1993: 87–8).

Many of Wilson's keynote speeches during his 1963–4 leadership of the Labour Party in Opposition were concerned with science and technology, and the manner in which these were deemed integral to the modernisation of the British economy and the achievement of social progress. One of the most notable of these speeches was that delivered at Labour's 1963 Annual Conference in Scarborough, when Wilson sought to equate socialism with the application of science and technology, arguing that both were potentially progressive because they could foster social advance and improvement to liberate humanity from ignorance and poverty. This, however, required that scientific and technological developments were planned, and utilised to serve the majority, because 'technological progress left to the mechanism of private industry and private property can lead only to high profits for a few ... and to mass redundancies for the many' (Wilson, 1964a: 18; see also

Wilson, 1964b: Chapter 4). It was in this speech, linking science, technology and modernisation to economic growth and social progress, and *inter alia* to socialism, that Wilson spoke of the new Britain 'that is going to be forged in the white heat of this revolution', while insisting that 'the commanding heights of British industry' could no longer 'be controlled ... by men whose only claim is their aristocratic connection or the power of inherited wealth or speculative finance', but would henceforth have to be placed under the control of 'democratic planning' (Wilson, 1964a: 27, 28).

This keynote speech attracted numerous plaudits in the press, with The *Guardian*'s labour correspondent, John Cole, averring that Wilson's peroration constituted 'the best platform speech of his career' (The *Guardian*, 2 October 1963), a judgement endorsed by *The Times* (2 October 1963), while the *New Statesman* (4 October 1963) even suggested that Wilson had delivered 'the most important speech made by a British politician for many years'. Meanwhile, *The Economist* (4 October 1963) alluded to 'Mr Wilson's clamber upwards into very valuable statesmanship'.

Of course, if only with the benefit of historical hindsight, it is evident that the premise that science and socialism were intrinsically linked was arrant nonsense, as Paul Foot (1968: 150–3) trenchantly pointed out five years later, but, as with so much that Wilson said or did, such speeches were intended to be symbolic rather than substantive, and in this regard served three interlinked objectives.

First, Wilson's perorations about science and technology as the basis of economic revival and social progress were supposed to render the Labour Party electorally attractive to the burgeoning middle class, particularly the rapidly growing strata of administrators and managers, along with scientists and technicians themselves. Second, but inextricably linked to this vital objective, Wilson's efforts at linking the Labour Party with science and technology underpinned the strategy of depicting the Conservative Party as old-fashioned and out of touch with the modern world. Third, as we will note later, the attempt at linking science and technology with socialism was also part of Wilson's mode of party management, during his first period of Opposition leadership, in seeking to transcend or redefine ideology; instead of traditional divisions between left and right, Wilson sought to demarcate the Labour Party from the Conservatives largely in terms of new opportunities and progress for the many versus entrenched privileges and defence of the status quo for the few.

Wilson's efforts at crafting a more favourable public persona were aided, in 1963 and early 1964, by two other developments. First, the Conservative Party opted for Sir Alec Douglas-Home to replace Harold Macmillan as their leader and Prime Minister, following Harold Macmillan's resignation owing to ill-health. The much older, and aristocratic, Douglas-Home inadvertently reinforced Wilson's attempt at portraying himself as a young, dynamic, forward-looking leader who was intent on creating a modern and meritocratic Britain for the latter half of the twentieth century. It was not difficult, therefore, to depict Douglas-Home as even more aristocratic and atavistic than his 'Edwardian' predecessor, Macmillan, hence Wilson's barbed reference to the 'fourteenth Douglas-Home', a jibe that was also intended to reinforce Wilson's growing reputation for sharp wit and clever put-downs.

The second development during the 1963–4 period that aided Harold Wilson's public image and communication skills was the increasing importance of television broadcasting, this being the decade in which TV ownership increased dramatically. Not only did television offer Wilson ample opportunity to make clear to millions of viewers the marked differences between himself and Douglas-Home, the new Labour leader also recognised that TV appearances could help to counter the entrenched anti-Labour bias of most of the national daily newspapers. Ultimately, though, Wilson seemingly became 'convinced that what he said on television was less important than the impression he gave and what he looked like' (Cockerell, 1986; see also M. Williams, 1972: 119).

By the early 1970s, however, Wilson was somewhat less proficient as a public communicator, not least because of the lower profile he adopted in the aftermath of the 1970 election defeat. The sparkling wit of 1963–4 was less prominent, and manifested itself only sporadically during the 1970–4 period, such as when Wilson was asked by a journalist whether Labour would be conducting an inquest the party's 1970 defeat, to which he retorted that: 'There is no post-mortem when there is no body' (quoted in Hatfield, 1978: 37). As one of his biographers notes, Wilson 'would do his bit on the big occasions, usually be present for the Prime Minister's questions, but his appearances in the House of Commons were less frequent than when he had last been leader of the opposition' (Ziegler, 1993: 372).

Not only did Wilson partially withdraw from public life in the immediate aftermath of the 1970 defeat, in order to write his record of the 1964–70 Labour Governments, he also reasoned that there would be little for Labour to gain by attacking the newly elected Conservative Government too vigorously too soon: 'We can't do anything this year' (quoted in Ziegler, 1993: 372), he claimed, particularly as the Heath Government would probably enjoy a political honeymoon; but he also believed that if Heath persevered with the 'Selsdon Man' programme, then 'the Tories will be in a horrible mess sometime next [1972] year', whereupon Labour could regain the electoral advantage (C. King, 1975: 83). In the meantime, Wilson stated that Labour's approach now it was in Opposition would be to 'wait for each new development of policy, wait watchfully and keenly, but we shall not rush into condemnation for the sale of it' (HC Debates, 2/7/1970, vol. 803, col. 57).

Not surprisingly, Wilson's reluctance to provide more active and focused leadership in the aftermath of the 1970 election defeat dismayed and frustrated many of his Parliamentary colleagues, and fuelled suspicions that he was a broken man who would soon resign. Some of Wilson's colleagues, such as Richard Marsh, complained that the Labour leader 'takes little part in the business of the House, but embarrasses new members by recounting the brilliant speeches he made years ago' (quoted in C. King, 1975: 88), while another acquaintance, George Caunt, feared that Wilson was a 'burned out case who will get drunk on his memories' (quoted in Ziegler, 1993: 356). Similarly, Douglas Houghton, Chair of the PLP, lamented that in the aftermath of the 1970 defeat, Wilson appeared to have 'no inspiration or enthusiasm to impart', content, it seemed, to 'dwell on the glories of the recent past', but offering 'no vision of the future' (quoted in C. King, 1975: 103), while another former ministerial colleague, Ray Gunter, observed that the post-1970 Labour leader was 'a very different man from the old Wilson' (quoted in C. King, 1975: 139).

Concern that Wilson was becoming personally and politically withdrawn following the shock of the 1970 election defeat naturally prompted some of his closest colleagues to urge the Labour leader to launch a counter-offensive to re-establish his authority and put Heath under more political pressure, which would also serve to rally and re-energise Labour MPs. Thus did his PPS, Frank Judd, urge Wilson to embark on a public campaign throughout the country, to boost his own profile and popularity, and thereby capitalise on Heath's increasing political problems and declining popularity. Such a campaign, Judd envisaged, would entail visiting factories, coal mines, ship yards, shopping centres, etc, 'being sent to listen to and talk directly with ordinary folk' (MS Wilson, c.914, Judd to Wilson, 6 November 1970).

Public policy platform

In his first period as Opposition Leader (1963–4), the political context greatly helped Harold Wilson in crafting a public policy platform that simultaneously provided the Labour Party with a semblance of unity, while clearly distinguishing itself from the Conservatives by making Labour appear dynamic, forward-looking and progressive, and depicting the Conservative Government as dated, tired and out of touch. Certainly, political circumstances at this juncture proved highly propitious for Wilson and the Labour Party in four main ways. First, Wilson was elected Labour leader after the party had experienced the divisions occasioned by Gaitskell's 1959 attempt at rewriting Clause IV, in order to abandon Labour's formal commitment to public ownership, and the reversal, at the party's Annual Conference in 1960, of a formal commitment to unilateral nuclear disarmament. Wilson was able to devise a series of policy proposals, however vague or vacuous (particularly with hindsight), which seemingly diverted the party's attention away from such internecine conflicts, and instead rally behind a public policy platform with which most Labour MPs could endorse, and which could be interpreted favourably by the party's different ideological tendencies.

Second, a General Election was due in 1964, which enabled Wilson to benefit from a semblance of party unity, which had been lacking in Labour's Parliamentary ranks in recent years. The prospect of electoral victory against an ailing Conservative Government served to foster a renewed sense of shared purpose among Labour MPs, which in turn ensured that Wilson's policy platform benefited from considerable initial goodwill in the party. The imminence of the next General Election effectively encouraged most Labour MPs to rally behind the party's new leader, and this further provided Wilson's public policy platform with a favourable political context.

The third way in which the political circumstances in 1963–4 proved highly propitious to Wilson's advocacy of a new public policy programme for the Labour Opposition was the Conservative Party's own change of leadership, with Alec Douglas-Home replacing Harold Macmillan in October 1963. Inadvertently, Douglas-Home's age and social background served to imbue Wilson's purported 'modernisation' programme, and its emphasis on science and technology, with enormous significance, not least by apparently lending considerable credence to Wilson's depiction of Labour as a reinvigorated and forward-looking party, and which thus contrasted starkly with the seemingly exhausted and backward-looking Conservative Party.

The fourth way in which the political circumstances in 1963–4 proved highly beneficial to Harold Wilson's advocacy of a new public policy programme for the Labour Opposition was the intellectual climate, for a range of academic critiques pertaining to Britain's sluggish economy, antiquated political institutions and lack of social mobility or opportunities were canvassed during the early 1960s, all of which reflected and reinforced many of the policies championed by Wilson when he became Labour leader, most notably those pertaining to economic planning and reform of Britain's political institutions.

One crucial way in which Wilson sought to meld economic modernisation with political and institutional reform was through proposals for the creation of new ministries. In particular, a Ministry of Technology was viewed as a vital means of driving the scientific and technological progress that Wilson now depicted as inextricably linked to 'socialism', and a such, it has been suggested that this proposed Ministry was to constitute 'the main instrument of state intervention' (Jones, 1996: 78), through the state-sponsored promotion of industries-based science and/or technology. At the same time, though, Wilson also envisaged a new Department of Economic Affairs (DEA), which would be responsible for economic and industrial planning, while simultaneously providing a counter-weight to the Treasury.

Meanwhile, Wilson's (and thus Labour's) social policy programme placed enormous emphasis on widening opportunities and facilitating greater social mobility, primarily through reform of Britain's education system. This was most apparent through the Labour Opposition's advocacy of significantly extending comprehensive schooling in place of grammar schools, while also expanding higher education. The latter was to be achieved in three particular ways, namely: creating several new universities, in towns such as Blackpool, Burnley, Doncaster, Halifax, Redruth and Watford (although the building of these particular universities was subsequently abandoned owing to financial stringencies), establishing a 'University of the Air' (which soon became known as the Open University), and creating a number of polytechnics.

This proposed educational expansion was intended both facilitate both an economic and a social objective. Economically, wider educational opportunities were supposed to contribute towards a reversal of Britain's relative economic decline, by providing employers with a more skilled or highly qualified workforce. This was supposed to help to revitalise Britain's sluggish economy, and underpin the steady economic growth that social democracy depended upon to achieve its wider goals and objectives. It was also envisaged that the expansion of higher education would foster the increased number of administrators, scientists and technicians that Wilson envisaged were integral to the modernisation of Britain.

Socially, educational expansion was intended to increase social mobility, by providing pupils and students from working-class backgrounds with many more opportunities to obtain post-18 academic or vocational qualifications. This would ensure that Britain became much more meritocratic; what you know, rather than who you know, would increasingly shape citizens' life chances and employment opportunities, thereby breaking down class barriers and the disadvantages that had hitherto been endured by virtue of family background and socio-economic deprivation.

Of course, there was a crucial electoral consideration informing this public policy platform, because Wilson was cognisant of the need for the Labour Party to broaden its appeal beyond the traditional working class. The affluence of the 1950s had fostered a widespread assumption that much of the British working class was enjoying a process of *embourgeoisment*, and was thus less inclined to identify with Labour as strongly as in the past. Subsequent psephological studies challenged this assumption, but during the 1960s, it was a widely held perspective, not least in much of the Labour Party itself, and therefore underpinned internal debates about electoral strategy.

If sections of the working class were apparently turning away from Labour as a consequence of affluence and consumerism, then it was imperative that the party seek new sources of electoral support. Given that the traditional middle class had *never* been enamoured with the Labour, the party ostensibly faced a serious electoral predicament. Wilson discerned that the solution lay in appealing to the new sections of the middle class that were expanding during the early 1960s, most notably the administrators, scientists and technicians, along with other professionals likely to benefit from the expansion of higher education. Not only did many of these occupational groups constitute the personnel of Wilson's envisaged scientific and technological revolution, they were also assumed to be amenable to a public policy programme that attacked the allegedly out-of-date and out-of-touch 'establishment' (of which the Conservatives were deemed the political representatives) forever looking back nostalgically to a sepia-tinged past.

However, during his second term as Opposition leader, Wilson struggled to replicate his former success in crafting a distinctive and effective public policy platform. Instead, whereas in 1963–4, Wilson had been widely viewed as an innovative party leader who skilfully seized the initiative in devising a range of polices that simultaneously unified the Labour Party and seemingly provided an electorally attractive alternative to the policies of the ailing Conservative administration, the 1970–4 Wilson often seemed bereft of originality and inspiration. Not only did he increasingly seem to be responding to political initiatives pursued by others, most notably, of course, the Conservative Government led by Edward Heath, but his responses often seemed to be motivated primarily by the imperative of maintaining the unity of an increasingly fractious PLP riven again by a reinvigorated left–right power struggle. It should also be noted, though, that immediately after the 1970 election defeat, and in order to forestall a shift to the left, Wilson insisted that 'there will be no lurches of policy from what we did in Government', although he added that 'I hope there will be some healthy developments of new thinking' (quoted in Hatfield, 1978: 38).

The tardiness in devising a distinctive policy platform during 1970–4 owed much to Wilson's own partial disengagement from active party leadership in the first year of Labour's period in Opposition. The unexpected election defeat in June 1970 seemed to plunge Wilson into a state of depression and despair, to the extent that many of his closest colleagues expected him to resign as Labour leader, with Labour's Chief Whip, Robert (Bob) Mellish, predicting (in December 1970) that 'Harold Wilson would not be leader of the Leader of the Labour Party by the end of 1971' (Benn, 1988: 322, diary entry for 31 December 1970).

However, there was no discernible likelihood of an imminent leadership challenge, in spite of the disillusion that different sections of the PLP apparently felt with Wilson's leadership. Nonetheless, his low profile was a cause of considerable concern among some of his Parliamentary colleagues, to the extent that Frank Judd implored Wilson to have 'an honest heart to heart' talk with the party, while also offering a few of his morale-boosting 'classic jibes' against the Conservatives (MS Wilson, c.914, Judd to Wilson, 13 September 1970).

Much of Wilson's attention was initially focused on writing a personal record of the defeated 1964–70 Labour Governments (Wilson, 1971), reflecting, it seems, his concern to present his version of events, and thereby perhaps repair some of the political damage to his reputation accruing from the failures and problems experienced during his premiership. Yet in looking back over the previous six years, Wilson failed to look forward to the next four, and as such, policy initiatives passed both to the Heath Government and to Labour's increasingly organised and vocal left.

Not surprisingly, for most of this period, it was the Heath Government that set the political agenda, and which appeared to offer a form of technocratic modernisation through institutional reform and innovation – the very theme that Wilson had promoted in the mid-1960s. Moreover, on two notable policies pursued by the Heath Government, Wilson found himself obliged, largely for partisan reasons, to oppose measures very similar to ones which his Government had pursued just a few years earlier. Such instances, of course, merely reinforced the views of those critics who deemed Wilson to be an unprincipled opportunist and political chameleon for whom short-term pragmatism and tactical considerations all too often took precedence over strong principles and strategic vision.

For example, one of the key legislative items of the Heath Government was the 1971 Industrial Relations Act. The 1966–70 Wilson Government had itself introduced a Bill in 1969, based on the white paper *In Place of Strife*, to place statutory curbs on unofficial strikes. This Bill was withdrawn in face of hostility from many Labour MPs, particularly those sponsored by trade unions, but Wilson himself had originally deemed the Bill essential, and Labour's 1970 manifesto had alluded to new legislation to: 'Overhaul negotiating and dispute procedures' and facilitate 'legally binding agreements' where employers and trade unions mutually sought such deals. Yet a couple of year later, the Labour Party bitterly opposed the Industrial Relations Bill, although admittedly, Wilson himself adopted a relatively low-profile, and let the party's employment spokeswoman, Barbara Castle, along with sundry Labour backbenchers, pursue most of the party's Parliamentary attacks on the legislation.

However, it was the issue of British membership of the European Economic Community (EEC) that subsequently caused serious problems for Wilson in terms of crafting a credible and consistent public policy platform that was also commensurate with the maintenance of Labour Party unity. Back in 1967, while Prime Minister, Wilson had formally tendered Britain's second application to join the EEC, although like the previous application (submitted by the then Conservative Prime Minister four years earlier), this had been vetoed by the French President General de Gaulle. Yet when the 1970–4 Heath Government made Britain's third application for EEC membership, Wilson found himself in an extremely awkward political position, because ideological divisions within the PLP had subsequently deepened, with many on the party's right in favour of Britain joining the EEC, and Labour's increasingly prominent left opposed. Wilson's solution, in terms of a public policy response, was to oppose British membership of the EEC on the grounds that the terms and conditions negotiated by Heath were unacceptable. However, this stance was strongly shaped by Wilson's need to manage intra-party divisions over Europe, as we will note below, and as such, it represented another Wilsonian tactical response rather than a position based on principle.

One notable policy initiative emanating from the Labour leadership during this period, in conjunction with the trade unions, was the 'social contract', which constituted an agreement between the party and the unions over a range of economic, industrial and social polices that would be enacted by the next Labour Government, in exchange for voluntary restraint by the trade unions *vis-à-vis* wage claims (TUC–Labour Party Liaison Committee, 1973; see also Hatfield, 1978: Chapter 5; A. Morgan, 1992: 415–21; Warde, 1982: 145–7). In essence, the 'social contract' entailed the trade unions agreeing not to pursue inflationary pay claims, in return for which the Labour leadership would legislate to enhance employment and trade union rights, including repeal of the Industrial relations Act, while also improving the social wage (that is, welfare provision).

Party management

As noted above, Wilson's initial skills as a political communicator, and the public policy platform adopted, were both integral to overcoming, or avoiding, intra-party divisions between Labour's left and right. During Wilson's first term as Opposition Leader, the type of polices that Labour canvassed, and the discourses that Wilson deployed to explain and justify them, were carefully crafted and contextualised to render them amenable to the Labour Party's left and right alike, and thereby transcend intra-party ideological divisions. Certainly, the emphases on economic and industrial planning, modernisation of Britain's educational and political institutions, scientific progress and technological advance, all of which were *inter alia* intended to facilitate the recovery of the British economy, and thereby foster the economic growth necessary to finance many of Labour's social objectives, were amenable to favourable ideological interpretation by both the left and the right of the Labour Party.

The revisionist or social democratic Labour right viewed many of these policies and objectives as commensurate with their own vision of a fairer, more prosperous, society, attained through state regulation and planning of the economy (albeit largely as an alternative to, rather than dependent upon, further large-scale nationalisation), modernising political institutions to enhance their efficiency, and reforming the education system in order to widen access and promote equality of opportunity. This was intended to increase social mobility, which would primarily benefit the poor and disadvantaged, and in so doing, transform Britain into a meritocracy in which socio-economic backgrounds and divisions became less inhibitive and important. This, for Labour's social democrats, was the key to creating a classless, more egalitarian, society, rather than through left-wing shibboleths such as a major expansion of public ownership and even higher taxation of the rich and big business (both of which were deemed likely to prove counter-productive if pursued further).

Labour's left, meanwhile, was enthused by Wilson's professed commitment to state-sponsored economic and industrial planning, which the left viewed (or chose to interpret) as a means of controlling, and ultimately, transcending or superseding, capitalism. Indeed, some on the left assumed that planning would necessarily entail an extension of public ownership, in order to bring key industries under state control, ...and thereby ensure that they served the wider common good, rather than merely the interests of senior industrialists and shareholders. The left was also heartened by Wilson's professed commitment to political modernisation, which could be interpreted as a willingness to eradicate the overwhelmingly Conservative majority of hereditary peers in the House of Lords, and the Oxbridge-dominated 'elitist' civil service. Add to these the formal commitment to expanding comprehensive education *vis-à-vis* grammar schools, and it is perhaps easy to understand why the left chose to believe (however erroneously) that Wilson was intent on attacking institutions of apparent class domination or privilege, and thereby pursuing radical egalitarianism.

Certainly, in the immediate aftermath of Wilson's 1963 Conference speech linking science with socialism, a *Guardian* (5 October 1963) editorial declared that 'Labour [could] fairly claim that it has not been more united, personally and doctrinally, since 1945', while one of Wilson's Parliamentary colleagues, Richard Crossman, claimed that the new Labour leader had 'provided the revision of Socialism and its application to modern times which Gaitskell and Crosland had tried and completely failed to do. Harold has achieved it' (quoted in A. Morgan, 1992: 246). Certainly, the technocratic approach canvassed by Wilson, coupled with the emphasis on 'public enterprise', seemed to indicate that 'the old argument about nationalisation and private enterprise was left behind' (Shore, 1993: 89), whereupon both the Labour left and right chose to view Wilson's stance as an endorsement of their own perspectives and policy prescriptions, and assume that the new Labour leader was, at heart, 'one of us'. Or, as Noel Thompson has noted: 'Wilsonian speeches told the left what it wanted to hear, but party policy served to reassure the right', for 'while the idea and rhetoric of planning had a strong resonance with the left, the type of planning proposed ... was something that could be accommodated by the social democratic right' (Thompson, 2006: 63; see also Anderson, 1964: 16).

Needless to say, such interpretations (however naïve or mistaken) did much to foster a fragile party unity as the 1964 General Election loomed, leading the eminent labour historian Kenneth Morgan to claim that as a consequence of Wilson's leadership of the party during 1963–4: 'The dismal background of Labour's years of fratricide was set aside' (K. Morgan, 1992: 252).

The second aspect of Wilson's astute management of the Labour Party during 1963–4 was his allocation of Opposition front bench portfolios – or rather his lack of allocation, for upon becoming leader, 'Wilson had inherited an almost wholly Gaitskellite Shadow Cabinet and he wisely left them and their portfolios undisturbed' (Shore, 1993: 89). Yet he sought to assuage the left by declaring that he was 'running a Bolshevik revolution with a Tsarist Shadow Cabinet', a claim that somehow 'seems to have been taken seriously' (K. Morgan, 1992: 251). Nonetheless, the modernisation programme that Wilson promoted would also entail the creation of new ministries and thus new ministerial posts or portfolios, which enabled him to promise seemingly prestigious roles to senior Labour figures if and when the party won the imminent (1964) General Election.

As noted above, the aftermath of the 1970 Election defeat, and Wilson's initial semi-withdrawal from public life while he wrote his account of the 1964–70 Labour Government, facilitated a steady increase in intra-party factionalism and internecine power struggles, these being reinforced by the increasing strength and vociferousness of the left on Labour's National Executive Committee (NEC) and at the party's Annual Conference. In this context, 15 months after the June 1970 Election defeat, Frank Judd was exhorting Wilson to give a clear, firm lead, both to bolster his own authority, and because failure to do so would mean that 'the infighting between an apparently disorganised crowd of individuals will inevitably predominate', thereby spreading disillusioning throughout the labour movement (MS Wilson, c.914, Judd to Wilson, 24 September 1971).

According to Pimlott (1992: 573), although the 'post-1970 division was less serious than many ... the tensions were powerful, and the rivalry deep', which meant that 'the tenuous unity that was maintained until the February 1974 election required all Wilson's ingenuity and contortionist skill', but 'at a cost to his reputation, to his morale and to his appetite for office'. In this context, Wilson found it much more difficult than in 1963–4 to manage the PLP, for whereas in the mid-1960s he had had the advantages of being a new Labour leader facing an ailing Conservative Government with ageing and seemingly out-of-touch leaders, and with a General Election imminent after over a decade in Opposition (which greatly facilitated an outward semblance of party unity to provide 'one last heave'), the 1970–4 Wilson led a party that had just lost an election to a Conservative Party itself now led by a seemingly dynamic young leader espousing technocratic modernisation and institutional reform.

In spite of simmering intra-party tensions and despondency, Wilson was not vulnerable to a direct leadership challenge following the 1970 Election defeat, not least because there were, at this juncture, no candidates who were either willing to put themselves forward or would have been likely to fare any better than the incumbent at holding the PLP together. For example, a leading figure on Labour's right, Roy Jenkins, would never have secured the support of the left had he stood against Wilson, just as left-wingers such as Tony Benn, Barbara Castle and Michael Foot would have been anathema to the Labour right. In this context, Wilson found himself leading a party whose disparate factions and tendencies increasingly criticised him (often for not doing more to 'stand up to' the other wing of the party), but who were not able or willing to field a credible candidate against him in a leadership contest.

Consequently, whereas back in 1963–4 Wilson had been able to seize much of the initiative in terms of canvassing policies that could be interpreted favourably by virtually all sections of the PLP, and thus fostered a sense of unity, the 1970–4 era saw Wilson increasing struggling to manage a more disputatious Labour Party in which traditional left–right divisions were once again becoming wider and deeper. Yet, exasperatingly for Wilson, the more he contorted himself to adopt policy positions that would serve to assuage or appease the different sections of the PLP, the more these different wings chided him for opportunism, or for not siding with them on specific policies or issues.

This was most evident in the aforementioned stance that Wilson adopted over Edward Heath's application for British membership of the EEC, for whereas Wilson himself had applied in 1967, he subsequently opposed Heath's application on the grounds that the terms the latter had negotiated were unacceptable. This stance was adopted primarily in order to manage a PLP characterised by increasingly deep divisions between the (mostly) pro-EEC tight and the anti-EEC left, yet far from earning Wilson plaudits from the PLP for his efforts at holding together over such a divisive issue, his compromise position resulted in scorn from left and right alike. Both wings of the PLP felt deeply dismayed, and even betrayed, by Wilson's failure to endorse their respective stance; the right generally wanted to support Heath's approach, thereby securing a bipartisan approach to securing British membership of the EEC, while the left wanted Wilson to reject British membership outright. As such, in offering *qualified* opposition, on the grounds that the terms and conditions of EEC membership negotiated by Heath were not acceptable, Wilson inadvertently – or unavoidably – fuelled resentment on the left and right of the PLP simultaneously.

One particular episode concerning the EEC issue neatly illustrated how Wilson's efforts at pacifying the left and right of the PLP merely served to antagonise both equally. When it became apparent that Heath's Conservative Government was likely to grant the party's MPs a free (unwhipped) Parliamentary vote over the issue of Britain's membership of the EEC on the terms he had negotiated, Wilson initially intimated that Labour MPs would also enjoy a free vote, a stance strongly favoured by pro-EEC MPs on Labour's right. However, under pressure both from Bob Mellish, the party's Chief Whip, and the increasingly strident Labour left, Wilson apparently reneged on this commitment in a hastily convened special meeting of the Shadow Cabinet (which Roy Jenkins, Deputy Leader and staunch pro-European was unable to attend) on 18 October 1971, at which it was agreed that Labour

MPs would be subject to a three-line whip to oppose EEC membership on the terms and conditions attained by Heath. This decision was endorsed the following morning by a meeting of the PLP, at which 159 Labour MPs voted in favour of a three-line whip to oppose the Government, while 89 voted against (favouring a free vote).

As Ben Pimlott explained, this particular episode irked senior figures on Labour's right and the left alike: 'Jenkins because he considered Wilson cowardly for permitting a whipped vote, [Tony] Benn because he thought Wilson cowardly for proposing a free one' (Pimlott, 1992: 590). However, Wilson's manoeuvrings over the EEC issue attracted some grudging admiration from an editorial in The *Observer* (3 October 1971), which remarked that while 'Some people admire the dexterity with which Mr Wilson has handled the European issues, others are appalled at his cynicism. But everyone must recognise his success in keeping his party united when it might well have been torn apart.'

Meanwhile, in order to 'manage' divisions within the PLP over the EEC, Wilson also promised that a Labour Government would hold a referendum on continued membership on the terms agreed by Heath, yet when such a plebiscite had originally been mooted by Tony Benn, back in November 1970, Wilson had flatly rejected the proposal.

There were two other main ways in which Wilson sought to manage and maintain party unity during the 1970–4 period, namely the development of the 'social contract', and, as in 1963–4, the judicious appointment of Shadow Cabinet posts and portfolios.

The 'social contract', as noted above, enshrined a series of policy commitments that were intended to appeal to the left and right of the PLP alike. However, it was also expressly intended to unify the 'political' and 'industrial' wings of the British organised labour movement, namely the Labour Party itself and the trade unions. Labour's Parliamentary leadership evidently hoped that the 'social contract' would simultaneously heal the divisions caused between the party and the unions during the late 1960s (arising from union hostility to statutory incomes policies and *In Place of Strife*), while also persuading the electorate that Labour could work harmoniously with the trade unions – a key factor in the context of the Heath Government's repeated clashes with them in the early 1970s, and the ensuing industrial conflict thus engendered.

With regard to effecting party management through key appointments or endorsements, two particular aspects warrant brief mention. First, Wilson gave his support to Roy Jenkins when the latter stood for election to the post of Deputy Leader immediately after the 1970 Election defeat, while exhorting Barbara Castle not to stand against Jenkins. The Labour leader was anxious that as a prominent figure on the left, Castle's candidature might exacerbate ideological tensions within the PLP, whereas formal PLP unity (and, arguably, his own position) would be better served 'by pinning down a potential opponent. ... He wanted to bind the Right to him; the last thing he wished for was to be shackled to a reconstituted Left' (Pimlott, 1992: 570). Wilson then backed Jenkins again the following year, when the latter was challenged from the left by Tony Benn and Michael Foot. In both cases, Wilson was presumably acting in accordance with the principle of keeping one's friends close and one's enemies closer.

Second, when Jenkins resigned as Deputy Leader in April 1972 – joined by a handful of other shadow junior ministers on the right of the party – ostensibly because of the [Labour] Shadow Cabinet's decision to support a referendum on Britain's membership of the EEC, Wilson used the consequent mini-reshuffle to appoint James Callaghan to the key post of Shadow Foreign Secretary. This was a shrewd move, because although Callaghan was clearly on the right of the PLP on many issues – and had previously been viewed by some as potential rival to Wilson – he had also adopted an increasingly (albeit pragmatically) cautious line on the EEC as the Labour Party overall became more sceptical or even hostile during the early 1970s (Pimlott, 1992: 581). Callaghan's overall stature and experience in the PLP (and his potential appeal to the trade unions, having opposed *In Place of Strife* back in 1969) rendered him a potentially useful ally in shaping Labour policy *vis-à-vis* the EEC, while also prising him away from the 'Jenkinsites', some of whom were deeply dismayed by Callaghan's shifting stance over Europe and his support for the referendum.

Emotional intelligence

In Wilson's case especially, it is difficult to distinguish between the personal and the political, for while he has generally been viewed as an arch-pragmatist, it is difficult to determine the extent to which this derived from his own personal aversion to conflict and disagreement, or was primarily motivated from an understandable political desire to maintain the ideological unity of the PLP by avoiding contentious decisions or policies that might reignite intra-party disagreements.

Although Wilson was intelligent, as evinced by his educational background and qualifications, he was certainly not an intellectual. On the contrary, he seemed to share the quiet contempt that many senior Labour figures have felt towards political theorists and 'ivory tower academics'. On one occasion, for example, he boasted that he had never read beyond the first three pages of volume one (of three) of Karl Marx's major work, *Das Kapital*, an assertion that was clearly intended to convey the image of a Labour leader who was more interested in practical policies for the real world than abstract ideas and theories adumbrated by left-wing thinkers.

This anti-intellectualism was also closely associated with more general public persona that Wilson cultivated, as we noted above: down-to-earth, provincial (in a positive way) and in touch with 'ordinary folk', even though he had received a grammar school and Oxford education.

During his first term as Opposition Leader, before he had seemingly become exhausted or exasperated by the demoralising vicissitudes of being Prime Minister, Wilson initially appeared to be a benign and inspiring character, one who was an open and approachable party leader. Having swiftly crafted a public policy platform that appeared both to have unified the PLP, and made imminent electoral victory seem highly likely, Wilson's early leadership exuded a relaxed confidence and affability which, along with a rapier wit that was often directed against his Conservative opponents, galvanised many of his Parliamentary colleagues after twelve years languishing in Opposition. Tony Benn was among those greatly heartened by the character and style of Wilson's early leadership, deeming him to be 'an excellent chairman ... [who] gets on well with people, and has some radical instincts, whereas Gaitskell had none' (Benn, 1987: 5, diary entry for 14 February 1963). A few weeks later, following a bilateral meeting with Wilson, Benn reported that it was 'a delight to find him so relaxed and easy', particularly as Gaitskell 'used to be so tense and tired' (Benn, 1987: 9, diary entry for 25 March 1963). During the next two months, Benn remarked apropos Wilson: 'What a change from Hugh. That man knows how to get the best out of people', and that: 'He has a very sure touch' (Benn, 1987: 13, diary entries for 29 April and 3 May 1964). Another Labour parliamentarian claims that during 1963–4, 'Wilson proved to be an outstanding leader of the Opposition ... assured in the House, fluent on television ... a professional to his finger tips' (Radice, 2002: 125–6).

By contrast, during the 1970–4 period, Wilson had, perhaps not surprisingly, lost much of his former confidence and sureness of touch. Three main reasons account for this personal transformation. First, the events and crises with which the 1966–70 Labour Government had to contend had naturally proved emotionally and politically exhausting, and prevented the Labour Party from accomplishing many of the political objectives and policy goals with which it had contested the 1964 and 1966 elections. Consequently, the energy, enthusiasm and quiet self-confidence that had characterised Wilson's leadership in 1963–4, and which had so impressed some of his senior colleagues, steadily dissipated.

Second, but inextricably linked to the last point, the 1966–70 Labour Government's responses to these events and problems often caused disagreements and tensions within the PLP, often between left and right, but sometimes – most notably with regard to incomes policies and *In Place of Strife* – between Labour MPs who were sponsored by a trade union and those who were not. There were also discernible differences in attitudes over aspects of social liberalism (the so-called permissive revolution) such as abolition of the death penalty, divorce and homosexuality, with Labour's growing number of younger, middle-class, university-educated MPs often proving more enthusiastic or relaxed about such reforms than some of their older, proletarian party colleagues, the latter more likely to harbour morally or socially conservative views on lifestyle or sexual issues. The cumulative effect of such divisions and tensions was to make management of the PLP increasingly difficult from 1966 onwards. This alone would have taxed Wilson's leadership skills and tireless efforts at maintaining party unity, but it meant than increasingly he found himself criticised by different sections or wings of the PLP for his stance on specific issues, often simultaneously.

It was largely in this context that his pragmatism, necessitated by the maintenance of Labour Party and Cabinet unity, earned Wilson a growing reputation for being a 'shifty' political operator devoid of political principles, and who was, instead, an opportunist primarily focused on short-term tactical considerations. The increasing criticism which was directed against the Labour leader from various of his colleagues, right up to Cabinet rank, during the latter half of the 1960s, itself fuelled a growing defensiveness and insecurity in Wilson. Indeed, a few critics were not averse to suggesting or implying that Wilson was suffering from paranoia, particularly as on some occasions he interpreted criticisms of his decisions or stance as evidence that their were plots against him, which merely compounded his increasing defensiveness and growing irascibility towards various colleagues, even to some of those who had hitherto been close to him.

Third, the loss of the 1970 General Election understandably shook what remained of Wilson's self-confidence so that, coupled with the cumulative impact of the two factors we have just noted, the Harold Wilson who led the Labour Party in Opposition until 1974 was, for much of this time, a rather different character from the 1963–4 version. As previously mentioned, Wilson's initial response to the 1970 Election defeat was to retreat somewhat for the first year, while he wrote his record of the 1966–70 Labour Governments. Not surprisingly, though, many of his senior colleagues interpreted this political reclusiveness as an indication that Wilson had lost his personal drive and determination, and would imminently announce his resignation. Others close to him, who did not expect or want him to resign, were nonetheless deeply concerned about the impression that would be created by Wilson's self-imposed semi-exile, with Frank Judd warning Wilson of the need to avoid giving critics (in the party and beyond) the opportunity to claim that he is 'defensive, petulant and bitterly preoccupied with Ted Heath's success' (MS Wilson, c.914, Judd to Wilson, 13 September 1970).

Conclusion

In spite of his affability, down-to-earth manner, enthusiasm and sparkling wit in 1963–4, the enduring image of Harold Wilson has been dominated by subsequent developments, with the trials and tribulations of his 1966–70 premiership, and his subsequent leadership of the 1970–4 Labour Opposition, providing ample examples for those who have wanted to condemn him by depicting him as a crafty opportunist and devious political operator who was devoid of genuine political principles, and who was invariably concerned much more with short-term tactics rather than long-term strategy or vision. The sundry guises and stances adopted by Wilson prompted one commentator, Walter Terry, to refer to the 'ten faces of Harold' – Huddersfield Harold, American Harold, Nationalise 'em Harold, Capitalist Harold, etc (*Daily Mail*, 19 June 1964; see also Sandbrook, 2006: Chapter 2), alluding to the different personas that Wilson seemed to adopt at different junctures and on different occasions, to the extent that no-one could be confident about who the 'real' Harold actually was. Terry wryly added that some of Wilson's Parliamentary colleagues wondered whether 'ten faces' was a conservative estimate.

Meanwhile, even in 1963–4, some on Labour's revisionist right, such as Bill Rodgers, disliked and distrusted Wilson, whom they believed lacked the admirable qualities they ascribed to Gaitskell: 'Where Gaitskell was straight, Wilson was tricky. Where Gaitskell had vision, Wilson was the super-tactician' – although Rodgers candidly admits that some of his 'resentment towards Wilson' derived simply from the fact that he challenged and then replaced Gaitskell, whom Rodgers had greatly admired and respected (Rodgers, 2000: 73). From the left, the *New Statesman* (30 June 1972) lambasted Wilson's leadership, claiming that he 'stands today as the principal apostle of cynicism, the unwitting evangelist of disillusion. There have been just too great a number of tawdry compromises.'

Yet whatever Wilson's personal defects and political deficiencies, it is hard to imagine any other Labour leader faring better during these two periods. Certainly, the increasingly fractious nature of the PLP during much of Wilson's leadership would similarly have limited the room for manoeuvre and options of any other Labour leader. Tragically for Wilson, it was the deepening divisions and concomitant personality clashes between the left and right of the PLP that often obliged him to adopt seemingly cynical or unprincipled positions and policy stances, but which then attracted accusations from both wings of the Labour Party about his shallow opportunism and shameless pragmatism. Of course, in any political party, when one faction or tendency accuses the leadership of failing to pursue the correct or ideological consistent policies, what they often really mean is that their leader is not adopting the stance or policy position *they* want adopted or pursued.

It is thus difficult to envisage how Wilson could have acted differently and proved more successful in leading the Labour Party in Opposition in 1963–4 and 1970–4. Had he sided more often or more openly with the left, it would have earned even more bitter recriminations from senior figures on Labour's right, such as Roy Jenkins, possibly to the extent of prompting an open split in the PLP and the formation of a breakaway party (as occurred in 1981, when Jenkins and three other former Labour Ministers – the 'gang of four' – formed the Social Democratic Party). Yet had Wilson opted to side unequivocally with the revisionist right, this would similarly have provoked fierce denunciations and accusations of betrayal or selling-out by the increasingly organised and vocal left. In either case, Labour's chances of winning the next General Election would have been greatly diminished, due largely to the British electorate's understandable reluctance to vote for a clearly divided party.

Wilson evidently understood this vital fact better than many of his critics, and so strove ceaselessly to adopt compromise positions that would hold the PLP together, and maintain an outward semblance of party unity. It was not an attractive or edifying spectacle, but electorally and politically it was absolutely necessary. Yet in struggling to hold the Labour Party together, Wilson was often compelled to adopt or shift policy stances that sullied his own reputation, and resulted in a tarnished legacy.

6
Alec Douglas-Home, 1964–5

Michael Hill

Alec Douglas-Home holds two unfortunate British political records: he is the shortest-serving post-war Prime Minister, with just 364 days separating his appointment and his defeat in the 1964 General Election. In addition his tenure as Leader of the Opposition, between October 1964 and July 1965, was even shorter than his spell as Prime Minister and consequently, Douglas-Home also has the dubious distinction of being the shortest-serving Leader of the Opposition of the post-war period, excluding temporary occupants such as George Brown, Margaret Beckett, John Major and Harriet Harman. This short time at the very top of the Conservative Party means that Douglas-Home is largely passed over in literature covering the period, as he is sandwiched between Macmillan's high-water mark of one-nation Conservatism and Heath's failed attempts at ideological renewal (Evans and Taylor, 1996: 101–40).

This chapter suggests that Douglas-Home's chances of any degree of success as Leader of the Opposition were undermined not just by the fact that he lost the General Election of October 1964, but also because the Conservative Party remained deeply troubled about the means by which he had acquired the party leadership and premiership in October 1963. In addition the chapter identifies two other dimensions that explained why his tenure was so short. First, his weaknesses in terms of public communication, and second that Douglas-Home showed little personal ambition to withstand the criticism and fight to retain the role.

The circumstances around Sir Alec Douglas-Home's appointment were and indeed still are a matter of controversy and debate: as a consequence his legitimacy and mandate to lead the Conservative Party was always a matter of dispute. This is not the place to go into detail about the war of the Macmillan succession. However, some Conservatives alleged that Macmillan had manipulated the process of choosing a successor from his hospital bed: the backbench Conservative MP Humphrey Berkley claimed that he and his colleagues were asked a loaded question: 'If there is deadlock between Rab [Butler] and Quintin [Hogg] would you accept Alec Home?' (Punnett,

1992: 41). These accusations had serious consequences for Douglas-Home's leadership as:

> the controversial means by which he had acquired the party leadership had been divisive in equal measure: both the figurehead of the libertarian right, Powell, and the articulator of the one-nation left, Iain Macleod, refused to serve in the Douglas-Home government. Their refusal undermined his credibility as the newly installed party leader.
>
> (Heppell, 2008a: 34)

Macleod later made public in an article in the *Spectator* magazine his objections to the way in which Douglas-Home acquired the leadership. Macleod claimed that the succession process had been rigged by Harold Macmillan and a 'magic circle' of Old Etonians who had conspired to stop R. A. Butler and make one of their own Conservative leader (D. R. Thorpe, 1996: 344). He also argued that by choosing Douglas-Home the Conservative Party was:

> proposing to admit that after 12 years of Tory government no one amongst the 363 members in the House of Commons was acceptable as Prime Minister.
>
> (Heffer, 1998: 327)

Macleod's article not only caused deep discontent and resentment within the party, it also undermined the credibility of the Conservative Party as a modern political institution as it exposed the 'customary processes' as being 'inherently rigged to the advantage of social unrepresentative elites and to the disadvantage of more meritocratic and socially representative Conservative parliamentarians' (Garnett, 2005: 196–7). The manner of Douglas-Home's accession to the leadership highlighted the Conservative Party's obsolescence and sounded the death-knell of the traditional methods of choosing the Conservative Party leader (Evans and Taylor, 1996: 131).

Despite the controversy Douglas-Home's main rivals for the leadership, Hailsham [Hogg] and Butler, agreed to serve under him. Had either refused it would have fatally undermined Douglas-Home's leadership from the outset (Watkins, 1998: 76). Nevertheless Douglas-Home had a difficult job ahead of him. He a little under a year in which to prepare the Conservative Party for a general election, which it duly lost. Several factors contributed to the defeat: first, Douglas-Home's Government suffered from the economic legacy of the Conservative's previous two election victories. Evidence of relative economic decline undermined their appeal and the attempt to address this by seeking membership of the EEC, and being rebuffed undermined their credibility further. Rejection left the Conservative Party without a convincing narrative for modernisation (Turner, 1996: 346).

Moreover, by 1964 the party looked divided and out of touch with the public mood of the early 1960s. The public has also grown bored of a long period being ruled by the same party and there was a palpable feeling that it was 'time for a change'. The Conservative Party's new leader could make no difference to this desire for change, as the aristocratic Douglas-Home seemed, to many people, to be from the same mould as Macmillan and reinforced the harmful 'grouse moor' image of the party (Gilmour and Garnett, 1997: 204). Although he avoided much of the blame for losing the election, defeat in 1964 'effectively disabled Alec Douglas-Home as a long-term leader, confirming him as a stop-gap who was bound to give way sooner rather than later' (J. Campbell, 1993: 166).

Public communication

The impression that Douglas-Home's leadership would inevitably be temporary was reinforced by his poor communication skills. Not only was he uncomfortable with old-fashioned political campaigning 'on the stump' but he also failed to get to grips with and came across poorly on the relatively new and increasingly important medium of television. In Douglas-Home's memoirs he confessed that, while he recognised that television was an essential tool of political communication, he was nevertheless ill at ease on television and that 'I could not conceal my distaste for the conception that the political leader had also to be an actor on the screen' (Douglas-Home, 1976: 203). In addition, he was poor at memorising speeches, and television producers thought that teleprompters would be too complicated for Douglas-Home to use (K. Young, 1970: 213). These shortcomings made him nervous, which caused his lips to dry out, and to moisten them Douglas-Home constantly pushed his tongue out like a lizard (Dutton, 2006: 66). He was also unfortunate that his looks were not suited to the television technology of the day. In his memoirs, he recounted an amusing and revealing off-screen conversation with a makeup artist:

Q. Can you not make me look better than I do on television?
A. No.
Q. Why not?
A. Because you have a head like a skull.
Q. Does not everyone have a head like a skull?
A. No.

(Douglas-Home, 1976: 203)

Things were little better when Douglas-Home, reverted to more traditional campaigning methods and spoke at public meetings. His inability to read from a script led reporters to joke that they 'were clubbing together to buy him the other half of his half moon glasses' (Howard and West, 1965: 116).

In addition, although Douglas-Home could perform well when facing a friendly audience, or when speaking about foreign affairs, he was very poor at dealing with heckling. This easily threw him out of his stride, leaving him unable to react quickly enough to regain control of the situation. As a result Labour Party managers tried to ensure that Labour activists were present at all Douglas-Home's public meetings and interrupted him as loudly and often as possible (Dutton, 2006: 81).

Finally, Douglas-Home did not have the Parliamentary skills needed by an effective Leader of the Opposition. For set-piece debates Douglas-Home preferred to write his own speeches and could not engage with his speechwriters at the Conservative Research Department, who in turn found it difficult to write speeches for him (Ramsden, 1996: 215). In addition, he could not cope with the more pugnacious Harold Wilson: at the despatch box Douglas-Home frequently stumbled over the names of colleagues or over details of policy, which made his supporters nervous every time he stood up to speak (Evans and Taylor, 1996: 130; Ramsden, 1998: 380). He called computers 'imputers', and during one speech he inadvertently gave Geoffrey Ripon a knighthood (Ramsden, 1996: 215). In addition Labour employed the same heckling and jeering tactics that so discomforted Douglas-Home at public meetings, further undermining his performance in Parliament (K. Young, 1970: 222). Douglas-Home's Parliamentary shortcomings when Prime Minister could be dismissed as 'lofty disdain stemming from a desire not to besmirch his high office' (Evans and Taylor, 1996: 130). However, as Leader of the Opposition:

> his defects as a parliamentarian were now far more damaging than when in office. He was too much of a specialist and he lacked the speed of repartee or the ability to coin phrases which enable a politician to cut a figure in the House of Commons.
>
> (Blake, 1998: 297)

Douglas-Home refused to indulge in knockabout attacks on Wilson that would have helped rally backbench Conservative support. He also refused to attack government policy that might be right, just to make his backbenchers happy (Gilmour and Garnett, 1997: 218). This laid-back attitude to Opposition led Douglas-Home's first biographer, Kenneth Young, to write of Sir Alec that:

> the sheep looked up to the shepherd and were not fed. ... It is likely that he simply did not hear the plaintive ba-ba-ba from the patient sheep so far from the purlieus of Westminster.
>
> (K. Young, 1970: 226)

These defects led Labour's Richard Crossman to note in his diaries that Douglas-Home was 'totally ineffective as Leader of the Opposition; and there are already to-ings and fro-ings about who shall replace him and how it shall be done' (Dutton, 2006: 88).

Public policy platform

Whilst Douglas-Home was further to the right of the party than his predecessor Macmillan, he was still a long way ideologically from the likes of Enoch Powell. Douglas-Home's political philosophy, such as it was, was also rooted in his patrician background. With limited trust in the voters' ability to understand politics Douglas-Home believed that Conservatism was simply about 'doing the right thing at the right time' (Douglas-Home, 1976: 187). As he had little interest in the formulation of policy Douglas-Home decided to delegate the task, even though the party leader traditionally took a leading role in the policy-making process. Consequently, Edward Heath was put in charge of a rapid policy review in readiness for a snap General Election, taking over the chairmanship of both the Advisory Committee on Policy and the chairmanship of the Conservative Research Department from Butler (J. Campbell, 1993: 167).

As another General Election could be imminent, the party did not have the time to conduct an in-depth analysis of why it lost in 1964; rather it needed some eye-catching new policies to counter the perception that it was tired and had run out of ideas (J. Campbell, 1993: 170). Initially Heath set up twenty small groups made up of Conservative MPs, and outside experts from business and academia: the groups were initially told to report back within six months (Garnett, 2005: 206). By early 1965 Heath had set up over thirty small groups, involving over 100 Conservative MPs, studying different policy areas and making recommendations. These were then sent to the Advisory Committee on policy to be collated and approved before being sent to the Shadow Cabinet. As chairman of the ACP Heath saw every policy paper before it was passed to his senior colleagues (J. Campbell, 1993: 172). As a consequence of the growing scale of the policy review, together with the perception that there would be no election until 1966 at the earliest, no new policies were finalised during Douglas-Home's period as Leader of the Opposition. This lack of new policy, together with Douglas-Home's back-seat position in the policy-making process and the correspondingly high-profile role played by Heath was to have serious consequences for Douglas-Home's ability to manage party tensions.

Party management

Douglas-Home was given the credit for the party's better than expected performance at the General Election in which the Conservatives narrowly missed out on a fourth consecutive election victory (Dutton, 2006: 87). Indeed, there were surprisingly few recriminations over the election result.

A mere nine hundred more votes in the right constituencies would have been enough for the Conservatives to retain office; many Conservatives were relieved the result was not much worse (Ramsden, 1996: 230). Moreover, polling carried out immediately after the election showed that although 49 per cent of the public thought that Douglas-Home should resign, 40 per cent that thought he should not. Of known Conservative voters 56 per cent wanted him to stay. Another survey of Conservative parliamentarians taken in February 1965 found that less than a quarter believed that the party would do better with another leader, and even those MPs who wanted Douglas-Home to resign did not wish to force him out (J. Campbell, 1993: 174).

When forming his initial Shadow Cabinet (known then as the Leader's Consultative Committee, the LCC), Douglas-Home took care to spread the jobs around so that no potential leadership contenders should have too much prominence and be seen to be the heir apparent (J. Campbell, 1993: 167). Consequently the LCC included R. A. Butler shadowing foreign affairs and Reginald Maudling continuing with the Treasury brief, while Edward Heath was tasked both with shadowing George Brown's Ministry for Economic Affairs and also developing future Conservative policy. The prodigal Enoch Powell and Iain Macleod were brought in from the cold: Powell shadowed Transport, while Macleod was to lead the opposition to Labour's steel nation-alisation programme (D. R. Thorpe, 1996: 378). In February 1965 Butler left politics, having accepted a life peerage and the mastership of Trinity College, Cambridge (Ramsden, 1996: 232). In the consequent reshuffle Edward Du Cann was appointed Party Chairman, in a move that seemed designed to modernise the party's image, while William Whitelaw's appointment as Chief Whip was welcomed by many backbenchers who had become increasingly disenchanted with Martin Redmayne (Dutton, 2006: 89; Ramsden, 1996: 232). Maudling was promoted to deputy leader and Shadow Foreign Secretary, which improved his all-round experience. However, Douglas-Home also made Heath Shadow Chancellor, which had the effect of improving Heath's posi-tion relative to Maudling. The controversial 1965 Finance Bill ensured that the economy became a high-profile issue and Heath boosted his leadership credentials by mounting a strong offensive against the proposals (Gilmour and Garnett, 1997: 217). In addition, Maudling had little familiarity with foreign affairs and soon found himself overshadowed by Douglas-Home's vast experience (J. Campbell, 1993: 168). Iain Macleod, another possible successor to Douglas-Home, also found himself marginalised as, constrained by their small majority, Labour delayed their plans to renationalise the steel industry (Ramsden, 1996: 232).

Although Douglas-Home wanted to remain as leader and there was no immediate will within the party to force him out, there was still some residual bitterness over the way in which he had acquired the leadership. Douglas-Home realised that the old system of informal consultation could not continue, saying that he 'didn't think that any election by the same methods would ever carry any public confidence again' (Punnett, 1992: 44). Therefore a new formal system for electing the party leader would have to be set up. However, Douglas-Home did not intend the new system to be used in the immediate future, hoping rather that the party could be made to look more modern and democratic, while he continued as leader (Garnett, 2005: 197). Douglas-Home was also pressed by Humphrey Berkley, who suggested a secret ballot of MPs or an Electoral College and asked Douglas-Home to set up a small committee to consider which process should be adopted (D. R. Thorpe, 1996: 378–9). Douglas-Home acceded to Berkley's request and set up a committee consisting most of the central characters from 1963: Douglas-Home, Butler, Hogg, Macleod, Lord Dilhorne and Redmayne (Dutton, 2006: 89). One of the matters for consideration was whether the ballot should be restricted to MPs, or whether it should be opened up to include the wider party. In the end the idea that Conservatives outside the House of Commons should play a formal role in selecting the leader was rejected on the grounds that it ran the risk of imposing on the party in the Commons a leader whom a majority of MPs would not have chosen (Shepherd, 1995: 386). It was also felt that as the leader was bound to be an MP, the best-placed people to judge the respective strengths and weaknesses of leadership candidates were their fellow MPs (Shepherd, 1991: 163). Consequently the committee decided to limit the participation of Conservatives outside the Commons:

> to a consultative (and thereby) token role. This consultative role was based on the assumption that the views of the party membership, constituency chairs, and Conservative peers, could be expressed to Conservative parliamentarians, prior to the holding of the ballot. By feeding their views into the process at the pre-ballot stage, it negated the fear of the wider party being able to override the choice made by Conservative MPs.
>
> (Bogdanor, 1994: 83)

These consultations, according to one committee member, were 'complete nonsense, but they help make the rest of the party feel better' (Shepherd, 1991: 163). Restricting the franchise to Members of Parliament also had the added advantage of allowing the selection process to be completed in a relatively short time, with even the longest campaign taking just two weeks, thus avoiding prolonged and possibly divisive campaigns (Punnett, 1992: 55). The new rules for selecting the party leader were approved during February 1965 by both the Shadow Cabinet and the 1922 Committee. The system eventually chosen allowed for up to three ballots of MPs:

> A single ballot would be sufficient, provided that the leading candidate enjoyed an overall majority plus a minimum lead of fifteen per cent

over the runner up. If no one jumped these hurdles, the slate would be cleaned for a second ballot. Prospective candidates could hold back from the initial contest, if they calculated that no outright winner would emerge and preferred not to declare themselves at the outset. An overall majority was still required, and the top three candidates would go forward to a final run off if necessary. This third ballot would allow MPs to declare a second preference, ensuring that a clear winner would be found once the least popular candidate had been eliminated.

(Garnett, 2005: 197)

The requirement for a candidate to achieve a majority plus 15 per cent of those who voted, in order to win after one round, was designed to ensure that the winner had a clear and decisive mandate to lead the party. Crucially the original rules were only designed to operate when there was a vacancy for the leadership. There were no provisions for Conservative MPs to challenge an unpopular or failing leader (Punnett, 1992: 55–7). Douglas-Home could have used the new system to his own benefit by resigning and standing for the self-created vacancy (John Major's tactic in 1995): as there was at the time no obvious candidate to replace Douglas-Home he may well have won a renewed and undisputed mandate (Gilmour and Garnett, 1997: 218; K. Young, 1970: 225). A *Daily Telegraph* poll of Conservative MPs conducted on 7 February 1965 found the 75 per cent of Conservative parliamentarians wanted Douglas-Home to continue as leader. If he did resign, 35 per cent wanted Maudling, 28 per cent wanted the still-available Butler and a mere 10 per cent favoured Heath.

By not using the new rules to renew his mandate Douglas-Home made a serious political misjudgement from which he could not recover (Ramsden, 1996: 234). The security of his position was partly dependent on wider electoral considerations. His rivals and critics had been constrained by the possibility of having to fight another General Election in the near future, which gave the Conservatives no option but to unite around Douglas-Home. As Campbell noted, 'for all his limitations Sir Alec was a unifying figure, while a divisive leadership contest might tempt Wilson to catch the Opposition in disarray by calling a snap election' (J. Campbell, 1993: 175).

However, Harold Wilson's announcement in June 1965 that there would not be a General Election that year removed that constraint. It therefore gave the Conservatives both the freedom and time to choose a new leader and gave the new leader time to establish himself (Baston, 2004: 253). That weekend a story appeared in the press claiming that 100 Conservative parliamentarians were involved in a plot to remove Douglas-Home and that one of the alleged ringleaders was Anthony Kershaw, who had been Heath's Parliamentary Private Secretary when the Conservatives were in Government (*The Times*, 13/7/1965: 12). The story was denied, but the suspicion was that Heath's supporters had overplayed their hand. Although there was no suggestion that Heath was involved one Shadow Cabinet member told the *Daily Telegraph* that 'Ted must have known about it: he did not stop it' (J. Campbell, 1993: 176). Moreover, Douglas-Home's supporters became alarmed that Heath's dominant role in the policy review was undermining Douglas-Home's position as leader, as Heath became seen as the modern face of the Conservative Party. Some Conservative MPs believed that the whole policy review process was designed to advance Heath's leadership ambitions (J. Campbell, 1993: 12–173).

Douglas-Home's position had already been undermined in March 1965 by the loss, to the Liberals, of a by-election in the formerly safe seat of Roxburgh, Selkirk and Peebles, a seat close to Douglas-Home's Kinross constituency, which greatly unsettled Conservative MPs (Dutton, 2006: 90). This led Alan Watkins, writing in *The Spectator*, to ask, 'how much longer can Alec Douglas-Home continue as leader of the Conservative Party? After the loss of Roxburgh the question really does not have to be asked. It asks itself' (Shepherd, 1995: 394). The Roxburgh, Selkirk and Peebles by-election was not just significant for the result: the defeated Conservative candidate, Robin McEwan, was an old Etonian Scottish laird and a personal friend of Douglas-Home. Thus, Roxburgh, Selkirk and Peebles refocused attention on the aristocratic and out-of-date image of Sir Alec that many Conservatives believed was damaging to the party (Fisher, 1977: 118). The issue of the leadership was discussed by the LCC on 31 March, when Douglas-Home asked for the Committee's support, but said that the most important thing was the unity of the party and that he would immediately stand aside if his continued leadership caused divisions within the Parliamentary Party. Douglas-Home's colleagues were for the most part supportive, but had differing views on the best course of action. Lord Carrington suggested working harder to get the press onside; Peter Thorneycroft argued that Douglas-Home submit himself to a vote within the party, while Enoch Powell thought that 'there was a danger of getting over-excited about the whole situation – time would do its work' (CPA 31/3/1965).

However, unrest within the Parliamentary Party continued, and on 5 July a motion signed by 25 backbenchers, mostly Heath supporters, was put to the 1922 Committee, asking for a debate on the question of the leadership. Douglas-Home was informed that party feeling was running against him (D. R. Thorpe, 1996: 386). Douglas-Home was also influenced by a William Rees-Mogg article in *The Sunday Times*, which appeared on 18 July, titled 'The Right Moment for Change'. Mogg argued that it was unlikely that the Conservatives could win the next election under Douglas-Home and that it was time for him to give way to a younger man. Douglas-Home had:

> played the sort of captain's innings one used to see in county cricket before the war. There were then in most counties good club players, often

fresh from university, who were appointed captain because they were amateurs. They lacked the professional skills and they never had very high averages. But occasionally ... they would come in ... and see their side past the follow-on.

(D. R. Thorpe, 1996: 387)

In addition to Rees-Mogg's article, Labour's lead in the polls had increased from 2 per cent to 4.6 per cent (Dutton, 2006: 92). Moreover, Douglas-Home was appalled to discover that opinion poll findings also showed he was regarded as being less honest than Wilson (Baston, 2004: 253). As a consequence, Douglas-Home announced his resignation to the 1922 Committee on 22 July. He made it clear that it was his decision and that he had resigned to preserve the unity of the Conservative Party (Ramsden, 1996: 236). Forcing Douglas-Home out of the leadership was, arguably, as big a mistake as choosing him as leader in the first place. It was always likely that Labour would win the next General Election, whenever it was called. Therefore it would have been better for the Conservative Party to go down to defeat under Douglas-Home, thus allowing his replacement to start with a clean slate (Gilmour and Garnett, 1997: 219).

Emotional intelligence

Douglas-Home's cognitive style, his understanding of politics and of the electorate together with voters' perceptions of him were inevitably coloured by his social background. He was born into an aristocratic Scottish family whose peerage dated back to the fifteenth century: the family owned two baronial mansions and 100,000 acres of land, which were tended by 70 staff (Dutton, 2006: 1–2). Consequently Douglas-Home never experienced many of the things that many people took for granted:

> Sir Alec filling a boiler or standing in a queue in the pouring rain waiting for a bus was inconceivable. He did not borrow books from the library; the books flooded in, mint new, from the authors and publishers. He did not try to make ends meet: they met.
>
> (K. Young, 1970: 187)

In the context of the mid-1960s Douglas-Home seemed to be a figure from a bygone age, remote and out of touch. Iain Macleod once remarked that if Douglas-Home was '... asked about unemployment he would probably think his questioner was referring to a shortage of ghillies' (Shepherd, 1995: 368). This remoteness from the lives of ordinary people became publicly apparent when Douglas-Home made a serious gaffe during a television interview on the BBC's *Election Forum* programme, in which the party leaders answered questions submitted by viewers. In a reply to a question about pensions Douglas-Home said:

> over and above the basic pension, in future years, we will give a dona-
> tion to the pensioners who are over a certain age because they are in the
> greatest need.
>
> (D. R. Thorpe, 1996: 366)

Douglas-Home's aristocratic upbringing also gave him a strong sense of *noblesse oblige*, which in the world of 1960s politics could be a double-edged sword. On the positive side Earl Swinton highlighted Douglas-Home's 'hon-esty, sincerity and integrity', and believed his character was 'what every man in public life would wish to be' (Garnett, 2005: 54). Likewise, Margaret Thatcher, a junior minister in Douglas-Home's government, believed that he was 'a manifestly good man – and goodness is not to be underrated as a qualification for those considered for powerful positions' (Thatcher, 1995: 130). The belief that Douglas-Home was a 'good man' was not confined to his Conservative colleagues. As Hennessy noted, one left-wing Labour MP admitted that

> I could never feel highly critical of Alec Douglas-Home, I don't know
> how anybody could. He was a good guy. Contrary to what most people
> think, decency counts for a lot in politics, especially between people on
> opposite sides of the House.
>
> (Hennessy, 1997: 241)

However, this honesty and goodness could also prove to be a drawback. It was the underlying reason for Douglas-Home's refusal to attack everything that Labour did, as 'opposition for opposition's sake', a policy that upset many of his backbenchers, who believed that they were duty bound to robustly oppose all of Labour's programme and consequently undermined Douglas-Home's ability to manage the party. Sir Anthony Acland, former head of the Diplomatic Service, who worked with Douglas-Home in the Foreign Office, believed in doing the right thing for the country and then, much lower down the scale, doing what was right for the Conservative Party (Hennessy, 1997: 243).

Although Douglas-Home's decency was not in doubt, he could be sen-sitive, proud and thin-skinned (K. Young, 1970: 227–8). Consequently the internal party debate and press speculation over his leadership easily wore down his will to fight for his position. At the 31 March meeting of the LCC, which discussed his leadership, he told his colleagues that he was 'beyond the point of suffering personally'. Douglas-Home also seems to have had a sense of entitlement derived from his background and his time as a sen-ior Conservative politician. In his biography he argued that his reluctance to face down the Conservative MPs who wanted to replace him was because 'I had been chosen as Leader to fight the Socialists, and I did not see why I should now be asked to battle with my own side' (Douglas-Home, 1976: 220). Later, Douglas-Home told Kenneth Young that 'I didn't see why, after doing Commonwealth and Foreign Secretary and Prime Minister, I should, so to speak have to fight for position as leader of the opposition. It didn't attract me. ... If I'd been ten years younger I'd have seen it through' (K. Young, 1970: 232). Harold Macmillan, Douglas-Home's predecessor as party leader, put it rather differently, saying that he 'didn't have enough fire in his belly – he wouldn't say bugger off' (Dutton, 2006: 110).

Conclusion

Judged by the criteria above Douglas-Home can in many respects be seen as a failure as Leader of the Opposition. Because of the manner in which he acquired the leadership in 1964, his legitimacy was questioned and consequently he lacked authority and credibility, both within his own party and with the wider general public. This was exacerbated by his inability to communicate his party's policies and vision: he was a poor performer in Parliament, in public and on television. These poor communication skills combined with his aristocratic background led people to perceive Douglas-Home as out of touch, as an anachronism who belonged to a bygone era. Douglas-Home's image fared even worse when he was compared to the younger, working-class and grammar school-educated Harold Wilson.

Furthermore, his limited conception of Conservatism meant that Douglas-Home played virtually no part in his party's policy renewal process, leaving the majority of the work to be done by Edward Heath. This, together with Douglas-Home's principled refusal to oppose the Government for Opposition's sake, upset many Conservative MPs who wanted their leader to take a tougher stance against a Labour Government with a small majority and to articulate a vision of Conservatism that could return the Conservative Party to power. Finally, Douglas-Home's unwillingness, or inability, to fight his corner led him to resign when a different course may well have seen him securely confirmed as party leader.

However, this critique of Douglas-Home needs to be tempered in one important respect. Despite his failings as a Leader of the Opposition he was able to keep the party united, and also successfully resolved the question of how the Conservative Party chose its leaders. In doing so he ended the 'magic circle' and began the process of 'democratisation' of the leadership of the Conservative Party, instituting an election procedure that survived, with minor changes, until 1998.

7
Edward Heath, 1965–70 and 1974–5

Mark Garnett

Edward Heath fought four General Elections as Conservative Party leader, and his record exhibits a curious symmetry. He led the party into two elections in which its chances of overall victory were negligible: not long after he became leader (1966), and very close to the end of his stint (October 1974). In between, he fought one election that he seemed certain to lose, but prevailed against the odds (1970); and another (February 1974), which most people expected the Conservatives to win, but instead resulted in a narrow defeat that was heavily freighted with consequences for Heath and his party.

Inside a decade, Heath entered three election campaigns – those of 1966, 1970 and October 1974 – as Opposition Leader. The differing circumstances covered almost all of the scenarios that might confront a leader hoping to win office – with the conspicuous exception of the challenger with every reason to expect a comfortable victory. Thus the snap election called by Harold Wilson in March 1966 interrupted Heath's period of probation as leader, and given the unpromising context his party was always likely to forgive anything short of a humiliating defeat. In June 1970, by contrast, Heath's position was on the line; a failure to unseat Wilson, by however slender a margin, would have terminated his leadership. By the election of October 1974 the vigorous underdog of 1970 had dwindled into a tarnished figure who had presided over an inglorious government before losing office in an election called at a time of his own choosing (February 1974). In this second 1974 election Heath was once again facing a contest that had been called by Harold Wilson in order to improve his Parliamentary position; but by that time most Conservative MPs were ready to contemplate a change of leader (even if they did not relish the prospect of a new ideological direction). Even if the Conservatives had won enough seats to form the largest part of a coalition (their only realistic chance of returning to office), Heath would have come under irresistible pressure to step aside.

The chapter proceeds by examining Heath's record as Opposition Leader in each of its three phases; a brief survey of his spell as Prime Minister

(1970–4) is included in order to explain the difficulties that faced him when his party returned to office. However, since most commentators agree that Heath was, to an unusual degree, the author of his own mixed fortunes, some preliminary remarks are necessary on his character and career up to the time when he became Opposition Leader in August 1965.

Early career 1950–65

Heath's origins and early life have been chronicled many times: the son of a small builder and a ladies' maid, brought up on the Kentish coast; a grammar schoolboy of prodigious application, who won an organ scholarship to Balliol College; a student who took every opportunity to travel, witnessing among other things a Nazi rally at Nuremburg; an early opponent of appeasement, who campaigned against the official Conservative candidate in the famous 1938 Oxford by-election; a brave and highly efficient soldier who ended the Second World War with every prospect of transcending his relatively humble background and aiming for a successful career in public life (Blake, 1998: 299; Ramsden, 1996: 386–8). A more recent revelation is that before the war Heath had briefly kept a diary, which proves his firm commitment to what later became known as 'one-nation' views. The diary was discovered by researchers helping Heath with his memoirs, but to their frustration he failed to make use of this fascinating document. It was left to his official biographer to quote from the diary, providing some flavour of the political outlook that underpinned the whole of Heath's political career, notwithstanding the series of 'U-turns' that are associated with his short spell as Prime Minister (Ziegler, 2010: 29, 40).

Elected to Parliament in 1950 for the Bexley constituency, Heath soon became a member of the One Nation group of Conservative MPs. Considering his political outlook it seemed a natural place for him, but he played an insignificant role in its activities. This is easily explained because although One Nation did pursue a political agenda of sorts it was as much about pleasure as business. Heath had no interest in social activities of that sort, partly because he was relatively poor but mainly because he always preferred the company of people who were bound together by a sense of common purpose (Seawright, 2005: 73–5). From that perspective, the surprising thing is that Heath ever joined One Nation at all.

Thus while Heath could be frivolous when he wanted to be – often, it must be said, when others thought he was being serious – he was essentially 'unclubbable'. As a result, it was somewhat surprising when, after just a year in the Commons, he became a Conservative whip. This job, after all, requires a high degree of social dexterity. However, Heath proved a great success. During the war he had demonstrated an ability to carry out orders transmitted to him from higher up the hierarchy; and in a Conservative Party whose disciplinary apparatus still bore military hallmarks, he was deservedly both effective and popular. In 1955 his efforts were rewarded by promotion to the post of Chief Whip, and in that role he played an important part in guiding his party through the choppy waters of the Suez Crisis, as well as smoothing the difficult transition from Anthony Eden to Harold Macmillan in 1957 (Lindsay and Harrington, 1974: 192).

Heath's ministerial career began in 1959, and in the following year he was promoted to the Cabinet as Lord Privy Seal. His main task in that post was to negotiate British entry into the European Economic Community (EEC), a policy that he endorsed whole-heartedly and eventually brought to fruition, although this part of his story is not of central relevance to his record as Opposition Leader (Blake, 1998: 286). When Britain's first bid for EEC membership was vetoed by the French in 1963 Heath was transferred to the Board of Trade, where he aroused considerable controversy within Conservative ranks by steering through the abolition of Resale Price Maintenance (RPM), to the horror of many Conservative-supporting shopkeepers (Ramsden, 1996: 387–8).

Thus when the Conservatives lost power in the 1964 General Election Heath was widely regarded as a forceful, modern-minded politician who would not shy away from tough decisions. His opponents during the RPM battle might have come to regard him as abrasive and even divisive, but other colleagues remembered him as an emollient Chief Whip who was almost the epitome of a good team-player (Ramsden, 1996: 381–2). On the face of it, Heath seemed to possess all the qualities of a successful party leader; certainly, after the Conservatives went into Opposition after the 1964 General Election, MPs could be forgiven for thinking that he was ideally equipped to lead his party against Labour's Harold Wilson, who had also shown himself to be tough-minded and who came from a similar social background.

Heath duly won the party leadership after Alec Douglas-Home stepped down on 22 July 1965. Douglas-Home's departure was involuntary, and after he had announced his decision to the backbench 1922 Committee, one MP from the traditionalist wing of the party complained that 'The rotters' eleven has won' (Garnett and Aitken, 2002: 68). Since Heath's supporters were widely blamed for destabilising Douglas-Home, this was an instructive response (Gilmour and Garnett, 1997: 218). With the removal of Douglas-Home – whose background, manners and outlook amounted almost to a caricature of the old-style Tory – the party had opted for a radical change of ethos. When Heath was chosen, narrowly, in preference to the former Chancellor Reginald Maudling, the *Economist*'s editor Alastair Burnet noted that his party was showing its 'instinct for power'. However, Heath would not be able to count on the reservoir of support that enabled Douglas-Home to stay in post for ten months after the electoral defeat of October 1964. Heath was hardly an unpolished representative of the proletariat – indeed, he was far more cultured than most well-heeled Tories. But although he ended his life in the Cathedral Close at Salisbury, the characters in Anthony Trollope's *Barchester Towers* would have been unanimous in rejecting any idea that Heath was a *gentleman* – the status that was so crucial to the Victorians, and continued to matter even in the Conservative Party of the early 1960s. True, Heath was not the first Tory leader with questionable qualifications in that regard – even Disraeli had been viewed with distaste by the party's grandees, and not just because of his Jewish ancestry. But this precedent only meant that Heath would have to show something like Disraeli's ability in order to retain his position; as Burnet noted, the party 'will remain united behind him just as long as his pursuit of power looks promising' (J. Campbell, 1993: 184). Although Heath was the first Conservative leader to be given a democratic 'mandate' by his colleagues, by implication his position would become difficult to sustain if he lost the backing of a substantial number of MPs. The 1965 rules for electing the Conservative Party leader did not have a formal mechanism for challenging incumbents, but it was assumed that when they became a liability they would voluntarily stand down (or would be persuaded to do) in the wider interests of the party (Fisher, 1977: 147–8). Douglas-Home himself had been forced out just six months after the decision to let the Parliamentary Party choose its leader in a secret ballot; and unlike Heath, Douglas-Home had the kind of pedigree that muted dissent in the ranks, and certainly made it easier for leaders to survive temporary political setbacks.

Leader of the Opposition, 1965–70

When Heath over from Douglas-Home, the Conservatives were well aware that they could be out of office for at least five more years (Ramsden, 1996: 386). Labour had achieved an overall majority of only four seats at the 1964 General Election; but a master-tactician like Wilson could be expected to maximise the advantages of his position in order to choose the most pro-pitious date for a new election. By choosing Heath, though, Conservative MPs felt that they could at least score enough points to keep Wilson on his toes, and hopefully confine Labour to another slender margin of victory next time round (Lindsay and Harrington, 1974: 236–48).

However, John Campbell was only exaggerating slightly when he wrote that 'Heath's election as Tory leader was a triumph which quickly became a protracted nightmare'. A key problem was Heath's 'public personality – stiff, odd, tense and humourless' (J. Campbell, 1993: 189). Even amid the general acclamation of his rise to the leadership, there had been ominous hints that Heath might be difficult to sell to the electorate, not to mention to elements within the Parliamentary Party who thought that 'his four years as chief whip have left him with a manner that some of his colleagues frankly describe as authoritarian' (*Illustrated London News*, 7/8/1965). A leader who was difficult to like – and whose rise from humble origins was a source of resentment rather than deferential admiration – could only hope to win grudging respect from his fellow MPs if he landed effective blows on his opposite number. Heath had won favourable notices for his organisation and leadership of the attack on Labour's 1965 budget (J. Campbell, 1993: 168). However, it turned out that this campaign was very different from the spontaneous debating skills upon which Heath would have to draw in his direct duels with Harold Wilson. It was soon apparent that Heath would find it difficult to land a blow on the quicker-witted Wilson, and on television he came across as wooden, even to those who valued his obvious sincerity.

Although the Powellite Patrick Cosgrave was being unfair when he claimed in 1973 that the Conservative Party had chosen Heath 'in one of those fits of profound superficiality which often characterise its activities', those Tory MPs who congratulated themselves on their ability to choose a suitable leader for a meritocratic age had miscalculated (Cosgrave, 1973: 435). In reality, what they should have sought was an individual who could rise to the new challenges of a *media* age; yet in plumping for Heath they selected someone who was ill-equipped to perform effectively on radio, let alone on the now-dominant medium of television. Despite the efforts of well-intentioned advisers, Heath never took very seriously the notion that he should try to modify his style. Political interviews and (in particular) party political broadcasts were serious occasions in which the tone should never be lowered. As a result, even in relatively good times Heath too often sounded as if he was lecturing the public rather than wooing them, and over time the impact of such orations was bound to wear off among a public audience which had heard similar messages so often before (Garnett, 2005: 199).

Forty years later, Conservative MPs who had opted for Heath for the wrong reasons might have corrected their mistake by unseating him before he could fight a General Election (Garnett and Aitken, 2002: 85). In those more merciful days, at least the party could derive some satisfaction from Heath's well-known abilities as an organiser. Even before the 1964 General Election he had been placed in charge of the Advisory Committee on Policy, and established more than thirty groups to review the party's stance on a wide range of issues. The deliberations were condensed into a policy document (*Putting Britain Right Ahead*), which was published for the following year's Party Conference and formed the basis of the 1966 Party Manifesto, *Action Not Words* (Garnett, 2005: 205–10). The general character of these publications resembled 'a Commander-in-Chief's staccato orders for a massive offensive on all conceivable fronts' rather than attempts to win support from an increasingly demanding electorate (Gilmour and Garnett, 1997: 225). The 1966 Manifesto was far more concise than Labour's, but this economy with words was only achievable at the expense of space that could have been devoted to the creation of an over-arching 'narrative' that explained why people should not give Wilson's Government a second chance. In this context it was unsurprising that a senior figure within the party would issue a protest; the spokesman on Colonial Affairs, Angus Maude, went public in January 1966 with his concern that the Conservatives were beginning to 'talk like technocrats' (*The Spectator*, 14/1/1966). For such insubordination Maude (a founder-member of the One Nation Group) was dismissed from his front-bench position.

In his memoirs, Heath brushed off the result of the 1966 General Election, in which Labour was re-elected with a majority of 96. 'The result', he wrote, 'was disappointing, even though few of us expected to win' (Heath, 1998: 282). According to one acute observer, 'there was only limited discernible criticism of Heath personally' at the time (Rhodes James, 1972: 99). However, if the Labour lead had crept over a hundred, serious questions might have been raised about Heath's leadership. As it was, he survived to fight another day, well aware that his restive party would be less forgiving next time round.

In the wake of the electoral setback of 1966, Heath consoled himself with the thought that Wilson would have to provide the voters with tangible evidence of success if he was to secure a further term of office. Typically, Heath also felt that his party's chances would be brighter in the next contest because 'we had the opportunity of developing further the thorough policy review which had been started in 1965' (Heath, 1998: 282). He also refreshed his front-bench team, bringing forward younger MPs like Geoffrey Rippon and Peter Walker, who might compensate for some of his own weaknesses in terms of public communication. Unfortunately for Heath, within his truncated Parliamentary Party the decision to push forward relatively inexperienced MPs aroused dissatisfaction among more seasoned representatives who thought that they had been overlooked. It was not surprising when the leader's allies were dubbed 'Heathmen', as if they constituted a specific faction within the party – especially because Heath himself habitually treated MPs outside the new 'magic circle' in a dismissive fashion (Roth, 1972).

Ill-feeling among disappointed colleagues is a perennial problem for any party leader. However, between 1966 and 1970 Heath faced far more serious difficulties caused by the nature of his party rather than any maladroit management of his own. Even before the 1966 General Election Heath and his Chief Whip, Willie Whitelaw, had been unable to prevent a three-way split within the Parliamentary ranks on Labour's proposed imposition of oil sanctions on the illegal regime of Ian Smith in Rhodesia (Garnett, 2005: 195). The official line was to abstain – hardly a satisfactory compromise on such an emotive subject – but 31 Conservatives supported sanctions while 50 voted against (Ramsden, 1996: 288–9).

Divisions over Rhodesia coincided with attitudes on racial matters, and in the late 1960s this subject was becoming highly sensitive at home as well as abroad. Before the 1966 Election Labour had introduced a Race Relations Bill as a sop to its liberal wing, which was deeply troubled by new restrictions on immigration from the 'new Commonwealth'. The provisions of this legislation were mild, but almost all Conservative MPs voted against it. In February 1968 14 liberal Conservatives, including the Shadow Chancellor Iain Macleod and the young Michael Heseltine, voted against the Government's panic-stricken Commonwealth Immigration Bill, which limited the access to Britain of Asians expelled from Kenya. Two months later, Wilson introduced tighter measures to outlaw racial discrimination; and this time it was the turn of the right wing to break ranks. Despite a Shadow Cabinet agreement to present Conservative objections to the Government's Bill in measured terms in order to minimise intra-party dissent, Enoch Powell delivered a speech in Birmingham that predicted civil strife and quoted private correspondence, which claimed that an elderly white female constituent was afraid to go out because of harassment from local immigrants (Garnett, 2005: 195–6).

Heath was outraged, not least because Powell had caused embarrassment before and now seemed to think that he was licensed to speak out without fear of dismissal. On this occasion Powell had overstepped the rational limits of dissent; if he had not been sacked, at least four senior front-benchers (Macleod, Quintin Hogg, Edward Boyle and Robert Carr) would have resigned, and very few of those remaining would have relished the prospect of continued collaboration with Powell. The latter's supporters could argue that Macleod had committed a similar offence by voting against the Commonwealth Immigration Bill – indeed, some Powellites could even insist that Macleod's offence was more serious, since Powell's Birmingham speech was an attack on legislation that his senior colleagues also opposed. Probably one reason why Macleod survived was that Heath and others secretly shared his distaste for discriminatory legislation, and felt that (as a former Colonial Secretary) he really could be granted a licence to rebel on that issue. More importantly, though, Macleod did not conduct himself in a manner that was certain to alienate fellow front-benchers who were already struggling with their consciences (Garnett, 2005: 195–6).

Heath must have been relieved at this chance to remove Powell from his Shadow Cabinet team. But if he thought that he had nullified the leadership challenge of the man who had stood against him (with derisory results) in the 1965 leadership contest he was quickly disabused. Tens of thousands wrote letters supporting Powell and/or vilifying Heath, testifying to pent-up resentment against a political establishment that was apparently inactive in the face of a serious threat to British identity (Blake, 1998: 306). This reaction, and the spectacle of meat porters from the East End of London marching on Westminster, might have jolted Heath's belief that most Britons shared his own interpretation of moderation and rationality. In fact, the events of 1968 encouraged him to think that he should fight even harder on behalf of an undemonstrative majority that was in danger of being drowned out by the voice of extremism. In the long term Powell's 'Rivers of Blood' speech did mark a turning point, in that many right-wing

Tory MPs could now hope that the party would receive enthusiastic public backing for an alternative strategy, so long as it was presented by a candidate who was a Powellite without being Enoch himself.

In the medium term, the controversy over Powell's intervention might even have helped the Conservatives (Ramsden, 1996: 405–6). Although their opinion poll advantage over Labour was gradually eroded after April 1968, for the next eighteen months their rating was either above or very close to 50 per cent, according to the Gallup organisation. Ironically, the party performed well in Powell's heartland of the West Midlands, so that in the Midlands as a whole it won 51 seats in 1970 as compared to 35 in 1966. Against this, according to Robert Rhodes James, some Conservatives in other areas felt that Powell's continued identification with the party cost them support (Butler and Butler, 2000: 241, 271; Rhodes James, 1972: 277).

While arguments about Powell's precise role in the Conservative victory of June 1970 can never be settled, most media commentators decided that it had been a one-man show. The *Daily Express*, for example, felt that 'the Tory victory was attained by the new Prime Minister's own guts and determination'. Even the *Guardian* conceded that 'Mr Heath's victory is his own'. The personalised flavour of the coverage partly reflected the sense that this, as the *Telegraph* put it, had been an unusually 'Presidential' campaign (Butler and Pinto-Duschinsky, 1971: 343–5). One suspects, though, that national newspapers, which had anticipated a Labour victory on the basis of recent opinion polls, had been caught on the hop, and rationalised the shock result in the way they found most congenial (and simplistic) – that is, that the British public, having been generally unimpressed by Heath's earnest approach to Opposition since 1965, had suddenly warned to him and responded to his urgings that the country was being betrayed by Wilsonian gimmickry.

Heath had good reason to mistrust the media. At the beginning of 1970 it had helped Harold Wilson in his attempt to portray Heath and his colleagues as reactionaries, encapsulated by the collective sobriquet of 'Selsdon Man'. This referred to a Shadow Cabinet meeting at the Selsdon Park Hotel near Croydon in Surrey, where Heath and his colleagues had attempted to find an overall 'narrative' that might connect the ideas thrown up by the party's continuing policy reviews. No such themes were discovered, but the media had been encouraged to think that the meeting was important, so something had to be said to the assembled reporters before the politicians departed. It was decided that law and order was the safest bet, and this duly captured the headlines in the Sunday papers even though the subject had barely been discussed at Selsdon Park (Heath, 1998: 301).

Although Heath was alarmed by coverage of the Selsdon Park meeting and Wilson's attempt to portray him as a right-winger of Neanderthal tendencies, once again it has been argued that the result was beneficial in that the Prime Minister and the press managed to bestow upon the Opposition exactly the coherent image it had been lacking (Garnett, 2005: 213). However, the opinion polls at the time showed both Labour and the Conservatives holding steady. There was, though, a notable improvement in Heath's personal ratings. This probably owed less to Selsdon Park than to Sydney–Hobart – the gruelling boat race that Heath and the crew of *Morning Cloud* had won in the month before the sterile Shadow Cabinet meeting. It was fairly typical of Heath's luck that although he gained some credit for having skippered his boat to a remarkable win, relatively few people understood the prestige of that contest in racing circles and it produced no lasting benefit even in the year of an unusually 'Presidential' General Election.

Heath would have been less than human if he had not been affected by the lavish praise of the press in June 1970. But although he was not free from personal vanity, he knew that the credit for his party's success should be shared with close colleagues who endorsed his own, highly rational view of the world. The party, in short, would not have won without the collective effort behind the policy review, which continued up until the election. As a result of this unprecedented exercise, Heath could feel that his party was better prepared that any other Opposition in British political history (Garnett, 2005: 205–18).

However, from the outset more sceptical opinions had been voiced within the party. For example, Geoffrey Block of the Conservative Research Department (CRD) had expressed the view at the time of Selsdon Park that 'we will have to win the next general election in spite of, rather than with the aid of, our manifesto'. According to Block, this was not a disaster since 'Few people read manifestos' (Ramsden, 1996: 301). But the fact that party insiders could express such views casts an ironic light on the publicity given at the time, and subsequently, to Heath's unprecedented policy-making exercise. The overall results, at their best, could only work in an ideal world. Thus, for example, Conservative policy on trade union reform was devised in (limited) consultation with senior trade unionists. But if such officials had been able to control the response of their grass-roots members the policy would have been unnecessary; indeed, if trade unionists had been rational in Heath's sense, they would have accepted Labour's earlier proposals for reform in the workplace (Barbara Castle's *In Place of Strife*) and the problem would have been resolved before Heath came to office. By contrast, on inflation, which probably inflicted the greatest damage on the Heath Government, the party's policy before 1970 had barely progressed beyond wishful thinking (Garnett, 2005: 214).

At least Heath entered the 1970 General Election campaign backed by a skilful team of media advisers, and he did have a snappy phrase to mollify voters who were worried about inflation. At an election press conference he read out a brief that promised that a specific Conservative policy would 'at a stroke, reduce the rise in prices' (Heath, 1998: 304). The phrase had been carefully crafted: the abolition of Labour's Selective Employment Tax

(SET) would make prices rise *more slowly*, rather than reducing them over-night. But the words 'at a stroke' had been chosen deliberately, to create the impression that Conservative policies would have an immediate impact on the rate of inflation; and if that persisted at a high level after the election, the Conservatives could hardly complain that the offending phrase had been distorted when Labour critics used it against him. The 1970 Manifesto contained an unwise repudiation of the 'philosophy' behind the use of incomes policy as a means of containing inflation. This meant what it said – that is, that Heath disliked the idea of incomes policy, not that he would never resort to such measures if they seemed unavoidable. But to his crit-ics (especially on the right) such semantics were irrelevant; in their eyes it looked as though Heath had ruled out the prospect of an incomes policy, and when his Government felt constrained to implement such a policy they bitterly resented this 'U-turn' (Ramsden, 1996: 406–10).

A similar problem for Heath was created when his opponents in all parties quoted his apparent pledge that Britain would not enter the EEC without the 'full-hearted consent' of the British people. Actually in the original text Heath had included Parliament as well as the people, in line with the orthodox view that the British legislature was entitled to speak on behalf of the voters even on crucial constitutional questions. However, a more mundane form of words would have suited Heath better, since the notion of 'full-hearted consent' could easily be used to back the argument that the UK should not have entered the EEC without a referendum.

The impact of office, 1970–4

One could conclude simply that Heath was a politician out of tune with the times: for the most part he could not communicate with the voters, but on the rare occasions that the message got through he had chosen words that were open to misinterpretation. For whatever reason, however, the Conservatives were elected under Heath's leadership; and then the real troubles began. The bare facts suggest that, after an almost uniquely inglorious spell in office, Heath called an early election in February 1974 and lost, albeit by a narrow margin. However, the chief themes of his pre-miership are relevant to an account of his subsequent period as Opposition Leader, and thus deserve to be examined here (for full accounts of the Heath Government, see Ball and Seldon, 1996; Holmes, 1997).

Broadly speaking, Heath's main perspective in office was international rather than domestic. In other words, unlike his predecessors, he was try-ing to answer Dean Acheson's challenge about Britain's failure to find a role since the Second World War. His answer was that Britain should stop pretending to be a first-rank global power, and carve out a constructive role within the developing European Communities. As such, his priority was to take Britain 'into Europe', but the realisation of his vision would only be positive for his country if it was in good health economically, with its manufacturing sector able to bear the brunt of open competition with other European nations, especially Germany.

This plan was perfectly sensible on paper, but during Heath's period in office it was subjected to two unpredicted blows. The first – the collapse of the Bretton Woods arrangements, which had governed the global economy since 1945 – was just about sustainable, even if one of its effects was to reduce the value of sterling relative to other currencies. However, Heath's fixation with the conditions under which Britain would join 'Europe' encouraged him to stimulate demand within the domestic economy, and this process was in full swing when the second blow landed. Britain was far from being self-sufficient in its oil consumption, being unable as yet to exploit the North Sea supplies that were to bolster the regime of Heath's nemesis, Margaret Thatcher. Thus, when the price of oil increased almost four-fold over the course of 1973 (thanks to the decisions of producers in the Middle East before and after the Yom Kippur War between Arab states and Israel), the result in Britain was unprecedented price inflation across the board. The National Union of Mineworkers (NUM) delivered the *coup de grace* to the Heath Government; at the time their economic importance (thanks to the oil crisis) and their moral status within Britain as a whole (because of memories of past conflicts when they had been perceived as virtuous underdogs) were high enough in combination to make them the likely winners in any conflict with Government. In February 1974 Edward Heath was persuaded to ask the electorate for a new mandate that would strengthen his bargaining position with the miners; and his reluctant gamble backfired (Blake, 1998: 315–17).

Superficially, the Heath Government could be summed up in the fact that out of eleven 'states of emergency' declared in Britain under legislation passed in 1920, five were called in that fleeting period between June 1970 and February 1974. As a result, Dominic Sandbrook had good reason to choose *State of Emergency* as the title of his account of Britain under Heath (Sandbrook, 2010). The characteristic Heath response in times of trouble was to deliver sombre addresses to the nation on television, often appealing to the latent public spirit of his audience to pull the country through its current difficulties. While his sincerity was palpable, Heath betrayed his ignorance of the national psyche at such moments; if public spirit had meant very much to Britons in the early 1970s it would not have been necessary to announce so many states of emergency. Heath's admirers might have deplored the unfortunate turn of events that landed such a well-intentioned administration with so many scenarios (like the prospect of unemployment rising above one million) that only hard-hearted ministers could have addressed without giving at least the appearance of weakness. However, while the Heath Government was undoubtedly unlucky, to a considerable degree it merely paid the price for its over-elaborate preparations in Opposition.

In practice, Heath and his ministers proved to be adept at improvisation; but prior to the 1970 General Election they had given the distinct impression that only shallow politicians like Harold Wilson ever had to improvise, and the electorate had good reason to feel that the Conservatives had not delivered on their promises (Kavanagh, 1996: 359–90).

One crucial constituency that was entitled to feel short-changed was the Conservative Party itself – estimated at the time to consist of at least a million members (Butler and Butler, 2000: 141). To many grass-roots activists it must have seemed that Heath and his colleagues were taking their continued support for granted in their anxiety to govern on 'One Nation' principles. Since the 1980s members of the party have concentrated their fire on Heath's drive for membership of the European Community (EC), although at the time this approach commanded much greater support in the constituencies as well as the Conservative-supporting press. More serious were domestic policy decisions, which could almost be seen as a strategy to alienate the whole of the grass-roots party by degrees. Opponents of nationalisation would be irritated by the failure of the Heath Government to 'roll back the state' more than a fraction; its efforts at denationalisation certainly compared very unfavourably to the state's procurement of Rolls-Royce, support for Upper Clyde Shipbuilders and the Mersey Docks and Harbour Board, culminating in the 1972 Industry Act, which even moderate Conservatives would find difficult to distinguish from Labour Party policy (Norton, 1980: 90–8). A more successful administration might have been able to justify a radical reform of local government that resulted in a drastic redrawing of county boundaries, but in the context of the early 1970s this was more often taken as another initiative of a government that was alien to the traditions of the Conservative Party and the country as a whole. Even the horrific breakdown of law and order in Northern Ireland, which Heath handled with remarkable skill in tandem with his Secretaries of State Willie Whitelaw and Francis Pym, was seen in some quarters as the prelude to a tame surrender of British authority to people who were no better than murderous criminals.

A second term as Leader of the Opposition, 1974–5

Since 1997, Conservative Party leaders have announced their intention to resign in the immediate aftermath of electoral defeat. Edward Heath was not prepared to interpret the result of the February 1974 General Election in the same light. The statistics provided him with some justification for staying on: the Conservatives had actually won a higher share of the vote than Labour (37.9 to 37.1 per cent); and since Wilson had fallen short of an overall Parliamentary majority there was some sense in allowing Heath to carry on as leader until the Government asked the country for a more secure mandate, or a viable coalition agreement was made that would give Labour a workable majority for the foreseeable future.

Unfortunately for Heath, the failure of the first-past-the-post electoral system to deliver a clear winner in February 1974 added a new error to the considerable charge-sheet being compiled by his internal opponents. It was his constitutional duty in such circumstances to stay in Downing Street until he had exhausted any chance of forming a coalition with other parties; but (like Gordon Brown in 2010) his failure to evacuate Number 10 as soon as the nation's verdict became apparent was held against him. Margaret Thatcher, for example, noted in her memoirs that Heath's 'horse-trading was making us look ridiculous. The British dislike nothing more than a bad loser' (Thatcher, 1995: 239). This testimony is by no means discredited by Lady Thatcher's own conduct after losing the confidence of her party in 1990. What Thatcher's admirers in the press later described as 'the longest sulk in history' had apparently begun a year before Heath started to snub the only person who had possessed sufficient courage to mount a serious challenge to his leadership.

When asked why he had not resigned in February 1974, Heath told the present author that he had wanted to prevent the right wing from taking over the party, a view shared by the backbench MP Julian Critchley who had warned in the previous year that a defeat for the Conservatives would transform them into 'the party of the aggrieved motorist' (Critchley, 1973: 410). The obvious rejoinder was that if Heath had stepped aside someone else who broadly shared his views would have had a much better chance of succeeding. His refusal to stand down in February seriously impaired the prospects of his faithful lieutenant, Willie Whitelaw, who would now have to show unflagging loyalty to a regime that was obviously failing while others could register their suggestions for policy departures, either openly or in coded messages (Heppell, 2008a: 61–6).

To his credit, Sir Keith Joseph chose the former approach, delivering a series of speeches in which he attacked his party for having allowed Labour's 'socialists' to retain the ideological initiative in British politics, whether or not they won elections. Joseph included himself in this indictment, but clearly the main culprit was his party leader. Consistent with his desire to criticise the recent performance of his party, Joseph had refused to accept a specific brief inside the Shadow Cabinet after the February election, and instead was entrusted with a vague policy-making role. Addressing a less incendiary issue than immigration, Joseph could not be accused of following Powell's example; but his collective offences were surely more serious than Angus Maude's imprudent comments about Heath's 'technocratic' tendencies back in January 1966. Pleas for restraint, rather than threats, were the only weapons Heath and his allies could deploy as Joseph continued to ridicule the economic philosophy and practice of the previous Government (Denham and Garnett, 2001: 238–63). The impression that Heath had lost control of his party was enhanced by his own maladroit decision to back an amendment to Labour's first Queen's Speech, on a proposal to jettison

Stage III of his Government's statutory incomes policy. If this had succeeded, Wilson would almost certainly have been able to secure the promise of a dissolution of Parliament from the Queen, and comfortably win the ensuing general election. More likely, the Conservatives would have been humiliated in the vote on Stage III, which at least 40 of their own backbenchers despised on ideological grounds. Heath was fortunate that this egregious mistake was nullified by Labour's decision to retain Stage III in the short term (Gilmour and Garnett, 1997: 293–4).

On returning to Opposition the outgoing Cabinet was reshuffled rather than refreshed – even Alec Douglas-Home stayed on as Shadow Foreign Secretary – underlining the impression that this was a team that was waiting for a new election rather than hoping to seize the political initiative. Policy groups were re-established, and, contrary to the practice between 1964 and 1970, backbench opinion was strongly represented. Heath, however, made sure that policy ideas on the economy remained under his control. To a considerable extent the resulting proposals represented the party's attempt to mollify critics who thought it had been divisive in office, and were influenced by the reflections of a specially convened survey panel (Kavanagh, 2005: 221). Thus the Industrial Relations Act would not be revived once Labour had repealed it, and the approach to incomes policy was a closer reflection of Heath's real views – a voluntary policy was seen as the best way forward, and statutory measures would only be taken if all else failed. The most eye-catching ideas were in the field of housing, where a cap of 9.5 per cent was proposed on mortgage interest rates, and council tenants of more than three years would be allowed to purchase their properties at a considerable discount. The Shadow Minister for the Environment, Margaret Thatcher, was not entirely happy with these policies, and was even more disenchanted when Heath insisted on a pledge to abolish the rating system of local government taxation (Butler and Kavanagh, 1975: 62–4, 244–9). However, being saddled with controversial policies certainly did no harm to Mrs Thatcher's public profile.

Between his two 1974 defeats, Heath did at least manage to enhance a reputation for far-sighted statesmanship, which was already impressive enough for impartial observers. His visit to China in May was much more sincere in intention than Richard Nixon's cynical trip of 1972. However, the real implications were obscured by the blaze of transient publicity accorded to the Chinese gift of two giant pandas to London Zoo – a gesture that proved that the Communist leadership in Beijing was more media-savvy than the Leader of the British Opposition (J. Campbell, 1993: 635). While Heath was respected in China, his own party was growing more disorderly. Gradually Heath and his advisers accepted that, since the electorate was clearly disillusioned with both main parties, the suggestion of a government of national unity might prove enticing; but confusion reigned over whether or not such a government, under overall Conservative direction, would encompass both Labour as well as the Liberals. In the end, it seemed as if Heath was hoping to secure a majority for his party, but that after winning he would defy the expressed wishes of the electorate and try to form an administration 'that would transcend party divisions' (Behrens, 1980: 27–8). Lurking in the leader's mind was the possibility that unless the Conservatives won a clear Parliamentary majority – thus obviating the need for a deal with the other parties – his own position would be too weak to ensure that he would be accepted as Prime Minister of a coalition government. Even his closest political friends wanted Heath to announce his readiness to step down as Conservative Party leader if the election proved inconclusive and potential coalition partners found him objectionable. At the beginning of September, while Heath was wrangling with the various scenarios and hoping for a solution that would reconcile his personal ambitions with the best interests of his party, the new version of his yacht *Morning Cloud* was wrecked by gale-force winds. Two crew-members were lost, including Heath's godson Christopher Chadd. Sixteen days later Harold Wilson called a General Election for 10 October 1974.

In 1966, when Edward Heath fought his first election as leader, the Tories won 253 seats. In October 1974 their tally (admittedly on a lower share of the national vote) was 277. Yet the reaction within the party could scarcely have been more different. Instead of being the untried champion who had inherited a cause that was already lost, Heath was now the long-term incumbent who had led his party into three defeats out of the four elections he had contested – and, after the sole contest he had managed to win, his decisions had not been greeted with universal applause, even within his own party.

It was not surprising that Heath's final stint as Opposition Leader was dominated by a campaign to unseat him, focused initially around the backbench 1922 Committee whose chairman, Edward du Cann, had fallen foul of Heath in the previous decade and was briefly seen as a possible successor (Fisher, 1977: 147–9). The campaign bore institutional fruit, in a reform of the rules governing the choice of party leader. Previously an election could only be held when there was a vacancy at the top; now the logic of the changes introduced since 1964 was taken to its extreme, and just two Tory MPs (a proposer and a seconder, who could remain anonymous) would be needed to precipitate a leadership contest at the beginning of every Parliamentary year. When Du Cann decided not to challenge (apparently because of rumours about his business activities), Keith Joseph emerged as the most likely standard-bearer of the right. If Joseph had really thought of himself as a leader-in-waiting, at this point he would have abandoned his series of iconoclastic speeches in favour of orthodox orations. Instead, Joseph delivered a further speech in Edgbaston (close to the scene of Powell's 1968 'Rivers of Blood' sensation) in which he implied that Britain's 'human stock' was endangered by the propensity of the poor to breed and transmit socio-economic disadvantages from one generation to the next (Denham and Garnett, 2001: 275).

In the final savage irony for Heath, the process of attrition that whittled down the list of potential challengers removed the vulnerable ones and left him with the person who was not inhibited by personal loyalty, unorthodox business dealings or public displays of ideological idiosyncrasy. The idea of a woman leading the Conservative Party was a challenge to many traditionalists, but not more so than the notion of a low-born male had been in 1965. Novelty value was just one of the ways in which Mrs Thatcher's path to the Conservative leadership had been smoothed by the career of her one-time friend, Edward Heath.

Conclusion

On the face of it, the indictment against Heath seems heavy – not simply in terms of his performance as Opposition Leader, but as a person who saw himself as possessing the essential qualities for effective stewardship of his party's fortunes whether in or out of office. On the presentational side, he was too inflexible to master the demands of the media in a television age, often appearing robotic when a touch of humanity would have reassured voters facing difficult circumstances. When he and his advisers did unearth memorable phrases, all too often these were capable of various interpretations and could be used against him.

In terms of party management, Heath deliberately courted disaster by failing to observe the trivial courtesies of social engagement with members of his Parliamentary Party. In retirement, he continued to behave in a similar fashion, even though he must have been aware that he was no longer important enough to win fair-weather friends. A highly sensitive (not to say vulnerable) person who had learnt to live without real intimates, he treated human encounters as part of a game; anyone who was self-confident enough to ignore the iciness of an introduction to Ted Heath was accepted, while those who looked disappointed or annoyed were spurned. This weird manifestation of insecurity could be restrained and concealed when Heath was a valued underling, but once he became leader he regarded it as the essential test of whether or not a member of his team was truly loyal. Such eccentricities in a leader might just about be manageable if the party is completely united on ideological grounds; but once divisions on principle become apparent any personal idiosyncrasies become insupportable.

Heath did oversee a policy review of unprecedented diligence. However, as previously noted, this turned out to be a handicap rather than an advantage once his party had returned to power. In Opposition Heath had given the impression that he and his colleagues possessed a plan to revive Britain's fortunes; and once the ideas generated by the policy review proved unenforceable, voters decided that Heath was too inflexible to improvise a workable Plan B.

Although Heath verified the dictum of his fellow One Nation Group member Enoch Powell, and ended his political career in failure, his record of unfulfilment is more interesting than most. In fact, his failure was dictated by the assumptions of Conservative MPs who elected him as leader in the first place. While they thought that their party's image would be improved by the election of a candidate who typified the values of a 'meritocratic' society, they overlooked the more pressing need for someone who could cope with the demands of the electronic media. In this respect Heath was probably more proficient than his predecessor Alec Douglas-Home; but it would have been difficult to find anyone who looked worse than Douglas-Home on the dominant medium of television.

Heath's inability to play up (or, rather, down) to the media would probably have proved fatal to him even if he had not faced so many serious challenges during his short time in Downing Street. Unable to grasp the political implications of social change, he imagined that in a 'meritocratic' age political showmanship had no future, whereas in reality it was becoming increasingly important for aspiring leaders. Taking Heath's career and views as a whole, it is reasonable to conclude that the Conservative MPs who elected him in 1965 had chosen a man who rejected the ideas of the past without considering whether or not his own approach to politics was still relevant. Heath would have been the perfect party leader in a genuine 'age of reason'. To Heath and his supporters this might have looked imminent in the Britain of 1965, but by 1975 even they had to admit that the prospect had receded.

8
Margaret Thatcher, 1975–9

Philip Norton

Margaret Thatcher entered the record books as the first female leader of the Conservative Party and as the longest continuously serving Prime Minister in modern British history. She was leader of the party for fifteen years (1975–90) and Prime Minister for eleven-and-a-half (1979–90). We are here concerned with the four years she spent as Leader of the Opposition.

There are two hypotheses as to the relationship between Margaret Thatcher as Opposition Leader and Margaret Thatcher as Prime Minister. The first hypothesis is that one leads naturally to the other – in essence, a Whig interpretation of history: Margaret Thatcher crafted an intellectually coherent philosophy – one that was to take shape as Thatcherism – which was to prove popular and was able to craft an electoral base that was sufficient to establish Conservative hegemony in the polls and to lead to a period of uninterrupted Conservative rule. This hypothesis has been influential in prompting criticism of later party leaders who have failed to lead the party to victory.

The other is to see the two as primarily distinct periods, with Thatcherism and predictable Conservative victory at the polls not deriving from what happened before, but rather as a consequence of what happened after Margaret Thatcher strode across the threshold of 10 Downing Street in 1979, after Labour lost the election. What was to become the Thatcher era was not predictable from Mrs Thatcher's period, a somewhat troubled period, in Opposition.

Dennis Kavanagh has elsewhere addressed the first hypothesis and found it wanting (Kavanagh, 2005: 219–42). Though the period spent in Opposition was a formative one for Margaret Thatcher – being party leader was necessary but not sufficient for achieving her goals – she neither forged a clear philosophy nor established strong and consistent electoral support for her beliefs and her party. She did not transform the party into a party destined for victory, though – rather like David Cameron thirty years later – she was to render it at least not unelectable (Norton, 2009: 31–43). That, however, was no guarantee of success.

What delivered victory to the Conservative Party in 1979 was the 'Winter of Discontent'. Labour had been clawing back support until the trades union unleashed industrial action that heavily impacted on the Government's support (Butler and Kavanagh, 1980: 29). Had Prime Minister James Callaghan opted for an election in October 1978, there was a distinct possibility that Labour would have won. 'If that had happened', writes Dick Leonard, 'and she [Thatcher] had gone down to defeat, she would most probably have been dumped in short order by the Tories, and would have rated no more than a footnote in the history books' (Leonard, 2005: 308). In essence, she became party leader because of the failings of Edward Heath and Prime Minister because of the misjudgement of James Callaghan.

The Thatcher legacy derives from her Premiership rather than from her period leading the party in Opposition. It was only as a result of being Prime Minister that she established an international reputation. 'She became more readily recognised worldwide than any figure in British public life, except perhaps the most prominent, or notorious, members of the royal family' (E. Evans, 1997: 2). However, until she entered Downing Street, she was little known outside the UK. She is the only modern British politician to generate an eponymous philosophy. A veritable library has been written on Thatcherism (see, for example, Gamble, 1988). However, the philosophy emerged from the Premiership rather than the other way round. Though Margaret Thatcher espoused a distinctive set of beliefs, Thatcherism did not develop as a discrete philosophy until she was ensconced in Government. Perhaps ironically, its coherence was first discerned not by adherents to Margaret Thatcher but rather by her opponents. It was Marxists and opponents within her own party, such as Sir Ian Gilmour, who identified a distinctive and essentially un-Tory set of rigid principles (Hall and Jacques, 1983; Gilmour, 1992). She was to acquire a reputation as the 'Iron Lady'. Although the term itself was coined in 1976 by the Soviet army magazine *Red Star*, it did not resonate until she was in office. She proved a doughty fighter against communism, alongside US President Ronald Reagan, and acquired her reputation as a defender of British interests through the Falklands conflict in 1982. Before she entered Downing Street, she was seen as a shrill politician, no match for Labour Prime Ministers Wilson and Callaghan. Margaret Thatcher as Leader of the Opposition was seen in a very different light from Margaret Thatcher as Prime Minister.

Indeed, initial concerns as to her leadership provide the basis for exploring the different aspects of her period in Opposition. As Patrick Cosgrave wrote:

> The four points of consideration of her leadership – its initial hesitancy, the refusal of some to serve or express loyalty, the puzzled distance between her and the Party organisation, and the question of how she would set about both establishing her authority and hammering out

rejuvenated policies – all caused headaches for herself and those around her. The initial flush of delight and pleasure faded from many parliamentary cheeks. Rumours of plots and coups were rife, and the press in general allowed her very little time to adjust to her new circumstances.

(Cosgrave, 1978: 183)

Public communication

When Margaret Thatcher was elected as party leader in 1975, she was little known beyond the confines of Westminster, other than for her period as Education Secretary under Edward Heath. Heath was better known and certainly the preferred candidate in the leadership contest, including among Conservative local associations (Gardiner, 1975: 192). Thatcher was also relatively inexperienced. She had stepped forward to contest the leadership only when a more experienced figure, Sir Keith Joseph, had decided not to take on Heath. She had only held the one Cabinet post. She was not a confident performer in the House of Commons. 'Despite some successes earlier in her career, from her maiden speech to her recent put-down of Denis Healey, Mrs Thatcher was never comfortable in the Commons, particularly in opposition' (J. Campbell, 2000: 318). Though she was assiduous in preparation – as leader, she had a small team of MPs to assist in preparing for Prime Minister's Question Time (Lawson, 1992: 14; Tebbit, 1989: 182–3) – she came across as someone prone to hector the House; she was well prepared, if anything over-prepared, but not especially good in the cut-and-thrust of spontaneous debate. She tended to lack subtlety and humour.

Margaret Thatcher realised some of the problems. 'Even outside the House, when addressing an audience my voice was naturally high-pitched, which can easily become grating' (Thatcher, 1995: 295). After she became leader, she took lessons from a voice coach. However, within the House she faced two kinds of problems. The first was her dislike of reading from a text. She thought the problem was exacerbated by the fact that initially there was sometimes little of substance to say – 'The difficulty at this point was that we *had* no credible alternative to offer' (Thatcher, 1995: 297) – and that she lacked authority in the House: 'you need to have acquired considerable authority in the House – the sort usually accorded only to Prime Ministers, and not always to them – to get through reading a text without a barrage of barracking and interruption' (Thatcher, 1995: 297). She conceded that she never managed to score more than a draw against Harold Wilson and his successor, Callaghan, in the House (Thatcher, 1995: 313). As a result, records John Campbell, 'she spoke less and less frequently in the House' (J. Campbell, 2000: 344).

Her appearances outside the House were not always without their problems either. She was not a natural media performer. She disliked appearing on television. 'Winston was never on television', she said, 'certainly never interviewed on it' (A. J. Mayer, 1979: 134). She also had to battle with some in the press who had trouble accepting her as a serious Leader of the Opposition. An initial positive reception, influenced by the novelty of her success, gave way to more negative coverage: 'many reporters, and not a few parliamentarians, continued to believe or began to express the notion that some ghastly and nightmarish mistake had been made, and that time would see a reversal to the natural state of affairs' (Cosgrave, 1978: 171).

Public communication was not sufficient to generate a sustained lead in the opinion polls. Though the party variously led Labour, sometimes by a large margin (by over 14 points in July 1977, for example), by the summer of 1978 Labour had clawed back much of its support, even in some polls claiming a lead. Though one poll gave the Conservatives a seven-point lead another shortly afterwards showed a Labour seven-point lead. In the October, Labour held the seat of Berwick and East Lothian in a by-election. In terms of who would make the best Prime Minister, Callaghan regularly led over Thatcher – 'and some surveys even showed that the Party would gain more support with Heath as leader' (Kavanagh, 2005: 225). The economy had begun to improve. Had Callaghan called an autumn election, there was, as we have noted, every possibility Labour would have won.

Public policy platform

Margaret Thatcher had to walk a tightrope in developing party policy. On the one hand, she had offered Conservative MPs a new direction in policy. She had challenged Heath in Cabinet, not least over his U-turn on economic policy in 1972 (Norton, 1978: 93). She had a committed band of neo-liberal supporters. She was keen to shift the party in a neo-liberal direction.

On the other hand, she was relatively isolated at the head of the party. She had inherited a Shadow Cabinet that was loyal to Heath. It was, in the words of one of them, 'an unsatisfactory forum' (Nott, 2002: 173). Despite removing some members, she was not in a position to craft a Shadow Cabinet that was committed to her views. Though some of the inherited Heath supporters, such as William Whitelaw, proved loyal to her leadership, they were not of her way of thinking. She was not in a position to impose her views. Nor did she always try. She might have decided opinions but there was also a practical streak. As one of her later Cabinet colleagues was to put it, 'She recognised a brick wall when she saw one' (former Cabinet minister to author).

Her will to achieve her goals and her recognition that she could not expect to carry her colleagues with her produced a personal style at variance with how she structured the party's policy-making process. As her Shadow Chancellor, Geoffrey Howe, recalled, 'Margaret became increasingly adept at using an unheralded public utterance as the means of signalling a policy shift away from some previously agreed balance' (Howe, 1994: 103).

One celebrated occasion was in 1978 when she said city dwellers feared being 'swamped' by immigrants. These utterances put pressure on colleagues, leading at times to some modification of policy, but she still had to work within established channels for developing party policy.

She began by following the practice adopted by Conservative leaders in earlier periods of Opposition. A series of policy groups were set up, drawing on members from different sections of the party and outside experts. Unlike policy groups set up by Heath in Opposition, they operated on a relatively light rein and were concerned more with the principles to govern policy rather than the detail of policy (Norton and Aughey, 1982: 230). A subcommittee of the Shadow Cabinet, chaired by Sir Keith Joseph, was set up to consider the proposals before they were submitted to the Shadow Cabinet (Patten, 1980: 19–20).

The two principal policy documents that were produced were *The Right Approach* in 1976 and *The Right Approach to the Economy* the following year. Though stressing the limitations of government, there was no embrace of an unbridled market economy. There was a recognition of the case for responsible pay bargaining and a voluntary pay policy. There was little mention of some of the policies that were later to be features of a Thatcher Government, such as privatisation. *The Right Approach to the Economy* – the result of deliberations in the Economic Reconstruction Group chaired by Sir Geoffrey Howe – envisaged the Government reaching a view about the scope for pay increases following discussion with 'major participants in the economy'. This embrace of some form of tripartism did not endear the document to Mrs Thatcher, who insisted that it be published under the names of the authors rather than as an official party document. However, when it was well received in the media and at the Party Conference, she rather warmed to it. 'Within three weeks, Margaret was ready to adopt our text as her own', noted Sir Geoffrey Howe. 'Nothing, I thought, succeeds like success' (Howe, 1994: 101).

Thatcher was influenced not only by what came up through the party but also what came in from outside the party. In 1974, she and Keith Joseph had established the Centre for Policy Studies (CPS), a think-tank designed to offer alternative policy advice to that coming through Conservative Research Department. 'The CPS became the furnace in which the new economics was forged' (Ridley, 1991: 8). It was led initially by Alfred Sherman, a former Communist who exhibited all the dogmatism of a convert. It was a significant, though not the only, influence on economic policy (Riddell and Haddon, 2009: 14–15). 'Alfred helped Keith to turn the Centre for Policy Studies into the powerhouse of alternative Conservative thinking on economic and social matters', recalled Thatcher (Thatcher, 1995: 251). It drew in many free-market thinkers, 'by no means all of them Conservative', in order to challenge the prevalent dogma that favoured Government intervention (Thatcher, 1995: 252).

As leader, Thatcher may have had to embrace the policy agreed within the party, but her own views were being shaped by the CPS as well as by bodies such as the established Institute for Economic Affairs – where she had regularly lunched – and the newly created Adam Smith Institute. This was essentially a new era, that of the think-tanks. The party's own policy-making structures lost their near-monopolist role within a more crowded and competitive market growing to influence the leader of the Conservative Party. The leader proved a willing target. The consequences of this influence, though, were yet to fully emerge. *The Right Approach* was a party publication. Pamphlets from the CPS had no official status.

Party management

As Heath's own former Parliamentary Private Secretary, Kenneth Baker, laconically recorded, 'The Parliamentary Party got rid of Ted because he was a loser' (Baker, 1993: 45). Though Margaret Thatcher had a committed group of neo-liberal supporters, and drew support disproportionately from the right of the Parliamentary Party, she was elected in large measure because of who she was not rather than because of who she was (Cowley and Bailey, 2000: 599–629; Heppell, 2008a: 51–69). She had the courage to challenge Heath in the leadership contest and she reaped the reward for so doing. Heath had led the party to two consecutive General Election defeats, was increasingly detached from his backbenchers and was unwilling to shift from the line he had taken in Government. Pressure mounted among MPs for him to be subject to re-election, and the rules were duly changed to enable such a contest to take place. Heath consented to the change believing that he would be re-elected. Thatcher proved the only senior frontbencher willing to challenge him. She was given little chance of success, but after an effective campaign run by Tory MP Airey Neave – and a complacent campaign by the Heath camp – she achieved 130 votes against 119 for Heath (Heppell, 2008a: 59). Heath duly withdrew from the race and Thatcher emerged triumphant in a second ballot against other contenders.

Thatcher was essentially a late candidate, following Joseph's decision not run, and when she was elected, the party was unsure as to the likely consequences. She was largely an unknown quantity:

> Colleagues who had seen Mrs Thatcher as an industrious but lightweight junior found it hard to adjust to the idea of such a naive and unsophisticated politician in the role of leader. Even those who had campaigned for her were not sure what they had persuaded the party to elect, and the party in the country did not know her at all.
>
> (J. Campbell, 2000: 312–13)

Just as the party did not know her, she did not know the party especially well either, certainly in terms of its structure and operation. Though a politician, she had been trained as a chemist and a lawyer. She had no managerial training. She had little knowledge of party management, especially at the national level. She approached it from a position of ignorance. As Cecil Parkinson recalled, 'When she became leader she knew little about the workings of the party or the House for that matter. … When I became Party Chairman I discovered that Central Office was as much of a mystery to her as it was to the rest of the Party' (Parkinson, 1992: 144).

In terms of the party organisation, she did not so much change it as work around it. Upon becoming leader, she removed some leading figures, primarily the Director-General Michael Woolf, and put her own people in to head Central Office and chair Conservative Research Department (which was also physically moved from Old Queen Street to Central Office) (Lewis, 1975: 140–1). However, there was no fundamental restructuring of the party. Rather, she worked within existing structures to bolster support among activists and the Parliamentary Party.

The party faithful initially remained loyal to the displaced leader, but were to be won round by the new leader's speeches at the Party Conferences and her engagement with party members. Simon Jenkins suggests:

> Thatcher's personality steadily broadened. She found set pieces best, especially party conferences. These were staged with panache by a team involving the dramatist Ronald Millar and the Billy Graham alumnus Harvey Thomas. They were professional and American in style but patriotic and British in content.
>
> (S. Jenkins, 2006: 48; see Millar, 1993: 230–49)

As Nigel Lawson observed, she was unusual among the party's leaders in actually liking the party and its members:

> Harold Macmillan had a contempt for the party, Alec Home tolerated it, Ted Heath loathed it. Margaret genuinely liked it. She felt a communion with it, one which later expanded to embrace the silent majority of the British people as a whole. What was initially an unusual and rather endearing trait was eventually to become part of the hubris that led to her nemesis.
>
> (Lawson, 1992: 14)

One model for understanding relationships within the Conservative Party is that of the 'traditional family' model (Norton and Aughey, 1982: 242–3). Whereas previous leaders may have been akin to distant – and, in Heath's case, stern – fathers (though Douglas-Home was a much-respected one), Thatcher was akin to the fussy and concerned mother. She spent time with party members, visiting constituencies and making her presence felt at Party Conferences.

She maintained contact with back-benchers. She made a point of dining in the Members' Dining Room at least once every two weeks and would occasionally venture into the Members' Smoking Room. She was not one for late-night social gatherings. 'Margaret's more of a luncher', said one Conservative MP. 'Like Ted, she doesn't care much for small talk' (A. J. Mayer, 1979: 157). However, unlike Heath, she was accessible. She was careful to avoid the approach taken by her predecessor. She needed her MPs. They were her power base. They had put her in office and could remove her from office. She was the first leader to be subject to annual re-election. Throughout her period in Opposition, and in her first term as Prime Minister, she maintained close contact with Members. In Opposition, she regularly briefed the Business Committee (the officers of back-bench committees and front-benchers not in the Shadow Cabinet) and made sure that other Shadow Cabinet members did likewise (Butler and Kavanagh, 1980: 67). As one far from loyal back-bencher, Julian Critchley, was later to record, 'she has more support on the back-benches, which is her natural constituency, than any other party leader I have known' (Critchley, 1986: 126).

Though most MPs were to prove loyal to the leader, they did not always prove loyal to the party's policies. The Parliamentary Party divided on a number of issues. The most divisive was that of Rhodesian sanctions. When the order for renewal came before the House, the party line was to abstain, but a number of Tory MPs voted against – 15 in 1975, 19 in 1976 and 27 in 1977. However, opposition was more pronounced in 1978, when 116 voted against, the most sizeable dissenting lobby in the party's post-war history (Norton, 1980: 377–9, 455–6). Two front-benchers who voted against gave up their posts.

Members were also divided on the issues of devolution and European integration. When it was decided to issue a three-line whip against the Second Reading of the Scotland and Wales Bill in December 1976, Alick Buchanan-Smith resigned as Shadow Scottish Secretary, and was joined by his deputy, Malcolm Rifkind. Both of them were among five Conservatives to vote for Second Reading; a further 29 (including Ted Heath) abstained from voting (Norton, 1980: 211–12). Several Tory MPs opposed to devolution voted for amendments to the Bill, where the party line was to abstain. Tory MPs opposed to further European integration also voted against the party line, not least on the European Assembly Elections Bill. Although front bench advice was to support the Bill, 16 Tories voted against Second Reading in November 1977 and several maintained their opposition during the Bill's passage. During the course of the Parliament, more than 90 per cent of Tory MPs voted against the party line on one or more occasions; 10 per cent voted against twenty or more times (Norton, 1980: 452).

The divisions, though, did not cause lasting rifts. The splits within the Conservative ranks were embarrassing but were overshadowed by the extensive revolts within the ranks of the Labour Party. There was unprecedented dissension by Labour MPs (Norton, 1980: 431–6). The nature of the Tory party was also a benefit in that it remained, in Richard Rose's terminology, a party of tendencies rather than one of factions (Rose, 1964: 33–46). Though MPs deviated from the party line on a number of occasions, the composition of the dissenting lobbies differed from issue to issue. On the Labour benches, there was a clear factional divide. The Conservatives also benefited from the fact that some of the Shadow Cabinet members handling the issues proved good at listening to back-benchers and following a line that reduced tension. Willie Whitelaw, Francis Pym, and Leon Brittan proved their worth, not least on issues such as devolution. The party was divided, though not as divided as it might have been without some adept leadership on the front bench.

However, there was one division that did prove persistent throughout Thatcher's period of Opposition – and was to follow her in office – and was essentially factional, albeit largely a one-man faction. Ted Heath never accepted his ejection from the leadership by someone he regarded as inadequate for the job. He proved a vocal, if not an organisational, rallying point for those within the party not prepared to accept the Thatcher leadership. Though they were a declining number, they created a running sore. Heath had a poor attendance record in the Commons, but he did on occasion appear in order to deliver a critical speech. Perhaps more damaging to the party's public image was his appearances at Party Conferences, where he failed to respond to attempts to support the leadership and on occasion rallied against it. 'The party conference of 1978 did not so much bring a rift into the open, for it was embarrassingly evident already, as formalise it', wrote Philip Ziegler. 'Heath came close to denouncing Thatcher for irresponsibility' (Ziegler, 2010: 519). Heath's speech was not well received by those in the party – if anything it served to mobilise support behind Thatcher – but it fed media interest as well as reflecting public opinion (Ziegler, 2010: 521). It served to increase public awareness of a conflict as well as reinforce perceptions of the Conservatives as moving away from the centre. A poll showed that the party would have a better chance of winning the forthcoming general election if it was led by Heath (Harris, 1988: 81). Thatcher may have won over her party, but she had yet to convince the electorate. Election victory was not seen as assured, certainly not under her leadership.

Emotional intelligence

What set Thatcher apart was her personality and leadership style. 'Any account of Thatcherism must include a consideration of the "Thatcher factor", which recognizes her strong personality and a leadership style which is both self-confident ands dogmatic' (Brown and Sparks, 1989: xi). This applied both in Opposition and Government. What separated the two periods was that only in Government did her strong personality emerge as an electoral asset for the Conservative Party.

Young and Sloman used the title *The Thatcher Phenomenon* in a work on Margaret Thatcher (Young and Sloman, 1986). This is a useful term for understanding the impact of Margaret Thatcher on British politics. As we have noted, there have been a great many works on Thatcherism. There have also been a great many on Margaret Thatcher. The key to Conservative success once Thatcher was in Downing Street was not Thatcherism but Thatcher (Norton, 1987: 21–37). She did not craft either a Thatcherite electorate (Crewe and Searing, 1988: 361–84) or a Thatcherite Parliamentary Party (Norton, 1990: 41–58). What she did deliver was a particular style of Government and the ability to convey a sense of direction.

Her style of leadership was to be a benefit for most of the period of Government. However, it proved less beneficial, at times notably harmful, towards the end of her Premiership – contributing fundamentally to the fact that it was the end of her Premiership – as well as during her period in Opposition. As Butler and Kavanagh observed of her as Opposition leader, 'Her attitude of certainty could make her overbearing in discussion. ... Even her friends acknowledged that she approached conversations as an intellectual exchange rather than an opportunity to empathise' (Butler and Kavanagh, 1980: 66–7). She was seen as confrontational and abrasive. This concerned some Conservative supporters such as columnist Peregrine Worsthorne: 'The Conservative tradition was one of tolerance. As a potential national leader Mrs Thatcher needed to demonstrate a greater sympathy and understanding with the views of ordinary people, even if she disagreed with them' (Butler and Kavanagh, 1980: 67).

Her style initially confused her colleagues. As Jim Prior recalled,

> At first some of us thought this tendency of Margaret's to make new policy on television was simply a matter of inexperience. But it was her way of making certain she got her way. We did not fully appreciate at first that she was a strong, determined leader which she subsequently turned out to be.
>
> (Prior, 1986: 107)

She was able to get her way on occasion not only by her determined approach but also by employing her femininity. She was surrounded by a body of men who were unaccustomed to having a woman in such a powerful position. They were unsure of how to handle her. She played this to her advantage. Douglas Hurd recalled of Francis Pym:

> Throughout, Francis found his dealings with Margaret Thatcher difficult. Her habit of leading every discussion with a firm statement of her own views bumped up against his natural reluctance to argue with a woman.
>
> (Hurd, 2003: 243)

However, although she was not lacking in feminine guile, her approach did limit her capacity to achieve her goals. Her confrontational approach irritated members of the Shadow Cabinet. Equally important, her single-minded focus on policy goals meant that she tended to neglect the interests of her supporters. She showed remarkably limited interest in the process of promotion within the party's ranks. She kept Heathites in the Shadow Cabinet. She did not give preferment to some of her most avid Parliamentary supporters. Although in Government she was to place neo-liberal allies in the key economic ministries, she still left promotion to and within ministerial ranks to the whips. The consequence in Government was to be a disproportionate number of 'damp' MPs serving in ministerial office (Norton, 1990: 55).

This reflected the leader's concentration on goals rather than processes. It was said of Churchill that he was fascinated by politics rather than by policy. Margaret Thatcher was much more concerned with policy – or at least policy goals – than she was with the nitty-gritty of politics. Though she realised she had to fight and cajole to get her way, she was at times a little naïve when it came to the actual structures through which she had to operate to get her way. She had to rely at times on those around her to do the work on her behalf and to advise her as to what was and was not wise in terms of party reaction.

Though naïve at times about processes, there was some realisation of the political realities. She had to fight to get her way because she could not impose her will. She had to carry with her leading figures who were not of her persuasion. She could not afford to lose them nor could she afford to be so daring in policy that it scared the electorate. 'She often remarked that she had to win the argument of power before she could win the argument of policy. Her entire leadership was a conversation between the two' (S. Jenkins, 2006: 50). Sometimes the balance between the two may have become a little out of kilter, but she nonetheless was not blind to the context in which she had to operate. She may be party leader but she lacked the levers and the authority that came with being Prime Minister. As a result, she was wary of moving frontbenchers – 'except when circumstances forced her hand' – and the only significant reshuffle of the Shadow Ministerial team was in 1978 (Butler and Kavanagh, 1980: 68). She had a reputation for talking too much in Shadow Cabinet, and was prone to interrupt, but this can be interpreted as her way of ensuring that reluctant members went along with what she wanted. As Butler and Kavanagh note, she was less forceful than Heath, but she could hardly afford to be as forceful: she had not yet occupied Downing Street (Butler and Kavanagh, 1980: 68).

Conclusion

Though the Parliamentary Party under Margaret Thatcher harried the Labour Government between 1975 and 1979, and did so with some effect, the Labour Government was its own worst enemy (Ridley, 1991: 12–13). It was badly split and presided over the Winter of Discontent. In the event, it signed its own death warrant. Margaret Thatcher had presided over a party that was at least electable, and it was elected because it was not the Labour Party.

People were unsure as to what they were getting with the new Government. Thatcherism had not emerged as a coherent philosophy. As one of Thatcher's leading supporters was to concede,

> ... the full nature of 'Thatcherism' was not known to the electorate in 1979. Nor was it fully understood within the parliamentary party. ... To the extent that that people knew of Margaret Thatcher's policies, many thought that she would be pushed off them by the old hands still in her Cabinet.
>
> (Ridley, 1991: 13)

What was forthcoming was thus not apparent. Support for the Conservatives may have been reasonably broad, but it was not deep. Electors were voting on the basis of retrospective rather than prospective evaluations: that is, they were voting against Labour rather than for the Conservatives (see Whiteley, 1983: Chapter 4). They had some idea of what the Tories were promising, but were less clear as to what they would deliver. 'After a short time in office ideology has always tended to yield to practicality' (Butler and Kavanagh, 1980: 340, 344). Those electors – and members of the Parliamentary Party – who thought (sometimes hoped) Thatcher would be another Edward Heath were to be proved wrong. That she would prove to be so very different was not obvious when she made the transition from Leader of the Opposition to Prime Minister. One could anticipate a continuation of her style of leadership, but not its consequences. After Margaret Thatcher strode over the threshold of No 10, British politics changed in a way that few could have predicted based on her period as Leader of the Opposition.

9
James Callaghan, 1979–80

Stephen Meredith

> Jim Callaghan told me within a week of the election that
> he planned to stay on as Leader of the Labour Party for
> eighteen months – 'to take the shine off the ball' for me.
> I did not complain, nor would I have changed Jim's mind
> if I had. ... I did not look forward to the idea of succeed-
> ing him as Leader of the Labour Party in Opposition; I had
> seen that there is no more difficult job in British politics.
>
> (Healey, 1990: 466)

James Callaghan falls into the small category of British Prime Ministers
who remained as party leader and Leader of the Opposition after a General
Election defeat, and the even smaller category of Premiers who had not
previously performed the role. In Callaghan's case, as is generally the norm
in the circumstances, it was only for a relatively brief period and in a highly
disputatious and factional party context, and these factors obviously remain
of paramount significant in any evaluation of Callaghan's Opposition leadership style and performance.

Contrary to personal inclination, Callaghan remained as Leader of the
Opposition for a period of just eighteen months between May 1979 and
October 1980, primarily to oversee the 'inevitable post-mortem' and allow
election of a suitable successor as party leader (Labour Party, Parliamentary
Committee Minutes, 15 October 1980). The difficulties of his previous
Labour administration and subsequent defeat in the 1979 General Election
left him a hamstrung 'caretaker' leader of a discordant and divided party.
Accounts have presented Callaghan, largely out of a sense of duty, as 'merely
holding the fort' for a more suitable leader; an experienced hand to steer
the party through stormy waters and to keep the party together, resist the
clamour for left-wing reforms and ensure election to the leadership of his
preferred successor, Denis Healey, rather than a candidate of the Labour
left (Callaghan, 1988: 565; Conroy, 2006: 136; McKie, 2005; K. Morgan,

1997a: 702–3; Rees, 2001). Callaghan's post-election leadership interlude has also been treated relatively lightly in comparison with earlier (and later) periods of his political life (see, for example, Callaghan, 1988; K. Morgan, 1997a, 1999; Shaw, 1996), or viewed as largely a failure on the dimensions of strategic party leadership providing the rationale for him to remain in the post after the 1979 election defeat; as 'essentially wasted time' in attempting to stem the tide of left-wing demands for greater internal democracy and maintain party unity (Conroy, 2006: 136–7; K. Morgan, 1999: 148; Shaw, 1996: 164).

Callaghan's stewardship indeed coincided with a period of intense conflict and momentous change inside the Labour Party after 1979, and the chapter attempts a re-evaluation of his leadership and party management style and performance in a challenging and confrontational party and political context. It suggests that Callaghan's leadership perspective and strategy in Opposition at this intricate juncture of Labour's politics derived from a defensive instinct to resist what he perceived to be the fundamental threat of radical, divisive and ultimately unpopular party presentation and policy, informed by a sense of duty and traditional principles and priorities of solidarity, party unity and moderate responsive leadership, and as such can be judged with mixed success in severely restrictive circumstances.

After a series of senior government posts carried out with mixed degrees of success, Callaghan had been elected simultaneously to the leadership of his party and Prime Minister in the strange circumstances surrounding Harold Wilson's resignation as Labour leader and Prime Minister in 1976, defeating Michael Foot in a final ballot of Labour MPs only. Callaghan, of the leadership contenders, most clearly represented a centrist, unifying position and, although only second choice of many Labour MPs, promised to be the least divisive in a relatively factionalised party context. Although Callaghan's abbreviated three-year Premiership was consistently under pressure of economic and political circumstances, and he was subject to the intense scrutiny and criticism of a resurgent left in Labour's National Executive Committee (NEC) and Party Conference, perhaps only towards the end of his tenure did he lose a sure touch for the mood of the limits of the party. In the face of International Monetary Fund (IMF) conditions that threatened to split and destabilise his Government, Callaghan managed to keep ministers together across the intense and prolonged Cabinet debates to achieve the loan. Labour's fragile political position was managed and upheld by a Parliamentary pact with the Liberal Party and, for a period, he accomplished the often fraught and delicate balance of national economic and party and wider labour movement interests in the face of severe internal opposition to public spending cuts. As the lifespan of the political arrangement with the Liberals ran out, failure to confirm an early General Election for October 1978, when treating the Trade Union Congress (TUC) to his own (misattributed) version of Vesta

Victoria's old music hall favourite, 'Waiting at the Church', and subsequent decision to continue with an anti-inflationary prices and incomes policy, proved significant misjudgements as ensuing and sustained industrial (re)action characterised the following (in)famous 'winter' (McKie, 2005; *The Times*, 5/9/1978).

In the well-known story of persistent inflationary pressures, wage restraint, public spending cuts and industrial strife that beset the Callaghan Government in the winter of 1978–9, his Labour administration came tumbling down in the wake of the so-called 'winter of discontent'. Ultimately, Callaghan's authority and Labour's claim to work effectively with the trade unions were destroyed in the upsurge of industrial unrest. A 'beleaguered and battered' Callaghan was forced to call an election that his party had little chance of winning following a vote of no confidence in his Labour Government and was succeeded by Margaret Thatcher as Prime Minister. Callaghan's Government was swept away in the emerging wave of full-frontal Thatcherism, along with the 'gentler, consensual, non-confrontational approach that he represented' (McKie, 2005).

In the turbulent period of British and Labour politics that followed, Callaghan appeared out of step with the new polarised politics of right and left; a Labour King Canute feebly attempting to stem the tide of seemingly inexorable left-wing thrust in the institutional and policy-making apparatus of his party (and 'new right' populism in the country). He remained as Leader of the Opposition in the context of a party in which the left had steadily grown in influence and repudiated many of his Government's policies, and Callaghan appeared to be able to exercise little authority as the left were able to reform party institutions and an influential segment of party opinion eventually departed Labour to form a new alternative vehicle of moderate revisionist social democracy.

His post-election stewardship of the party exposed him not so much as a 'caretaker' or 'night watchman' as a 'lame duck' Leader of the Opposition. While his party engaged in the internecine warfare that came close to damaging its credibility as a potential party of government, Callaghan was a sitting target of left-wing retribution in the organs of the party (Healey, 1990: 475; McKie, 2005). Callaghan appeared to be both out of step and out of sympathy with many of policies emerging in the new party environment, particularly those that repudiated his essential tool of incomes policy (Benn, 1990: 599; 1994: 10, 26) and favoured withdrawal from the European Economic Community (EEC) and unilateralist nuclear disarmament. He resigned as party leader after eighteen months, shortly after the 1980 Party Conference had voted for a new system of election of the party leader, involving an electoral college of trade unions and Constituency Labour Parties (CLPs), as well as Labour MPs (Labour Party, 1980: 184–94, 298). To some extent, his hand was forced by the decision to extend the franchise for party leader into the wider organs of the party, and his 'timely' resignation ensured that his successor would still be elected by MPs only, presumably in the hope that a 'moderate' successor would be elected by the more 'moderate' Parliamentary Party (Healey, 1990: 476). When Michael Foot rather than Denis Healey was elected as his successor by Labour MPs under the old system in November 1980, the tactic had largely failed.

Party management

In Callaghan's case, the issue and priorities of party management cannot be separated from the wider challenge of resisting the oncoming battalions of the left in the party apparatus and related ideological and policy conflict in the battle for the 'soul of the party'. His approach can be broadly characterised as consolidationary, or rather as defensive and reactive, and one in which both strengths and weaknesses can be identified in his leadership within a highly restrictive political context. As Morgan (2007) suggests, Callaghan 'embodied, if anybody does, the traditional values of solidarity. That is what he symbolised. ... He had a very strong sense of class, of us and them, a strong sense of the Party'. Morgan also suggests that both as Prime Minister and party leader his natural style was collective and collegiate. He was sensitive to the new developments of the 1970s that threatened the broad consensual nature of the party. He very much believed in the party being led from the top and wasn't 'a great grass-roots man', and in this respect differed sharply from the left and Tony Benn, and even some others on the so-called right of the party such as Roy Hattersley. It wasn't a case of 'the leaders lead and the followers follow', but neither was he in favour of redefining the essential working structure of the party. His view of the party was 'very much that it was controlled responsively and sensitively with control at the centre', in the traditional manner 'by the leaders of the party but in conjunction with the trade unions ... he always felt that a very close liaison with the Trade Unions was an absolutely essential and stabilising force'. While he felt Labour should evolve, he regarded it as a 'traditional and rather conventional party' representative of the majority of people, and in this sense should develop in a broadly consensual way, remote from the dramatic and potentially damaging transformation to party structure and policy being proposed. In this sense, he was also decidedly 'anti-group' and unsympathetic of internal party factionalism and obsessions of both left and right and the danger to party unity they represented. He expressed a variety of objections, both theoretical and rational, to attempts to 'democratise' the party and participation (K. Morgan, interview with author, 1997b; also see Labour Party Manifesto Group Papers, LP MANIF/1; Meredith, 2007: 74). Unfortunately for Callaghan and his ability to manage the party in the traditional manner, trade union support had seemingly run out. They had largely been converted to the cause of constitutional change and notions of internal party democracy and were determined on an extension of the franchise (Labour Party, Parliamentary Committee Minutes, 19 March 1980; 18 June 1980; 3 November 1980).

Eric Shaw (1994: 17–18) describes the period surrounding Callaghan's leadership of the party in Opposition between 1979 and 1981 as reflecting a 'paralysis of leadership power' within the context of Labour's wider 'crisis of governance'. He suggests that the notion of Labour as a 'highly pluralist organisation' came clearly to the fore as the traditional dominance in the party of the Parliamentary leadership, based on right-wing majorities in key institutions, disintegrated after 1979. This upheaval reconfigured the balance of power in the institutions and policy-making machinery of the party, and the process of transformation overshadowed and inhibited Callaghan's party management and policy development strategies. Deprived of the authority it had previously enjoyed in other organs of the party, the leadership was largely unable to halt the refashioned NEC demand for constitutional reforms and adoption of policies to which it was in principle opposed. According to Shaw, Callaghan's inability to dissuade Conference, taking its lead from the NEC, from adopting left-wing positions on party constitutional and major policy issues 'demonstrated the extent to which the authority of both the Leader and [Parliamentary] front bench as a whole had dwindled'. In Callaghan's own words, the new left-wing shift and mood of the movement following the ignominious fall of his Labour administration was used to 'fetter the Parliamentary Party and to organise factions to replace Members of Parliament with whom they did not agree', and provoked an 'atmosphere of mistrust and cynicism in which the motives and actions of Party Leaders were continually questioned' (Callaghan, 1988: 565). For those who privileged the relative autonomy of the Parliamentary Party and its leadership in a representative democracy and the crucial role of the party leader in its link with the electorate, in which '[h]is personality and authority are of immense importance', it seemed 'absurd' to commit him to a policy with which he fundamentally disagreed. Leaders have a central role in this respect, and Callaghan as Labour's leader was 'always ahead of Mrs Thatcher, and was trusted, respected and liked' (Benn, 1990: 581–2; Healey, 1990: 473–5). Nonetheless, with a left-wing-dominated NEC in the constitutional box-seat determined on a course of party institutional and policy reforms, Callaghan confronted a hostile and constrictive environment in his attempts to manage and lead the party in Opposition.

Given intra-party tensions over the proposed changes and their implications, neither was it the case that Callaghan was subject solely to the force of the left. Defending their traditional position and influence, those on the so-called centre-right of the party were equally vocal in their support of the constitutional status quo. Roy Hattersley and Bill Rodgers in Labour's Shadow Cabinet, for example, implored its representatives on the Commission of Enquiry on a new electoral college to elect the party leader and oversee the party manifesto to attempt to resist excessive NEC proposals as far as possible, and expressed their 'hope that not all the moves to compromise would be taken by the PLP Leadership'.[1] Other 'moderates' expressed their hope that the Commission as a whole would be resilient and sensible, but 'the Leadership must be free to negotiate' (Labour Party, Parliamentary Committee Minutes, 22 May 1980). Others considered this to be an unlikely prospect, as it was felt that the NEC had 'rigged' membership of the Commission to recommend constitutional changes to the Party Conference. While trade union representation on the Commission reflected a balanced range of party opinion, the NEC had appointed seven left-wing representatives and the Parliamentary Party were allowed only two (Callaghan himself and the Deputy Leader, Michael Foot), resulting in a 'built-in left-wing majority'. It was felt that the NEC, with its own left-wing majority, was oblivious to the arguments of the Parliamentary leadership and was determined to gain further constitutional concessions in the form of an electoral college (Healey, 1990: 473–4; Shore, 1993: 132).

Rodgers and David Owen blamed Callaghan directly for the Commission of Enquiry's eventual recommendation of an electoral college. They essentially accused him of betrayal of the Parliamentary Party in the negotiations, which represented a fundamental challenge to Callaghan's residual authority and prestige as party leader. They had not agreed to the concessions made and were opposed to the principle of an electoral college, and 'they were now to be told they could not choose the Leader and Deputy Leader, and would have to accept a rolling Manifesto from the NEC/PC which would have to be endorsed by an electoral college'. It was their view that they looked to the elected leader of the party for leadership, and believed that the party leader 'should not have moved from the position adopted by the Parliamentary Party in the evidence ... submitted to the Commission. There was the great danger of the PLP "selling the pass" while the NEC remained resolute. No compromise was possible. The battle was on to protect Parliamentary democracy'. From their perspective, 'it would be hard to defend the idea of an Electoral College', and while they were 'sure the PLP representatives had fought hard for the status quo ... sometimes it was better to fight straight and lose'. Callaghan regarded this view as 'naïve', as there was 'no true trade union support for the status quo' and highlighted the pressure to which they had been subjected during the Commission. He adopted a characteristically pragmatic and hard-headed response in the prevailing party context, indicating key principles of solidarity and party unity and the need to absorb minimal change. He argued that it was 'difficult to defend the selection of the Leader by MPs only on principle – even the Conservative Party nowadays selected its leader on a wider basis'. The leadership further explained that the so-called 'straight fight' proposed by Rodgers would have resulted in an alliance of the NEC and trade unions, 'the worst possible split imaginable', and there was the danger they could end up with something far worse than the current compromise in which 'the NEC would not have absolute power over the Manifesto and the Electoral College would have a membership of 50% PLP members'. Although the 'form of the new proposal was not ideal ... it could be made tolerable and reputable', and there was no particular merit in 'merely going down fighting', but there 'had to be eventual victory' (Labour Party, Parliamentary Committee Minutes, 22 May 1980; 18 June 1980; Labour Party, Manifesto Group Papers, LP MANIF/1; LP/MANIF/19; Rodgers, 2000: 195–6; Shore, 1993: 133).

Callaghan was also sharp to accuse them in turn of plotting to endanger the unity of the party in their alleged 'complicity' in Roy Jenkins' call for a new party of the 'radical centre'. Denis Healey goes as far as to suggest that the decision of the Commission of Enquiry at Bishop's Stortford was the moment that the Social Democratic Party (SDP) was born and formally split the Labour Party (Healey, 1990: 474; R. Jenkins, 1982: 26–7; Shore, 1993: 133–4). Precise points of departure in the formation of political parties are always contentious, but Owen's comments elsewhere of 'Jim let us down' and 'too late Harold + Jim are the mugwumps of the L.P.' certainly offer a perspective on views of Callaghan's party management from the social democratic right and their likely (brief) future in the Labour Party. Particularly, they were concerned that the party had been allowed to drift too far away from its traditional 'philosophical and organisational development' and 'roots in the people of this country and its commitment to Parliamentary government'. It had reached a situation in which a 'handful of trade union leaders can now dictate the choice of a future Prime Minister', and the imposition of a manifesto by a minority that 'does not reflect the broad aspirations of Labour Party members [and] ... Labour voters', and results in a programme that cannot be sustained in government and 'provides endless disillusionment when it is not implemented'. Ultimately, a narrow sectionalist approach would undermine Labour's identification with the 'development of a cooperative, neighbourly and altruistic society', and the lack of a credible and 'acceptable socialist alternative' would open the way to 'divisive and often cruel Tory policies' and the 'individualistic uncooperative, isolated, selfish society' of the Thatcher project dominating the 1980s (Owen Papers, D709/2/17/1/2; D709/2/17/1/3; *Guardian*, 1/8/1980).

In the circumstances, evaluation of Callaghan's party management skills and performance is overshadowed by the constraints of an antagonistic and highly polarised party context. Ultimately, he proved unable to contain the clamour for institutional reform and crippling levels of disharmony in the party. His collective and collegiate approach and seamless roots in the wider party had seemingly deserted him, or at least were broken on the back of a deeply hostile and rancorous intra-party environment. His leadership authority, already weakened owing to the perceived limitations of his previous Labour administration, was further challenged by the advance and demands of the left in the key institutions of the party. While he attempted to concede and absorb some of the new developments in the spirit of party unity and the prospect of longer-term solidarity, he encountered both uncompromising pressure for change from the left and the recriminations of the party's social democratic right, some of whom were determined on leaving the party to form a new vehicle of moderate liberal social democracy.

Public policy platform

Again during Callaghan's brief period as Leader of the Opposition, issues and problems of policy development cannot be separated from the task of resisting the dual challenge of the left to the party's institutional hierarchy and policy platform. On the back of NEC-sponsored left-wing advances in the key policy and decision-making forums of the party, a raft of policies broadly associated with the left, including the shift to a unilateral defence policy, withdrawal from the EEC and a far greater interventionist economic strategy and extension of public ownership, swept through the Party Conference between 1979 and 1981. The development of the party's policy programme in this direction not only provided a final straw in the defection of influential centre-right figures to the SDP but, partly owing to the insistence of Callaghan's successor, Michael Foot, not to compromise Conference resolutions, infilled the party's infamous 1983 General Election manifesto, described as 'the longest suicide note in history' (Hope, 2010; Labour Party, 1983; K. Morgan, 1997a: 714; Shaw, 1994: 16–17). Under pressure from the centre-right and other anxious members of the Parliamentary Party to resist the left's onslaught on the two related fronts in 'a struggle for the control of the party', Callaghan appeared to be increasingly 'out of date', a 'fixer from the past unable to point any new directions for the future'. To both the new left and revisionist right, his leadership 'represented Old Labour, a dying generation of old-style social democrats, or perhaps simply "Labourism", an economist creed of support for the working class rather than a doctrine for the conquest and mobilization of power' (K. Morgan, 1997a: 707–8, 714–15). In the febrile atmosphere after 1979, it seemed that his perennial values of 'partnership and consensus', constructed around his identification with the precepts of a mixed economy, social welfare and a level-headed union alliance of the post-war consensus, had become unfashionable (Meredith, 2008: 126–7; K. Morgan, 1999: 148).

Callaghan has been described as generally a cautious man in the policy sphere. He was cautious over newer Labour policy initiatives that departed from its traditional 'labourist' and 'economist' concerns. He was unconvinced by constitutional reform and the move for devolution, ambiguous over Europe and, with his emphasis on 'family values', had not fully embraced recent liberal social reforms. After the experience and consequences of Labour's prior period of office and subsequent election defeat, his ambitions as party leader in opposition were strictly limited. In terms of policy development, Callaghan's approach was as much defensive as pro-active, focused as he was on resisting the twin challenge of the left but, according to Morgan (1997a: 756; 1999: 149; 2007), neither was he merely the 'limited machine politician' of popular legend. He was not just a 'managerialist', and more than just the 'pragmatist' that he is commonly called (Meredith, 2008: 174–5). He was also a politician 'with an ideology'. He believed himself to be a democratic socialist, but it was different socialism from that of the new Labour left of the early 1980s, which regarded him rather as a traitor to socialism. Caught between the revisionist socialist stools of left and right, it seemed that his particular set of values for a socialist and fairer society did not chime with the (new socialist) times.

Tired from the endless tide of internal conflict and with his hands increasingly tied by the emerging balance of power and realignments in the party, Callaghan was unable to mount a credible challenge to the left's policy platform in the same way that he very largely failed to halt the left's assault on the power apparatus of the party. One small hint of success at the 1980 Party Conference was to defend the existing system of jointly determining the Party Manifesto between NEC and Shadow Cabinet rather than the NEC alone, but his plea to delegates to '[for] pity's sake, stop arguing' indicated the level to which he had been reduced in his attempts to counter dissent and maintain some semblance of party unity. Much less grandly and almost despairingly, he was calling for, in Gladstone's (and Churchill's) words, 'a blessed act of oblivion' to end the discord (Garton-Ash, 2009: 201). Otherwise, he viewed the future direction of party policy with the same degree of pessimism with which he regarded the constitutional issues of mandatory selection of MPs and a leadership electoral college as largely 'lost causes' (K. Morgan, 1997a: 717–18; Shore, 1993: 134).

Eric Shaw argues that 'Callaghan's inability to dissuade Conference from approving these constitutional reforms and adopting left-wing positions on major policy matters demonstrated the extent to which the authority of both the Leader and the front bench as a whole had dwindled'. Moreover, the inability of the party leadership to effectively utilise its resources and mobilise opinion to undermine the case of the left in party deliberations simultaneously frustrated senior Parliamentary colleagues affronted by a full-frontal assault on their traditional sovereignty. In the circumstances, Callaghan complained to an aide that 'I have as little authority in the PLP as I have in the NEC', to which the response came, 'the left are the masters now' (Shaw, 1994: 17; 1999, 153; P. Jenkins, 1987: 113). Callaghan's situation appeared hopeless, caught between the warring party interests, and bringing to mind David Marquand's famous and potentially separatist reflection that

> [t]o pretend, in this situation, that socialists and social democrats are all part of the same great Movement – that Shirley Williams and Bill Rodgers ... have more in common with Tony Benn and Eric Heffer ... than

they do with Peter Walker or Ian Gilmour or Edward Heath – is to live a
lie. But it is a lie which the Labour Party has to live if it is to live at all.
(Marquand, 1979: 17–18)

He claimed that respective positions on core policy issues – 'incomes
policy, prices policy, taxation policy, trade policy, industrial policy and
European policy' – were 'not merely different, but irreconcilably opposed'
(also P. Jenkins, 1981; Labour Party, Manifesto Group Papers, LP MANIF/6;
Rodgers, 1979: 429–34). The Common Market remained a particularly
thorny issue and had divided the party in interesting ways for a generation
(Meredith, 2011). Although attempts were made to reduce its significance
in the party's internal and external forms to avoid potentially further debili-
tating divisions, pro-European social democrats were further angered and
blamed Callaghan for 'moving the Party increasingly into a position where
it appears to be against membership on principle and ready to consider
pulling out' (Labour Party, Manifesto Group Papers, LP MANIF/19). The
development of party policy on Europe in this direction has often been held
as a major factor in the formal split in the party in 1981, although Labour's
broader policy shift to the left after 1979 caused similar tensions and hard-
ening of a clear social democratic identity (Crewe and King, 1995: 106–7;
Desai, 1994: 145–60).

With the left dominating the key policy conduit of the NEC and mood
of Conference, the policies that worked their way through Labour's policy-
making machinery after 1979 were of a distinctly socialist flavour alien to
Callaghan and the dominant tradition of revisionist social democracy of
the post-war period. The left had drawn succour from their seeming vindication as (largely impotent) critics of the 1974–9 Labour Government and
apparent bankruptcy of traditional revisionist social democracy. The decline
of the Government and subsequent election defeat transferred the initiative
to the left-wing NEC which, through its various subcommittees, was
constitutionally responsible for the formulation of policy. It was now able to
promote an extensive 'socialist alternative', gestating since the economically
radical *Labour's Programme 1973*, as the basis of Labour's policy platform,
culminating in *Labour's Programme 1982*, and ultimately the 1983 Election
Manifesto. Consequently, with Tony Benn in the vanguard as head of the
NEC's influential Home Policy committee, the left pushed through a host
of economically interventionist and regulatory policies favouring stricter
economic planning, industrial democracy and targeted extensions of public
ownership. These included reflationary policies, labour law, import and
exchange controls and withdrawal from the EEC. The reliance on Callaghan's
pet incomes policy as a mechanism to combat inflation had been swept way
'as simply a form of wage restraint designed to ensure that workers bore the
main brunt of economic [recession]' (Shaw, 1994: 7–15; Shore, 1993: 127–8).
To Callaghan and others in the predominantly centre-right leadership, the

development and presentation of such a programme in rapidly changing international and domestic circumstances only suggested disaster but, in the context of the newly reconfigured party, were unable to halt the journey to electoral 'suicide'.

On the other hand, beyond his preferred but seemingly broken anti-inflationary instrument of incomes policy and general identification with the achievements of post-war Labour, and shorn of the comfort of moderate trade union co-operation, it is not clear that Callaghan offered the prospect of a clear and coherent vision of policy to counter the left's (or revisionist right's) more packaged product. Despite Kenneth Morgan's championing of Callaghan's firm ideological foundations, these appeared to be rooted in the past in the defence and maintenance of the old shibboleths of the post-war social democratic order. Almost isolated as party leader, the prevailing balance of power militated against even Callaghan's defensive and 'consolidationist' strategy. His key lieutenants were similarly hamstrung. Deputy Leader Michael Foot was never likely to 'pursue a nationwide campaign against the left', and Callaghan's preferred successor, Denis Healey, was unable to directly challenge the new electoral college proposals as he needed to retain the support of trade union leaders to endorse him in any future leadership contest, while at the time failing to build bridges and alliances with putative allies (Healey, 1990: 475, 477; K. Morgan, 1997a: 715, 717, 719; 2007). Modest, pragmatic adjustment to the changing milieu was not acceptable to the newly triumphant left in the NEC, nor to the generation of 'post-Croslandite' Labour revisionists keen to defend their hard-earned pro-European spurs and to review core elements of Labour's economic and industrial politics. It was his return to the backbenches that allowed Callaghan a greater degree of freedom and contribution to policy, particularly in international affairs in terms of economic collaboration and defence and security issues, including one last conspicuous stab at the left's (and party's) unilateralist platform (Benn, 1994: 496–7; Callaghan, 1988: 565–6; K. Morgan, 1997a: 706–7, 720–1, 727–9).

Public communication

With obvious notable exceptions, Callaghan demonstrated undoubted skills as a public communicator, often in difficult circumstances, and felt it to be one of his core political strengths. In addition to his ability, for the most part, to communicate a message of calm and reassurance, the 'personal touch' was regarded as the essence of his charm, even in the darkest days of his Labour Government.[2] Perhaps aware of his advantages in this respect, Callaghan was the first Prime Minister to indicate his willingness to take part in a televised debate during the 1979 General Election campaign with the Leader of the Opposition, but it was the Conservative leader's refusal to participate that denied the public their first opportunity to see the two party leaders battle it out face to face (Labour Party, NEC Minutes, 23 May 1979). Identification with the 'touch-stone of public opinion' was a constant feature of Callaghan's political method and appeal. It offered a guiding principle in his opposition to attempts to 'democratise participation' after 1979. He believed the Labour Party should move in a consensual way that reflected and did not depart too far from the 'majority of people', and was unsympathetic to 'groups running around' flogging their minority wares. His connection and claim to familiarity with public opinion 'was a gut sense sort of thing of how he felt people worked, and the very important test ... would be his sense of his constituency. He was a tremendously devoted constituency person'. This relationship was a steady force on his career. He 'felt he really understood his constituents and had a deep intimate knowledge of their problems, and that was what the country was like broadly speaking'. His personal rapport was such that 'people seemed to take him at his word. ... He would pronounce on some occasions that "that's what they are saying in the working men's clubs" ... and they appeared to take him at his word'. It didn't always express itself in liberal progressive form in issues such as immigration, but both he and evidently others felt that he possessed 'intuitive feeling' for the mood of mainstream opinion (K. Morgan, interview with author, 1997b; 1997a: 308–9, 515–16).

It is probably true that Labour's natural constituency in the country identified more readily with Callaghan's easy bonhomie than with the apparent aloofness of Roy Jenkins or urgent dissent of Tony Benn. He carried this geniality into his own television interviews during the 1979 Election campaign and, in ethic and presentation to the electorate, 'Callaghan was Labour's campaign' in the sense that 'he was far more popular than the party'. Here he was able to effect his reputation as a national rather than party leader, and communicate his core traditional values of community, neighbourhood, family, a safe society and unity of the nation as a whole. His personal popularity and public rapport easily out-shone that of Margaret Thatcher (K. Morgan, 1997a: 516–17, 691–3), but popularity and a one-man election campaign were not enough to convince the electorate of his party's fitness to govern. Unfortunately, his generally silky skills of public communication continued to reap little reward as Labour entered Opposition. His communication talents and approachable quality, a major factor in his political progress, mixed with an often assertive (and sometimes 'grumpy') temperament (K. Morgan, 1997a: 133–4), fell on largely deaf ears. Engaged as he was in vicious, time-consuming intra-party struggles, he had little in terms of Labour's positive national message to convey. While exhorting colleagues to unite and recognise the fundamental strengths and values of the party, he focused largely on delivering a negative anti-Conservative and anti-Thatcherism message (Labour Party, Parliamentary Committee Minutes, 15 October 1980). Callaghan continued to stand for and communicate traditional values and an 'abiding commitment to partnership and co-operation'.

He was perceived more widely as a 'conservative mediator' who attempted 'to run Labour by consent'. He was considered to have retained his dignity in the face of much adversity, and continued to represent a reassuring image to those unconvinced of the ideological politics of right and left (K. Morgan, 1997a: 720; *The Times*, 16/10/1980). To this effect, Callaghan's relative popularity and public rapport remained intact, but his party, its philosophy and the nature of its appeal had passed him by, at least temporarily.

Emotional intelligence

As some other contributions to the volume emphasise, there is a sense in which issues of personality and politics are often treated with caution. However, there is also a sense in which personality and personal style of leadership intersect with institutional, ideological and sociological factors in determining political direction. For instance, recent debates concerning the relative power of the Prime Minister in the British political system have encouraged a shift away from a focus on personality to consider the structured relationships and institutional resources and constraints of their office and role (Richards and Smith, 2002: 203, 224–5; Smith, 1999: 2–3, 13–14). However, it is also clear that the nature and performance of leadership can be shaped by the personality and style of a particular leader. According to the current Cabinet Secretary, Sir Gus O'Donnell, 'the style of [a] Prime Minister is very important ... John Major ... had a very collegiate style ... Tony Blair ... had a strong emphasis on stock takes and delivery. ... There is a personality element' (House of Lords, 2010). Peter Hennessy has contrasted the distinctive 'destiny' styles of Thatcher and Blair and 'more collective' styles of leadership of Major and Callaghan (House of Lords, 2010). According to one pioneer of the analysis of personality on political action and decision-making,

> [t]here is a great deal of political activity which can be explained adequately only by taking account of the personal characteristics of the actors involved ... political actors ... loom as full-blown individuals influenced by all of the peculiar strengths and weaknesses to which the species ... is subject, in addition to being role-players, creatures of situation, members of a culture, and possessors of social characteristics.
>
> (Greenstein, 1967: 629)

These insights can be reinforced even in a collective framework if the characteristics of individual leaders can also be located in some of the latter context and particular political situation (Theakston, 2007: 41).

Callaghan's personal political style has been described as palpably 'collegiate'. His leadership of the party and government was considered to be much 'more open than under Harold Wilson', and he brought a general sense of calm to his role, capable of arousing great trust among different constituencies. As noted, he utilised a collective style, 'quite unlike Tony Blair and ... quite unlike ... Wilson'. Under Callaghan's leadership, it 'was felt that the atmosphere changed'; there was no 'kitchen cabinet', and little concern about 'leaks and moles' (K. Morgan, 1999: 149; 2007; Benn, 1994: 26; S. Williams, 2009: 226, 247). Conscious of the need to maintain unity, and at least contain the swing to the left in the party after 1979, he continued in a broadly collective spirit to concede to and absorb what he hoped would be inevitable but limited change (Labour Party, Parliamentary Committee Minutes, 16 June 1980). Even so, the particular context of Labour's politics brought the limitations of his personal style into stark focus. Labour's polarised and confrontational politics of Opposition presented a largely alien context in which Callaghan's ameliorative personal qualities appeared out of date. In left-wing circles, his avuncular charm, easy personal manner and ability to induce trust were interpreted as surrogates for caution, moderation and radical timidity (Benn, 1994: 26; K. Morgan, 1997a: 759). Whatever concessions he made to the left over constitutional reform and European policy were met with equally bitter recriminations of weakness and betrayal from Labour's 'departing' social democrats. Maybe, Callaghan's major incremental failing stemmed from one of his key political strengths, as he appeared to lose his sure personal touch and 'matchless feel for opinion in the unions and constituencies'. Consequently, his core base in the party evaporated with it. Already, 'the man who [almost intuitively] understood the trade unions' had risked their wrath in his arguably mismanaged handling of wage claims in Government, and subsequently appeared unable to comprehend the shifting mood of the trade union movement in which its links, or at least identification, with mainstream Labour Party policy seemed more fragile. The unions had never been 'more powerful' and 'difficult to rein in' and, in Callaghan's mind, never more in need of strong, moderate centrist leaders (K. Morgan, 1999: 149; 2007; Shore, 1993: 117, 133–4).

Callaghan resisted much of the more bullish approach of a Denis Healey in the new antagonistic environment, but was summarily accused of failing to mobilise both his courage and traditional Labour forces to 'take on' the left directly and forcefully (Shore, 1993: 126, 134). Whether, of course, it was possible to effectively mount a challenge to the triumphant left at this point remains a moot point. Maybe, his personal qualities and leadership style were ill-equipped for a straight fight in heavily loaded circumstances but, as Morgan (1997a: 719–20; 2007) suggests, neither is it clear that an alternative leader such as Healey, who was far less experienced in terms of party management, lacked a solid base in the party and was confrontational in his personal style, would have fared better in managing Labour's trajectory: the 'Labour Party was almost beyond leadership by this stage', and 'perhaps demanded more than any leader, especially one aged 68, could have offered at the time'. This was a transformation that emerged ultimately from wider structural and sociological factors of a calamitous electoral defeat, the challenge of moderate revisionist social democracy and the culmination of long-term socio-economic change. Callaghan did not have these 'advantages' to help 'control' the party but, in 'hopeless circumstances ... did his best to fight, more consistently ... than ... Healey or others on the centre-right', some of whom jumped ship altogether in disillusionment and defeat. In the cause of party unity and a 'better tomorrow', he displayed characteristic qualities of movement solidarity and collective development which, it seemed, had become quickly unfashionable. His consensus politics and style appeared ill-fitted and impotent in the newly 'ideologised' party (and national) political environment.

Conclusion

The death throes of Callaghan's Labour Government in the latter half of 1978 and early 1979 appeared to have tarnished its leader's record irrevocably, and the subsequent fall-out and introspection over the perceived limitations of the Government and election defeat and the future of the party overshadowed and significantly impeded his leadership in Opposition. Callaghan, contrary to his natural instincts, but fuelled by his quest for solidarity, remained as leader for perhaps longer than a Leader of the Opposition wisely should in such circumstances. During the period of the climatic 1980 Party Conference, Callaghan was explicitly acknowledging the complete erosion of his leadership authority and feelings of weariness and detachment (Labour Party, Parliamentary Committee Minutes, 15 October 1980; K. Morgan, 1997a: 702–3, 718; Rodgers, 2000: 1888; Shore, 1993: 135). There were some small strategic successes, such as the defence of Shadow Cabinet input in the Manifesto (Shore, 1993: 134–5), and perhaps confusing and stalling the left in the timing of his resignation before the new rules of leadership election kicked in. Ultimately, he failed in his avowed aim to resurrect the party in the image of a responsible leader of the centre-right, and the party set itself on a course of civil war that almost extinguished Labour as a political force.

Subsequent reassessments have to some extent 'recovered' Callaghan's reputation against the context and constraints he faced, both in Government and Opposition, appreciative of his personal qualities, skills of party and national management and as a public communicator, while not losing sight of errors of judgement and limitations of his leadership in this respect. As had been demonstrated in his capture of the party leadership in 1976 in a heavily 'factionalised' contest and party environment, he was able to garner a cross-section of support from disparate political camps as the 'natural unifying candidate', and was 'more personally approachable than Healey' and offered 'more weight than [Tony] Crosland'. In the context of party ideological and institutional constraints of the period, 'credible "consensus leaders" such as Callaghan' were 'better able to unite the warring party factions' (R. Jenkins, 1991: 434; Radice, 2002: 4, 234). His effective characteristics included a general belief in calm, cautious progress, a consensual approach to national economic management and a 'candour' and 'straightness' in his personal dealings and public communication. Unlike the perceived 'omniscience' of his predecessor Wilson, Callaghan was able to present himself as 'humanly fallible' (McKie, 2005; also see Benn, 1994: 26; Healey, 1990: 343, 475).

Callaghan had appeared to realise that history was now running a certain (different) way,[3] and that there were new challenges ahead to combat this recent thrust.[4] Unfortunately, the new mood of the party following the frustrations of Government and election defeat was resistant to these urges. He possessed considerable resources of (Labour) leadership, including his 'matchless feel' for the trade unions and constituencies and a broad 'open style' that grounded him in the party, as well as a disposition that provided him with useful a rapport with the general public (K. Morgan, 1999: 149). Whether Callaghan utilised his leadership resources to full effect in Opposition remains a moot point given the equally considerable institutional constraints and restrictions on his freedom of manoeuvre. According to his sympathetic biographer, his party had become virtually ungovernable and 'beyond the powers of any individual to reform', but at least Callaghan attempted 'to educate his errant comrades, unlike say … Healey'. It was not unusual for Labour to undergo a sharp swing to the left after election defeat, but the 'party left of 1980 was a radically different beast to the essentially parliamentary Bevanites or Tribunites of the past' (K. Morgan, 1997a: 706–7; 1999: 149). The social democratic right, already divided within itself and intrinsically threatened by the radical shift to the left (Meredith, 2008: 173–81), responded in an equally belligerent and critical manner. The notion that that 'Jim will fix it' in favour of them had largely evaporated. Consequently, assessments of Callaghan's handling of party affairs in Opposition after 1979 have varied from damning indictments of his strategic failings, ebbing and increasingly obsolete personal and political qualities, and lack of 'toughness' and protection of vulnerable Labour MPs in the heightened circumstances (Rodgers, 2000: 188; Shore, 1993: 127, 135; S. Williams, 2009: 273–4), to more contextualised representations attempting to mitigate these charges and manifest lack of success against structural conditions that would have tested the skills of any leader, and which took the 'shock therapy of Thatcherism' and threat to the party's very life to reform (K. Morgan, 1997a; 1999: 148–9).

Notes

1. They were already smarting from the agreement in principle of the 1979 Party Conference to what they perceived to be anti-Parliamentary NEC proposals for

constituency party reselection of Labour MPs and privileging the NEC in decisions over the Party Manifesto (Healey, 1990: 473; Labour Party, National Executive Committee Minutes, 27 June 1979).
2. Callaghan's allegedly casual response to questions about 'mounting chaos' in the country on his return from an international conference as Prime Minister in January 1979, or at least the way it was famously represented in the press as 'Crisis, what crisis?', did little to promote a mood of calm and reassurance in the heat of the 'winter of discontent'. His reassuring public manner was increasingly viewed as inappropriately relaxed to the point of complacency in critical circumstances. Neither could his earlier seemingly dismissive and brusque treatment of political allies in announcing his decision not to hold a General Election in September 1978 (itself often considered to be a fatal strategic error) be considered a public relations success (K. Morgan, 1997a: 661–2; 1999: 147).
3. He had remarked to the head of his Downing Street Policy Unit, Bernard Donoughue, during the 1979 General Election campaign as his party drifted towards almost inevitable defeat, 'there are times, perhaps once every thirty years, when there is a sea-change in politics. It then does not matter what you say or what you do. There is a shift in what the public wants and what it approves of. I suspect there is now such a sea-change, and it is for Mrs Thatcher' (cited in K. Morgan, 1997a: 697; also see Donoughue, 2003: 277; 2009: 483–4, 492–3; Rees, 2001; Sandbrook, 2008; Watkins, 2008).
4. He had of course recommended a dose of 'New Realism' in his (in)famous 1976 Blackpool Conference speech, indicating that Labour needed to shift its intrinsic belief 'that you could spend your way out of a recession and increase employment by cutting taxes and boosting government spending' at the expense of 'injecting a bigger dose of inflation into the economy, followed by a higher level of unemployment as the next step' (Labour Party, 1976: 188). 'New Realism' was a term coined by Peter Jay, the major architect of Callaghan's epoch-defining speech, and subsequently adopted by Mrs Thatcher (Beckett, 2009: 337–9).

10
Michael Foot, 1980–3

Ed Gouge

Michael Foot became Leader of the Labour Party in November 1980, after the resignation of James Callaghan, and led the Labour Party until just after the disastrous General Election defeat of June 1983, through one of its most difficult periods. Divisions within the party between right and left but also within the left, the creation of the new Social Democratic Party, the infiltration of the party by the Trotskyite Militant Tendency, the Falklands War and the need to construct an alternative to the new Thatcher Government were all problems that Foot faced in this short period as Leader of the Opposition. Despite sympathetic biographies by Mervyn Jones and Kenneth Morgan, the perception of Foot has been of a weak leader, out of touch with changing political circumstances, running an out-of-date General Election campaign, based on policies that would not be acceptable to the electorate. Labour's long period out of office after Foot's tenure as leader seemed to confirm these judgements but, from a longer perspective, Foot's role can be re-examined.

The perception of Foot as a poor Leader of the Labour Party contrasts with his previous achievements in politics, for no Labour Leader came to the office with such a long political career, stretching back to his first Parliamentary candidature in Monmouth in 1935 and his election as an MP in 1945. He was a distinguished journalist, writer and editor for the *London Evening Standard* and co-authored the influential 'Guilty Men' in 1940, a powerful polemic against the pre-war appeasers. He took part in a well-known TV panel programme, wrote extensively on political and literary topics and was acknowledged as one of the best Parliamentary and platform speakers of the post-war period. He was associated with the Bevanite left and, rejecting political office for a long period, followed radical causes, in particular nuclear disarmament, and was a critic of the 1964–70 Labour Government on issues such as Vietnam and wage restraint. He decided, successfully, to stand for the Shadow Cabinet in 1970, and Wilson made him Shadow Leader of the House with responsibility for opposing the European Communities Bill. After the Election victory of 1974 he was made Secretary of State for

Employment and then Leader of the House when Callaghan became Prime Minister in 1976. In both roles he impressed Labour MPs in helping to keep the Government together in difficult times, seeing through the Social Contract with the trade unions and then the devolution legislation. He had become effectively Callaghan's deputy.

Foot was the last Labour Leader to be chosen by the Parliamentary Party alone. Although the Labour Party had agreed at the 1980 Conference to change to an electoral college system of choosing the leader, the details had not been decided. Denis Healey, on the right of the party, was the obvious successor and declared his intention to stand with every expectation of gaining the support of a majority of MPs. Tony Benn considered standing as the candidate of the radical left, but his closest supporters argued that the old system was illegitimate and that he should argue for a new leadership election once the electoral college details were agreed (M. Jones, 1994: 452). Peter Shore and John Silkin were the main candidates from the centre-left. Michael Foot had not intended to stand and had already encouraged Shore to put himself forward.

The prospect of a Healey victory and the danger of it splitting the party further began to energise a range of people. Healey's reputation for abrasiveness led many people to doubt his capacity for leadership in the current situation, and even Callaghan had said privately to David Owen when he had appointed Shore as Shadow Foreign Secretary that it was because he wanted more competition for the leadership when he stepped down (Owen, 1991: 421). Ian Mikardo phoned Foot to tell him that he had a duty to stand because Shore would lose, Stan Orme tried to persuade Shore and Silkin to stand down in his favour, Clive Jenkins of the union ASTMS organised a union delegation to go and see Foot, and Stuart Holland put together a list of MPs who would vote for Foot and not for Shore (M. Jones, 1994: 449). Once Foot decided to stand, Neil Kinnock organised the campaign and, although a majority of MPs were on the right, Foot beat Healey on the second ballot by 139 votes to 129 in November 1980. Some MPs no doubt feared that Healey would have divided the party even more deeply, and some may have felt that they would be better protected against reselection by Foot. A handful may have hoped that the result would speed up the creation of a breakaway party, which they would then join (Crewe and King, 1995: 74). Nevertheless, the vote does suggest support for Foot in the centre of the party based on his ministerial record and personality.

Foot took over as leader at a difficult time for the Labour Party. The 1979 General Election defeat had seen the Labour vote fall to its lowest percentage share since the war, and the perceived failure of the Wilson and Callaghan Governments led to immediate criticism of the leadership. At the 1979 Party Conference the Labour Government was immediately publicly criticised by the Chair, Frank Allaun MP, and by Ron Hayward, General Secretary of the Party since 1982, for its failure to implement party policies

(M. Jones, 1994: 438). Even David Owen, in his biography, admitted that Conference decisions had been completely ignored by Labour Governments and this had led Conference to then pass even more radical proposals (Owen, 1991: 421). This lack of trust between leaders and the party was the basis of the proposals, around which the left united, for mandatory reselection of MPs, election of the leader by the whole party and control of the next Election Manifesto by the National Executive Committee. This campaign for constitutional change and the adoption by the NEC of a left programme in May 1980 launched a bitter battle between left and right for control of the party and led a group of leading figures on the right to consider creating a new party. Callaghan had effectively given way on reselection of MPs and election of the leader to the annoyance of the right, and Foot became leader with these bitter conflicts now deeply engrained in the party.

Public policy platform

The problems of the 1974–9 Labour Government are indicative of a general crisis of European Social Democracy in the late 1970s (Patterson and Thomas, 1986). The Labour leadership since the war had been able to put together a policy package, not that different from the Conservatives, which involved Keynesian demand management to prevent unemployment and stimulate growth, and welfare spending based on this economic growth, with Crosland's *The Future of Socialism* providing the theoretical justification, taking his view that post-war managerial capitalism was efficient. Never entirely successful, these policies no longer seemed able to cope with the economic crisis that the 1974–9 Labour Government faced. The other major economic tool that could be used was a prices and incomes policy, but the Labour Government's Social Contract came to grief when, in 1978, Callaghan decided that the wage limit should be 5 per cent and the trade union leaders were unable to prevent their membership from launching a wave of strikes.

The failures of the Labour Government of 1974–9, and indeed that of 1964–70, created a policy vacuum as Labour went into Opposition and, although Foot continued to defend the Labour Government, there were those on both wings of the party who pointed to the problem. For Owen, the leading people on the centre and right of the party were 'exhausted after years in government and intellectually demoralised' with no response to the challenge of 'flexible patterns of production, the demand for lower taxation and individual aspirations or the crisis of confidence in British industry' (Owen, 1991: 418). He also felt that because both right and left in the party were horrified by Thatcherite policies, it made it difficult for people on the right of the party to include any aspect of market ideas into their proposals. This meant that the right played little part in policy thinking during the Foot period, other than to criticise ideas coming from the left, and the development of social democratic ideas took place in the SDP – and not that successfully there either. The left, on the other hand, had developed a more comprehensive programme than at any time since the 1930s (Seyd, 1987: 24). On becoming Leader, Foot had a set of policies in relation to economic intervention, withdrawal from Europe and nuclear disarmament that he broadly agreed with. Immediately after his election, he made unemployment, rapidly rising towards 3 million, and nuclear disarmament the two great issues that he wanted to emphasise.

Gerald Kaufman's often-quoted assessment of the 1983 Election Manifesto as 'the longest suicide note in history' has rather clouded analysis of the policies adopted by the Labour Party between 1979 and 1983. Labour won the February 1974 Election on a left-wing Manifesto and the failure to carry this out, as well as the deteriorating economic and international situations, led the left to look for even more radical policies. Stuart Holland's *The Socialist Challenge*, published in 1975, was a response to Crosland (Wickham-Jones, 2004: 29). According to Holland, the economy was now dominated by multinational monopolistic firms that were able fix prices at a high level in their own class interests. His solution, drawn from French and Italian experience, was to create a National Enterprise Board, which could buy a stake in part of an industrial sector, and so force it to become more competitive, and which could enter into planning agreements with firms about investment levels or labour practices in return for public funding (Wickham-Jones, 2004: 34–5). These ideas became part of what became known as the Alternative Economic Strategy, which included reflation of the economy to reduce unemployment and import controls over finished goods so that the reflation would not merely produce a balance of payments crisis (Seyd, 1987: 28–9). Holland recounts that both Jenkins and Rodgers showed interest in the proposals, and Callaghan had told him that he would have looked to implement planning agreements if he had won the 1979 Election but says that once the right found out that the left supported his ideas they dropped them (Holland, 2004: 163–6). The left was also proposing withdrawal from the European Economic Community or a major renegotiation of the Treaty of Rome and a 'non-nuclear' policy to impact on the deteriorating situation as a result of the intensification of the Cold War.

Foot faced a number of problems in developing policy. He had a staff that dealt almost entirely with press and party matters with hardly any capacity for policy development, and the one real policy adviser was Henry Neuberger, seconded from the Treasury to deal with economic policy (K. Morgan, 2007: 384–6). Foot had to spend a good deal of time in developing compromises between the policies coming from the party and the views of the corresponding PLP spokespersons. In 1982, for example, a one-year freeze on council rents agreed by the NEC met with opposition from Gerald Kaufman so that Foot had to persuade him to accept it (R. Evans, 1982); then Benn's Home Policy Committee proposed the nationalisation of the four main clearing banks, and Foot had to use the NEC to prevent it becoming party policy (Bevins, 1982b). In addition, party matters took up huge amounts of time that could have been spent on policy, for example, a meeting of the NEC in the summer of 1982 to discuss action against Militant took seven hours (Routledge, 1995: 153).

The task of constructing a policy platform that would appeal to voters was not impossible, and a poll of trade unionists for MORI in 1982 showed 58 per cent support for withdrawal from the EEC, 74 per cent for import controls and even 42 per cent for unilateralism (Bradley, 1982). Foot, however, was not able to turn the Alternative Economic Strategy into an understandable set of policies that would appeal to voters. Early on he was able to portray the Government as fanatical monetarists unconcerned with the impact on the economy and was able to use the concerns of the Confederation of British Industry, economic commentators and even some Conservatives to back up his attacks, but he increasingly concentrated on the evils of unemployment, which was the argument with which he felt most comfortable. This kept up support in Labour's industrial heartlands but failed to make an impact in the marginals, including mixed constituencies such as Dartford or Loughborough, which Labour had held through the 1950s but had lost in 1970 and 1979. The report by Geoff Bish, Head of the Research Department, after the election concluded that Labour had failed to develop a policy programme that accurately reflected the concerns and needs of ordinary voters (Butler and Kavanagh, 1984: 278). By the middle of 1982, Foot was returning to the idea of reviving the Social Contract, but this was associated in the public mind with the trade unions who were now unpopular (Webster, 1982). Foot was also unable to develop an effective line of attack against the SDP. They were either presented as traitors or as Conservatives in disguise. The line that might have been more effective, which was that the SDP represented the elements of previous Labour Governments that had failed, was not possible because of his loyalty to those Governments and because it might have alienated Labour voters and MPs on the right.

In contrast to economic policy, Foot fully understood nuclear disarmament as a result of his long association with the Campaign for Nuclear Disarmament. He was capable of winning the intellectual arguments about the need for a policy of 'no first strike' and the dangerous escalation brought by Cruise and SS20 missiles in Europe. He was reasonably effective in 1981 in presenting Thatcher as a leader who was taking no interest in disarmament and who merely followed American policy in areas such as El Salvador and a rapid reaction force in the Gulf. He was not, however, able to develop a clear line that the public could follow. The first problem was that he was a unilateralist by conviction and would never deny it when taunted by Thatcher, allowing her to say that he would leave Britain defenceless. The other problem was that the Labour Party Conference had passed unilateralist and multilateralist resolutions and, in addition, Foot needed to keep Healey on board. Therefore policy hovered between unilateralism and multilateralism, with uncertainty as to what a Labour Government would actually do. Nevertheless, a policy of opposing Cruise missiles (the same as many other European Socialist parties), not proceeding with the Trident programme that would upgrade Britain's nuclear deterrent (the same as the SDP), and being ready to put Britain's current Polaris system into disarmament negotiations might have held together (M. Foot, 1984: 76–8). In 1982, Argentina's invasion of the Falklands reinforced the view that Labour was not interested in defending Britain. The issue was at first a major embarrassment for the Government because they had taken away the naval protection of the islands that the Labour Government had maintained, and Foot took a strong line on opposing a dictatorship and sending a Naval Task Force to liberate the islands. He was reined in by Healey and by left opposition to the Task Force and was pushed into a stance of seeking to negotiate with the UN, with uncertainty as to whether he would use the Task Force (K. Morgan, 2007: 411–13). Calls from Benn and the hard left for the withdrawal of the Task Force gave the impression that Labour would not liberate the Falklands. The nationalistic fervour in the popular press once Britain had defeated Argentina transformed the opinion polls and put the Conservatives in a clear lead, where they remained until the General Election. The final problem for Labour's defence policy came when, in the General Election, Callaghan, deciding that he could not justify Labour's policy to voters on the doorstep in Cardiff, publicly attacked the proposal to abandon Trident (K. Morgan, 2007: 433). Foot and Healey kept up a show of unity but the damage was done.

Public communication

The problem, in looking at Michael Foot as a public communicator, is in trying to explain why someone who had been widely seen as a great journalist, a brilliant platform speaker and one of the greatest-ever Parliamentary performers failed to resonate with the public and, by the second half of 1982, was registering only 14 per cent support in opinion poll satisfaction ratings as Leader of the Labour Party. Foot was the master of both the written and the spoken word. Kenneth Morgan considered *Guilty Men* to be the finest political tract since Wilkes or Paine (K. Morgan 2007: 278) but, of course, in the 1980s hardly anyone read political tracts. He was a brilliant speechmaker, and many considered his Parliamentary speech defending the Labour Government, in its last few days, against a no-confidence motion to be one of the finest that they had ever heard. Frances Beckett recounts how, when Foot was Leader and came to talk to the Agricultural Workers' Union at St Albans, he was confronted by demonstrators against his Northern Ireland policy:

> As he started his speech, he seemed old, hesitant, appealing to his tormentors to allow him first to address rural affairs, promising he would

not leave without addressing their concerns. They knew that they had to let him do this, or the crowd would turn against them. He talked about rural affairs for a while, then without warning moved swiftly on to an angry, passionate, fast, fluent defence of his Ireland policy. They were a second too slow, and by the time they started to try to shout him down, he had the initiative, and beat them over the head with his fury and his idealism. He won hands down. So much for the weak leader the press talked of.

(F. Beckett, 2010)

On another occasion, after his plane had been delayed at Oslo airport for four hours in 1982, he kept the passengers entertained with a mainly non-political commentary and jokes (Bevins, 1982a). The problem was that Foot was not interested in images and, by the 1980s, television was all important both for its visual images and the key messages that could be put across. It is uncertain whether Foot showed much interest in television. After watching Foot quote critical newspaper reports on the Government's economic policy at Prime Minister's Questions, Frank Johnson said: Foot 'is probably the last party leader to regard the press as the best source of news. ... God bless him. When he goes, the dark night of television current affairs will close in on our leaders for good' (F. Johnson, 1982). Foot's style was to set out his views at length and then to listen carefully to someone with different views put theirs to him. At press conferences Jim Mortimer felt that he was good at presenting the main theme and answering questions, though Clive James, observing him during the 1983 campaign, felt that he rather lectured the press (James, 1983). However, on television, this produced a rambling style when crisp replies and sound bites were needed. He improved over time but, as Barbara Castle commented, television interviews are not like an opportunity to give speeches but more like a job interview. Because Foot was well-read with a long memory, in many ways, he knew too much for the modern television world. He would often use literary and historical references that made him seem remote to the electorate. The Gadarene swine appeared in an interview with Brian Walden, and a speech in the Darlington by-election led him to remember it as a good Quaker town.

Foot took little interest in his personal image. Older leaders have been able to stay in power in democracies once established as the Prime Minister, but it is difficult in the television age for them to appear as new and dynamic. Just as Mrs Thatcher was having her voice and hair changed to create a new image, Foot appeared in photographs with a stick and old-fashioned looking clothes. Alan Watkins, when he first met him, said he looked like 'an unfrocked Methodist minister' (Watkins, 2010). Foot had to face a more hostile press than any other party leader, except perhaps Baldwin. Determined to prevent a left Labour Government, the Conservative press were determined to portray Foot as a doddering old fool. For the Cenotaph ceremony he bought a new coat, which the Queen Mother complimented him on, but, because it looked a bit different, the press were able to turn it into a CND-inspired duffle coat and an insult to the war dead. Bernard Levin wrote of 'Michael Foot, half blind and at least a quarter crippled', a phrase that he would probably not get away with today in an age more sensitive to disability (Anon., 2004).

The 1983 General Election was the culmination of this dislocation between the Foot style and modern campaigning. It was the last British election in which a political party looked to base its campaign on major public meetings. Foot spoke effectively to large groups of enthusiastic supporters, but little thought was given to managing how the television news was portraying him. Mrs Thatcher gave few public speeches and her appearances were carefully stage-managed to look like a triumphal progress (Butler and Kavanagh, 1984: 271–2). Labour's campaign was badly managed with a large campaign committee of some thirty people, which failed to develop any strategy. Labour did use opinion polling, at the suggestion of Bob Worcester of MORI, and this pointed to the problems, but the campaign had no real ability to respond to them (Butler and Kavanagh, 1984: 276). Roy Hattersley found that one day the graphics for his press conference did not arrive and the next they slid off the screen as the cameras filmed them (Hattersley, 1995: 241). In his postscript on the 1983 Election, Michael Foot himself quotes from a piece written for the *Sun* by Jon Akass, a former colleague from the *Daily Herald*, and it is worth repeating some extracts here (not quite in the same order as the original):

> Having pursued Mr Michael Foot all week and listed to him for hours ... I cannot for the life of me see what he is doing wrong ... he is far too old now to change his act ... and I have seldom seen a more polished version than in the past few days ... it is a very good act and it might have lasted him a lifetime if he had not made the mistake of becoming Party Leader ... and yet every opinion poll brings the same mournful message. ... I fear the explanation might be simple and terrible. It might be that Michael Foot has gone out of fashion.
>
> (M. Foot, 1984: 53–4)

Party management

Foot probably had to spend more time on party management than any Labour leader has, before or since. Peter Shore has said that, 'No leader of the Labour Party, not even George Lansbury in 1931, inherited so disastrous and bankrupt an estate as did Michael Foot in November 1980' (Shore, 1993: 137). On the right of the party he had to deal immediately with the likely defection of leading figures to form a new Social Democrat Party, which might have triggered a major move of members and MPs out of the party. The breakaway of a group of leading politicians is not something that any party leader had had to deal with since the 1930s. David Owen had been Foreign Secretary, Bill Rodgers had been the Transport Minister, Shirley Williams, who was widely liked in the party, had been Education Secretary, and Roy Jenkins, although already largely detached from the Labour Party, had been Chancellor of the Exchequer. Previous examples of such splits – the Liberal/Liberal National split in 1933, the desertion of Ramsay MacDonald from Labour in 1931, the Lloyd George/Asquith split in 1916 and the Liberal Unionist break from the Liberals in 1886 – had each led to electoral disaster for the party involved. Despite the serious implications that the creation of a new party would have, it is doubtful whether Michael Foot could have done more to prevent it happening. The idea of leaving the Labour Party was already well advanced by the time that Foot became leader, and in a letter to the *Guardian* on 1 October 1980, Owen, Rodgers and Williams warned that there would be a case for a new democratic socialist party if Labour continued to abandon its democratic and international principles. Both Owen and Rodgers bitterly attacked Callaghan at the first Shadow Cabinet after the Bishop's Stortford meeting when Callaghan had conceded the new system of electing the leader. At the Shadow Cabinet after the NEC had adopted *Peace, Jobs, Freedom* with its policy shift to the left, Callaghan had said that he could not support these policies but that he only wanted a low-key response (Owen, 1991: 432).

The election of Foot as leader was another factor in the decision of the three to go, and Foot failed to reappoint Rodgers as Defence spokesperson because of the differences between them on disarmament, but it was probably Healey rather than Foot who could have influenced the course of events. Owen felt that if Healey had run an aggressive leadership campaign and clearly opposed the electoral college, then, even if he had lost, he would have been in a position to mobilise the right later and Owen would have stayed. However, Healey had already decided that too aggressive an attitude towards Callaghan might lose him the leadership (Owen, 1991: 458). Shirley Williams also comments on Healey's low-key campaign in her autobiography, writing that at a meeting with MPs on the right he had merely argued that they had to vote for him as there was no one else they could vote for (S. Williams, 2009: 278). The Wembley Conference on 24 January 1981 at which the method of electing the leader was agreed provided the opportune moment, and the Limehouse Declaration the next day made the break fully public. Foot had talked to the three the previous August and again on 21 January. Rodgers felt that Foot had no proposals and that the January meeting was a waste of time (M. Jones, 1994: 459–60). Owen conceded that Foot genuinely wanted them to stay and argued that the left had had a long period when it had had to accept control of the party by the right, and so why were they not prepared to do the same. Owen says that he asked Foot if they could oppose the policies in public, but Foot became more vague and then said that the left had between elections but then kept quiet during the election itself (Owen, 1991: 477). Foot was not ready to accept that they were definitely leaving until they actually had, and still wrote to Williams and also spent a good deal of time talking to John Cartwright, the Woolwich MP, but by late February decided that he could do no more and began to develop a public attack on the group. The new Social Democratic Party was launched on 2 March with 12 MPs, and the staged defection of other MPs followed later. Foot was relieved that it was only this many and defended potential defectors against their parties and continued to talk to them (M. Jones, 1994: 461). In the end, although there were 27 SDP MPs by the time of the 1983 General Election, the creation of the SDP did not have a great effect on Labour Party organisation. Only a few councillors or members of constituency general committees joined the SDP, who found that most of its membership was new to politics and mostly in professional and managerial occupations, while Labour was recruiting new members who more than made up the losses. The main impact was electoral.

Despite winning the leadership campaign, Foot faced a Shadow Cabinet and Parliamentary Party that were predominantly on the right, but managed to keep their support over the next two years. Two factors were important in this. The first was that Foot, though supportive of left policies, never really saw the need for the party reforms and had, with Callaghan, tried to delay their implementation. He had a strong sense of the need for the independence of MPs, both from their party and from the Executive, and was a traditionalist in relation to Parliament, opposing the introduction of the new Select Committee system as taking power away from the individual MP on the floor of the House. His *Guardian* article in September 1981 argued that Conference decisions were to be respected but could not be regarded as absolute and binding in every particular and upon every Labour MP in all circumstances, for MPs had a loyalty to their fellow MPs, to their political judgement and to their country (M. Jones, 1994: 470). He regularly supported sitting MPs who were threatened with deselection with letters of recommendation, and so Foot could reassure MPs on the right that he would look to limit the impact of the constitutional reforms, while to the party he could show that he accepted aspects of them. This was helped by acceptance by key figures on the right of the electoral college, and on 13 November 1980 Hattersley put a motion to the Shadow Cabinet to this effect, with the Parliamentary Party having 55 per cent of the vote and a provision for CLPs to ballot members at a specific meeting (Owen, 1991: 459). This passed, though not without dissent, the Shadow Cabinet and the PLP.

The second factor in reconciling Foot to the right was his relationship with Healey. Foot had always defended Healey's role as Chancellor, when his public expenditure cuts were widely criticised in the party, and indeed always defended the record of the Wilson and Callaghan Governments. Foot and Healey had had a good relationship in Government and, after a short while, developed a partnership as Leader and Deputy Leader. Healey recounts that, at first, he argued with Foot in Shadow Cabinet, but a colleague asked him not so and they then sorted out differences one-to-one. Healey said: 'When we disagreed, I think he tried hard to meet me half-way' (Healey, 1990: 481). Healey distanced himself from SDP policy positions, for example renouncing Chevaline, Trident and Cruise, while Hattersley argued for equality of outcome in the debate on social policy when the SDP were arguing for equality of opportunity (K. Morgan, 1987: 323, 330).

The Wembley Conference in January 1981 agreed a formula of 40 per cent of the vote for the unions and only 30 per cent for MPs, when Foot had wanted 50 per cent. He was persuaded by Kinnock not to speak first to influence the Conference, in case he lost and his authority was undermined, but this was probably a mistake (Westlake, 2001: 170). Foot's objectives after the Wembley Conference and the SDP breakaway were to stabilise the party by not taking the constitutional reforms any further and preventing the deselection of existing Labour MPs, thus allowing the party to concentrate on promoting the left policies that had been carried by Conference. During 1981 this brought him into conflict with Tony Benn and those on the left who wanted to push party reforms further and remove those who did not support the new party programme. The federal structure of the Labour Party means that power bases outside the PLP are available for a rival leader to appeal to groups in the party, as Benn did (P. Williams, 1978: 54). Foot could not rely on the support of the party machinery during this battle. The NEC had a majority of Benn supporters in early 1981, while the influential Home Affairs and Organisational subcommittees were chaired by Benn and his ally, Eric Heffer, respectively. Foot could not even rely on the staff at Walworth Road, Labour's headquarters, where there were a number of Benn supporters (K. Morgan, 2007: 396). Jim Mortimer, the new General Secretary, did not have a political background and the skills to cope with the party infighting that ensued (Healey, 1990: 501). In the end, Foot's success in defeating the 'Bennite rebellion' depended on his understanding of the creative tension between the different elements in the party, and the split that emerged between a 'soft left' that provided a base for him on the NEC and in the PLP and the 'hard left'.

After the Wembley Conference, Benn discussed the situation with his supporters and decided, now that the new electoral college was in place, to stand against Healey for the Deputy Leadership. Foot asked him privately not to stand, but Benn made the formal announcement on 1 April 1981 (M. Jones, 1994: 446). The relationship between Benn and Foot had never been close. Foot had considered Benn's criticism of the Labour Government, while he was a Minister in it, as disloyal, and Benn felt that Foot had failed to take a stand in Cabinet on issues such as the IMF loan (K. Morgan, 1987: 287). Benn had come to see Parliament as irrelevant, with the action by workers and other groups outside Parliament as the main basis for the advance of the left, in contrast to Foot, Bevan and Castle who regarded Parliament as a key arena for political struggle. Benn was quite happy to accept the support of anyone on the further left, including Trotskyites, whereas Foot's anti-Communism and the need for Labour to distance themselves from the extreme left had been a key part of his philosophy since the late 1940s (K. Morgan, 1987: 301–2).

Benn's decision to stand for the Deputy Leadership was deeply divisive for the left of the party. Criticism from Joan Lester, Stanley Orme and Frank Allaun was echoed by Alex Kitson, the Chair of the Party, and even Eric Heffer. Tribunites such as Neil Kinnock argued that Healey had no real power as Deputy Leader and was not embarrassing Foot by any of his public statements (M. Jones, 1994: 446–8). Foot publicly criticised Benn and challenged him to stand as Leader instead (M. Jones, 1994: 469). The long period of the Deputy Leadership election from April to the Annual Conference in the autumn meant that divisions in the party were in the public eye for most of the year. It also affected party discipline in Parliament. In May, a potential Conservative backbench revolt on the Defence White Paper, on which the Shadow Cabinet had decided to abstain to make it easier for Conservative MPs to vote against their Government, was overshadowed by Benn and 74 Labour MPs who defied the party whip to vote against because of the mention of nuclear weapons in the document (K. Morgan, 2007: 398). Foot and the Shadow Cabinet tried to get Benn to accept collective responsibility, but he refused. Arguably Foot should have taken a stronger line. After the Defence vote he did not ask junior spokespersons to resign. After refusing to accept collective responsibility, Benn remained frontbench Energy spokesperson, and in November embarrassed Foot by committing the party to renationalising the oil industry without compensation (K. Morgan, 2007: 401).

Foot had decided early on that a third candidate in the Deputy Leadership election might help to divert some votes away from Benn, and told Roy Hattersley this when he complained that Foot had not come out in support of Healey (Hattersley, 1995: 230–1). Silkin stood as the third candidate, and this allowed Kinnock, Orme, Lester and other MPs to adopt the strategy of voting for Silkin and then abstaining, thus distancing themselves from the Bennite left. This decided the election but, nevertheless, the final result was hardly a triumph for Foot, with Healey winning by only 50.4 to 49.6 per cent, and raised questions about Foot's failure to clearly support Healey. In the other elections at the 1981 Conference, however, the hard left was in retreat with the trade unions ready to exercise their votes to restore the balance in the party. Eric Varley, the right candidate, defeated Norman Atkinson for Treasurer and five places on the NEC went to the right. This still did not guarantee Foot a loyal base on the NEC but it did give a right/ soft left majority that could prevent further constitutional changes (Shore, 1993: 145). Kinnock, Judith Hart, Lester and Short voted with Foot and the right to defeat a proposal to give control of the Manifesto solely to the NEC.

Foot still tried to make peace with the hard left by having Heffer and Benn remain as Chairs of the Organising and Home Policy Committees of the NEC, but John Golding, who was organising for the right, made sure that they were removed (M. Jones, 1994: 416).

Foot might have been able to divert public attention from divisions in the party after the end of 1981, but further party management problems developed, none of which were resolved satisfactorily. Bob Mellish, the right-leaning Labour MP for Bermondsey, was to stand down at the next election. The local party had moved to the left and selected Peter Tatchell, who was a gay rights campaigner at a time when no MP had admitted publicly to being gay, and had called for 'more militant forms of extra-parliamentary action'. Mellish had portrayed Tatchell to Foot as more extreme than he was, and Foot was upset by the suggestion that Parliament was ineffective (M. Jones, 1994: 479). An SDP MP asked a question about the article in Prime Minister's Question Time, and Foot intervened to say that 'the individual is not an endorsed member of the Labour Party and, so far as I am concerned, never will be' (Thomas-Symonds, 2005: 44). It was clearly a mistake for Foot to promise to remove a candidate who had been legitimately selected by the local party. Frank Allaun immediately said to him, 'You have made the most serious mistake of your life'. Foot, recognising this, was upset (M. Jones, 1994: 480). On 16 December the NEC met to endorse Tatchell as candidate and, with Kinnock making it an issue of confidence in Foot, did not endorse him by 15 to 14 (Adams, 1992: 418). The decision not to endorse Tatchell did, however, lead to an angry action from the left and a large number of resolutions from constituency parties, and the local party chose Tatchell again anyway when Mellish forced a by-election. The by-election campaign in February 1982 was a vicious and homophobic one, which produced a disastrous defeat at the hands of the Liberal Democrats (Tatchell, 1983). By the summer of 1982, with poor opinion polls and by-election defeats, there was open talk of removing Foot who was increasingly spending media interviews defending his leadership (Michael Foot Leadership Papers a).

The next problem that Foot faced was that of the Militant Tendency. The NEC had considerable evidence by 1975 that they were a Trotskyite group, but neither Wilson nor Callaghan wanted to create publicity by attempting expulsion, especially as the 1979 General Election neared (Thomas-Symonds, 2005: 31–2). However, by 1980, Militant controlled the national organisation of the Young Socialists and Liverpool City Council, and had prospective Parliamentary candidates selected in a handful of constituencies. The issue was a difficult one for Foot personally. He had faced threats from the right majority in the 1950s to take action against him and other Bevan supporters, and he always felt that sectarian minorities should be defeated by argument rather than by expulsion. However, by the end of 1981 he was convinced, especially by large number of letters from members, that Militant were intimidating people at party meetings and preventing free speech (Shaw, 1988: 226). In December 1981, on Foot's initiative the NEC voted to hold an Inquiry into Militant, and in June 1982 it confirmed the entryist nature of the organisation. Foot's action in not endorsing Tatchell had alarmed many on the left into thinking that expelling Militant would be the prelude to similar action with other left groups. Chris Mullin, then editor of *Tribune*, felt that Foot had now become a prisoner of the right on the NEC and in the PLP (Mullin, 2010: 26). The only realistic action that Foot could take, if another party war was not to break out, was to expel the five leaders of Militant, not because of their political views but because they had a separate programme (Thomas-Symonds, 2005: 47). Even so, the procedural and legal difficulties meant that this was not achieved until after the General Election, with consequent media coverage through 1982 and 1983.

Emotional intelligence

Those who knew Michael Foot recall him with affection. For Ken Livingstone, he was 'the nicest man I ever met at a senior level in politics' (Parkinson and Griffiths, 2010). Ian Mikardo, a fellow left-wing MP from the 1945 intake, talked of Michael Foot 'whose friendship has been one of the most precious things in my life' (Mikardo, 1988: 90–1). Barbara Castle, though uncertain in many ways about his election as party leader, reflected that he was a 'tolerant, civilized and cultivated' politician who would take a future Labour Government to the left (Martineau, 2000). The private letters to him from MPs both of the right and left demonstrate empathy and sympathy for the difficult time that he was having with the party, even those from MPs who later joined the SDP (Michael Foot Leadership Papers b). These impressions may have been coloured by the fact that he always had time for people. He made sure that he was available to talk to MPs in the tea rooms at the House of Commons and this, no doubt, helped to stem the flow of MPs into the SDP. He was always seen as straightforward, and neither those on the right such as Hattersley and Healey nor on the left such as Benn and Tatchell, though they might disagree with his decisions, ever had any complaints about being misled or betrayed. These qualities of honesty and readiness to listen no doubt helped keep the different groups in the party together but they did not help Foot to control the party. Michael Cocks, Labour's Chief Whip during the period, recounts that Michael Foot had many qualities and was capable of inspiring people, but 'infighting was not one of them and the party battles sapped his strength as a leader' (Cocks, 1989: 83). In the end it was John Golding who organised the removal of Benn and Heffer from the NEC Committees, and not Foot.

Foot was portrayed by his enemies in the Conservative Party and the right-wing press as naïve and, more kindly, by *The Times* in its profile when he became leader as 'the last romantic'. His obituaries portrayed him as an idealist and man of principle quite unlike the politicians of the present time. In reality, Foot was a mixture of the romantic and the realist. He was much happier dealing with the great moral issues of unemployment and nuclear disarmament than the details of policy. Kenneth Morgan, otherwise a sympathetic observer, said he appeared as a rhetorician rather than a creative politician (K. Morgan, 1987: 284). He had a tendency to see current problems in terms of battles fought long ago. At Oxford in the 1983 Election campaign he talked about the Lord Chancellor, Quintin Hogg, as the candidate who had stood for appeasement in the Oxford by-election of 1938, which was true, but allowed Hogg to say 'the old boy has clearly lost his marbles' (K. Morgan, 2007: 432). Perhaps General Galtieri seemed like Mussolini and David Owen like the 'traitor' Ramsay MacDonald but, of course, new situations may need different responses. Roy Hattersley, after an evening discussing with Foot his favourite literary and historical figures, concluded that 'Michael believes that people he likes share his views' (Hattersley, 1995: 241). This led him to see things it terms of rights and wrongs.

However, when problems did have to be sorted out, he was ready to be a realist. His friend, the historian A. J. P. Taylor, said that in times of crisis he could be seen steering a path down the middle of the road (K. Morgan, 1987: 279). Foot worked hard to keep the Labour Government going by bargaining with the Liberals and the Nationalist and Irish parties, and as Leader he sought to reconcile conflicting views and keep the Labour Party intact. This was, no doubt, essential given the state of the party but it also had its limitations. Barbara Castle felt, that like Wilson, Foot made a fetish of party unity at the expense of policy formation (Martineau, 2000). Taking the middle road meant that he was not leading the party in any particular direction.

Conclusion

We have to conclude that Michael Foot's period as Leader of the Opposition was a failure. When he became Leader of the Labour Party he faced a Conservative Government whose economic policies were broadly unpopular, but Foot was temperamentally unsuited to developing a policy platform adapted to a changing electorate or to television as the principal medium for electoral communication. Labour lost the 1983 Election badly, and none of the three aims that Foot and the Labour left supported – an alternative to economic liberalism, withdrawal from the European Union or nuclear disarmament – have ever been adopted by British Governments.

Foot inherited acute problems of party management, although he would probably not have become Leader but for these problems. Despite some mistakes, such as the impetuous decision not to endorse Tatchell and the cautious decision not to give a lead to the Wembley Conference on a preferred option for the selection of Leader, he strove to reconcile competing factions and produce a sort of party unity by the time of the 1983 General Election.

This was enough to maintain Labour support in its heartlands and keep the SDP/Liberal Alliance in third place, if only just. The 1983 Election campaign was a shambles, but Kinnock did not do greatly better with a smoothly run campaign in 1987. In the end, however, Foot's successes in preventing mass defections to the SDP, compromising between right and left, creating the soft left and starting the expulsion of the leaders of Militant may justify Neil Kinnock's assessment of him as 'the man who saved the Labour Party'.

11
Neil Kinnock, 1983–92

Simon Griffiths

> Neil
> you made me feel
> hope
> even though the electorate
> said nope.
>
> John Hegley, 'Happy Easter, Mr Kinnock'
in The Guardian, 18th April 1992

Neil Kinnock has the unenviable title of being the longest-serving Leader of the Opposition in the post-war period. He was elected on 2 October 1983 and stepped down on 18 July 1992, after his party lost its fourth consecutive General Election – the second under Kinnock's leadership. Yet by the time Kinnock stepped down, the party was almost unrecognisable from the one he inherited – less divided, with a set of policies more attractive to the wider electorate, better presented and on the cusp of regaining power after over a decade out of office.

Kinnock's reputation has changed since 1992. The past is viewed through the changing lens of the present. One's view on Kinnock is also affected by the lens one uses to assess New Labour and the relationship between Kinnock and the post-1997 Labour Government. However, I argue that a broad review of the literature shows that Kinnock's reputation has undergone something of a decline and rise since 1983: seen by many as the 'saviour of the Labour Party' upon his election as leader, it reached a nadir in 1992 after two election defeats, before rising sharply as changes begun under Kinnock were seen to reap electoral rewards under Tony Blair.

After the disastrous 1983 general election, in which the Labour Party, under Michael Foot, received less that 28 per cent of the popular vote, Kinnock was overwhelmingly elected leader. He received over 71 per cent of the party's vote; winning in every section of a college of unions, MPs and party members. Seen as a candidate from the left, although no longer the hard left, Kinnock formed a 'dream ticket' to unite a fissiparous party with

Deputy Leader Roy Hattersley, from the right of the party (Westlake, 2001: 237). *Marxism Today* ran a front cover of Kinnock as Superman, ready to save Labour (Fielding, 1994: 593). After a car crash in 1983, which Kinnock was lucky to survive with only minor injuries, he commented, 'Someone up there likes me'. The comment caught the mood of the time and was widely reported (R. Harris, 1984: 223; Westlake, 2001: 236). The following nine years were to prove more difficult.

Emotional intelligence

Kinnock is often described as one of the most personable, good humoured and eloquent politicians of his generation. Yet, in a sympathetic biography published after the 1992 Election defeat, Eileen Jones reported that

> Kinnock's personality was said to be one of the reasons for Labour's fail-
> ure. It was widely held that he was sufficiency disliked by a proportion
> of the electorate to allow the re-election of a none-too-popular govern-
> ment during a recession. He was, said his detractors variously, ruthless,
> arrogant, autocratic, devious, untrustworthy – even being Welsh was con-
> sidered by some to be a character defect. One commentator maintained
> that he had endured more public insults over a longer period than any
> other figure in British public life.
>
> (E. Jones 1994: 11)

In a critical account of Kinnock's tenure, Heffernan and Marqusee reported a poll that found that 'dislike of the leader was quoted by nearly two in five non-Labour voters as the main reason they would not vote for the Party' (Heffernan and Marqusee, 1992: 303–4).

Kinnock's personality is, very noticeably, a product of his class and national-ity, both of which are different from that of most Westminster commentators. David Marquand has written: 'in a sense true of surprisingly few of his pred-ecessors, Labour's ethos is also [Kinnock's] ethos. He is unmistakably and unaffectedly a product of the working-class culture of the South Wales valleys, with all the strengths and weaknesses that that implies' (Marquand, 1999: 205–6). The popular caricature of Kinnock, propagated in the media, was of a brawling, boisterous, charming, silver-tongued 'boyo' most at home in a work-ing men's club. Early accounts of his time as Leader of the Opposition stress this bonhomie, and see it as a vote winner. The flip side of this caricature is the accusation that Kinnock was not 'heavy-weight' enough to be Prime Minister.

This lack of gravitas was said to be epitomised in Kinnock's performance at the Sheffield Rally days before the 1992 General Election. As Heffernan and Marqusee note, 'Carried away, he cast aside eight years of self-imposed gravitas to disport himself before the adoring throng in the manner of a pop star or a boxing champion. ... Sheffield proved a public relations disaster'

(Heffernan and Marqusee, 1992: 319). (Kinnock himself had said that he had unthinkingly responded to cheering supporters with a yell of 'well, alright?' in the same way that he had seen The Everly Brothers and Johnny Cash doing – BBC, 2009.) For some commentators the over-confidence of the Sheffield Rally and the exuberance of Kinnock's performance is one of the reasons Labour lost the election. To defenders of the campaign it was a minor blip. As the party's public relations adviser, Philip Gould, wrote, 'Of the many that have been given, the Sheffield Rally on 1 April 1992 is the least convincing reason for losing the election. ... It was barely on the news and was hardly noticed. It did Labour little or no harm. The voters had bigger fish to fry' (Gould, 1998: 148).

Kinnock was undoubtedly aware of the accusation that he was 'lightweight'. Many commentators at the time noted that he seemed to be subjugating the more ebullient aspects of his personality to appear more statesmanlike. Hughes and Wintour argued that the bid to get Labour elected 'forced [Kinnock] to shut down part of his character, and some of his beliefs, probably for good' (cited in E. Jones, 1994: 209). Ken Livingstone argued that voters never entirely believed this front. Discussing Kinnock's appearance on the satirical show, *Have I Got News for You?* after the 1992 Election loss, Livingstone commented,

> He went back to being the Welsh boyo as if there hadn't been an intervening nine years. Of all the non-professional comedian guests they've had on, I thought he was the best, with all these snappy one-liners he'd forced himself to drop. And one of the reasons people didn't want Kinnock was because they recognised the person they were seeing was false, he had shed half his personality.
>
> (cited in E. Jones, 1994: 17)

Yet Kinnock was always a more serious, contemplative individual than the caricature allowed (Drower, 1984: 150). Fed by a hostile media, voters found it hard to accept a more rounded account of Kinnock. As the journalist John Humphrys noted,

> I don't see why a politician should be remote. We are prepared to accept the elite and arrogant in a politician, yet not so much the down to earth. I suspect that aspect of him, being one of the boys, is what people associate with being lightweight, although I don't see why you have to be aloof to be taken seriously.
>
> (cited in E. Jones, 1994: 17)

Others have alleged an anti-Welsh element to the media's account of Kinnock. The week after the 1992 Election the former Labour Minister, Barbara Castle, wrote that 'I was interested to detect some racist undertones emerging during the campaign. Neil's "unfitness to govern", it appeared, had something to do with his being Welsh. Tories don't respect the Welsh whom they regard as a nation of plebs and poets' (quoted in E. Jones, 1994: 14). John Humphrys largely agreed, noting that 'There is a kind of latent anti-Welshness among the English and that is his bad luck, that and his [ginger] hair colour' (quoted in E. Jones, 1994: 17). As James Thomas has argued, Kinnock suffered from this anti-Welsh rhetoric far more than other Welsh politicians because his personality traits lent themselves to anti-Welsh caricature. While he used his 'brawling boyo' image and rough working-class Welsh background to his advantage, the image also made him an easy figure for the press to portray as 'an unstatesmanlike, intellectually lightweight, over-emotional figure' who could not be trusted. Kinnock, Thomas added, was particularly vulnerable to the accusation of untrustworthiness because he had shifted to the right on a number of issues, including disarmament and nationalisation, during his leadership (Thomas, 1997). Kinnock was ruthlessly caricatured by the media, and it is his skills at getting his message across to which I now turn.

Public communication

There are at two apparent paradoxes concerning Kinnock and public communication: the first relies on differing interpretations of his skills as a public speaker. On the one hand, Kinnock is 'arguably the finest orator in modern British politics' (Kellner, 1992: 6) – a speaker so beguiling that Joe Biden, the current US Vice President, plagiarised parts of his speech in his run for the Presidency in 1988 (Kellner, 1992: 7–8). Yet on the other hand, Kinnock was often seen as ineffective in Parliament – particularly against Thatcher – and was attacked unkindly as a 'Welsh Windbag' (Kellner, 1992: 1).

Kinnock first made a name for himself in the national Labour Party through a series of Conference speeches during the 1970s (A. Morgan, 1992: 337). Commentating on his Conference speeches as leader, Peter Kellner wrote, 'At his best, [Kinnock] refines his speeches to remarkable effect' (Kellner, 1992: 2). Kinnock admits to working hard to develop these skills. He describes how he spent 'much of this life searching for words' and was not afraid of 'painting pictures' and using 'illuminating language' in the tradition of Aneurin Bevan or Michael Foot, whose purpose, he argues, was not to be 'orators' (a word his dislikes for its implication of artifice) but to be 'advocates, conveyers of inspiration and understanding' (Kinnock, 2011).

Perhaps the best-known example of Kinnock's rhetorical powers came in his 1985 Conference speech against the far left Militant Tendency, which controlled several Labour councils at the time. Kinnock famously argued:

I'll tell you what happens with impossible promises. You start with far-fetched resolutions. They are then pickled into a rigid dogma, a code, and you go through the years sticking to that, out-dated, misplaced, irrelevant to the real needs, and you end in the grotesque chaos of a Labour council – a *Labour* council – hiring taxis to scuttle round a city handing out redundancy notices to its own workers. I'm telling you ... – I'm telling you and you'll listen – you can't play politics with people's jobs and with people's services or with their homes.

(Kellner, 1992: 91)

This was Kinnock at the height of his rhetorical powers, using repetition, alliteration, image and sound bite to establish the dominance of the leadership over the party's far left. A poll conducted two days after the speech found that Kinnock had overtaken Margaret Thatcher for the first time as the person electors thought would 'make the best Prime Minister'. His rating had climbed fourteen points in just seven days (Kellner, 1992: 5). To Kellner 'a clear message emerges: that when Kinnock enjoys sustained television exposure, and when voters are given the opportunity to judge him directly, he wins admirers' (Kellner, 1992: 9).

Yet, as many commentators note, at times Kinnock let his words run out of control. As Kellner remarked: 'even his closest friends wince at his tendency to stretch a succinct statement into an elasticated tangle' (Kellner, 1992: 1). This was particularly clear at times in the House of Commons against Thatcher. Nowhere was this more obvious than in the emergency debate over the future of Westland – a failing UK aviation manufacturer – which was causing divisions in the Conservative Party and even threatening the Prime Minister's position. As the journalist Hugo Young wrote, 'Rarely has so inviting a target been so easily missed' (Westlake, 2001: 390). Kinnock acknowledges self-deprecatingly his own 'inadequacy' against Thatcher, but notes 'environmental features' that caused him difficulties, especially in the early days of his leadership. He commented that 'I couldn't be as nasty to Thatcher as she deserved, because she was a woman and nearly twenty years older than me. ... I was brought up to believe ... that real men are courteous. ... But in that bear pit, courtesy has a very limited currency, especially when the times demand that you lash out' (Kinnock, 2011). He also noted that the Conservatives were immensely well-organised in their barracking, which caused him problems in his early days as Leader. It was only later that he developed a technique of speaking close to the microphone and focusing on the audience at home rather than the House of Commons (Kinnock, 2011).

These seemingly contradictory interpretations of Kinnock can be explained in a variety of ways. First, to a degree, the areas in which Kinnock excelled were not those of the media age. His skills as a public speaker were honed in noisy debating societies and in conference halls: forums in which the modern media has not fully intruded. As Kellner notes, 'By William Gladstone's standards, Kinnock has always been a model of brevity. But modern politics, and today's media, demand different standards' (Kellner, 1992: 2).

This can be overstated, and Kinnock was aware of the importance of the sound bite, although he argues that it is unhelpful to reduce politics to it (Kinnock, 2011). Second, as I noted above, Kinnock exudes the ethos of the Labour Party and Labour traditions. As David Marquand has written,

> The language of 'our people', which can so easily sound false or patronising, comes naturally to him because they really are his people. The myths and symbols of Labourism, which he manipulates with such artistry, are his myths and symbols: that is why the artistry is so successful.
> (Marquand, 1999: 205–6)

For those who appreciate the 'myths and symbols of Labourism' the speeches are moving and convincing; for many voters outside that ethos they are alien. Finally, as implied above, Kinnock faced a generally hostile media, which was quick to focus on perceived failings and resort to caricature. It is to Kinnock's relations with the wider media that I now turn.

This is the second paradox in Kinnock's public reputation. On the one hand, Kinnock was demonised by large sections of the press, famously – although by no means exclusively – by The *Sun*, which led on the morning of the 1992 Election with the front page rather clumsily proclaiming 'If Kinnock wins today will the last person to leave Britain please turn out the lights'. On the other hand, he spearheaded the professionalisation of the Labour's Party's public relations, rebranding the party and presenting a more professional corporate image.

During the 1980s the Labour Party's presentation became increasingly slick. After the disastrous election of 1983, Kinnock and his office went about radically improving the way in which the Labour Party presented itself. Peter Mandelson was appointed the party's first Director of Campaigns and Communications in 1985. He brought in Philip Gould, a public relations consultant, to work with him and began to assemble a Shadow Communications Agency, the existence and function of which were ratified by the Party's National Executive Committee in 1986. Mandelson enjoyed close relations with Kinnock's office. The Shadow Communications Agency pioneered the use of qualitative surveys – 'focus groups' – in the party. Mandelson in particular cultivated close contacts with chosen journalists, 'spinning' stories in ways favourable to the leadership, sometimes at the expense of the left (Heffernan and Marqusee, 1992: 212–13). The Campaigns and Communications Department gained ever greater power within the Labour Party. It accounted for over half of the twenty-five new posts created by the party in the two years following the 1985 reorganisation. Its budget rose from £35,000 in 1983 to over £300,000 by 1986 (Heffernan and Marqusee, 1992: 214). Fruits of the investment in public relations were seen in the party's new branding: the Labour rose replaced the red flag; there was better staging of the annual conference; and slicker party political broadcasts were produced – notably 1987's 'Kinnock: the movie', by Hugh Hudson, who had recently directed *Chariots of Fire*.

The rebranding of the party came from the top. Asked about the party's new image, Kinnock replied that he learnt the importance of presentation from a maxim in a George Bernard Shaw lecture. Shaw had argued that the socialist message would be illuminated by the best means available, so they dispensed with 'damp meeting halls, faded notices and smudged leaflets' in favour of 'colourful, intriguing and attractive' presentation. Kinnock argued that from the time he started running the student Socialist Society, he used the best available means of communicating available. He recalls how he decided on the new image of the Labour rose, a version of the logo used by the Norwegian Labour Party, and asked Mandelson to arrange for new logos to be designed. (Kinnock recalls pointing out the exact rose in his father-in-law's gardening catalogue.) The anecdote shows both how the branding of the party was integral to Kinnock's tenure and the extent to which he was involved in the detail of decisions about that redesign.

Yet despite the professionalisation of the way in which the Labour Party's presented itself to the media and outside world, the media were hostile and Kinnock, in particular, was ruthlessly attacked. In his review of Labour, the tabloids and the 1992 General Election, James Thomas argued that between 1979 and 1992 the popular press was more hostile to Labour than at any time in the post-war period (Thomas, 1998). One explanation for this relates to the ownership of the British media. Kinnock was certainly no friend of Rupert Murdoch's. Martin Westlake recounts Kinnock's response to Murdoch's claim that he was a 'menace to freedom' at a meal in the late 1970s because of his pro-union views. Kinnock had told Murdoch that he was 'a menace to democracy; not press barons in general – they come and go – but you personally' (Westlake, 2001: 712). Kinnock did not believe that Murdoch would have remembered the incident. However, Kinnock does concede that part of the attack upon him could have been down to his views on press ownership (Kinnock, 2011). The 1992 Labour Manifesto committed a future Labour Government to 'establish an urgent enquiry by the Monopolies and Mergers Commission into the concentration of media ownership' (Westlake, 2001: 712). Thomas concludes that although there were more fundamental reasons for Labour's defeat in 1992, the tabloid press campaign almost certainly made the difference between a Conservative victory and a hung Parliament (Thomas, 1998).

Party management

Pippa Norris argued that 'The overriding goal of Neil Kinnock's leadership, the central thrust behind the policy changes and organisational reforms, was to purge Labour of its image as an extremist and divided party' (Norris, 1994: 173).

The loss of the 1979 General Election under James Callaghan, with, at that time, the worst result in the party's post-war history, saw a shift to the left within the party (Jefferys, 1993; Seyd, 1987; J. Smith, 1992; Whiteley, 1983). The centre of gravity shifted further leftwards after the split in 1981, which saw the creation of a new Social Democratic Party, its Parliamentary presence made up almost entirely of politicians formerly from the right of the Labour Party. After 1979, the left sought to 'change Labour's Constitution in order to make the leadership more accountable to the party outside Parliament' (Garner and Kelly, 1998: 114). The result was a shift in power away from the Parliamentary Labour Party (PLP) and towards party activists. Mandatory reselection of MPs by Constituency Labour Parties (CLPs) was introduced (Koelble, 1991: 101ff) and the PLP lost its exclusive right to elect the party's leader and deputy – Kinnock himself had won the leadership under a new electoral college of unions, the PLP and CLPs.

Kinnock's election brought with it a style of leadership, which was to transform the Party's internal power relations (Shaw, 1994). As Uwe Jun argued, Kinnock initially pursued two specific goals (Jun, 1996: 66–7). First, he aimed to decrease the dependency of MPs on delegates in the constituencies. The intention was two-fold: to extend democracy and to curtail the influence of activists in favour of more moderate rank-and-file members (Shaw, 1994: 117). In line with this goal, Kinnock proposed the adoption of the 'one member, one vote' principle in constituencies for reselection of Parliamentary candidates, rather than the power being held by the executives within local parties. This aided moderate MPs who were threatened with reselection. It also provoked fierce resistance from unions and party activists, who had only recently won their powers, and Kinnock failed to win support for the move at the 1984 Annual Conference. As Martin Westlake wrote, 'Whatever criticisms might be advanced against Kinnock, the failure to learn from mistakes was not one of them. In some ways it was fortunate that his most important defeat happened so soon in his leadership. It was not repeated' (Westlake, 2001: 276). It was not until 1990 that one-member one-vote ballots among local party members were finally agreed by Conference (Westlake, 2001: 501).

Kinnock's second goal was to curtail the role of the unions within the party organisation (Alderman and Carter, 1994). The extent of union influence on the party was seen to be a barrier to reform and electoral success. In 1990 Kinnock took steps towards achieving this goal through a reduction in the share of the union block vote in conference decisions from 90 to 70 per cent (Westlake 2001: 501) and an agreement that this would be reduced further, as party membership increased, until parity was reached with the CLPs. In this fight Kinnock was also helped by greater support from a new generation of union leaders that emerged who increasingly supportive of the party leadership (Jun, 1996: 68).

As Jun wrote,

> The point of departure for these specific goals of Kinnock's reforms was thus the intention to increase the power and authority of the party leadership, to expand its independence, and to achieve greater control over campaigns, presentation and co-ordination of party activities.
>
> (Jun, 1996: 68)

Kinnock recalls how he spent much of a frustrating first term dealing with issues internal to the management of the party – in particular leading the fight against Militant. It was only after internal battles within the party were largely won that the argument could be made on policy. In establishing his control over the party Kinnock was successful. As Jun argued,

> Kinnock succeeded in securing control over the power centres within the party: the Parliamentary Party, the National Executive Committee, and the annual conference. The hard left no longer had any influence on political decisions, it was reduced to an isolated and helpless rump.
>
> (Jun, 1996: 68)

Public policy platform

The 1983 Manifesto, issued under the leadership of Michael Foot, was famously dubbed the 'longest suicide note in history' by Labour MP, Gerald Kaufman. The poorly presented assortment of radical policies, set out at length, included the repeal of Conservative legislation on industrial relations; the return to public ownership of local authority services; a massive programme of house-building; positive action for ethnic minorities; abolition of the legislative powers of the House of Lords; cancellation of Trident; an explicit refusal to deploy Cruise missiles; the removal of nuclear bases from Britain; and withdrawal from the European Economic Community (EEC).

After 1983 Kinnock set about moving the party back to the centre. Reflecting on his time as leader and the policy changes that were introduced, Kinnock stressed the importance of 'fidelity to a body of convictions', but in policy terms that meant 'doing practical things in practical ways'. Policies have to be feasible. As Kinnock commented 'unless [policies] satisfy the feasibility test you'd be better off taking up stamp collecting – you'd do less harm' (Kinnock, 2011). Between 1983 and 1987 the party dropped opposition to council house sales; reduced the importance of nationalisation; and committed Labour to membership of the EEC and to remaining in NATO (while opposing US nuclear weapons being placed in Britain). A second significant defeat in 1987 convinced Kinnock and the leadership that they had not gone far enough. Bryan Gould, a member of Kinnock's

Shadow Cabinet, told a Labour Co-ordinating Committee shortly after the 1987 defeat that 'The popular appeal of policies must be a prime consideration, not an afterthought' (Heffernan and Marqusee, 1992: 215). In 1987 a further drive to reform the party began, with a wide ranging policy review. This review dropped the party's commitment to unilateral nuclear disarmament and reformed the annual conference and National Executive, curtailing local parties' ability to influence policy. The general election loss also led, in 1988, to a new statement of aims and values. This allowed a much greater role for the market in the economy (a prelude to Tony Blair's abolition of Clause IV of the Party's constitution, which had theoretically committed Labour to 'the common ownership of production, distribution and exchange' since 1918).

Critics made much of the apparent volte-face in Kinnock's own position on many of these policy issues. It also opened up Kinnock to the charge that his focus was on getting into power at the expense of his beliefs. It led to The *Sun's* unkind depiction of 'Crafty Kinnock'. The satirical show *Spitting Image* linked it to Kinnock's verbosity, with a puppet of Kinnock singing to a Gilbert and Sullivan Operetta, 'You ask what I believe in and I have simply no idea / which is why I'm rather given to this verbal diarrhoea.' Despite the media attacks, the Labour Party began to pull ahead in the polls. Popular policy shifts from Labour coincided with the introduction of the unpopular 'poll tax' by the Conservatives. For Kinnock, however, the peak in popularity was too early. After forcing Margaret Thatcher out of office in November 1990, the Conservative Party had almost 17 months to pull back the polling deficit, and to the surprise of many it won the 1992 Election with a workable majority.

Kinnock's attempt to move the party to a more popular centre ground must be seen against a difficult international backdrop. Even critics, such as Heffernan and Marqusee, note that these were inauspicious times for progressive political parties, arguing that,

> Labour's failure at the ballot box on the 9th of April [1992] was part symptomatic of a worldwide crisis of socialism, which would have caused serious difficulties for Labour under any leadership. It was the result also of a string of industrial defeats stretching back over a decade, and reflected the prolonged shrinkage in trade union membership and influence. Britain's economic decline had removed the material basis for Labour's previous achievements in office. Within the framework of a market-dominated economy, it had become harder and harder to offer a convincing progressive alternative.
>
> (Heffernan and Marqusee, 1992: 1)

The accusation that Kinnock moved the party too far to the centre seems thin after New Labour. Kinnock was a moderniser, but one indubitably in the Labour tradition. It is this view of Kinnock – as a moderniser still located in the social democratic or socialist tradition – that has gone a long way to rebuilding his reputation in the years after New Labour.

Conclusion

The headline electoral data covering Kinnock's period in office is not impressive. Between the elections of 1983 and 1992 Labour's share of the vote increased from 27.6 per cent to 34.4 per cent, a rise of only 6.8 per cent, well below the 37 per cent won in 1979, which had been Labour's worst performance since the 1930s. Moreover, the 6.8 per cent rise that occurred under Kinnock seems to have been mostly taken from the SDP–Liberal Alliance, which in the same period saw its vote fall 7.6 per cent; the Conservative vote fell a mere 0.5 per cent (Fielding, 1994: 598–99).

The aftermath of the 1992 General Election saw Kinnock's reputation at a low ebb. Fielding sums up this view in an article published in 1994. He noted that:

> Neil Kinnock was leader of the Labour Party for nearly nine years, during which time Labour lost the general elections of 1987 and 1992, each by substantial margins. Instead of helping his party enter government, Kinnock became the longest-serving leader of the opposition. It is not surprising, therefore, that Kinnock's impact on the Labour Party is generally conceived in unfavourable terms. Not only did the party under his leadership fail to win power, but he is considered by many to have been the single most important cause of Labour's 1992 defeat. In comparison with previous Labour leaders Kinnock's record appears even more wretched. Although Hugh Gaitskell also failed to win an election, he is at least credited with remaining faithful to a set of consistent beliefs throughout his political life. While Harold Wilson is said to have possessed few principles, this is partly compensated by the fact that he was able to win four general elections. In contrast, Kinnock is seen as lacking both principles and the ability to win.
>
> (Fielding, 1994: 589)

Viewed through a historical lens, however, the changes introduced under Kinnock are sometimes given more credit. By the late 1990s there was a revisionist take, that while it was true that the Labour Party under Kinnock did not win a general election at least Kinnock laid the foundation for Labour's landslide victory in 1997. Electorally, Roy Hattersley claimed that, Kinnock saved Labour from destruction and ultimately ensured that it remained electable. Kinnock has indeed been described as the 'architect' of the party's later success (Jones, 1994: 210). Writing in 1998, the moderniser Philip Gould wrote of Kinnock that,

Without him, there would be no modern Labour Party, no huge Labour majority. He was and is a giant of a man who through the power of his personality lifted Labour into the modern era. He made the first great modernising breakthrough. He took Labour from the pathetic, unelectable shambles he inherited in 1983, with a Conservative majority of 144, to a party on the brink of government just 20 seats short of a hung parliament.

(Gould, 1998: 142)

Peter Kellner goes even further, arguing that 'When Kinnock became its leader, the Party's long-term survival was in doubt' (Kellner, 1992: 10). Less than five years after he stepped down Labour had won the biggest landslide of the post-war period.

Ideologically, Kinnock is seen as introducing a modernised form of social democracy to the party and breaking with a rigid adherence to dogma. While Blair undoubtedly drew on aspects of Kinnock's inheritance (Corthorn, 2004), part of the revival in Kinnock's reputation is down to his distance from elements in New Labour. In a reasonably sympathetic account, the historian Ross McKibbin notes that

Whether we think Kinnock was the saviour of the Labour party or its gravedigger depends very much on what we think of New Labour, and how far we agree with Hattersley that Kinnock was seeking not to abandon socialism but to introduce a new and improved form of it. Somebody had to disembarrass Labour of the infantile disorders of the early 1980s and Kinnock did that very well. As a result his successors were able to exploit the Conservative party's various disasters in the following decade. Kinnock, furthermore, did not (does not?) share New Labour's overt or covert admiration for Thatcher. He retained a moral critique of the 1980s unfashionable in the contemporary Labour party.

(McKibbin, 2002)

One could say that Kinnock's reputation as party leader has followed a U-shape. From the high hopes of 1983, when *Marxism Today* depicted him as Superman, flying in to rescue the Labour Party, it fell to the nadir of 1992 and his second consecutive election loss. Yet, since that time, Kinnock's reputation has risen again, first, as it became clear that the ideological 'modernisation' and media professionalisation begun under his tenure reaped rewards for Blair; and second, when many in the Labour Party became increasingly sceptical at the ideological direction Blair was taking, Kinnock's reforms appeared more grounded in the Labour tradition than those of his successor. The election of Ed Miliband as party leader, a social democrat who sees himself in the revisionist tradition and who was supported by Kinnock, perhaps marks a high point in Kinnock's reputation – the culmination of efforts started a generation before.

Kinnock's account of the two sides of his legacy summarises it best. On European Election Day in June 1999, an old man attracted his attention – 'immaculate, regimental blazer, regimental tie, sparkling white shirt, trousers with cut-your-finger creases on them'. The man said, 'Tell me Mr Kinnock, the way I see it is, if you hadn't done what you did, we wouldn't have a Labour Government.' 'Very kind', Kinnock answered. 'No, no', the man continued. 'I want your opinion on that. What's your view on this? If you hadn't made the changes you made in the Labour Party, there's no way we could have won the 1997 general election.' 'Well', Kinnock demurred, 'Tony and others are kind enough to say that and I take a degree of pleasure' ... The man stopped him: 'No, What I'm trying to say is, if it wasn't for you then Blair couldn't be in Number 10 Downing Street'. 'Well, that's what people tell me and I suppose it's right', Kinnock agreed. 'There you are', said the man triumphantly. 'You're the bastard we've got to blame!' (Kinnock, 2011).

Acknowledgement

I would particularly like to thank Lord Kinnock for allowing me time to interview him for this chapter.

12
John Smith, 1992–4

Mark Stuart

John Smith shares with Hugh Gaitskell the unhappy distinction of having died while serving as Leader of the Opposition. The Labour Party tends to revere its fallen leaders, and Smith is no exception. The very place of his burial – among the Scottish kings on the holy island of Iona off the West Coast of Scotland – has, over the years, helped to create an almost saintly image of the former Labour leader. People, especially on the left of the Labour movement, want to hold on to an idealised image of Smith, as an example of what a 'good' Socialist Labour Government would have been like had he lived to be Prime Minister, even though Smith was actually an old-fashioned figure hailing from the Labour right. Had he lived, Smith would have succumbed to the perennial cries of betrayal that inevitably beset every Labour Prime Minister in office.

However, while Smith has been revered, he has also been largely forgotten in terms of the narrative of how Labour modernised itself in Opposition in the period from 1983 to 1997. Smith's short period as Labour leader from 1992 to 1994 is often viewed as an interregnum between two reforming Labour leaders, Neil Kinnock and Tony Blair, a period in which the process of modernisation ground largely to a halt. Rarely in politics is one reforming leader followed immediately by another one. However, the view of Smith as an opponent of change has gained credence because the recent history of the Labour Party has been almost exclusively penned by New Labour arch-modernisers, such as Philip Gould and Peter Mandelson, keen to portray 1994 as 'Year Zero'. Everything before then is seen as irrelevant. The aim of their narrative, as Gould puts it in the sub-title to his book, is to set out 'How the Modernisers Saved the Labour Party' (Gould, 1998). Who can really blame them? Smith's death, though tragic, gave the Labour Party a rare opportunity to renew itself entirely, reborn as New Labour. But as a result, Smith has been largely airbrushed out of history. So, Smith has been both revered and forgotten in equal measure.

This chapter attempts to measure the success or otherwise of Smith's truncated period as Leader of the Opposition from 1992 to 1994, deploying objective criteria to discover his strengths and weaknesses. However, before doing so there needs to be some awareness of his inheritance. His election as Labour Party leader on 18 July 1992 needs to be set against the backdrop of electoral defeat. It is worth recalling the utter sense of demoralisation that befell ordinary Labour members following their party's fourth successive electoral defeat. There was a general feeling of hopelessness, that if the Labour Party could not win in 1992, when would it ever regain power? Moreover, Neil Kinnock had overseen a long and difficult period of modernisation, in terms of both internal and external reforms, which had by-passed many of the party's existing structures and overturned long-held beliefs on issues such as nuclear disarmament and the extent of state ownership. In order to make those changes, Kinnock had stepped on many people's toes in a movement that has always liked to see itself as instinctively anti-leadership. As Larry Whitty, the General Secretary of the Labour Party, wrote in September 1992:

> It was clear from my vantage point that over the latter years of Neil Kinnock's leadership there were serious breakdowns in communication and empathy between the Leader and various key elements in the Party. This was, for the most part, not due to any deliberate decision to reduce contacts but just that they got squeezed out.
>
> (Whitty, 1992)

John Smith's first task was therefore to repair the strained relationship between the Leader's Office and the Labour movement more generally. Before Smith's leadership is assessed more fully, it is important to establish from the outset that almost every character trait he possessed and almost everything he did was in sharp contrast to that of his predecessor. Neil Kinnock and John Smith were two completely different personalities, who had emerged from wholly different routes through the Labour Party. Neil, as with so many Welsh politicians, had earned his trade on the stump, becoming a brilliant platform speaker, whereas John Smith's debating skills best suited the House of Commons. Neil was a great party organiser, a National Executive Committee (NEC) man who knew the rules of the Labour Party inside out; John actively disliked committees and long meetings, had very little knowledge of the party's rulebook, and was not on the NEC until he became leader. It wasn't entirely his fault – he'd twice tried to get elected in the early 1980s, but right-wingers couldn't get elected in those days. Neil had been a rebellious backbencher in the 1970s, whereas John had served loyally in Government. Indeed, the two had clashed over devolution in the House of Commons. And because they had emerged via separate routes in the party, they had no common hinterland to build on when John became Shadow Chancellor in 1987. Neil rarely mixed socially with other members of the Shadow Cabinet, his only real friend being Bryan Gould. Whereas

Neil tended to be tense and insecure, John had tremendous self-confidence, and had the charm and the bonhomie to get on with his Shadow Cabinet colleagues. In his burning desire to transform the Labour Party into an electable force, Neil had no time for playing touchy-feely with junior MPs, whom he later termed 'salonistas' – lazy, armchair opponents of change. Years later, Kinnock expressed his view of how the Labour Party needed to be run:

> It is important that the Leader likes (or loves) the Party enough to max-imise its chance of winning. Sometimes the affection can only properly be transmitted through a firm grip on the back of the Party's neck.
> (Neil Kinnock, correspondence with author)

The problem with this kind of juggernaut, or cudgel, style of leadership is that it has a limited lifespan. Too many people get upset. And yet, after what might be termed the Smith pause for breath, Tony Blair essentially resumed Kinnock's 'reform or die' leadership style.

The marked differences between Neil and John didn't stop there: while Neil worked tirelessly as Labour leader, John adopted a more relaxed approach. All along, Neil's basic objection to John was that he thought John was lazy. Just after Neil stood down from the leadership, Neil thought what a rare treat it would be to go to the cinema in the afternoon. As Neil and his wife Glenys sat down to watch the film, Neil noticed a man in front of him eating an ice cream. It was John Smith (David Hare, correspondence with author). In short, the two men were, in the words of Roy Hattersley, chalk and cheese (Stuart, 2005).

Public communication

Smith's skills a public communicator best revealed themselves in debates in the House of Commons. His skills had been honed, first as a student politician in the Glasgow University Union, and then as an advocate in the Edinburgh law courts. Murray Elder, John Smith's Chief of Staff, sums up the roots of Smith's Parliamentary skills:

> John's whole adult life, whether as a debater at Glasgow winding up a long debate, as a criminal lawyer, persuading a jury that a man was not guilty of murder, or in the Commons in the 1970s making devolution policy on the hoof from the Dispatch Box, had taught him how to be convincing in front of an audience.
> (interview with Murray Elder)

His debating strength lay not in being flamboyant, but in building up a well-argued factual case. It would not be hard to compile an impressive compendium of Smith's great Parliamentary performances as Leader of the Opposition. Early on, he was presented with an open goal. On 16 September 1992, Black Wednesday, Britain fell out of the Exchange Rate Mechanism (ERM). Smith's conclusion that day was devastating, referring to John Major as the 'devalued Prime Minister of a devalued Government' (HC Debates, 24/9/1992, col. 22). But perhaps Smith's very best Parliamentary performance occurred on 9 June 1993 when he attacked the Prime Minister's 'botched' reshuffle, following the resignation of the Chancellor, Norman Lamont:

> If we were to offer that tale of events to the BBC light entertainment department as a script for a programme, I think that the producers of 'Yes, Minister' would have turned it down as hopelessly over-the-top. It might have even been too much for 'Some Mothers Do 'Ave 'Em'.
> The tragedy for us all is that it is really happening – it is fact, not fiction. The man with the non-Midas touch is in charge. It is no wonder that we live in a country where the Grand National does not start and hotels fall into the sea.
>
> (HC Debates, 9/6/1993, col. 292)

Although having the ability to perform well in the House of Commons is not the only attribute required of a Leader of the Opposition – as William Hague discovered to his cost from 1997 to 2001 – as Hilary Armstrong, Smith's Parliamentary Private Secretary, and later a Chief Whip under Tony Blair, points out, 'performance is a lot of the job' (interview with Hilary Armstrong). The late Michael Foot agreed that, especially in a situation where there is no immediate prospect of a return to Government, 'getting the Labour Party in a good mood [in the House of Commons] is an essential part of the role' (interview with Michael Foot). And if the leader is commanding in the House, then the backbenchers can have confidence in him (or her). Frank Dobson recalls that John Smith 'exuded an air of competence, always looked like he would cope, was unlikely to lose an argument in the House of Commons, and was perceived as a winner' (interview with Frank Dobson). In 1986, Smith had won the *Spectator*/Highland Park Parliamentarian of the Year award, largely for his successful harrying of the Government over the Westland Affair. The contrast with Neil Kinnock's tendency to botch the big Parliamentary occasions, most notably over Westland, could not have been more stark.

Whereas Smith excelled in the House of Commons, living on his sharpness, put him on a Labour Conference platform, and he could be very dull indeed. As Anthony Howard observed on Smith's death, '... the platform was never his [Smith's] métier, any more than the House of Commons was Neil Kinnock's' (Howard, 1994). Howard pointed out that making a good Conference speech involves getting the jokes right and getting people to laugh and applaud at the right times – it was all too pre-prepared to suit John Smith's impromptu style of speaking and debating. To take one example, only five days after his demolition of John Major over devaluation, Smith's attack on the Prime Minister at the Labour Party Conference fell flat: 'We were promised a *New Statesman* and what have we got instead? A *Spectator*' (Labour Party Conference Report, 1992: 101).

But if Smith was a dull Conference speaker, he came across well on television, cultivating the air of a safe Scottish bank manager figure, building on his period as Shadow Chancellor, 1987–92, portraying himself as a man who wouldn't dare gamble with the nation's finances. Labour sorely needed such an image following on from Kinnock's dangerously flamboyant style, something that had worried the general public. As Simon Hoggart puts it, Smith's priority was to appear as 'un-Kinnock' as possible (Hoggart, 1994). Smith was very comfortable with his chosen political style, deliberately modelling himself on unshowy political heroes such as Clement Attlee and Harry Truman (Hoggart, 1994). James Callaghan was also someone whose 'Father of the Nation' political style John had watched and learnt a great deal from (interview with Leo Beckett). The paradox was that this reassuring image concealed the real man underneath. Whereas Neil Kinnock had unwisely allowed his passion to bubble up to the surface, Smith made a point of keeping such outbursts private.

If Smith had another failing as a political communicator, it was in his rather naïve and old-fashioned attitude towards the modern media and political campaigning. It was later said, at least in a work of fiction, that Smith thought that '*Newsnight* was the most watched programme on television' (Kominsky, 2002). Apocryphal or not, Smith belonged to an older generation who believed that the primary role of a politician was to convince the electorate that their view, and that of their party, was the right one. Politicians should not merely conduct opinion polls to ascertain what median voters wanted, in order to obtain office. Smith had a strong dislike of focus groups. He dispensed with the services of Philip Gould's Shadow Communications Agency (SCA), which Kinnock had used so much. Nor did Smith like spin. According to David Hill, Smith's chief spokesperson, his leader had 'an innate detestation of trickiness with the press, and that was a large part of the reason he disliked Peter Mandelson, who like Gould, was cast out into outer darkness under Smith's leadership (Macintyre, 1999: 241). Smith had a perfectly user-friendly relationship with journalists, but he was not fixated or obsessed by it, in the way that New Labour became. He took the view that if the press wanted to contact them at weekends, then he was accessible. Equally, if they dared to telephone him on a Sunday morning, they would get a flea in their ear for being intrusive (interview with Elizabeth Smith). The result was a fairly low media profile. Such a profile however, would be unthinkable in today's 24-hour media age. Politics was changing, and still Smith refused to budge.

During his two years as leader, Smith's advisers regularly sent him confidential memorandums, pointing out that he wasn't doing enough to get his message across in the media (Stuart, 2005: 310–14). But Smith instinctively disliked repeating the same political message over and over again. The advocate in him had grown used to handing back the papers after a case was finished (interview with Lord McCluskey). Murray Elder was constantly frustrated after John had given a good speech on a subject. When he asked his leader, '"Shouldn't you follow that up?", John would say "It's finished, dealt with." His mind was always on the next issue' (interview with Murray Elder). Smith also tended to be stubborn when presented with new ideas. As Alastair Campbell recalls, 'Ach' was one of Smith's favourite words, 'his way of dismissing "fancy notions"' (A. Campbell, 1994). It was all in his head. He knew where he was going. Moreover, he didn't want to get cut off from the outside world. He actively disliked an entourage, and liked to get out there to meet-and-greet real people. Had he lived, it would have become more and more difficult to maintain that leadership style the closer he had got to Government. The entourage of advisers and spin doctors would inevitably have started to crowd around him. Almost every Leader of the Opposition lives under the illusion that they can retain a semblance of normality as Prime Minister. It never happens.

But the most important difference between John Smith and New Labour with regard to the media is that Smith had no time at all for Rupert Murdoch. His secretary recalls: 'He [Murdoch] was a no-no'. Just before his death, Hilary Coffman arranged for Andrew Neil, then editor of Murdoch's *Sunday Times*, to interview John Smith without first consulting him. Barrett recalls Smith's reaction when he heard about the interview: 'I thought he [John] was going to explode. But he wouldn't have let his staff down by cancelling it, so Andrew Neil became the last journalist ever to interview John Smith' (interview with Ann Barrett).

Public policy platform

If Smith were to be scored by the various criteria adopted in this book, then his lowest rating would undoubtedly be his ability to construct a public policy platform in Opposition. In some respects, that was down to his untimely death. Phase 1 of his leadership had always been about regrouping the Labour Party following its defeat in 1992, and setting up policy reviews of various sorts. Phase 2 – when Opposition policies would have been sold to the wider electorate – sadly never happened (interview with Margaret Beckett). That reality inevitably affects our ability to analyse Smith's policies as Labour leader.

In truth, Smith did have a strategy for his first two years as Labour leader. In the first year, his speeches focused on constitutional change, particularly but not exclusively the 'unfinished business' of Scottish devolution

(Smith, 1992). In the autumn of 1992, he asked Gordon Borrie, the former Director General of the Office of Fair Trading, to head up a Social Justice Commission, which, unluckily for Smith, didn't report until after his death (Commission on Social Justice, 1994). In the second year, the main public thrust was economic, culminating in attacks on John Major's promises not to increases taxes. The next phase, due to start in June 1994, would have been far more positive, setting out Labour's values to the electorate, with far more stress placed on projecting those ideas to the country at large.

But it is worth emphasising that there never was such a thing as 'John Smithism'. Smith was a political pragmatist by temperament and training. Whenever Smith had been asked as a politician to expound his 'big idea', he had always replied, 'A Labour Government' (E. Smith, 1994: 13). Unlike other Labour right-wingers of his generation, like Donald Dewar, Roy Hattersley and Gerald Kaufman, Smith spent very little time writing philosophical articles on the state of socialism. As a result, there are no set of Smith papers, hidden somewhere, outlining his beliefs. Smith had learnt a very simple yet fundamental set of values on his father's knee, which from his early adult life he saw best represented in the Labour Party, and from which he rarely deviated in later life. There was no changing him.

Smith was a committed Presbyterian, but was keen to keep his faith private. It was only when he became Labour leader that he was almost required to set out the moral basis of his beliefs. In March 1993, Smith gave the Christian Socialist R. H. Tawney Lecture, which became known as *Reclaiming the Ground*. Drawing on the ideas of Archbishop William Temple, he claimed that people had an obligation or duty to one another. In politics, that meant a duty to serve one's community and one's nation (W. Temple, 1942).

Despite Smith's attempt to set out his vision for the party, a widespread view developed during his leadership that he was moving too slowly when it came to modernisation. An impressive array of mainly younger figures in the Labour Party, including Tony Blair, Gordon Brown, Jack Straw and Philip Gould, believed that unless Labour's modernisation accelerated it risked being beaten again at the following general election (memo from Philip Gould to Murray Elder, 1993). In 1996, two years after Smith's death, Peter Mandelson upset many people in the Labour Party when he claimed that there was a sort of 'one last heave' mentality creeping into the party (Macintyre, 1999: 244–5). Is John Rentoul therefore correct to argue that the whole idea of New Labour was 'proposed and rejected under Smith'? (Rentoul, 1995: 5). In short, no. Smith felt in his bones that the Tories were finished, following 'Black Wednesday' on 16 September 1992, when Britain was forced out of the ERM. He was undoubtedly a cautious politician, who did not want to put everything in his shop window before an election. That natural caution had been shown in his controversial decision as Shadow Chancellor not to set out his Shadow Budget until just before the 1992 General Election. But that did not mean that Smith was in favour of total inaction. Alastair Campbell is right to describe the nuances of difference at the time as being between 'those frantic for change and those happy to play a longer game' (Brown, 1997: 228). Roy Hattersley argues that Smith most definitely did not belong to the 'one more heave' school. Rather, he was 'determined to modernise the party. But he wanted to bring the old principles up to date, not to replace them. He looked for intellectual improvements not ideological alternatives' (Hattersley, 1997: 374). He was a moderniser, but the argument was over the pace of modernisation.

Smith was found of telling a joke about two bulls standing in a field, eyeing up some cows on the hillside. The younger of the two bulls says excitedly: 'Let's run up the hill right now and shag one of them!' The older, wiser bull, replies: 'No, let's walk up the hill – and shag the lot of them' (Stern, 2004). That debate between older bulls or 'long gamers' such as Smith, John Prescott and Margaret Beckett, on the one hand, and younger, more 'frantic' bulls like Tony Blair, Gordon Brown and Peter Mandelson, on the other, was played out over the debate over the introduction of One Member, One Vote (OMOV) in 1993. Before he stepped down in 1992, Neil Kinnock had attempted to push through OMOV, but his authority as leader quickly evaporated. Critics of Smith claimed that he was moving too slowly, but it says something about his commitment to change that he was willing to risk the leadership of his party on the outcome of OMOV at the 1993 Labour Party Conference. Allies of Smith cleverly combined the resolution on OMOV with one supporting the introduction of a quota system for women, requiring half of winnable seats with no sitting Labour MP to choose a women candidate. The Manufacturing and Science Finance Union (MSF) delegation was opposed to OMOV, but had a long-standing commitment to all-women shortlists. Faced with this dilemma, the MSF delegation abstained. Their conversion was crucial in tipping the vote the leadership's way because they held 4.5 per cent of the votes, and the eventual winning margin was only 3.1 per cent. Smith was also helped enormously by John Prescott's conference speech in favour of OMOV. The 'levy-plus' scheme finally agreed wasn't pure OMOV as Blair wanted, but it was a workable OMOV that survives today. Moreover, the change was hugely significant in terms of the Labour Party's image because it showed that Labour now believed in democratically-arrived-at decisions at Party Conferences, rather than union barons casting block votes.

The accusation from the modernisers is that a shocked and relieved Smith closed the shutters on any further reform of the party after OMOV (Sopel, 1995: 165; Rentoul, 1995: 342, 346–7; Naughtie, 2001: 48). Before his death, Smith faced separate calls from Jack Straw (in May 1993) and Neil Kinnock (February 1994) to completely rewrite Clause IV of Labour's 1918 Constitution. Smith was opposed to reforming Clause IV (Straw, 1993; Kinnock, 1994). He realised that it was no longer relevant, but he felt that it should remain part of Labour's heritage. In a rare use of a religious analogy, he commented to his policy adviser, David Ward, 'People need their icons, their altars. You can't make them change everything all of the time' (interview with David Ward). As Murray Elder explains, Smith had been explaining his attitude towards Clause IV to a group of Russians. Smith said that he wanted to move Clause IV to the side of the church, because it was no longer central, but people could still go and see it if they wished (interview with Murray Elder). In other words, it should be allowed to wither on the vine. In a telephone conversation, Smith told Jack Straw that he would be 'stirring up a hornet's nest' if he went ahead with the publication of his Clause IV pamphlet. Straw went ahead anyway. In a private meeting between the pair, Smith lost his temper. 'Amidst raised voices, I sought to take my leave', recalled Straw. '"You can take this with you too", he [Smith] shouted, as he threw the envelope containing my pamphlet at me' (Jack Straw in correspondence with the author). Party unity meant everything to John Smith. Getting rid of Clause IV was more trouble than it was worth. Had he lived, Smith would have put his own imprint on it, based on his *Reclaiming the Ground* Tawney lecture, but he wouldn't have completely rewritten it.

Historically, OMOV was probably a more important policy change than Clause IV, the latter being a cosmetic exercise, a piece of symbolism designed to appeal to disaffected Tory voters, pondering whether to switch to Labour. Smith's reform, on the other hand, took real power away from union leaders – more so than at any time since 1918, especially in relation to the selection of Parliamentary candidates – and gave it back to ordinary trade unionists. It showed the voters that the old union barons could no longer fix things as they had done in the past, demonstrating that Labour had truly changed. OMOV was probably the most important single reform in Labour's history, but not as important as Kinnock's reforms taken as a whole. Such a conclusion is open to debate, but OMOV certainly cleared the way for Blair's eventual reform of Clause IV in 1995, in the sense that the hardest battle of all had already been fought and won by Smith (Stuart, 2004: 4–6).

The most difficult part of any attempt to analyse Smith's public policy platform concerns the development of economic policy after 1992. Was Gordon Brown, the new Shadow Chancellor, effectively in charge of economic policy, or was his predecessor, and now leader, the driving force? Hilary Armstrong believes that after 1992, 'Gordon did get frustrated that John was too slow' (interview with Hilary Armstrong). Murray Elder agrees, and believes that had Smith lived beyond 1994, there would have been 'very considerable' tensions between John and Gordon over whether to commit the Labour Party to freeze public spending at Tory levels in the first two years of a Labour Government. John was much more of the view that incoming ministers in a new Labour Government would need a bit of money to spend after a long period of Tory rule, whereas Gordon would have fought that view 'tooth and nail … there would have been a fierce battle' (interview with Murray Elder).

John Smith also retained a moral view that the better-off should pay more in income tax, whereas Brown argued the dangers of committing the party too early in the 1992 Parliament to a higher top rate of income tax. Instead, Brown expended a lot of time and political capital downplaying the idea of Labour as a high-tax party. Nor is it likely that Smith would have agreed with Brown's eventual policy of Bank of England independence, given his strong previous attachment to the idea of democratic oversight of Central Bank decisions (Stuart, 2005: Chapter 12). However, we are now entering the realms of 'what ifs'. Smith's views in 1994 might have changed by the time it came to 1997. We simply can't tell. Such matters will have to remain in the realms of counter-factual history (Stuart, 2003: Chapter 19).

Party management

If Smith scores poorly on his construction of a public policy platform, he more than makes up for it in terms of his skills as a party manager. Hilary Armstrong sees Smith as 'an acute politician' who was part of that tradition of Labour Party figures like Wilson and Callaghan who regarded party unity as vital (interview with Hilary Armstrong). Smith was a unifier. As a minister in the late 1970s, he had watched and learnt from Callaghan as he balanced the left and the right of the Labour Party, so much so that the overall complexion of Smith's Shadow Cabinets resembled much more that of a team put together by his former boss.

Although Smith started life as strong supporter of Hugh Gaitskell, he did not adopt Gaitskellite methods when running the party. Unlike Gaitskell, and indeed unlike Kinnock, Smith never set out deliberately to defeat one section of the party. Indeed, Smith's leadership was characterised by an incredible toleration of the left. The change in atmosphere was obvious from the moment that Smith became leader. The Leader's Office gave time to figures such as Dennis Skinner and Clare Short, after years of ostracism under Kinnock. In a way, it was harder for Kinnock, a figure originally from the left, to be forgiven for getting rid of cherished left-wing policies. John's relationship with the left was helped enormously by the fact that, although he hailed from the right, because of his consistency on most issues, the left knew where they stood with him (interview with Lynne Jones). Smith indulged Tony Benn, who had been his former boss at the Department of Energy in the mid-1970s. He retained a strong affection for Michael Foot, with whom he had worked as Minister of State at the Privy Council Office. Some figures on the right of the party were unhappy at the way Smith indulged the left, but Margaret Beckett argues that John always made a sharp differential between those people who were elected and those who were not. Every elected Labour member, in Smith's view, had a contribution to make.

Smith's style of party management was therefore a collegiate one, in which controversial issues such as the party's stance during the passage of the

European Communities (Amendment) Bill (usually known as the Maastricht Bill) in the 1992–3 session were hammered out collectively within the confines of the Parliamentary Labour Party (Stuart, 2006: 401–19). Everybody felt that they had had their say. Smith's approach to party management was akin to John Silkin's perception of it as a 'soft art'. Wilson's Chief Whip (1966–9) had fostered friendly relations with backbenchers, trying to persuade them of the leadership's line. As in Smith's case, the approach failed to prevent large Parliamentary rebellions, but it mitigated their impact (Shaw, 1988: 161).

But woe betide anyone who stepped over the mark. In such circumstances, Smith would turn into more of an old-fashioned tribal politician, reminding errant backbenchers of where their loyalties should lie. When a Labour backbencher tried to put a motion on a controversial matter to the PLP, Doug Hoyle, the PLP Chairman, failed to dissuade him. Smith said to Hoyle he'd handle the matter. To Hoyle's surprise, the rebel MP backed down. Hoyle asked Smith, 'How on earth did you do that?' Smith apparently replied, 'I threatened to throw the wardrobe at him' (interview with Alan Howarth).

If Smith knew how to handle the PLP, he was almost clueless when it came to dealing with the NEC. As Derek Foster, Smith's Chief Whip, recalls:

> Neil [Kinnock] knew the geography of the Party, where power was diffused within the unions. ... John was never terribly interested in that side of the Party, didn't understand how the Party operated, and therefore he occasionally got impatient with the NEC.
>
> (Interview with Derek Foster)

As has already been noted, Smith had no previous experience of the NEC on becoming leader, but he was lucky in that Kinnock had fought and won many of the hardest battles against the hard left. The NEC was now a different animal from the early 1980s. Votes were regularly won by 21 votes to 2, with only Dennis Skinner and Tony Benn voting against Smith's line. Larry Whitty confirms that it helped Smith enormously that he was never short of a majority on the NEC, and that the party was now in calmer times: 'Whereas John didn't want to interfere, Neil had to' (interview with Larry Whitty). Given his inexperience, Smith left Murray Elder in charge of co-ordinating the trade union elements within the NEC. In fact, real power over policy formulation had shifted away from the NEC to policy review groups, the new Joint Policy Committees (JPCs) and the National Policy Forum (NPF), which Smith launched in November 1992. Since the NPF had no power to initiate policy, and could only recommend changes to JPC positions, and since Smith chaired the JPC, power had shifted away from the NEC and into the hands of the leader. Writing in 1993, Peter Shore rightly concluded: 'No previous leader has enjoyed such personal and institutionalised control over party policy' (Shore, 1997: 180). Mark Wickham-Jones agrees that 'John Smith inherited a party structure in 1992 in which the authority of the leader was again paramount' (Wickham-Jones, 1996: 205).

Emotional intelligence

Probably Smith's greatest asset as a leader was his total self-confidence. Whereas his predecessor had a more sensitive personality, John harboured none of these insecurities. He was a normal member of the human race. In today's parlance, he would be known as a 'people person'. Smith used his personality to weld together a Shadow Cabinet of very differing personalities into an effective team. As Margaret Beckett explains:

> John was an unusual mixture of a team player and a team leader. There was no doubt that he was the one in charge. He had that rare quality of absolute self-confidence, but it was a naturally unassuming self-confidence. He was so confident in his own abilities, so secure in himself that he didn't need to feel challenged by anyone else in the team.
>
> (Interview with Margaret Beckett)

The upper echelons of the Shadow Cabinet comprised people as diverse as Robin Cook, Gordon Brown and John Prescott, none of whom got on particularly well with one another, but all of whom, quite remarkably, served reasonably happily under Smith.

As has been documented many times before, much of Smith's politics was conducted in the tearoom and bars of the House of Commons, or late into the night at Labour Party and trade union conferences. Smith was always willing to listen and made even the lowliest Labour official or backbencher feel wanted. As Frank Dobson recalls, 'John was a talkaholic; you could distract John just by having a talk with him' (interview with Frank Dobson). Hilary Armstong remembers numerous occasions when Smith would simply wander off in the House of Commons, and be found eventually speaking to the most unlikely person (interview with Hilary Armstrong). Quite simply, Smith remembered people. In West of Scotland parlance, he left 'wee mindings' for people everywhere he went, whether it was a box of chocolates for a hard-working constituency worker, or an invitation to an elderly Harold Wilson, now suffering from dementia, to a Labour Party reception. It is debatable whether this was a deliberate strategy on the part of Smith, or simply a natural trait. Under Kinnock's leadership, Smith had taken great care not to offend people. One of the Scottish Labour MPs at the time compared Smith's method of picking up allies as akin to 'climbing a mountain, leaving a bit of iron rations at staging posts along the way' (interview with Frank Dobson).

Therefore, under John Smith, and in contrast to both Neil Kinnock and Tony Blair, a more tolerant and inclusive leadership style was operated. Eric Shaw agrees:

> His [Smith's] style of leadership was more collegial, conciliatory and consensual than this predecessor, displaying a greater willingness to give leeway to Shadow Cabinet colleagues and to seek solutions which accommodated the various points of view within the Party.
>
> (Shaw, 1994: 224)

Conclusion

In conclusion, Smith's short period as Leader of the Opposition from 1992 to 1994 witnessed substantial policy reform in the shape of OMOV, but the pace of reform undoubtedly slowed compared to the frenetic pace of the Kinnock and Blair leaders. That should not surprise anyone: rarely does a reformer follow on from another reformer. There is often a pause in between.

Smith was a skilled House of Commons debater, but performed less well as a platform speaker. He excelled as a party manager, because of his strong people skills, and modelled himself on Labour unifiers like Wilson and Callaghan. In many respects, Smith was the last old-fashioned Labour Leader of the Opposition, blissfully and naïvely unaware of the impact that the advent of the 24-hour media was about to have on modern politics. His untimely death in May 1994 gave the Labour Party a unique chance to refresh and renew itself under Tony Blair, a dynamic new leader who was more comfortable with the media demands of being Leader of the Opposition.

13
Tony Blair, 1994–7

Stuart McAnulla

Occupying the position of Leader of the Opposition has often been described as the hardest job in British politics. Lacking executive power, and the resources of government, Leaders of the Opposition nonetheless have to attempt to both effectively challenge the current incumbents and present themselves as alternative Prime Ministers. Few Leaders of the Opposition have achieved these goals so comprehensively as Tony Blair did in his relatively brief period as Opposition Leader between July 1994 and May 1997. Indeed, by 1996 Blair had established a position of extraordinary political dominance in British politics, being widely seen as Prime Minister-in-waiting with consistently large opinion poll leads over the governing Conservative Party.

In many respects, Blair's inheritance upon becoming Leader of the Labour Party in 1994 was fortuitous. He followed a predecessor, John Smith, who had quietly guided the party on from the disappointment of the 1992 General Election defeat to establish itself as a credible contender for power. Under both Neil Kinnock and John Smith, reforms of Labour Party structure had given both greater autonomy and power to the leadership, and party policy had been transformed in a mainstream direction since the calamitous electoral defeat in 1983 (Driver and Martell, 2002: 6). Importantly, sterling's dramatic exit from the European Exchange Mechanism (ERM) in September 1992 had badly damaged the Conservatives' reputation for governing competence, and survey data suggested that Labour had become the party the public most trusted on economic affairs. Additionally, John Major's party had become deeply split over the issue of European integration, with internal division frequently spilling over into public spats. Major himself was often blamed for being unable to unite the party, and the Conservatives stumbled from crisis to crisis between 1992 and 1997 (Heppell, 2006).

This conjuncture of circumstances presented Blair with an excellent political context in which to present himself and his party as worthy of regaining office. At the same time, there were less convenient aspects to the challenges facing Blair. He was taking charge of a party that had lost four

General Elections in a row and whose 'core' support had been in long-term decline (Cronin, 2004: 402). The party had long been in an intellectually defensive position, struggling to find a response to the Thatcherite reforms of British politics that could achieve sustained public resonance. Though the party had recovered under Smith, there was no guarantee that this momentum would be sustained into a General Election campaign; indeed the party had seen many big poll leads melt away during fifteen years of Opposition. Blair himself had become leader at the age of only 41, with no previous practical experience of governing at any level. The high public profile he had established as Shadow Home Secretary under Smith was a major factor in quick ascendancy to the leadership, but he had been chosen more for his perceived potential electability rather than deep affection for him within the party. Though he had established a reputation for being willing to be 'tough' on public policy issues, as an individual he was still viewed by many as possessing a soft underbelly, hence the nickname 'Bambi' appeared. Thus as he inherited the leadership Blair had much to prove to his party, the wider electorate and indeed himself.

His approach to being Opposition Leader was shaped by his particular understanding of recent trends in British politics. In particular, he was convinced of the irreversibility of many of the far-reaching changes introduced by the Conservatives under Margaret Thatcher. Moreover, Thatcher's success and her decisive, conviction-oriented leadership had a strong influence on his own approach as a leader (Seldon, 2004). Blair was persuaded of the idea that in a newly deregulated economy the role of government had indeed altered to become one of being less concerned with direct interventions and more with ways of enabling individuals to compete in a global market. He was convinced that too many in the Labour Party were insufficiently in tune with these supposed new realities, and thus that preparing the party to regain office would involve considerable reforming energy and drive on behalf of the leadership. As an established member of Labour's 'modernising' tendency he believed that the approach that had been adopted by John Smith was too passive, and that further reform was necessary to fully convince people that Labour merited returning to office (Mandelson, 2010).

Emotional intelligence

Blair's period as Opposition Leader was greatly focused on the project of securing public trust in him both as a person and leader. He grasped that in an era in which ideological divisions were less pronounced than in the past, and where many more voters felt no strong loyalties to particular parties, issues of leadership and trust were becoming even more important to political competition. This context presented challenges that in many ways Blair was well-placed to meet, since he had long been someone who looked to gain recognition and popularity among others. In his younger years Blair had appeared in theatre and had his own rock band. Like many politicians who have risen to prominence, it is possible to explain Blair's drive for popularity in part with reference to his childhood and adolescent years. The death of his mother and illness of his father while he was still young may help account both for the approval that he sought through public life (Ahmed, 2003), as well the inner strength he displayed during stressful periods of his leadership. However, although the young Blair was skilled at ingratiating himself with others, he also had a rebellious streak and a willingness to question established orthodoxies. He was once threatened with expulsion from Fettes College, his independent senior school, and while at university he regarded himself as something of a social 'outsider' (Rentoul, 2001). Even when winning the Labour leadership in 1994, he retained something of these characteristics, since he had neither been a long-standing member of the Labour movement, nor did he venerate its complex traditions. Psychologically, he was well suited to the role of arch-party moderniser, willing to challenge conventions he thought archaic or politically disadvantageous, without undue concern regarding the internal hostility this might provoke. He was viewed by many (including himself) as having the kind critical distance from the party to discern what it had to do to win new support from 'middle England'.

Blair's efforts in this regard were founded upon huge reserves of self-confidence. Despite his young age and lack of governing experience Blair had challenged for the Labour leadership, even though he knew how much this move would upset his more senior ally, and would-be leader, Gordon Brown. An eerie recollection in Blair's memoirs describes how, shortly before John Smith died, Blair had a 'premonition' that Smith would suddenly die and that he would become leader (Blair, 2010: 61). Blair's charisma made a strong impression on Parliamentary colleagues, many of whom were quick to encourage him to challenge for the leadership when the opportunity suddenly arose. His self-belief was a great asset in his confrontations with the then Conservative Prime Minister John Major. Major was unsettled by the faith Blair displayed in his own abilities, something he resentfully attributed to the comparatively privileged education Blair had received (Foley, 2002: 15). However, while Blair was suitably combative in the House of Commons, in his interpersonal relations he tried to avoid protracted personal confrontations. Blair had risen within the party largely because of his perceived skills and charm, rather than through background manoeuvring or factionalism. He was not accustomed to, and had little appetite for, feuds and personal plots. He always found the process of disappointing people through Shadow Cabinet reshuffles difficult, and he tried to stay above the personal wrangles than often ensued between his close allies. Jonathan Powell argues that Blair was 'the master of constructive ambiguity', recounting how he managed to tell Jack Cunningham that his Shadow Cabinet role was changing, without the latter properly realising what had happened until hearing about it on television afterwards (Powell, 2010: 54). However, Blair was also aware that his modernising agenda would always create friction and opposition within the party, and so he looked to appoint people around him who could handle such pressure for him. He chose Alistair Campbell as his Chief of Communications not just for his media skills but because of his ability to be tough, or 'a hard nut' (Blair, 2010: 75), in the face both of the media and oppositional tendencies within the party.

Blair's deep belief in the essential correctness of his project for reforming the party was, however, qualified by an enduring anxiety concerning whether Labour would, in the end, win power (Seldon, 2004: 238). The public's apparent continuing suspicion of Labour on issues such as taxation played heavily on Blair's mind. The fear of losing the next General Election conditioned his entire three years as Opposition Leader. Even when Blair accrued huge leads in the opinion polls, and received widespread media plaudits, such good news fed anxiety that that the gains may be superficial, and could evaporate if and when the Conservative Party orchestrated a determined fight-back. Such anxiety could manifest itself in the form of high demands on his close colleagues (Campbell and Hagerty, 2010: 481) and in intensely concerned phone calls or notes to close advisers (Mandelson, 2010). However, Blair's unease also helps account for his high-energy approach to Opposition leadership, in particular his regular search to make moves or public signals aimed at assuaging residual public concerns about Labour. Paradoxically, Blair's moves to provide the electorate with reassurance that he was a safe pair of hands inspired him to take political risks that some might have deemed unnecessary, such as the change to Clause IV of the Labour Party Constitution (Powell, 2010: 33) (see discussion below). Yet Blair was of the firm belief that the leader had to be the author of party direction, indeed that he should personify the theme of 'change'.

Blair's perceived dynamism and youthful vigour were assets in his attempts to win goodwill from other political and media elites (M. Temple, 2006: 43). One of Blair's biggest concerns was the role that the right-wing press could potentially play in defeating Labour. Thus Blair believed it well worthwhile to court media baron Rupert Murdoch in the hope that his newspapers would give Labour a fairer deal in future political coverage than they had in the past. Again, Blair was taking a risk that not only might fail, but could provoke a hostile reaction from the left, many of whom regarded Murdoch as a political anti-Christ. Blair's success in winning Murdoch's backing was not merely the product of Blair's personal charm and carefully crafted speech to NewsCorp representatives at Hayman Island (Blair, 1995a). It also owed much to the fact that Blair genuinely did admire the kind of entrepreneurial success that Murdoch embodied and shared with him a desire for a 'true meritocracy' without prejudice against business (Rentoul, 2001: 780). More generally, Blair was inclined to be impressed by high achievers in the business and celebrity world, and did not shy from opportunities to associate himself with such individuals when politically expedient. The fact that Blair felt so at home in such company may be one reason he often became described as a 'celebrity' politician himself who would be associated with the fleeting mid-to-late 1990s cultural theme of 'Cool Britannia'.

Blair's interpersonal relations with other politicians were more mixed in their character. He was not considered a particularly 'clubbable' politician, and Parliamentary colleagues could sometimes find him distant and non-empathetic. He would sometimes lack sustained interest in the views of others, and had a 'sometimes maddeningly laid-back approach to policy discussion and decision-making' (Mandelson, 2010: 199). However, when he was so-minded Blair was capable of cultivating good relations across political dividing lines, most notably perhaps in his friendship with the leader of the Liberal Democrats, Paddy Ashdown. Blair looked to establish cordial relations with Ashdown in part, again, because he was so concerned that in the end Labour might struggle to win an overall Parliamentary majority. Thus Blair looked to lay the ground for a potential partnership between Labour and the Liberal Democrats in the event of a hung Parliament. However, the move was also a product of Blair's resistance to excessive Labour tribalism, which he felt had contributed to an unhelpful split between the two 'progressive' parties in the twentieth century. Blair's encouragement was a factor in Ashdown's decision to abandon the Liberal Democrats' policy of political 'equidistance' between the two main parties and to begin co-operating with Labour in collective discussions on plans for constitutional reform. Blair was skilful in tantalising Ashdown with the prospect of possible radical electoral reform following the 1997 General Election, without ever actually committing himself to supporting such a change (Ashdown, 2001). Though Ashdown was to later feel let down by Blair on this issue, the shared 'anti-Tory' emphasis of both parties in the lead-up to the 1997 election would bring significant gains for each (Russell and Fieldhouse, 2005: 198).

Blair had complex relations with his small team of advisers and close colleagues. His working 'den' was always affected by jealousies and rivalries, and thus he would take care to try to ensure people did not feel marginalised. In this regard Blair demonstrated considerable patience, being prepared to indulge tantrums and personal spats because of the high value he placed on the views of his team. He would endure Peter Mandelson's frequent 'walk outs' and Gordon Brown's erratic behaviour as he was convinced that both were huge assets to his project. So sensitive was Blair to Brown's bruised feelings on losing out on the leadership that he would even sometimes defer to Brown's judgement in arguments in the effort to keep him onside. In his everyday dealings with Alistair Campbell he would have extremely frank exchanges of views and even endure the occasional dressing-down (Campbell and Hagerty, 2010). Thus while in public Blair was quickly shedding his lightweight 'Bambi' image, and insisting in iron discipline within the wider party, in private he would put up with a good deal of adolescent behaviour.

Public policy platform

Tony Blair's impact on Labour policy while in Opposition was somewhat paradoxical. He became credited with having introduced radical change to the party's positions on key issues and preparing a credible policy platform for Labour's return to government. Yet, arguably Labour entered the 1997 General Election with few specific policy commitments and a set of rather vague aspirations. As Shadow Home Secretary, Blair had caught public attention by seeming to signal a shift in Labour thinking on crime, famously pledging to 'be tough on crime, tough on the causes of crime'. However, despite his overt stance as a hyper-moderniser, during his election campaign for the Labour leadership, Blair gave only limited ideas as to how he might seek to develop party policy. His leadership manifesto, *Change and National Renewal*, offered little fresh thinking (Riddell, 2005: 25). However, his campaign did introduce a moral perspective with a traditionalist stress on the importance of family life and respect in communities.

Blair was often accused of lacking substance, that he lacked clear conviction or ideological vision. An assessment of Blair's approach is complicated by the fact that he was 'one of the most porous politicians of modern times' (Foley, 2002: 241), willing to listen to new ideas and seeking to absorb elements of public opinion into policy calculations. Both Blair and fellow party modernisers were so concerned about voters' continuing mistrust of the Labour Party that a great deal of his time was spent emphasising the kinds of policies they would *not* introduce. Thus Blair would continuously seek to affirm that in Government he would not favour high taxation, nationalisation or excessively liberal social policies. As is discussed below, further effort was devoted to stressing the moderate and costed nature of any firm policy proposals they did make. However, Blair was also sensitive to the criticism that having jettisoned so much of previous Labour policy, the party now lacked a coherent guiding vision. Faltering attempts were made to plug this gap, though the common charge that Blair was primarily a power-seeker who lacked any distinctive guiding philosophy never disappeared.

For a brief period Blair appeared to endorse the idea of 'stakeholding', a term that was promoted by economists such as John Kay and the centre-left journalist Will Hutton (particularly in Hutton's best-selling book published in 1995, *The State We're In*). Hutton argued that companies should not be considered the exclusive domain of shareholders, but rather institutions that employees and customers had a direct 'stake' in. Stakeholding appeared to offer a concept through which Blair could convey both a critique of a Thatcherite obsession with profit, alongside an inclusive discourse that went beyond any outdated Labour notion of bosses versus workers. However, the way the term 'stake-holding' was quickly dropped exposed much about the cautious mind-set of both Blair and his Shadow Chancellor, Gordon Brown. Stake-holding was interpreted by some critics as resurrecting 1970s corporatism, and some business leaders were concerned that wider involvement in company affairs would undermine management. Blair quickly dropped reference to the term to avoid any risk that a more radical interpretation of what he actually intended by the concept could gain salience.

A more enduring concept in Blair's repertoire was that of community (Prideaux, 2005). As a firm Christian in his private life, Blair was attracted to ideas within Christian socialism, in particular the emphasis on responsibility to others and the community. He occasionally referenced Christian themes when challenging Thatcherite individualism, telling the Party Conference in 1995, 'I am my brother's keeper'. Blair drew upon themes from communitarian philosophy as part of the effort to distance himself from what he saw as the failures of both the traditional left and the new right (Bevir, 2005). In particular the communitarian emphasis on 'rights *and* responsibilities' was drawn upon to make clear Blair's unease with both the selfish materialism sometimes associated with Thatcherism, and also his discomfort with the excessively rights-oriented agenda associated with sections of the left. However, in important respects Blair followed through on the earlier intellectual moves by party modernisers under John Smith and Neil Kinnock. For example, Blair's approach to issues of social exclusion drew upon the work of the party's Social Justice Commission, which reported in 1994. The report provided grounds for rejecting both a Thatcherite 'deregulatory' approach to social issues and a more traditionally left-wing emphasis on levelling outcomes and incomes. Blair concurred with the report's advocacy of an 'investment' approach, which emphasised how individuals could be helped to prosper though access to training, education and other measures to include people in civil society.

On the economy, Blair was convinced that Labour had to ditch any residual aspirations for further state control of industry and to make the party's embrace of market capitalism overt and enthusiastic. In acknowledgement of his expertise the area, and broadly shared views, he was content to allow Gordon Brown to have a large degree of autonomy in formulating the details of economic policy. Both Blair and Brown came to believe that in an era of 'globalisation' traditional forms of intervening in the economy were being made obsolete by the growth of global competition and the integration of money markets (Hay, 1999). In many ways this involved an acceptance that much of what the Thatcher and Major Governments had done in economic terms was correct (Heffernan, 2001). In fact Blair's team began to discuss ways of further ensuring stability and low inflation through rules-based measures, including giving the Bank of England operational independence to set interest rates (although these plans were kept secret while in Opposition) (Blair, 2010: 89). However, Blair believed that social democratic goals of empowering individuals could be achieved with a new national emphasis on education and training, thus developing the 'supply side' of the economy. Thus while the state would eschew old-style Keynesian approaches, it would nonetheless be 'active' or 'enabling' in preparing people to compete successfully in the global market place. Blair was particularly keen to both reassure, and to attract new support from, the business community for Labour's plans. He spoke regularly to business leaders and city financiers, and businesses were invited to sponsor Labour Party Conference events. Aware of residual scepticism of Labour on economic matters, Blair devoted much of his time to spelling out the kinds of economic policies Labour would relinquish. In the effort to dispel the party's 'tax and spend' reputation, he made repeated criticisms of the tax-hikes being introduced by John Major's Government. On this issue Blair was even more conservative than his already highly cautious economic team. Blair overruled the proposal put forward by Shadow Chancellor Gordon Brown and his adviser Ed Balls that Labour should leave open the option of raising the top rate of personal taxation to 50p (Riddell, 2005: 32). By the time of the 1997 Election, Blair was explicitly promising that in Government he would cut corporation tax; introduce no increases in personal taxation; and would stick to the spending plans laid out by the Conservative Government for the first two years of its term.

Many of Blair's hopes for improving economic and social conditions under a Labour Government appeared to rest in improvements in education. Indeed at the Labour Party Conference in 1995 he famously declared that his three priorities would be 'education, education, education'. Despite the party's enduring popularity on educational issues, this was an area that caused several problems during Blair's years in Opposition. Blair signalled bold intentions for education policy through appointing as Shadow Education Minister David Blunkett, who, though emanating from the party's 'soft left', was rather traditionalist and conservative in his views on education and social issues. A key issue was the extent to which Labour should continue with the Conservative approach of stressing parental 'choice' and enabling schools to opt out of local authority control. These reforms continued to be opposed by many in the Labour Party on the grounds that they were likely to produce greater inequality of provision. To some extent both Blair and Blunkett sought to side-step the issue by declaring that 'standards, not structures' were what mattered and that improvement could be driven by planned initiatives such as those to improve literacy and numeracy skills in young children.

However, Blair's decision to send his son Euan to a prestigious grant-maintained school, the London Oratory, provoked widespread charges of hypocrisy. Yet Blair used the incident to signal that he was ultimately in favour of parental choice before political considerations, a view he reinforced when he refused to sack Shadow Minister Harriet Harman when she sent her son to a selective grammar school. The latter incident was testament to how far Blair would be willing to trust his own political instincts on issues if he felt there was a risk in alienating potential middle-class voters. Indeed Blair was 'in a minority of one' within his immediate office circles in defending Harman's decision, yet he believed sacking her would not only be wrong but would be viewed as out of touch with the everyday inclinations of key voters who look to provide their children with the best education possible (Blair, 2010: 88). Blair's willingness to upset educationists and teachers was further demonstrated by new policy commitments to close 'failing schools' and to rebrand grant-maintained schools as 'foundation schools' rather than return them to full local authority control.

In other policy areas Labour's plans tended to be less well-defined. Blair reinforced Labour's long-standing defence of the National Health Service, voicing opposition to development of the 'internal market' under the Major Government (Blair, 1996). He pledged to end the purchaser–provider split, yet the autonomy of trust hospitals would be maintained. Blair emphasised that Labour aspired to put much further investment into the NHS, but as with education this was always made with the caveat that this could only happen 'as resources allow' from economic growth. On welfare, the key policy initiative was the 'New Deal', a scheme that would give young unemployed the opportunity to take work or training. Controversially, if claimants did not 'exercise responsibility' and take up this offer they would lose benefits. The proposal was in part about signalling the party's new conceptualisation of welfare not as a means of simply distributing benefits, but rather a mechanism to support people to return to, or gain work. In fact Blair was worried about Gordon Brown's plans to finance the scheme through a one-off windfall tax on the privatised utilities (fearing it might tarnish efforts to ditch the party's tax-and-spend image), but in the end agreed to the measure.

Indeed Blair was not able to totally dominate party policy. He was relatively unenthusiastic, and in respects sceptical, about the plans for constitutional reform that had been established under John Smith. Yet he carried forward the party's commitments to introduce devolution in Scotland and Wales, a Freedom of Information Act and a referendum on electoral reform. This was done with caution, so, for example, in the case of Scottish devolution the party's position was modified to state that it would only occur if the Scottish public voted 'yes' in a referendum, and the new Scottish Parliament would only have modest tax-raising powers if ratified in a separate referendum question. Rather than heralding Labour's constitutional plans as revolutionary, Blair preferred to present them under the more neutral heading of the 'modernisation' of government. Caution and conservatism dominated Blair's approach to policy commitments to an extent that may have been counterproductive in the long term. Seldon (2004) reports how little practical policy development occurred in many areas during the period, and Blair himself has since argued that not enough was done in Opposition to prepare the ground for policies in Government (2010). However, at the time, the overriding objective for new Labour was winning office, and the general philosophy was that being sparse with detailed policy plans would help deprive the Conservatives of the ammunition they needed to mount a political fight-back.

Party management

Several concerns animated Blair's approach to party management. First was Blair's belief that the party as a whole was not sufficiently representative of wider public opinion. Low party membership was one manifestation of this, but more generally Blair was concerned that activists were insufficiently tuned into the concerns of regular people. Second, Blair believed that reforms of the party were an important part of presenting Labour explicitly as a party of the 'centre and centre left'. As is discussed below, Blair believed that the party had to be *seen* to be changing, rather than to merely claim that it had. Finally, Blair's approach to party management was shaped by a clear view of his own role as leader. He strongly believed that he should have a firm grip on the affairs of the party, and should cajole or even drag the party in the modernising direction he favoured. In these efforts he was aided by the way power had been centralised towards the leader in the Kinnock–Smith years, yet he wanted to secure even greater autonomy for the leadership within party structures.

Blair's decision to replace Clause IV of the Party Constitution was motivated in part by a desire to give the party 'electric shock treatment' (Gould, 1998: 218). An enduring concern for Blair was the fear that although he enjoyed considerable public popularity, his mission could be undone if opponents could demonstrate that his views and attitudes were far different from those of the wider Labour Party. This potential 'head and body' problem (Rentoul, 2001: 252) convinced Blair that he had to find a way to publicly indicate that the wider party were on board with his changes. Removing what many members had considered a key symbolic part of Labour's Constitution, with its commitment to 'common ownership' of industry, was viewed as a way of definitively showing that the mind-set of the party had changed. Blair knew that as the newly elected leader his political capital within the party might never be higher, and so he took the opportunity in his first full Conference speech to initiate the process of change. The risks involved with such a move were made clear when later at the same Conference a vote was taken ratifying the existing Clause IV. Yet Blair pressed ahead by announcing a national series of debates and discussions within the party regarding whether and how to replace the clause. The scale of work needed to ensure victory was made clear when the Labour group of Members of the European Parliament came out opposing change (*Herald*, 10.1.1995), as did some trade unions. However, Blair approached the campaign for change with energy and helped mobilise modernising tendencies within the party to make the case for reform. In addition to making the intellectual case for change, he could also appeal to the fact that as a new leader he had put his head on the block and needed support if his leadership were not to come to a quick end. Here he made use of the loyalty of his initially reluctant Deputy, John Prescott, to help make the case for change to sections of the party that were intrinsically sceptical towards Blair. The vote by the more traditionalist Scottish Labour Party in favour of change in March 1995 signalled that Blair was going to win nationally, as was confirmed a month later at a special Party Conference.

Blair's efforts to make the party more representative of public opinion also involved a membership drive. The recruitment success of his own local party in Sedgefield indicated to Blair that it was possible to broaden the party membership and also to reduce the domination of small cliques of activists. Indeed, under John Prescott's management, the party did manage to buck long-term decline in party membership, and numbers rose from 305,000 members in 1994 to 405,000 in 1997 (Marshall, 2009). Again, Blair saw not just the benefits for the party in terms of organisation and support, but also with regard to public perceptions. Indeed, he would claim that New Labour was almost 'literally a new party'. He was also keen to ensure that the broader membership were able and seen to give direct endorsement of the approach of the leadership, not just through having a vote on the Clause IV change, but also in a vote in 1996 to endorse the Draft Manifesto for the General Election.

The involvement of members in the policy process was also subject to significant change through the *Partnership in Power* reforms (Shaw, 2004). Blair was particularly concerned that previous Labour Governments had been embarrassed by the fact that Party Conferences would frequently vote against Government policy, thus projecting an image of disunity and internal division. Thus the Blair leadership proposed a more deliberative style of policy discussion within the party, incorporating its different sections, but enabling a rolling programme of discussions prior to any actual decisions at Conference. Crucially, no policies could be brought forward that contradicted actual or planned Labour Government policies. These reforms provoked bitterness and resentment within sections of the party, but were eventually accepted before the 1997 General Election (Cronin, 2004: 390).

Blair had little patience with factional battles within the party, or indeed deal-making or fixes. Party colleagues could find him 'unsociable, distant, direct and intolerant' (Foley, 2002: 156) in his approach to negotiation, and he had a tendency to view opposing opinions as inherently backward or insensitive to the electoral project of New Labour. His distrust of much of the party was reflected in his tendency to rely on a select group of colleagues for support and frank discussion. This group included Jonathan Powell (Chief of Staff), Alistair Campbell (Press Secretary), Peter Mandelson (adviser), Anji Hunter (Office Secretary) and, more problematically, Gordon Brown

(Shadow Chancellor). His revisionist outlook was also reflected in his choice of wider advisers, which included people who had previously left the party to join the breakaway SDP in the 1980s, such as Roger Liddle and Roy Jenkins. Indeed, Blair's approach to managing the party was in many ways vanguardist, with a leadership elite convinced of its own far-sightedness, driving the agenda and largely ensuring that this approach was adhered to in a disciplined way by the wider party. Andrew Rawnsley suggests that this 'control-freakery' (as it would become known) 'was a brittle carapace around a profound insecurity at the heart of the project and the personalities who shaped it' (Rawnsley, 2001: xiv). However, Blair's approach did provoke criticism, in particular for the way in which he had empowered individuals such as Alistair Campbell to take an often brutal approach to ensuring that colleagues remained sufficiently 'on message'. Claire Short spoke out against 'people who live in the dark' around Blair (Blick, 2004), a theme that was picked up too by the Conservatives when they sought to present New Labour as spin-obsessed and dangerously manipulative. Blair also had to clamp down on problems with Shadow Cabinet members leaking information or giving secret briefings (Blair, 2010: 102). However, set in the context of Labour Party politics in the 1970s and 1980s, what was striking about the Blair period was the absence of public splits and internal rows, with Blair in a position of exceptional dominance to assert his will upon the party. Significantly, for Blair party management was not just a matter of establishing efficient internal relations, it was also part of his wider goal of effective public communication.

Public communication

Next to the goal of winning the next General Election, effective public communication was arguably the defining objective of Blair's period as Opposition Leader. After the ERM crash in 1992, some in the party assumed that they could return to power via a 'one more heave' strategy of projecting leadership competence. However, Blair and his allies did not subscribe to this philosophy and were convinced that much more would need to be done to shift perceptions of the party among swing voters. Blair's approach had two essential components: (1) to make it abundantly clear to the public that the Labour Party had changed, and (2) to reassure voters that their interests would not be threatened by electing Blair as Prime Minister.

Blair's approach to political communication was shaped by several factors. One of these was the success in the United States of Bill Clinton's 'New' Democrats, who successfully overcame a long period of right-wing hegemony by being elected in 1992 (Gould, 1998). The way in which Clinton had repeatedly spelled out in obvious terms what was distinct about his politics as compared with traditional Democrats had a clear influence on the development of 'New' Labour. Blair built upon the more professional political communications that had developed under Neil Kinnock, and gave a key role to party pollster Philip Gould. The latter would seek to provide Blair with regular information on the concerns and perceptions of possible 'Tory switchers', thus helping Blair target his messages to the fears and aspirations of potentially crucial voters. Crucially, Blair's messages would be 'market-tested' so see how they were likely to be received, and sometimes tailored or revised in light of this information. Some argue that Blair's time as Opposition Leader witnessed the birth of the 'permanent campaign' (Riddell, 2005: 21) in Britain, with the leadership focused on public opinion and good communication with an intensity that traditionally only really happened around the General Election period.

In addition to the symbolism of changing Clause IV, Blair found other ways to make clear to the wider population how the party had changed. He managed to unofficially rename the party as 'New' Labour, initially through making this slogan the backdrop of the 1994 Party Conference. This marked another attempted to symbolise the way in which Labour had broken with its past, and had ditched the unpopular aspects of 'old' Labour (Coates, 2005: 27). This proved a very effective strategy as the phrase New Labour quickly passed into popular discourse on British politics. However, as Cronin notes, this move was not only about enhancing the party's electoral appeal, it was also a way of communicating the Blair leadership's refusal to concede the party's past to the interpretations favoured by party traditionalists (Cronin, 2004: 399).

A key element of Blair's approach to communication was to emphasise his own role as leader of the party, and to make himself central to the party's campaign imagery. In this regard his sought to project a type of 'presidential' appeal, someone who could be trusted because he was not particularly embroiled in the traditions of the party. Blair himself records:

> At every stage of this (and the decisions came pretty fast and furious) I was reconciled to fighting, and to leaving if I lost. The party had to know I was not bluffing. If they didn't want New Labour, they would get someone else. The country had to know that if I was going to be their prime minister, I would be 'of the party' but removed from it.
>
> (2010: 94–5)

This style was reflected in Blair's oratory, which would sometimes notably refer to himself in the first person and his audience in the third. He would not seek to dispel perceptions that he was the exclusive author of the party's direction, joking thus about how commentary about him had changed in his early months as leader: 'Last year I was Bambi. This year I'm Stalin. From Disneyland to dictatorship in twelve short months' (Blair, 1995b). Battles against sections of the party (for example, opposition to Blair's stance on education, see above) that resisted change were used as a means to seeking to reassure the public that they could at least trust Blair even if still harbouring doubts about elements of the party. Policy stances were directed with this goal in mind – for example, Blair scrapped the annual opposition of the party to renewing counter-terrorism legislation, helping quell any efforts to portray the party as 'soft' on terrorism. When the General Election approached, Blair drew upon focus group research that highlighted voters' concerns about politicians over-promising and failing to deliver. Thus the party released its 'five pledges' card, which committed New Labour to introduce only modest, costed reforms, such as reducing class sizes for primary school children.

More generally, Blair's success as Opposition Leader owed much to the way in which he could project himself to the electorate in a way that engendered trust. He achieved this in part through establishing himself as a statesman, through actions including the initiatives highlighted above. Blair also generally performed very well during Prime Minister's Question Time in the House of Commons, often out-scoring the troubled John Major. Blair used his skills as a barrister to command the attention of the chamber and to harry Major with a combination of sharp questions and witty reflections. He took full advantage of the Tories' splits on issues such as Europe and the eruption of numerous 'sleaze' incidents, at one point quipping resonantly, 'I lead my party, he follows his!' (HC Debates 1994–5, vol. 258, col. 256). Moreover, Blair would repeatedly return to questions of governing competence, exploiting Conservative failure over the ERM crash and playing to perceptions that Major had proved a weak, indecisive successor to Margaret Thatcher.

Perhaps Blair's greatest strength as a political communicator was also being able to combine this statesman-like appeal with an ability to come across as in touch with the wider public. Blair was particularly adept at cultivating a sense of 'closeness, intimacy and charm' (Grainger, 2005: 4), conveying himself as someone who spoke the language of ordinary people and shared their concerns. Blair's objective was in part to 'generate an identification of equivalence, rather than of some greater ideal to which we aspire' (Finlayson, 2003: 54). With Alistair Campbell's guidance he appeared on several popular television shows in which he could present himself to millions of viewers in a relaxed, apolitical context, unmediated by the interpretations of journalists or media commentators (Campbell and Hagerty, 2010: 304). Keen never to offend, Blair made use of his youthful charisma to generate an appeal that reached far beyond those groups of voters who might normally seriously consider voting Labour. He was prepared for, and indeed courted, the kind of intense scrutiny to which a potential Prime Minister in modern politics might expect. To this extent Blair knew he had to be eternally vigilant in every appearance, utterance and signal he gave throughout his period as Opposition. Although he was conscious of having to wear a metaphorical strait-jacket, he possessed an easy charm and (ostensibly at least) relaxed manner, which was not only able to withstand such tests but often to do so with flair. Though his messages were well prepared and carefully thought through, Blair also had an ability to spontaneously respond to awkward questions in a manner that could chime with the sensibilities of key voters. Blair knew that if he could continue to pass such examinations of his character this would go a long way to convincing the electorate that they could trust New Labour with their vote.

Conclusion

Thus Blair's tenure as Opposition was marked by a mix of bold moves and symbolic gestures, alongside a highly cautious approach to policy and campaigning. In some ways Blair's approach defied established theories that Oppositions win power by holding steady, appearing competent and capitalising on a government's mistakes. Blair certainly achieved these latter goals, but firmly believed that given Labour's recent past, a more profound recasting of the party's image was required. For many, Labour's landslide victory at the 1997 General Election provided vindication of the approach Blair adopted as Opposition Leader. Labour's win laid the ground for a thirteen-year period in office and a ten-year reign for Tony Blair as Prime Minister. Yet some on the left thought the price of success had been too high, arguing that under Blair little or nothing now remained of the socialist politics that had given the party historical purpose. In this view Blair's progress resulted from his effective surrender to the interests of powerful elites and neo-liberal economics. Others worried that under Blair a rather reactionary 'cult of leadership' had been established, reinforcing trends towards 'celebrity politics' and the victory of personal style over political substance. More measured critics voiced concern about the way political debate had been stifled through the constant emphasis on maintaining discipline in the party.

But were such sacrifices necessary for the project of winning back power? Was Blair's dynamic, highly personalised approach to leadership a necessary precondition of victory, or could a more conciliatory, John Smith-style of leadership also have proven electorally successful? It seems likely that Labour would not have obtained such an overwhelming electoral victory with another leader. What was most remarkable about Blair's achievement in Opposition was his ability to reach out to and attract support from people who would not previously have considered voting Labour. This owed much to Blair's own personal magnetism and his belief that only through projecting the idea that the party had radically changed could new supporters be won. It was not only Blair's public appeal that was crucial, but his ability to impress opinion-formers among elite groups, particularly the media. In this regard his ability to charm during interpersonal relations was a great asset. But Blair's accomplishments did not arise merely from forcefully leading his party, they involved standing apart from the party too. The 'presidential' aspects to Blair's leadership came relatively easily to a leader who was disposed to public performance and who genuinely did feel a sense of political and cultural difference from much of his party. He proved himself willing to push his own agenda with a steely determination buttressed by a helpful indifference to sacred aspects of Labour traditions. Here Blair was greatly aided by the wider party's desperation to win after a generation out of power. He was also fortunate to obtain the leadership at a time when many people had become profoundly disillusioned with John Major's Conservative Government.

Yet in an important sense Blair 'made his own luck' by squeezing enormous political advantage out of the opportunities that came his way. Through applying his rare mix of statesmanlike and 'celebrity' qualities he was able to overcome early doubts about his leadership and develop both an image and set of skills suited to the demands of modern politics. Commentators are divided upon the question of whether Blair in Opposition forged a newly viable form of centre-left politics, or whether he in fact squandered a golden chance to construct a genuine intellectual and practical alternative to the politics of Thatcherism. Equally, it is debatable whether Blair's period as Opposition Leader prepared the ground appropriately for a sustained period of Government, or in fact spent too much time on media communication to the neglect of preparing credible policies for public sector reform. However, in electoral and party-political terms at least, Blair's period in Opposition was a story of overwhelming success.

14
William Hague, 1997–2001

Nigel Fletcher

There are broadly two different schools of thought on the leadership of William Hague, the leader with the unenviable task of running the Conservative Party in the immediate aftermath of its landslide defeat in the 1997 General Election. The first is that of a young leader trying valiantly to instil a modernised approach into an outdated party, before being forced to retreat into a 'core-vote' strategy in the face of an impossible electoral challenge and opposition from within his own ranks. The second is of a traditional right-of-centre leader, the product of his Thatcherite inheritance, half-heartedly dabbling with cosmetic changes to improve his party's standing, while failing completely to begin the fundamental overhaul of the party that the Conservatives so urgently needed.

Both these extremes of view have their strong advocates, but while containing some elements of truth, neither convinces as a complete narrative. Politics is never quite as simple as that, and the reality must therefore lie somewhere between the two poles. Dismissing simplistic explanations and delving beyond the accepted wisdom that hindsight has given us is the first requirement in attempting a more realistic judgement of Hague's abilities and performance as leader.

The starting point has to be a proper appreciation of the challenges faced by the new leader, and the constraints under which he operated. This matters particularly in the case of Hague, whose inheritance was extremely tough. As he himself put it:

> I took over the party leadership in a situation we'd never been in before: We hadn't had such a heavy election defeat since 1906, and A J Balfour isn't around any more for me to ask him exactly how he felt about it! And indeed we hadn't been in opposition for nearly 20 years, so most members of the party didn't have any recollection of being in opposition. ... There were no people sitting in an office waiting to say 'This is what we're going to do today'. Now that's fine – I knew that was the position. Somebody has to take hold of it and say 'right – you come and work

for me; you come and do this – get those phones installed, start answering the letters'.

(BBC, 1999)

These last two points were real examples: when the new team arrived in the Opposition block at the Palace of Westminster, they found the phones had been disconnected. The task of organising an efficient office from scratch took such a long time that letters were frequently not answered for many months, according to Sebastian Coe, who as Chief of Staff (after a brief spell as deputy to Charles Hendry in the role) was tasked with helping bring order from the chaos (Snowdon, 2010: 47). George Osborne, as Political Secretary and Secretary to the Shadow Cabinet, did not have a proper list of telephone numbers for members of the Shadow Cabinet (Snowdon, 2010: 47).

These logistical difficulties afflict all new Oppositions, but were exacerbated by the length of time the Conservatives had spent in Government, which put the everyday reality of Opposition outside the personal experience of the vast majority of MPs and party staff. What was also unique was the scale of the electoral rout the party had suffered, as alluded to by Hague. The figures speak for themselves: the Conservatives' 9.6 million votes were the lowest total for the party since 1929; their 165 seats were the fewest the party had won since 1906; and their share of the vote, at 30.7 per cent, the lowest since the Duke of Wellington faced his electoral Waterloo in 1832 (Butler and Kavanagh, 1997: 244). This historically bad position created three general, overarching problems for Hague as leader before he even began: these were resources, credibility and legitimacy.

- **Resources:** The small number of MPs meant a restricted talent pool on the Conservative benches, from which Hague had to from his team. Policy adviser Daniel Finkelstein highlighted the lack of 'wise people', explaining that 'Many were simply not present in the aftermath, having lost their seats, and others drifted off, not to be seen in the wake of the storm' (Snowdon, 2010: 46). Many of the big beasts of the Major Government were not available, most notably Kenneth Clarke, who refused to serve, and Michael Heseltine, who ruled himself out on health grounds. When we consider also the number of former advisers and staff to MPs who also 'drifted off' with their bosses, the reduction in available personnel was significant.

  Financial resources were perhaps the most obvious pinch point. The amount of state support for Opposition parties ('Short Money') was then at a lower level than today, and was in any case calculated on the number of seats won, making the total even more inadequate. The party's own finances were in a terrible state, with Hague inheriting a huge deficit following the election campaign, which left the party virtually bankrupt. It was around £8 million in the red, and auditors warned the Party Chairman they might not be able to sign off the accounts (Snowdon, 2010: 48).

- **Credibility:** Such a resounding rejection by the electorate made a swift return to Government almost inconceivable, and as such, the Conservative Party in 1997 appeared to most people to be irrelevant. 'Absolutely nobody was listening to us', one Shadow Minister put it (private information to author). This presented difficulties given that one of the principal functions of an Opposition is to present itself as an alternative Government, ready to take over the reins of power, and to offer an alternative to the Government of the day. With no prospect of an imminent return to Government, pronouncements by Shadow Ministers lacked credibility, and the whole business of Opposition risked looking like a party going through the motions.

- **Legitimacy:** A particular problem for Hague was that of his own legitimacy. He had in many ways become leader by default – through having few enemies, and being the least divisive candidate (not the first or last party leader to benefit in this way). The fact that Kenneth Clarke had been the more popular choice in polls of party activists, and that Michael Portillo remained the 'King over the Water' for the party's right wing, clouded Hague's accession to the top job. Added to this was his relative inexperience as only a former junior member of the Cabinet, and his youth, which although seen as a potential strength in terms of voter appeal, unquestionably weakened his authority within the party.

Hague seemed to recognise his weak position by becoming the first leader ever to put his leadership to a confirmation ballot of party members. The result of this ballot was less than overwhelming, with a mere 44 per cent turnout delivering him 80 per cent support. As well as redefining the punch line to jokes about how many Tories it takes to have a leadership election, the mere fact of his having submitted to the exercise showed that Hague felt in need of a stronger mandate. Faced with all these dire problems, the new leader would have to have rare characteristics to tackle the task ahead. Did he have them?

Emotional intelligence

Evidence of Hague's cognitive style is gleaned from various points in his career. As a consultant at McKinsey, he reportedly impressed colleagues with his 'clear, rational approach to problem-solving and his conscientious attention to detail' (Nadler, 2000: 117). He certainly seems at this time to have demonstrated a capacity – and relish – for hard work and long hours, as well as the ability to 'compartmentalise' a range of complex issues and problems – all of which would seem to equip him well for the job of leader.

These traits certainly made him popular with civil servants when he became a minister. He was well suited to the businesslike approach of the Department of Social Security, and was considered a hard, but fair taskmaster. In this job and as leader, he set great store by good timekeeping, sticking rigidly to a timetable himself, and ensuring that meetings did not run over their allotted time. His staff soon discovered that one of the few things he was capable of losing his cool over was being kept waiting (Nadler, 2000: 144).

He was an early riser, and also developed the unusual (many would say eccentric) habit of practising transcendental meditation for twenty minutes each morning (Nadler, 2000: 117). All these characteristics seem to reinforce the accepted view of him as a driven, ambitious and slightly nerdy character, with a fascination for politics and the confidence of someone who knows they are destined for great things. This picture perhaps points to a high level of emotional intelligence, at least insofar as that term means a man in control of his emotions. As leader, his outward confidence and calmness were often remarked upon. Lord Coe says 'he was always calm under fire', and Lord Cranbourne once remarked that 'I only ever saw him lose his cool once – and that was when he sacked me' (Snowdon, 2010: 61). But this veneer seems to have hidden a certain level of insecurity. 'He is a loner', one of Hague's closest aides from that time volunteered as almost his first remark when questioned on the subject, confirming the contemporary impression formed by his biographer:

> Hague has always had the ability to elude close inspection. He remains an unusually private person, who friends and colleagues find frustratingly hard to read. He often uses humour to deflect criticism and control a conversation, but sometimes at crucial moments the jokes run out and he is left unable to make small talk. As leader his containment has been a mixed blessing, helping him to maintain an even temper but inclining him against developing relationships beyond the clique of his private office. Few people in the party feel they have established a rapport with Hague. ... Others just think he is socially awkward.
>
> (Nadler, 2000: 171)

Hague himself has since accepted much of this analysis of his personality as leader, telling an interviewer in 2003: 'Because I don't need much emotional support, I don't always appreciate other people need it. ... I don't think I was great at putting an arm round a colleague, or saying "Come and have a whisky"' (Elliot, 2011: 61). When asked about this comment more recently, he added: 'I've never needed other people to tell me whether or not I was doing well. ... I'm perfectly self-contained from that point of view' (Elliot, 2011: 61). The latter interviewer noted a distinct reticence when discussing personal matters, observing that 'The more personal the question, the more stilted our conversation' (Elliot, 2011:61). These traits – an inner self-confidence combined with a surprising lack of empathy – were in evidence in his management of the party as leader, and in how he performed in developing a policy platform and communicating it to the public.

Party management

Given his background as a management consultant, it might be expected that managing the party would be a challenge well suited to Hague's skills. But a political party is unlike any other organisation, and parallels with business are often misguided. Nevertheless, the skills he brought from his earlier experiences will have given him a store of knowledge on which to draw when putting together his team, and he certainly made the business model explicit with his appointment of former ASDA Chairman and new MP Archie Norman as Vice-Chairman of the party, charged with pushing through the reforms of its outdated constitution and structure. Norman set about this with brutal efficiency, recalling that 'I was going to deliver it and I didn't mind how much resistance there was' (Snowdon, 2010: 49).

The exercise in refreshing the party's democratic structures was ambitious, and its success was a significant achievement. It showed that Hague had the ability, when he wanted, to push through difficult decisions against internal opposition. The tactics he employed – balancing the divisive figure of Norman with the reassurance of Lord Parkinson as Party Chairman; conceding on specific points of detail in order to win the broader agenda; and using the anger of the party's membership at the behaviour of the party in Parliament to advance his agenda of change – were all fairly skilfully executed with a clear sense of purpose, and might have been thought to be signals of the approach he would take to the more fundamental reform of the party's policy platform.

His management of the Shadow Cabinet and Parliamentary Party throughout the remainder of his leadership was much less effective. He had signalled the level of discipline he expected among his Shadow Cabinet during the leadership election, when he had required a so-called 'loyalty test' on the European issue – a test that ruled out Ken Clarke joining his team. He also had his Chief Whip draw up and circulate a document entitled *Guidance for Frontbench Spokesmen* – a code of conduct similar to the Ministerial Code – and demanded that Shadow Ministers sign a declaration that they had read it (Fletcher, 2001: 27).

But while he was diligent in ensuring meetings were properly conducted and formalities observed, listening courteously to contributions in Shadow Cabinet and setting up subcommittees chaired by relevant Shadow Ministers, these structures did not reflect his method of taking important decisions. Tim Bale has noted that Hague

> was conflict-avoidant when it came to man-management – an individual trait that, as well as meaning he chaired rather than really drove

meetings, often saw him commit to a course of action in which really he had no faith, but which at the time seemed the best hope of keeping the peace.

(Bale, 2010: 210)

In reality, as noted above, his character inclined him towards management by clique, and this is what developed. He had also taken an early decision to move his office away from the House of Commons to Conservative Central Office – the ultimate political bunker at that time.

Sure enough, Hague came to rely increasingly on his inner circle of advisers, to the exclusion of Shadow Cabinet colleagues – a danger often seen with leaders in Government, but perhaps easier to avoid in Opposition. After the arrival of Amanda Platell as Communications Director in 1999 (along with her Deputy, Nick Wood) an unhelpful remoteness turned into a serious problem. Michael Portillo's return to the Shadow Cabinet could have defused the 'King over the Water' factor by tying him into Hague's team, but instead it became a source of hugely increased tension. Platell and Wood saw it as their task to protect the leader at all costs from threats, real and perceived, from Portillo and his allies, who included Shadow Foreign Secretary Francis Maude.

When Portillo and Maude complained they were being briefed against by the leader's team (which they unquestionably were), Hague refused to act (Snowdon, 2010: 70). His decision not to rein in his advisers in what Danny Finkelstein calls their 'very destabilising' feud with his senior colleagues was a symptom of a serious failure of leadership. He had allowed the relationship between the three most senior Conservatives in the party to disintegrate to the point that both Portillo and Maude threatened resignation, and his response to such reports now shows how dysfunctional the team had become: 'if they threatened to resign I largely ignored them. I wasn't going to deal with such stupidities and refused to speak to them' (Snowdon, 2010: 71).

This stubbornness and seeming inability to manage his colleagues extended to the wider Parliamentary Party as well. It has to be counted as a serious indictment of his stewardship that two Conservative MPs – Peter Temple-Morris and Shaun Woodward – crossed the floor to Labour during his tenure as leader. While their decisions can largely be attributed to more fundamental issues of policy direction, Hague's inept handling certainly played a part. In the latter case, the flashpoint was the party's divisive policy on retaining Section 28, the totemic legislation banning the 'promotion' of homosexuality. Woodward was sacked as the party's frontbench spokesman for London when he refused to back the stance, and crossed the floor to Labour shortly afterwards. His defection, as well as much anger from socially liberal Conservatives who remained, could have been avoided had the leader compromised by making the issue a free vote. The ability to use such a tactic when managing divisive issues, as Philip Cowley and Mark Stuart have observed, is one of the few luxuries an Opposition Leader enjoys (Cowley and Stuart, 2011: 180). Hague's failure to deploy such measures was symptomatic of a wider failure of leadership.

Public communication

Among Conservatives, Hague is credited with being one of the party's best communicators, delivering crowd-pleasing speeches at party functions and in the House of Commons. However, this view, which has also become accepted among most media commentators, disguises significant problems with his ability to communicate effectively with the public during his time as leader.

The forum in which Hague unquestionably excelled – the House of Commons – is a distinctly atypical environment compared with most modern forms of communication. The formal debating style is a world away from the informal, conversational manner that the public has come to expect in the television age. But Hague's jousting at Prime Minister's Questions and other set-piece occasions fulfilled an important role in bolstering his position within his Parliamentary Party and giving him credibility as an opponent of the Government. Sir Norman Fowler, who served in Hague's first Shadow Cabinet, having previously held office under Thatcher and Major, noted in his diary his impressions of Hague's response to Gordon Brown's second Budget:

> Gordon Brown sits down to a great Labour cheer and waving of order papers. A very difficult wicket for William. 'I don't see how he follows that' says Brian Mawhinney, sitting next to me on the front bench. But he does and with considerable effect. It is one of the best speeches I have heard an opposition leader make in response to a Budget. William does it better than either Kinnock or indeed Thatcher. He is the strongest debater we have had as party leader for a very long time. (*Tuesday 17 March 1998*)
>
> (Fowler, 2008: 194)

Despite such impressive performances, they had little or no effect on Hague's public image outside Westminster. Fowler noted that 'without such efforts Tory backbench morale in the 1997 parliament would have been markedly lower but sadly the impact never seemed to go wider' (Fowler, 2008: 194). Hague was also an effective platform speaker, but set-piece speeches such as the Annual Party Conference performance are directed predominantly at party activists and media commentators, with only small extracts intended as soundbites for television news.

Specific examples of Hague's failure to connect effectively with the public are numerous, and have become part of the accepted narrative of his leadership. They also lodged themselves in the public consciousness all too effectively, and remain there, even a decade on. In a rather unscientific experiment, a group of people were asked via the Internet sites Twitter and Facebook to give their personal summary of Hague's leadership. The following are some of the responses:

- 'He would have to have been something special to beat Blair at that time. Wasn't helped by daft *GQ* interview & blind Europhobia'
- 'Was in a no win situation, couple of infamous PR stunts that went wrong. Right guy at the wrong time'
- 'Claiming to have drunk 14 pints of beer a day ... says something about my generation. All I remember is the binge drinking quote'
- 'Baseball cap'
- 'Great PMQs, bad *GQ* interview'
- 'I'm afraid the most memorable thing for me is that hat'

While not necessarily representative of the wider public, these self-selecting respondents chose time and again to refer to public relations issues, and two in particular – the image of Hague wearing a baseball cap, and his claim in a *GQ* magazine interview to have drunk 14 pints of beer a day. These two incidents occurred at different points in his leadership, but both had the same root cause – attempts to make Hague appear more 'normal' that backfired and gave precisely the opposite impression.

The 'baseball cap' incident occurred on a trip to a theme park during a summer tour of the UK in 1997 specifically designed by Hague's advisers to allow him to be seen doing 'normal' things, to counter the 'nerdy' image he had developed during the leadership contest. This depiction of him as 'a *Hansard*-reading teenage conformist and tweed-jacketed Young Conservative' was, his biographer concedes, 'accurate and deadly' (Nadler, 2000: 211). Efforts to counteract it appeared forced and unconvincing. Although aides insisted later that the baseball cap had been intended not as a fashion statement but as a practical piece of headwear, the image haunts him to this day. A more deliberate photo opportunity shortly afterwards of William and Ffion sipping cocktails at the Notting Hill Carnival was also cruelly mocked. 'Neither Hague nor his team had the flair to pull off the art of rehearsed spontaneity', as Jo-Ann Nadler accurately puts it (Nadler, 2000: 212).

The most symbolically damaging of those early embarrassments was his response to the death of Diana, Princess of Wales. While Tony Blair seemed to speak for the mood of the nation in its hour of grief, Hague's performance was 'ill at ease, stiff and uncaring' and lacked empathy (Nadler, 2000: 213). In the rush to sort out the logistics of the TV appearance, no-one gave sufficient thought to the effect he needed to convey. It was a telling error – both in procedural terms, demonstrating the weakness of the Conservative media operation – and in what it showed about the new leader's skills.

While a confident and proficient public speaker, Hague simply lacked the instinctive ability to connect with the public anywhere near as effectively as Tony Blair, the opponent against whom he was unfavourably compared throughout his leadership, and who had set the standard for political communications in the age of 24-hour news and confessional TV interviews.

Public policy platform

On the face of it, Hague should have been well placed to deliver a root-and-branch overhaul of the Conservatives' policy platform. He had the time to do it, with very little expectation of an early return to Government, and had himself said he 'thought it would be a long haul and it would take two parliaments to recover' (Snowdon, 2010: 46). But his leadership was instead marked by what Tim Bale has summarised as 'tactics over strategy' (Bale, 2010: Chapter 3).

The beginnings of a coherent attempt at rethinking policy can be discerned in the first couple of years after 1997. There was the 'Listening to Britain' consultation exercise, designed to demonstrate the party was reflecting, and this was followed by the presentation in November 1998 of a strategy paper by Andrew Cooper entitled 'Kitchen Table Conservatives'. It set out a plan for demonstrating clearly that the party had changed, with eye-catching and symbolic gestures, which although modest (having a row with the Carlton Club was perhaps not a 'ten-thousand volt shock', as the paper claimed) were at least intended to signal a change in direction. Crucially, this also involved addressing the 'kitchen table issues' that people in the country were concerned about rather than the narrow interests that had obsessed the party in recent years, notably Europe.

Hague endorsed the plan in a meeting with senior staff, telling Cooper 'I agree with almost every word of it' (Snowdon, 2010: 54). He then had it presented to the Shadow Cabinet, telling them after very little discussion, 'This will be our strategy', and that they would be promoted and rewarded on the basis of how well they stuck to it (Snowden, 2010: 54). But the change in approach never happened: Shadow Cabinet members carried on as before, and even the leader failed to stick to it. Andrew Cooper now offers a revealing explanation of the demise of the 'Kitchen Table', pointing the finger firmly at the lack of leadership from the top:

> He had been elected leader on a reforming ticket, but he's not by nature and temperamentally a modernising person; he's traditional in most of his instincts and attitudes – he loves the rough and tumble of politics. It was almost like he wanted someone to give him an off-the-shelf way of doing it.
>
> (Snowdon, 2010: 56)

Having failed to advance the new strategy into a serious policy-making process, the leadership now reached what almost everyone involved agree was a tipping point. There were several factors leading into it. First, the humiliation of the 'Cranbourne affair', when Hague was forced to sack his Lords Leader for acting without authority in negotiations over Lords reform. This really shook him, bringing to head as it did the issues of legitimacy and weak authority that had plagued him since becoming leader. Then, much more seriously, was Peter Lilley's speech in April 1999, in which he attempted to move the party into exactly the territory the Cooper paper had endorsed, by seeking to acknowledge and move away from its perceived past hostility to public services.

The way the speech was spun, as a rejection of Thatcherism, was bound to cause a row, but what followed was a crisis of confidence that stopped the tentative policy development process in its tracks. As David Willetts has said, it was damaging because 'it raised the "no entry" sign over various party taboos, and it made it much harder to make changes to policy' (Snowdon, 2010: 61). Instead of developing the modernisation agenda, Hague decided to stick to familiar themes. In June, the supposed 'winning' of the European elections, on a hardline Eurosceptic platform, seemed to endorse this approach, and set the tone for a shift to right-wing populism. This coincided with the arrival of Amanda Platell and Nick Wood, who strongly pushed this new 'strategy'.

Any proper policy development process that had been beginning promptly died, replaced by a media-driven short-termism. The 'Common Sense' banner under which the party's programme would eventually be presented was in truth nothing more than a flag of convenience for the type of populist messages Hague was comfortable delivering. It was characterised by policies written from the newspaper headline backwards, and this approach lasted right up to the election, as a newspaper report from early 2001 makes clear:

> Such is the way Tory policy is made these days. It often has a cutting edge that the Government lacks. It is usually impeccably timed to coincide with public concerns, but like anything hastily assembled it has a tendency to fall apart embarrassingly quickly.
>
> (The *Times*, 24 February 2001)

The article went on to highlight changes in Conservative policy over drugs, Bank of England independence, the minimum wage and the 'tax guarantee'. Another key area of policy – pension reform, and in particular the 'rolling up' of Winter Fuel payments into the state pension – was summarily changed by the leader in a directive in early January 2001. After his daily team meeting, his office contacted the relevant Shadow Minister and Michael Portillo, telling them to 'reconsider' the policy, as 'he had formed the strong view that our position on Winter Fuel payments was unsustainable based on feedback from by-elections and polling data' (private information to author). Another key factor in this and other U-turns was reportedly the high level of correspondence being received on the issue from traditional Conservative voters (private information to author).

For major pieces of policy to be wholly rewritten just months before a General Election, on the basis of polling data and the leader's postbag, shows the short-termism and lack of confidence that passed for the party's policy-making. It certainly seemed to justify the jibe by Tony Blair that Hague was an opportunist 'Billy Band-Wagon'. A colleague of Hague sums up with stark bluntness the verdict on his policy-making skills: He 'didn't have a strategic sense, ... [he] wasn't actually interested in policy', but rather was 'reacting to newspaper headlines' (private information to author). It is hard to disagree.

Conclusion

The 1997 Election is often called a car crash for the Conservative Party. A better analogy might be a coach crash, given the number of dazed passengers left behind on the roadside afterwards wondering what hit them. Certainly the party's behaviour reinforced the analogy as the young and inexperienced driver was drafted to get the coach back on the road again. Although some basic structural repairs were carried out, no-one seemed willing to undertake the wholesale rebuilding that was required. Many did not even want to look under the bonnet, muttering 'It sounds OK to me' before climbing back aboard. Unsurprising, then, that as the coach limped on, every bump in the road was magnified, and the injured and traumatised passengers complained about the driver, who increasingly looked for the easiest and most familiar route, regardless of the direction it took them in.

With the benefit of hindsight – and of having seen the successful rebuilding of the party under David Cameron – it is easy to criticise Hague's efforts as superficial and ineffective, and his leadership as a missed opportunity. But while he certainly had flaws as a leader, circumstances played a huge part. His biggest failings – choosing short-termism over proper strategy, and rejecting evidence of the scale of changes required – are all explicable by reference to the prevailing climate in which he was operating. Disunity in the party and constant threats (real or perceived) to his position, combined with the uncharted territory of such low poll ratings, made short-term survival the priority, and a retreat to populist messages aimed at the party's core vote to appear the only viable course. Other leaders, no matter how gifted, would have faced the same pressures.

With the party in denial about the reasons for its defeat and considered an irrelevance by the public and media still obsessed by a hugely popular Government, any attempt at early recovery was arguably doomed to fail.

One of Hague's key advisers during this time certainly suggests that a modernisation project, no matter how authentic, would at that point have been 'wasted' and 'dwarfed by the scale of the challenge' (private information to author). The importance of timing within the political cycle cannot be disregarded, and William Hague drew the short straw of, as he himself puts it, 'the night shift'.

But we cannot wholly exonerate Hague by blaming his poisoned inheritance. There is no doubt that his emotional containment and private nature inclined him towards decision-taking by clique, and all the negative consequences associated with a bunker mentality. His aversion to direct confrontation led colleagues to doubt his sincerity, and made him appear at times duplicitous in dealings with them. Both these things aggravated the feuds and paranoia surrounding his leadership, which became self-perpetuating, and strengthened the perceived need for a 'survival strategy'.

Most crucially, Hague was not at heart a moderniser in the political sense. The management consultant in him could identify that structural changes to the party were needed, and these were carried out efficiently and effectively. But as an ideological Conservative, he was simply not comfortable with the scale of changes needed to the character and priorities of the party in which he had grown up. It would have been a hugely difficult task for any leader, putting them at odds with many in the party, and involving many fights and tests of strength. For William Hague, lacking in authority from the start, averse to confrontation and not himself believing in the changes, it would have been all but impossible. A modernising leader first has to embody change; Hague did not, and probably could not do so. When his narrow clique of advisers decided to 'Let William be William' they essentially conceded defeat (Bale, 2010: 97). Hague was the authentic voice of his party as it stood, and that was his – and their – biggest problem. His failure to modernise the party came down, appropriately perhaps, to pure market economics: having never bought the case for change, there was no way he could sell it.

15
Iain Duncan Smith, 2001–3

Richard Hayton

During the 1998 Party Conference *The Sun* famously pronounced the Conservative Party dead. As a Hague-faced parrot swung from its perch, the accompanying headline read: 'This party is no more ... it has ceased to be ... this is an ex-party'. The paper diagnosed the cause of death: 'suicide'. As things turned out, contra the original *Monty Python* sketch, the Conservative Party was not totally expired – it had not ceased to be, although it had slipped into a very deep slumber. After the trauma of landslide electoral defeat in 1997 a preference for closing its eyes to the enormous scale of the task of rebuilding its electoral appeal could perhaps be forgiven. No such excuse could be advanced following the deafening wake-up call sounded by the 2001 General Election. 'Labour's second landslide' produced another defeat of similar statistical magnitude, arguably the worst result in the Conservative Party's history (Geddes and Tonge, 2001: 2; Tyrie, 2001: 3). If any acclaim can be attributed to the Hague years it is that the doomsday scenario of further losses was averted. Although it remained on life-support, the Conservative Party had at least avoided the fate of the Liberal Party and inexorable decline to third-party status – political death in a first-past-the-post electoral system. But on almost any measure 2001 represented the nadir of the Conservatives' travails. In terms of seats the Conservatives made a nominal advance of one, although not at the expense of any other party (they regained Tatton, the seat vacated by the independent MP Martin Bell). The performance in terms of votes was little better. At the 2001 Election, the Conservatives received 8.35 million votes, over 1.25 million fewer than in 1997. On a substantially reduced turnout, the party's share of the vote advanced by one per cent, but the polls suggested that a higher turnout would have worked against them (Butler and Kavanagh, 2002: 251–64; Tyrie, 2001: 5).

The crisis facing the Conservatives in 2001 was also more than an electoral one. It was a crisis of ideology, mission and narrative. As Tim Bale (2010) has argued, under the leadership of William Hague short-term tactics prevailed over any coherent conception of a long-term strategy. The Conservatives under Hague failed to communicate a convincing narrative explaining to the electorate what Conservatism was for. In substantial part this reflected a failure of leadership, but more fundamentally it also stemmed from a long-term ideological crisis about the very nature of post-Thatcherite Conservatism (Hayton, 2012; Gamble, 1995). One manifestation of this was the sense of ambiguity surrounding Conservative attempts to articulate one of their most traditional themes and pillar of their electoral support: a clear sense of nationhood. The 1997 Election reduced the Conservatives to a rump of 165 MPs largely in the south and east of England, with no representation in Scotland or Wales. In spite of this status as the *de facto* English party the Conservatives remained wedded to a traditional idea of Britain – as Wellings (2007: 410) has argued, 'the historical merging of Englishness and Britishness continued to operate, leaving English nationalism without coherence'. However, in the evolving context of devolution to Scotland and Wales and the broader cultural trend of the emergence of a stronger felt and more clearly defined sense of English identity (Hayton, English and Kenny, 2009), the Conservatives were left without a clear conception of nationhood that they could communicate effectively to the electorate.

This difficulty was symptomatic of the Conservative Party's problems between 1997 and 2001. Unsure of its own purpose, and facing a centrist New Labour Government in its ascendency, the Conservative Party under Hague was unable to fashion a convincing response to the question 'why vote Conservative?' and fell back on a core-vote strategy lacking widespread appeal. Following Hague's resignation the Conservatives needed to identify a leader capable of formulating and conveying an answer to that question that would invigorate the party and enthuse the electorate. As Peter Snowdon later commented: 'If ever there was a time for an inspired leader to lift the Tories out of the gloom, it was now' (2010: 75). Who would answer the call for the Conservatives in their hour of need?

At the outset the odds-on favourite with the bookmakers was Michael Portillo, although it was 'not entirely certain that he would even enter the contest' (Alderman and Carter, 2002: 572). Portillo was one of only two men (the other being the former Chancellor, Kenneth Clarke) widely assumed capable of returning the Conservatives to power. Portillo had, however, caused substantial unease among former admirers on the right of the party who shared with Thatcher the view that he 'had "lost his way" since his conversion to "touchy feely" Conservatism' (Walters, 2001: 213). For the Thatcherites, Portillo's personal and political journey to an agenda of social liberalism and uncompromising modernisation was less a voyage of discovery and more the confused wanderings of a prodigal son yet to realise the error of his ways and return to the comforts of their ideological home. Had he been willing to compromise and sound a dog-whistle or two he would in all likelihood have made it to the final ballot of party members. Keen to secure a mandate firmly on his own terms he was unwilling to do so, and was eliminated by one vote (Hayton and Heppell, 2010: 429). As analysis by Heppell and Hill demonstrated, Portillo's inability to capture the votes of 'pure Thatcherites' proved fatal to his chances: 'it was their abandonment of Portillo that was critical to his elimination and the eventual election of Duncan Smith as party leader' (2010: 50). One Portillo supporter, John Bercow, suggested that the result could be easily understood: 'for Ken's Europhilia substitute Michael's socially liberal credentials'. For him, Portillo 'was clearly the modernising candidate in 2001', but the party 'wasn't ready for and wasn't signed-up to the idea that it needed fundamentally to change its approach' (interview with author).

In short, Iain Duncan Smith's election as Conservative Party leader was less a positive endorsement of either the man or his message, and more to do with who he was not and what he did not represent. In the final Parliamentary ballot he received less than a third of the votes available (54 out of 166 MPs supported him). Nonetheless Duncan Smith did achieve a clear victory over Clarke in the ballot of party members, securing 61 per cent of the vote on a turnout of 79 per cent. However, as Denham and O'Hara have highlighted, the party membership who ultimately selected the leader would have no say about his removal: the 'Hague rules' meant that just 25 MPs could force a vote of confidence, without even the need to nominate an alterative candidate (Denham and O'Hara, 2008: 66). Right from the start, his position as leader 'seemed precarious' (ibid.) – but what, if anything, could he do to enhance his authority and secure it?

In his seminal lecture 'Politics as a Vocation' the sociologist Max Weber (1918) identified three mainstays of legitimate rule: traditional authority; charismatic authority; and formal and/or legal authority derived from holding office. If a custom of deferential obedience was ever enjoyed by Duncan Smith's predecessors it probably died with the 'magic circle' – democratising the leadership selection procedure formalised the existing actuality that incumbents are ultimately beholden to the Parliamentary Party. The second source Weber noted, charisma – in his words 'a certain quality of an individual personality, by virtue of which he is set apart from ordinary men' – is perhaps more important than ever for the modern politician. But not even Duncan Smith's most loyal lieutenants would have suggested he was a man of flair with the ability to inspire a devoted following, and his own depiction of himself as the 'quiet man' was a tacit acknowledgement of this fact. Consequently, Duncan Smith needed to establish his authority through an astute management of the capacities available to him through his position as party leader, to reassure doubtful colleagues that he was indeed 'up to the job'. As noted elsewhere,

> having commenced his party leadership with a disputed mandate it was essential that Duncan Smith provided the following: first, a viable programme of policy renewal and strategic reorientation; and second, internal unity and effective political leadership.
>
> (Hayton and Heppell, 2010: 430)

Public communication

Iain Duncan Smith was an ineffectual public communicator. As Leader of the Opposition he had three main audiences to address: the Parliamentary Conservative Party (PCP), the wider party (i.e. the membership), and the electorate. In each case he failed to connect successfully, making little impact with the general public and losing the confidence of his Parliamentary colleagues and, eventually, the party members whose votes had installed him as leader.

Defeated leadership contender Michael Portillo commented that Duncan Smith 'wasn't able to perform at the necessary level, so he was desperately undermined by that, and that happened pretty much at once' (interview with author). In terms of the Parliamentary Party, this inability was rapidly exposed by Duncan Smith's performances at the despatch box of the House of Commons. For any party leader a key opportunity to rally the troops when the House was sitting was presented weekly at Prime Minister's Question Time. Armed with six questions, the Leader of the Opposition has the chance to expose the Prime Minister to sustained pressure and scrutiny. Duncan Smith's early performances were measured and overshadowed by international events. The announcement of his accession, originally scheduled for 12 September 2001, was delayed by 24 hours as a mark of respect following the terrorist attacks the previous day. In the aftermath of the 9/11 atrocities Tony Blair bestrode the world stage, and there was little for Duncan Smith to do other than offer his support to the Government's stated determination to stand 'shoulder to shoulder' with the United States in the 'war on terror'. As Geoffrey Wheatcroft later commented, as 'Blair played the new Churchill ... Duncan Smith could only trail in his wake, as he ineffectually did for months to come' (2005: 254).

Duncan Smith was perhaps also unfortunate that his immediate predecessor William Hague, for all his other weaknesses as Conservative Party leader, was universally recognised as one of the most effective Parliamentary performers of his generation, and a master of the quick-fire cut and thrust of PMQs. Unfavourable comparisons were inevitable, one of the politer ones being that Duncan Smith was 'Hague without the jokes' (Walters, 2001: 225). Perhaps partly in recognition of his own limitations as a debater, Duncan Smith consciously chose to adopt a less confrontational style than his predecessor, and determinedly stuck to topics that he supposed the public would like him to concentrate on, particularly the public services. This helped to reinforce his efforts to refocus the Conservatives' policy agenda (see below) but made little impression either within or beyond the Westminster village. As the months passed the rumbles of discontent on the Conservative backbenches grew, and the party leader was taunted in the House over his persistent nervous habit of clearing his throat – pitilessly satirised in *Private Eye* as Iain Duncan Cough.

Even as he struggled to satisfy the demands of his colleagues in the Commons, the wider party membership ought to have been Duncan Smith's natural constituency. Ideologically he was certainly one of them, an uncompromising Eurosceptic with traditionalist views on social and moral matters. In the past he had voted in favour of both hanging and caning, and was, as one *Telegraph* writer observed, 'a bit 1950s' (Wheatcroft, 2005: 255). In his hardworking campaign for the leadership he had also impressed members with solid performances at meetings up and down the country. Once elected, however, the most important platform for addressing the party membership was the Party Conference. Through guaranteed media coverage Conference also provides an opportunity to communicate to the electorate at large.

Barely a month after assuming the leadership Duncan Smith's first Conference was inevitably overshadowed by the storm clouds of war gathering over Afghanistan, already subject to aerial bombardment and about to face invasion from the American-led mission to overthrow the Taliban. His speech was in large part dedicated to September 11 and its consequences, although much of the remainder was an effort to refocus the Conservatives' attention on the public services. The *Daily Telegraph* (11.10.2001) loyally reported Duncan Smith's pledge to put public services first, although even through the eyes of their sycophantic leader writer – who discerned a vision 'at once more coherent, more original and more promising than anything the Tories have managed since the 1980s' – as Duncan Smith took the stage he appeared 'momentarily bemused' and 'began nervously'. The late Hugo Young similarly perceived that 'he seemed embarrassed to bestride the platform' and 'doesn't have a shred of excitement about him'. Young judged that

> Only the most desperate Tory acolytes could grace a speech of such stupefying dullness with acclaim for its fantastic strategic significance, merely because it committed the party to take state schools and hospitals seriously.
>
> (Young, 2001)

The 2002 Party Conference is best remembered for the pronouncement by the then Chairman Theresa May that the Conservatives needed to work to shed their image as 'the nasty party'. It also featured probably the most memorable phrase of Duncan Smith's leadership, when he urged his party: 'Do not underestimate the determination of a quiet man.' This undisguised effort to make virtue out of necessity was a direct acknowledgement of his own shortcomings as an orator, and it might have worked, had he been able to convincingly demonstrate his attributes as a leader in other ways. He could not, and when he returned to the theme the following year – announcing in a toe-curling tone that 'the quiet man is here to stay, and he's turning up the volume' – he found that it was a noise that few even in his own party wanted to hear. His foray into modernisation over, Duncan Smith pressed all the traditionalist buttons he hoped would appeal to his core constituency in the party membership. Simon Hoggart (2003) observed that it was 'road rage politics'; while in the opinion of another commentator: 'Duncan Smith knocked back his opponents by playing to every bigoted bone in the Tory body politic' and 'flunked' the real challenge, which was 'to get cheers for the new face the party needs to show if it is to crawl back towards power' (Glover, 2003).

For the modern politician the most important forum for communicating with the electorate is the news media. Television, radio, newspapers and increasingly the Internet provide space for political leaders to project their message to the public, albeit in most cases without any assurances as to how it will be filtered and presented. Unfortunately for him, Duncan Smith proved similarly ineffective as a media performer as he was in the House of Commons and on the conference platform. Through his efforts to develop the language of 'compassionate conservatism' and his stated desire to 'champion the vulnerable' Duncan Smith demonstrated an appreciation of the need to tackle one of the major electoral problems that the Conservative Party faced – namely, its nasty party image. However, his poor communication skills greatly hindered him in this task, and he made little progress – on most measures Conservative Party image data remained stubbornly negative (Hayton, 2008: 96–9).

As Richard Heffernan has argued, the media is an important leadership resource, 'but it is only one resource among many'. As he suggests, media attention, and even media management by spin doctors, is of little use to a leader who lacks other key skills and attributes. Heffernan notes: 'The stark reality is that while media image can help boost a prime minister's public standing, that public standing will inevitably trump that media image' (2006: 598). The same is true for Leaders of the Opposition. The media served to expose Duncan Smith's lack of aptitude as a communicator and his other shortcomings as a leader. As Snowdon suggests, he 'failed to get his message across because he failed to present it imaginatively and convincingly' (Snowdon, 2010: 93–4). This failure extended to each of the leader's key constituencies: the electorate, the party membership, backbenchers and even key figures in his Shadow Cabinet. Whatever the merits of his message it was poorly conveyed, inconsistently presented and largely ignored.

Public policy platform

Despite his reputation as a traditionalist hardliner, Duncan Smith showed signs of having heeded some of the lessons of defeat. Within weeks of being elected leader, he expressed his desire to re-establish the Conservative Party as 'the party of ideas' by launching a policy review (Seldon and Snowdon, 2005a: 259). Duncan Smith also sought to orchestrate a concerted effort by the Conservatives to reposition themselves as a party of the public services, an agenda that would outlive his leadership and be taken into the 2005 General Election and beyond. Members of the Shadow Cabinet made speeches and wrote articles on the subject of schools, hospitals and crime consistently over the four years following his election. Oliver Letwin, for example, made a series of speeches on the 'Neighbourly Society', a thoughtful form of Conservatism that sought to go beyond free markets (Letwin, 2003). The process of policy renewal made progress under Duncan Smith, and his record in this regard compares favourably to that of his predecessor (Seldon and Snowdon, 2005a: 259–62). By realigning the Conservatives' policy priorities Duncan Smith hoped to bring about a strategic reorientation of the party, so that it was once again seen to be speaking to issues of public concern and reoccupying the political centre ground dominated by New Labour. He recalled that: 'I had a sense that the public needed to instinctively begin to re-identify with the party that they felt cared about what they did – a big challenge' (interview with author).

He used his first anniversary as party leader to declare publicly his desire to defeat 'the five giants' blighting Britain's poorest communities. The targets he selected – 'failing schools, crime, substandard healthcare, child poverty, and insecurity in old age' – were less instructive than the language he chose to employ, which deliberately echoed that of the Beveridge Report of 1942 (Duncan Smith, 2002a; Seldon and Snowdon, 2005a: 260–1). The aim of this was not to win votes for the Conservative Party in the most deprived areas of Britain; rather Duncan Smith believed that: 'We needed to broaden the party out, stretch the elastic out a bit. And that meant going further and deeper than we'd been before' (interview with author). Arguably, only a figure from the right such as Duncan Smith could pursue such a strategy, as it drew criticism from that wing of the party (Cowley and Green, 2005: 52). As one early assessment of his leadership speculated, Duncan Smith's

> willingness to question some longstanding party totems suggests that the right-wing credentials that secured his election may yet enable him to institute a transformation of the Conservative Party, just as Neil Kinnock's left-wing roots helped him to initiate the modernisation of the Labour Party in the 1980s.
>
> (Alderman and Carter, 2002: 585)

Indeed, seven months into Duncan Smith's tenure his defeated opponent for the leadership, Ken Clarke – who during the contest had (accurately) labelled his opponent 'a hanger and a flogger' – declared himself 'surprised and delighted' by his party leader's efforts to move the Conservatives to the centre ground, particularly through his focus on poverty (Murphy, 2002).

Although Duncan Smith won some unlikely plaudits – he was also praised in late 2002 by Michael Portillo (2002) for resisting the 'constant temptation' of a right-wing populist agenda – the effort to renew the Conservative

Party policy platform was far from unproblematic. One difficulty was that in spite of the greater persistence of Duncan Smith compared to his predecessor, notable inconsistencies remained across a range of policy issues. This reflected the continued absence of a coherent overall narrative to bind the (albeit still embryonic) Conservative programme together. This disjointed approach flowed from the leader himself, as Duncan Smith 'oscillated' between a modernising and more traditionalist approach, in part simply in an effort to appease different elements within his own party (Bale, 2010: 159). The result was inconsistent signals to the electorate and the risk of appearing opportunistic. Some decisions, such as that to oppose the planned introduction of university top-up fees and the pledge to restore the earnings link to future rises in the state pension, prompted the latter fear even among some members of the Shadow Cabinet (Snowdon, 2010: 94).

Behind many of these difficulties lay a strategic dilemma that Duncan Smith was far from resolving, namely, how could the Conservatives balance their desire for lower taxes with the new dedication to public services? (A. Taylor, 2005: 144–53). This problem led to disagreement between the Conservative leader and his Shadow Chancellor, Michael Howard. To give credence to the public services narrative Howard wanted to reassure voters that the education and health budgets would be prioritised over tax cuts, by pledging to match Labour's spending plans (Snowdon, 2010: 94). This commitment was suddenly dropped in July 2002, as Duncan Smith caved in to pressure from the right-wing press and the right of his Parliamentary Party. This effectively neutered Conservative efforts to gain ground from the Government on these issues, as 'any criticism the Conservatives made of the two services the public most cared about could easily be countered by asking them (endlessly but nonetheless effectively) how precisely they planned to improve those services by spending less' (Bale, 2010: 159).

While some inchoate thinking by Duncan Smith undoubtedly contributed to this difficulty, had either Clarke or Portillo secured the Conservative leadership in 2001 they would have faced a similar dilemma over how to respond to the Blairite Labour hegemony. The context of a public perception of economic crisis and national decline, which had given Thatcherite solutions their electoral appeal, no longer applied. The Labour Party had successfully made the funding and improvement of public services the electorate's key concern, by accepting the free market in many areas but questioning the extent to which untrammelled market liberalism and privatisation could deliver them effectively. Even as market-based initiatives such as the Private Finance Initiative (PFI) were spread throughout the public services, Labour successfully preserved the mass state provision of health and education services free at the point of delivery. In this sense, the major accomplishment and legacy of the Blair Government was the fencing-off of a distinct public sector, and the apparent creation of a new consensus on the scope of the state in the early twenty-first century. Under Duncan Smith, like Hague before him, Conservative thinking on policy continued to be framed firmly within Thatcherite ideological parameters, and consequently the party 'evolved neither a convincing narrative nor effective statecraft' in answer to this quandary (A. Taylor, 2005: 152).

Party management

Duncan Smith's leadership was plagued by party management problems, many of which a more adroit leader might have sidestepped or defused. His downfall after little more than two years in office – which left the former Scots Guardsman with the ignominious honour of being the first Conservative Party leader since Neville Chamberlain not to take his party into a General Election – may have been avoided had he demonstrated a greater aptitude in this regard. Indeed, a key attraction to Duncan Smith's colleagues of his successor Michael Howard was the latter's reputation as a firm disciplinarian who would bring order to the Parliamentary Party. Some of Duncan Smith's party management problems undoubtedly derived from the fact that he was not the first-choice leader of a majority of his Parliamentary colleagues. Nonetheless, lacking the skill to make the best out of bad job, he contrived to make a difficult situation worse.

One episode, which served to illustrate both Duncan Smith's ineptitude as a party manager and the problematic context he faced, was the row that exploded over the ostensibly minor issue of the passage of the Government's Adoption and Children Bill in November 2002. The House of Lords had amended the legislation to the effect that only married couples could adopt children, and the Government sought to repeal these revisions in the Commons to grant unmarried and same-sex couples equal rights. For Labour and the Liberal Democrats, this was relatively uncontroversial (Dorey, 2004: 376). For the Conservatives, however, it was much more contentious, exposing once again tensions in the party between social liberals and social traditionalists, which had become a notable source of disagreement during the Hague years (Hayton, 2008: 169–99).

The dilemma for the party was whether they should follow prominent modernisers such as Portillo in taking a liberal view and accepting these different forms of family life, or continue to advocate the primacy of marriage, which for the majority of Conservative MPs remained their preferred model for raising children. The easiest way out of this difficulty for Duncan Smith would have been to allow a free vote, but as a staunch social traditionalist himself he instead chose to impose a three-line whip against the changes. The result was a public split and a leadership crisis that was 'almost entirely self-inflicted and eminently avoidable' (Cowley and Stuart, 2004: 357). Thirty-five Conservatives absented themselves from the Commons, and eight MPs defied the whip and voted against the party line. The eight included ex-leadership challengers Clarke and Portillo; four former Shadow

Cabinet members (David Curry, Andrew Lansley, Andrew Mackay and Francis Maude); and most damagingly, John Bercow, who resigned from the Shadow Cabinet in order to rebel (Cowley and Stuart, 2004: 357). This marked a turning point both for Duncan Smith's leadership and for party management of sexual/moral political issues in the PCP. In terms of issue management, the lesson for the Conservatives was clear: the party was divided, and free votes on 'conscience' issues offered the most effective means to prevent them from attracting media interest and becoming public displays of disunity. Duncan Smith adopted this tactic when, in March 2003, the Government once again brought forward legislation to repeal Section 28, and it was also used by Cameron and Howard.

Underlying the gay adoption row was a more fundamental intra-party disagreement that dogged Duncan Smith's leadership, namely, the debate over whether, and how, the party should seek to 'modernise' in an effort to rejuvenate its image and broaden its appeal. Back in 6th July 1998 *The Times* had argued that the key dividing line in the Conservative Party was no longer over Europe or between left and right, but that 'the real division is between liberals and reactionaries, modernisers and traditionalists, those armed primarily with principle and those whose first instinct is to take shelter in institutions'. Furthermore, for the Conservatives to regain power, the 'liberals must first win the battle of ideas within their party' (*The Times*, 1998). The leader went on:

> The more important argument the Conservative Party still needs to have is between those sensitive to changing times and those inclined to nostalgia. It is a battle, we believe, between Tory Mods and Rockers. In the Sixties the former were those comfortable with change, the latter those who followed old fads. It is the difference between those with a gaze fixed on new horizons and those either blinkered or still dreaming.

In other words, advocates of modernisation suggested that regardless of their personal preferences, electoral necessity demanded that Conservatives recognise the changing society in which they had to operate. The result of the 2001 leadership election, however, represented a clear defeat for 'the mods' – both candidates presented to the party membership (Ken Clarke and Iain Duncan Smith) eschewed the 'modernising' label, its chief advocate (Portillo) having been eliminated by the final ballot of MPs.

By his own admission Duncan Smith disliked the concept of modernisation, which he associated with a rejection of the core tenets of Conservatism. In spite of this he did actively pursue what he preferred to call a 'change' agenda. This left him in the ill-fated position of being attacked both by modernisers, who were unconvinced by his efforts to change the party, and by traditionalists, who felt that such moves went too far. Lacking a bedrock of support in the PCP Duncan Smith displayed 'an increasing tendency to match each modernizing move with something for the traditionalists' (Bale, 2010: 159) – an approach destined to infuriate rather than placate both camps.

Tim Bale offers a damning indictment of Duncan Smith's record at managing his party, noting that he: 'presided over a party that at times had descended into institutional chaos, a party that was unable to call on the services of many of its most talented individuals, a party that that eventually lost the confidence of the economic interests that funded it' (Bale, 2010: 193). It is impossible to effectively defend Duncan Smith against any of these charges. Major donors deserted the Conservatives, making it clear that they would not reopen their chequebooks until a new leader was in place. Heavyweight figures such as Clarke, Portillo and Francis Maude refused to serve under him, but even from the limited pool of talent available Duncan Smith's Shadow Cabinet appointments drew disproportionately from the right of the party. Finally, the leader's inability to prevent or contain the disunity and dissent that plagued the party was exacerbated by his own vacillations on strategy. To meet Duncan Smith's professed desire to 'change' the Conservative Party required a leader with a more coherent approach pursued with greater resolve than he was able to muster.

Emotional intelligence

Political scientists tend to downplay the significance of personality in politics, preferring instead institutional, structural or ideological explanations. Politicians themselves often denigrate the media for its seemingly ceaseless interest in the character of political figures – which allegedly comes at the expense of an adequate focus on policy or ideas. Yet the individual personalities of political leaders often play a crucial role in political outcomes: different characters shape events in quite different ways. Even in the case of perhaps the most imposing figure in post-war British politics, Margaret Thatcher, 'political scientists have lavished attention on Thatcherism and its impact, but they have not written much about the woman herself' (Garnett, 2007: 173). In the case of Duncan Smith in elite interviews and insider accounts his tenure led to the unavoidable conclusion that concerns over his individual character, aptitude and personality were at the forefront of his Parliamentary colleagues' minds when they removed him from office (see Bale, 2010: 134–93; Hayton, 2008; Hayton and Heppell, 2010; and Snowdon, 2010: 75–119). Indeed for some, these doubts were firmly in their minds during his leadership election campaign. As Bale diplomatically noted, 'Duncan Smith's biggest problem was that he was not renowned among his colleagues for being the sharpest knife in the drawer' (2010: 138). The perception that he was not up to the job dogged his leadership, and Duncan Smith did little to dispel it with his poor handling of various crises that he faced.

The previous section discussed how Duncan Smith induced a severe party management difficulty for himself through his decision to impose a three-line whip on what many regarded as a vote of conscience. Duncan Smith interpreted this rebellion as a conspiracy designed to destabilise his leadership, and compounded his initial error by seeking to reassert his authority through a crackdown on the dissenters. The next day he made a statement on the steps of Conservative Central Office calling for the party to 'unite or die'. In it, he declared that he had 'begun to reconnect the Conservative Party with the views and attitudes of contemporary Britain' – an odd claim given that many in his own party were concerned that his position on gay adoption was out of touch with modern Britain. Equally, he asserted that he was leading the party with unity in mind, 'respecting those who would like me to move faster and those who feel threatened by our moving at all'. However:

> Over the last few weeks a small group of my parliamentary colleagues have decided consciously to undermine my leadership. For a few, last night's vote was not about adoption but an attempt to challenge my mandate to lead this party. We cannot go on in this fashion. We have to pull together or we will hang apart.
>
> (Duncan Smith, 2002b)

The fact that Duncan Smith even felt the need to make an extraordinary appeal to the party barely a year into his leadership illustrated the perilous nature of his position, and it was strongly rumoured that he was on the brink of resignation (Brogan and Helm, 2002). The normally sympathetic *Daily Telegraph* described it as 'the most desperate day in the history of the Conservative Party' (H. Young, 2002). Kenneth Clarke attacked the party leader's handling of the 'entirely self-induced' crisis (Jones, Brogan and Peterkin, 2002), and within days a YouGov/*Telegraph* opinion poll revealed that 52 per cent of Conservative voters thought that the election of Duncan Smith had been a mistake. Moreover, 81 per cent of supporters and 75 per cent of party members thought he had mishandled the adoption issue by failing to allow MPs a free vote (Helm and Sylvester, 2002).

Duncan Smith's handling of this crisis is an interesting case-study in how he struggled to cope with the pressures of leadership. For Snowdon, it was after this 'desperate appeal for unity' that 'the Shadow Cabinet lost all hope' (2010: 107). Rick Nye, who was head of the Conservative Research Department at the time, noted that: 'the more pressure he was under, the more nervous he got and the more desperate he was to show he was in control' (quoted in Snowdon, 2010: 107). As Duncan Smith's insecurities grew, his judgement diminished. Increasingly mistrustful of those around him, a few months later he sacked Nye; Party Chief Executive Mark McGregor; and Director of Field Operations Stephen Gilbert from Central Office. This purge smacked of desperation and panic, and worse was to follow. The leader's choice of replacement for McGregor, former Maastricht rebel Barry Legg, reflected his increasing tendency to assign key posts to friends and close allies rather than to the best-qualified candidates available. His decision to announce Legg's appointment without even consulting the Party Board (which was technically responsible for it as Legg would be a party employee) provoked fury, and 'risked alienating the constituency representatives whose presumed loyalty was one of the main reasons why Tory MPs (who were also worried about appearing to stab him in the back while the country was at war) were staying their hands before the local elections' (Bale, 2010: 174). Legg lasted less than three months in the role before being forced out, and Duncan Smith was also obliged to back down over the removal of Gilbert who was 'reinstated following protests from the board' (Snowdon, 2010: 110). In attempting to crush dissent and shore up his own position, Duncan Smith's seemingly irrational decisions only served to further undermine it. His leadership style was a bizarre mix of a consensual balancing act, as he tried to please both modernisers and traditionalists at the expense of sticking to a clear agenda of his own, interspersed with dictatorial snaps that ultimately only served to highlight his lack of authority.

Conclusion

For any Leader of the Opposition the key test is the electoral one: can they return their party to power? Unable to convince his Parliamentary colleagues that they had any hope of victory under his leadership, Duncan Smith was denied the opportunity to take his party into a General Election, being removed by a vote of no-confidence in November 2003. This represented an ignominious failure on his part, and history will necessarily judge him harshly as a leader lacking authority in his own party, let alone in the country. Yet if he did not sow the seeds of electoral recovery he did at least begin to till the land, making a serious attempt to begin the process of policy renewal – work that he would continue out of office through the establishment of a think-tank, the Centre for Social Justice.

A poor public communicator and disastrous party manager, Duncan Smith was unable to persuade either his Shadow Cabinet or the Parliamentary Party of the virtues of his reorientation strategy. He was undermined by a lack of legitimacy, having secured the support of fewer than one-third of his Parliamentary colleagues in the 2001 leadership election. Duncan Smith had some success shifting the Conservatives' focus away from core-vote issues, although even this effort was undermined by wavering by the leader himself. His handling of the question of adoption rights for gay couples was a cataclysmic failure of party management, and became symbolic of the wider sense of his failure as leader. His tactical ineptitude brutally exposed ideological divisions and led directly to the end of his leadership. Despite his efforts to widen electoral appeal by developing the party's policies on public services and social justice, Duncan Smith was unable to gain support from the modernisers while precisely those efforts weakened his support among traditionalists. Encumbered by his own rebellious past, he could not inspire the confidence or loyalty of his colleagues. In short, Duncan Smith failed the most basic test of political leaders, namely, the need to establish and maintain his authority. The manner of his election granted him little authority in the PCP, and he proved unable to establish it through charisma, political skill or the through the exercise of his office. Without authority his leadership was doomed.

16
Michael Howard, 2003–5

Mark Garnett

In October 2003 the Conservative Party apparently rediscovered its much-vaunted instinct for self-preservation. Having experienced two demoralising electoral defeats in a row, senior figures within the party had no appetite for a third; and under their current leader, Iain Duncan Smith, there seemed to be little prospect that they could ever mount a serious challenge to the Labour Government. Their response to Duncan Smith's uninspiring speech to the 2003 Party Conference was rapid and ruthless. Under the new rules governing leadership elections, 25 MPs had to write to the Chairman of the backbench 1922 Committee in order to precipitate a vote of no confidence. On 28 October, the eve of the deadline for letters to be delivered, 41 MPs had already written. Duncan Smith lost the ensuing confidence vote by 75 to 90 (Denham and O'Hara, 2008: 92–100).

Thus far, the salvage operation had proceeded according to plan, even down to the relatively close confidence vote, which ensured that Duncan Smith (the choice of party members just over two years earlier) was dismissed but not humiliated. The next step was to choose a successor without a divisive contest that might land the party with another leader who, like Duncan Smith, failed to win a majority of votes from the Parliamentary Party. Press speculation centred on the Shadow Chancellor, Michael Howard, who was duly anointed as leader, unopposed, on 6 November 2003.

Howard took over when the Conservatives were lagging in the opinion polls behind an unpopular Labour Government, but only by around 5 percentage points. During his period as leader, the Government continued to suffer unpopularity, not least because of the Iraq War, and ill-concealed conflict between the Prime Minister Tony Blair and his Chancellor of the Exchequer, Gordon Brown. Even so, in the General Election of May 2005 Labour secured a third consecutive victory, by a margin of 3 percentage points (35.3 to 32.3) in the public vote and an overall majority of 66 Parliamentary seats. The election left the Conservatives with only 198 MPs – as Tim Bale has noted, eleven fewer than Labour had mustered after the 1983 General Election, which is widely regarded as a master-class in the art of alienating British voters (Bale, 2010: 252).

Yet despite this lacklustre outcome, early evaluations of Howard's leadership have varied widely, between forthright criticism and something approaching adulation. The unusual diversity of views on this period in Conservative Party history reflect differing responses to the personality of Howard himself, and contrasting assessments of the party's prospects when he took over as leader. Broadly speaking, those who take a negative view of Howard *and* think that the Conservatives were still realistic challengers for office in November 2003 regard him as an unfortunate choice. Those who respect Howard's abilities, and also believe that the party was facing extinction under Duncan Smith, are the most likely to hail him as the Conservative saviour. It could be argued that the latter perspective owes too much to subsequent events; if the party had not chosen David Cameron as Howard's successor, it might not have recovered sufficiently by 2010 to act as the senior partner in a Coalition Government after the election of that year – in which case the Howard interlude would lose much of its borrowed lustre. Howard's admirers can reply that he promoted Cameron and the future Chancellor of the Exchequer George Osborne, ensuring that one or the other of these youthful 'modernisers' would be well placed to win a leadership election when he stepped down; in the meantime, he ensured that their inheritance was more promising than the position he had accepted after Duncan Smith's deposition.

It is tempting for an academic commentator to pick out a path between these conflicting verdicts. In terms of the situation when Howard took over, it was understandable that Conservatives were dismayed to find themselves behind Labour in the opinion polls of autumn 2003, despite all the problems that the Blair Government had encountered. But while this was an indictment of Duncan Smith's leadership, and presented any incoming leader with a serious challenge, the fact remained that the Conservatives were not *far* behind. A leader who inherited an opinion poll deficit of around 5 per cent against a mid-term Government was faced with an uphill struggle. But defeat in the next election, whenever it might be held, was certainly not *inevitable*; and it cannot be argued that the Government's performance between November 2003 and May 2005 made the task much harder for Howard's Conservatives. As a result, it seems fair in Howard's case to base an assessment of his leadership on his own qualities and decisions: his ability to communicate with the public; the policy developments during his time as leader; his party management; and his cognitive style and emotional intelligence.

Public communication

In his acceptance speech in the modish setting of the Saatchi Gallery, Howard gave the impression that his party had learnt from its mistakes and was now prepared 'to preach a bit less and listen a bit more' (Bale, 2010: 197).

The speech, written by the 'moderniser' Francis Maude, suggested that Howard could be the answer to every Conservative's prayers. Here was a heavy Parliamentary hitter whose instincts lay with the right of the party, but whose rational faculties had been acute enough to detect a degree of resistance among the electorate to an additional dose of radical Thatcherite ideas in economic and social policy. Many Conservatives must have asked themselves why they had spurned the chance of plumping for such a figure back in 1997. Since then, of course, Howard had mellowed to a degree; but so had his party, and if he was so well suited to their needs in 2003, surely he had been no less apposite six years earlier? In fact, it could be argued that he was *less* suitable in 2003 than he had been in 1997; opinion polls after his elevation suggested that he would lose more votes for the party than he gained, and after their second election defeat the Conservatives should now have been looking for someone who had more proven vote-winning prowess. However, the 1997 leadership campaign was now history. The remaining question was whether Howard would live up to the flexible model of leadership that Maude had outlined for him in the Saatchi Gallery speech.

At the beginning of 2004 Howard and his advisers attempted to consolidate the favourable early impressions with a newspaper advertisement. Headlined 'I Believe', it featured a list of propositions that presented the Conservative leader as a man of principle – a refreshing contrast, by implication, to Tony Blair. The advertisement was certainly a success in financial terms, since a relatively small outlay produced considerable publicity and media comment (Bale, 2010: 204). However, while the appearance of a personal *credo* in this form suggested a revival of self-confidence within the Conservative high command, the content would have been more appropriate in the election pitch of a US Republican. In particular, Howard presented a stark opposition between the state and the embattled individual, forgetting that most British voters (including the key constituency of well-to-do pensioners) disliked many, but by no means all, state functions. The transatlantic tone was repeated in February, when Howard spoke of a 'British Dream'. Given Howard's background the intention was unexceptionable, suggesting that Britons, like Americans, should have the chance to fulfil their ambitions regardless of their origins. Yet in the British context the message of social mobility is rarely effective when the speaker seems to have discarded every aspect of his or her humble roots. By contrast, except when he attacked the public schoolboy Tony Blair for daring to lecture someone of his own, meritocratic grammar school background, Howard was fated to sound unduly self-satisfied when he spoke about his belief in an opportunity society. Even his spontaneous-sounding rebuke of Blair was remarkable mainly because it proved Howard's ability to discomfit the Prime Minister in the Commons; probably most members of the public who viewed the exchange continued to suppose that both leaders came from equally privileged backgrounds.

In his early months, then, Howard seemed to be aiming for a degree of public respect, rather than hoping to win the affection that was always likely to elude him, given his previous career. This was a shrewd strategy, since by the end of 2003 not even Blair himself could be deluded into thinking that he still enjoyed a special emotional bond with the British public. This meant that the Hutton Inquiry into the circumstances leading up to the death of the government adviser David Kelly was always going to be a crucial battle between the two leaders. If the Inquiry showed that the case for war against Saddam Hussein's Iraq had been distorted by Blair and his allies, Howard would be able to show that, if less outwardly likeable, he was the more trustworthy character – even though he and the majority of his party had supported Blair throughout the conflict, and Duncan Smith's public comments on the subject had not so much given the Government a blank cheque as granted it full powers of attorney.

In fairness to Howard, most commentators had shared his expectation that Hutton's verdict would be seriously damaging (if not devastating) to Blair. Even so, when it became clear that Hutton had vindicated the Government an experienced operator like Howard could still have turned the occasion to his advantage with sprightly footwork. Instead, in the ensuing (widely publicised) Parliamentary debate he spoke as if Hutton had reached the predicted conclusions, rather than the ones that had actually appeared in the report. While Blair was understandably relieved by Hutton's exoneration of his personal role in the build-up to war, the chance to turn the political fire against Howard was an uncovenanted bonus that he did not spurn. On his own account, Blair had sensed that the Opposition Leader was vulnerable to the charge of opportunism back in January 2004, when Howard had persevered with Duncan Smith's line of attacking the imposition of tuition fees for university students, rather than embarrassing the Prime Minister by announcing official Conservative endorsement of a policy that most Labour MPs disliked (Blair, 2010: 488–9). Now all the main news bulletins were showing concrete evidence that apparently supported Blair's central charge against Howard. The 'I Believe' advertisement, published less than a month before the Hutton debate, could now be seen as no more than a flimsy fig-leaf of principle. Although Howard delivered his 'British Dream' speech in the aftermath of Hutton, his chances of persuading the public of his unvarying sincerity had been seriously damaged, compounding negative memories of his ministerial mishaps.

Opinion polls suggested that Blair, rather than Howard, had been more seriously weakened by the Hutton Report (Bale, 2010: 207). Yet months before the Conservatives were defeated in the 2005 Election, Michael Crick could write that after Hutton 'Michael Howard's leadership would never look so threatening to the government again' (Crick, 2005: 445). Despite Howard's long-term infatuation with America, when he confessed that he would not have supported Blair before the war if he had known how the argument had been distorted, the Republican US Government felt that it could afford to snub him without fearing that it might have to deal with him as Prime Minister in the near future. His new line on Iraq, one seasoned journalist argued, 'looked not only intellectually unconvincing but slippery' (Wheatcroft, 2005: 268). Howard was a proud man who was likely to be more affected by self-criticism than by snap-shots of public reactions; if a majority of voters considered Hutton to have 'whitewashed' the Government, this was a small consolation if the incident as a whole had also demolished the Opposition Leader's carefully cultivated credibility. If Howard could no longer hope to allay public suspicions through set-piece speeches or party political broadcasts, he could always fall back on his assured performances in the Commons. After the debate on Hutton, he was acutely vulnerable even in that venue. There was an obvious temptation for him to abandon the inclusive course suggested by the Saatchi Gallery speech, and to revert to his 'comfort zone' of hard-line oratory, which had charmed his party in the 1990s. It is significant in this context that neither Tim Bale nor Peter Snowdon, in their meticulous accounts of the party's fortunes in recent decades, assess Howard's speech to the 2004 Conference – the single event of the kind that he addressed as leader, where he unveiled his 'Timetable for Action' and summarised his policy programme in just eleven words.

Public policy platform

In the early days of Howard's regime, his control over the Parliamentary Party seemed so absolute that he was not short of opportunities for policy innovation. A few days after his succession the philosopher John Gray pointed out that, as a man of the right, Howard was ideally placed to distance the Conservatives from their unappealing Thatcherite legacy (Gray, 2003). However, Labour's high command was unruffled by Howard's coronation. According to Peter Mandelson, 'It was a choice that Tony and I both felt, over time, would do us more good than harm. ... Howard would drift back to the Tories' right-wing comfort zone' (Mandelson, 2010: 381). While Howard undoubtedly had the opportunity, he lacked the inclination to challenge the core beliefs of the existing (and much-depleted) rank and file. The forthright brand of neo-liberalism that marked the 'I Believe' advertisement might have sounded distinctive had it been coupled with a more 'libertarian' approach to social questions; but Howard quickly showed that the authoritarian populism of his Home Office period had reflected his sincere convictions rather than a shallow desire for applause from The *Daily Mail*. Apart from opposing New Labour's (relatively) liberal attitude towards 'soft' drugs, and deploring the ubiquity of speed cameras, Howard even kept up William Hague's unprofitable campaign to allow greater freedom for homeowners in the means they chose to defend their properties (Bale, 2010: 205).

Tory modernisers who regretted Howard's inability to move beyond the old mix of economic 'freedom' and traditional moralising could argue that, even if one overlooked its philosophical incoherence, it was impossible to deny that a similar message had failed to impress the voters when purveyed by Hague in 2001. Howard could reply that, while the evidence of Labour's lingering 'tax and spend' propensities had been equivocal back in 2001, it was now obvious that the Government remained addicted to waste; he appointed the businessman David James to head a review of public spending in an attempt to prove the point and highlight the potential for tax cuts. However, on this subject the Tories under Howard were trapped between their wish to reassure the public as a whole that they would only eradicate 'genuine' profligacy, and the hope that party activists would be invigorated by the prospect even of token reductions in the (direct) tax take.

At the beginning of 2005 Howard and his Shadow Chancellor, Oliver Letwin announced proposals arising from the James review, which had identified £35 billion in potential savings. Of this sum, around two-thirds (£23 billion) would be ploughed into public services considered to be essential; £8 billion would be used to pay down government debt; and £4 billion would be allocated to unspecified tax cuts. The package seemed ideal for electoral purposes, combining compassion (redirecting revenues towards those in genuine need); prudence (keeping debt under control); and generosity (the tax cuts). However, to many voters it probably sounded too good to be true, and although memories of 1992 and 'Black Wednesday' were less potent, public confidence in Conservative economic stewardship was skin deep. Knowing that a General Election was likely to be held in May 2005, party strategists had developed the 'Timetable for Action' to convince the electorate that the Conservatives would hit the ground running with a programme of remedial policies as soon as the New Labour aberration had been brought to an end. A cynical observer might suggest that this was Howard's way of fulfilling his initial promise to provide his party with the *appearance* of a government-in-waiting, whether or not the public had any expectation of a Tory victory.

On the social side of the uneasy Thatcherite equation, Howard saw no reason to row back from the populist policies he had endorsed in the 1990s. His continuing faith in such messages was reinforced by Lynton Crosby, a virtuoso in the art of 'dog-whistling'. The party's most eye-catching posters in the 2005 Election campaign, which asked voters if they were thinking what the Conservatives were thinking, might have been more successful under a less shop-soiled leader. As it was, Howard's inability to persist with the personal reinvention of the Saatchi speech meant that even voters who were thinking like the Conservatives on subjects such as immigration or the travelling community were likely to think again when they realised that they shared some opinions with the much-maligned former Home Secretary. Howard's decision to keep talking about immigration is sufficient evidence that by the time of the election campaign he had given up trying to construct a policy platform that could reach far beyond the 'core' constituency targeted by Hague to so little effect in 2001. Although Howard's proposals were less draconian than his critics suggested, his pre-1997 reputation on this subject was widely regarded as the epitome of Tory 'nastiness'. For Labour, it was sufficient to remind voters of this reputation whenever immigration was mentioned; and if Howard had wanted to reach beyond the Conservative core he would have been well advised to leave the subject alone. Another toxic topic for Howard was Europe, where his party's equivocal policy was easily outflanked by the UK Independence Party. It was no accident that the Conservatives fared relatively badly in the 2004 European Parliamentary elections (even though they topped the poll), or that in that autumn's Hartlepool by-election they were beaten into fourth place by UKIP.

Party management

Howard's biggest advantage over Major, Hague and Duncan Smith was that he inherited a relatively united party, and his unopposed succession gave every incentive for his Parliamentary colleagues to minimise the level of dissent at least until the aftermath of the 2005 General Election. His initial decisions regarding personnel seemed to add substance to the phrase often used at the time, that 'the grown-ups were back in charge of the party'. He made shrewd appointments within his own encourage and in Central Office, bringing back Mrs Thatcher's old Political Secretary, Stephen Sherbourne, as his Chief of Staff, while giving the Political Secretary post to the capable and extremely loyal Rachel Whetstone, who had provided invaluable service when he was Home Secretary. Guy Black, the new Press Secretary, was well connected, and his relaxed style was a marked contrast to New Labour's (now departed) media supremo Alastair Campbell. The Conservative Research Department (CRD) was liberated from day-to-day dealings with the press and encouraged to resume its old role of developing longer-term policy ideas (Bale, 2010, 198–9). However, Howard's sure touch deserted him when he replaced the Party Chair, Theresa May, with a duumvirate of Maurice Saatchi and Dr Liam Fox. Presumably Howard thought that the different skills of Saatchi and Fox would prove complementary, but the relationship between them proved to be tense without being particularly creative. A later appointment, that of the Australian campaign guru Lynton Crosby to head up the electioneering effort, also produced mixed reviews. Nevertheless, Howard did tighten up the organisation he had inherited from Duncan Smith, and under his leadership significant steps were taken to repair the party's finances. In part, this was because of the decision to move Central Office out of Smith Square into cheaper premises on Victoria Street under the new, more dynamic name of Conservative Campaign Headquarters, but also owing to renewed investments by many of the donors who had deserted Duncan Smith.

Howard's front-bench team was deprived of Clarke, Hague and Portillo, all of whom refused to serve. While Clarke and Hague were supportive, and agreed to join John Major in an 'advisory council' (which assisted the impression of renewed party unity without seeming to do much advising), Portillo was increasingly semi-detached and used his prominent media profile to issue critical comments about the speed of 'modernisation'. Howard's Shadow Cabinet was certainly short of stars; neither was it overflowing with the leader's closest supporters. Andrew Lansley and Tim Collins were given responsibility for Health and Education respectively, but they were both outside the Shadow Cabinet and subordinate to Tim Yeo, another possible challenger to Howard who had gracefully declined to stand in the interests of unity. Yeo's appointment, implying that Heath and Education were simple subjects that could be handled by a single spokesperson with two deputies, was among the most baffling front-bench postings in modern times; the arrangement was abandoned in July 2004. Equally strange, albeit for different reasons, was Howard's decision to make Oliver Letwin Shadow Chancellor. The engaging Letwin had certainly helped to promote Howard's unchallenged 'coronation', and his intellectual gifts were undisputable; but his other-worldly demeanour and habit of musing aloud in public made him an ill-equipped sparring partner for Gordon Brown. While David Davis had to be accommodated (and was duly awarded the traditional 'hospital pass' of Shadow Home Secretary) Duncan Smith's supposed chief assassin, Francis Maude, was effectively blackballed because of resentment caused by his prominent role in arranging support for the no confidence motion. Howard did promote both David Cameron and George Osborne, but both were already well known to be rising stars, even if comparisons with Tony Blair and Gordon Brown were misplaced because they seemed to enjoy each other's company and were acutely aware of the need to avoid even the impression of divergence on personal or policy grounds. Instead, the apparent unity of purpose among the young Conservative 'modernisers' aroused resentment in some quarters against what was dubbed 'the Notting Hill set'.

Whatever his shortcomings in other respects, Howard did live up to expectations that he would restore some discipline to his Parliamentary Party. For example, he had no hesitation in withdrawing the party whip from the Cheshire MP Ann Winterton, who had been punished by Duncan Smith for relating a racist joke and now paid the supreme political penalty for a similarly unsavoury quip. During the 2005 Election campaign one of the party's Deputy Chairmen, Howard Flight, made unguarded comments about the possibility of major tax cuts if the Conservatives prevailed. By sacking Flight and ensuring that he was deselected as an official candidate, Howard nipped dissent in the bud. However, in previous months his Parliamentary Party had begun to fray at the edges; the mild-mannered and cerebral Europhile, Robert Jackson, defected to Labour, citing weak leadership as one of his motives. This followed the departure from the Shadow Cabinet of the maverick moderniser John Bercow, who accused Howard of being a 'control freak' who was unable to 'empathise with people' (Crick, 2005: 452).

Emotional intelligence

Taken at face value, the defiant comments of Jackson and Bercow seem contradictory. In fact, only Bercow came somewhere near the truth; Jackson's barb, one suspects, was designed to maximise the damage of his defection by attacking Howard in his sole remaining area of strength. Howard might have been unsuccessful in his attempts to communicate with the public, and this was attributable at least in part to the weakness of policy development under his leadership. Yet he excelled most of his post-war predecessors in his acquaintance with the twin imposters of triumph and disaster, and these experiences equipped him for the inevitable emotional challenges of party leadership – a role for which he had been rehearsing for so long.

More than a year before Howard's unopposed election, the journalist Hugo Young was tipped off that he had already seen 'a big chance for himself' amid the wreckage of the Duncan Smith leadership, and that he felt 'that he could lead the Tories back to credibility without winning the 2005 election. That should be their target' (Young, 2008: 790). But what, exactly, could be regarded as evidence that the party had made itself 'credible' again? As the election approached, Anthony Seldon and Peter Snowden reported that, despite continued talk of victory from the leader himself, some members of Howard's team considered that 'a gain of some 40 seats [compared to 2001] to just 200 MPs would be more than sufficient to show the success of Howard's leadership and ensure that he would stay on as leader' (Seldon and Snowdon, 2005a: 269). If the return of 200 MPs was really regarded as 'more than sufficient', then 198 should have been enough; and Howard's supporters could argue in May 2005 that the British electoral system had disguised what had actually been the closest race in terms of vote share since February 1974, when the contest had produced a hung parliament. However, on the same criterion it was still the third worst result for the Conservatives since 1832, and the fact that it was an improvement on the previous two contests was a mouldy crumb of comfort. Howard's instinct was to resign immediately. However, his desire to change the system of leadership selection (coupled with his fear of being succeeded by David Davis) persuaded him to stay on.

Until he finally stepped aside in December 2005, Howard endured an unpleasant period as caretaker leader. To adapt the usual ornithological allusion, he was not so much a lame duck as a wingless wonder, and even failed to push through reforms in the voting system that would have returned the final choice of leader to the Parliamentary Party. In such circumstances, to resume his place at the despatch box for the weekly ordeal of Prime Minister's Questions was proof of quite remarkable emotional resilience on Howard's part. His only consolation was that this interregnum gave him the chance to appoint George Osborne and David Cameron to Shadow Cabinet positions from which either (or both) could launch plausible leadership bids under the existing rules (for this period, see Denham and O'Hara, 2008: 104–29).

However, Howard's limitations as leader are best summarised as an insufficiency of 'emotional intelligence'. As we have seen, Howard was far more engaging in private than most voters would have imagined. Yet Ann Widdecombe's suggestion that there was 'something of the night' about Howard, which helped to thwart his leadership bid in 1997, hampered his attempts to build a more constructive relationship with voters between 2003 and 2005. As leader, he did try to open channels of communication with the electorate, particularly with the 'I Believe' advertisements and his invocation of a 'British Dream'. Such initiatives, though, might have been more successful if Howard had been more candid about his own success in overcoming the disadvantages of obscure origins; as it was, he only began to divulge the more dubious aspects of his family background when he learnt that his unofficial biographer, Michael Crick, had uncovered the truth about his grandfather (Crick, 2005: 38–9).

Apart from his failure to project a sympathetic image to the voters, Howard's emotional intelligence also proved wanting in his response to the case for 'modernisation'. As he put it himself after standing down as leader, 'I accepted a large part of the modernisers' thesis *intellectually*' (Bale, 2010: 197 (italics added)). Although he cited largely practical reasons for his inability to follow through on the logic of the modernising case, the real problem was his failure to embrace the approach with his heart as well as his head. Had he done so, he would have forced his party to confront the reasons for its unpopularity, instead of clinging to the hope that it could effect a change of Government while retaining the basic characteristics that had served the Conservatives so badly since 1992. Howard might have communicated more effectively with the public if he had built a policy platform on the social themes that had been explored under Duncan Smith, in order to develop a more convincing 'narrative' than the one offered by Hague in 2001. Instead, Howard gave the impression of wanting to restore the 'Thatcherite' formula for winning elections, even though a more clear-sighted observer would have grasped that the string of Conservative victories between 1979 and 1992 had depended heavily on negative evaluations of Labour (and the emergence of the Liberal/SDP alliance to split the anti-Conservative vote) rather than a wholehearted public endorsement of Thatcherism.

The evidence suggests that, whatever his other qualities, Howard simply lacked the imagination required from a leader who could bring his party back to office. This, presumably, was the underlying reason for the despair that modernisers felt after a strategy meeting in April 2004, when Howard insisted that practical problem-solving, rather than the unveiling of a 'big idea', was the way to win back power (Kavanagh and Butler, 2005: 38). Whether or not the modernisers had been realistic in convincing themselves that Howard would accept their case, they were surely right to draw the dispiriting conclusion even at such an early stage that the party could not hope to regain office under his leadership.

Conclusion

After the Election of 1997, the Conservative Party stood in need of a skilful caretaker leader who could maintain its role as a prospective party of Government despite the scale of its recent repudiation by the voters. Michael Howard would have been ideally equipped for this task; but the Parliamentary Party opted instead for what it regarded as youthful promise in the shape of William Hague. In November 2003 Conservative MPs thought that they faced disaster under Duncan Smith, and decided that the ideal caretaker should finally be drafted. However, after two election defeats they were ready to grasp at any evidence that the 'caretaker' might prove so adept at his role that he could make a credible application for the job of headmaster. From this perspective, Howard's Saatchi Gallery speech can be seen as the source of all the disputes about the nature of his leadership. It was cunningly crafted to mollify any party member who might be critical of the *coup* against Duncan Smith, but as a manifesto for a Howard leadership it promised far more than could ever be delivered. In all essentials, Howard remained the man whom the Parliamentary Party had rejected in 1997; even under favourable conditions his leadership skills were appropriate to keep his party in contention rather than winning an election. Between 1997 and 2001, that would have been enough; after the Saatchi Gallery speech it was likely to seem disappointing in the eyes of newly expectant Conservatives.

Howard's weakness as a public communicator was already well known when his fellow MPs elected him unopposed. Although he was an excellent Parliamentary performer, in the past he had alienated, rather than inspired, unaligned voters; and clearly this was one reason for his comprehensive rejection when he stood for the leadership in 1997. In his brief spell as leader he did little or nothing to address this defect (at least after the Saatchi Gallery speech). It can be argued that he had insufficient time to build a convincing policy platform; but some progress from the leading themes established by Duncan Smith might have been expected. Howard's failure to develop an appealing narrative can be attributed to the shortcomings of his cognitive style and emotional intelligence; crucial swing voters seemed to assume that he was still, in essence, the man who had been widely disliked in the 1980s, and, in essence, they were right. The depressing reality was summed up by an opinion poll of voters in key marginal seats, which found that less than half regarded Howard as a potential Prime Minister.

Even among Tory voters, fewer than a third believed that their party had any 'strong leaders' at all. It must have been particularly difficult for Howard to digest survey results like those produced by ICM for The *Sunday Telegraph* at the time of the 2004 Party Conference season, which indicated that despite Iraq Blair was regarded as more trustworthy than Howard by a significant margin (Norton, 2006: 47–8).

Once the election had been lost, Anthony Seldon and Peter Snowdon issued a blunt warning: 'To see the 2005 campaign, and Howard's leadership, as anything other than a complete failure is not only disingenuous: it is also dangerous if the Conservatives are at last to learn lessons and move forward' (Seldon and Snowdon, 2005b: 155). This seems unduly harsh, even if one takes into consideration the fact that the party might have picked an alternative leader to David Cameron, thus implying that Howard had failed even to perform the preliminary tasks of helping it to 'learn lessons' and thus begin to 'move forward'. Equally, Howard certainly did not deserve Peter Oborne's accolade of 'nothing less than the saviour of his party', as if he could not have done better (quoted in Bale, 2010: 255). His role, for instance, cannot be compared with that of Labour's Neil Kinnock, who kept his party alive *and*, despite far greater internal opposition than Howard had to face, introduced important reforms both of policy and procedure. Nevertheless, despite his limitations Howard deserves to be remembered as a leader who was willing to overlook previous humiliations and answer his party's call, even though it was never likely that he would lead it back to office. Although in the context of November 2003 it was equally improbable that the Conservatives were about to disappear as a significant political force in Britain, Howard's style of leadership did at least ensure that speculation on this subject was quelled. At the very least, his failure was more *instructive* than those of Major, Hague and Duncan Smith; for any clear-eyed observer, Howard's successor would have to be someone who could transmit the case for reform of the party with passion as well as rational argument.

Acknowledgement

I am indebted to Michael Crick and Andrew Denham for their comments on an earlier draft of this chapter.

17
David Cameron, 2005–10

Tim Bale

Despite the fact that it had been campaigning against a Prime Minister who had lost the confidence of the electorate, and against a Government that had presided over one of the sharpest downturns in recent economic history, the Conservative Party failed to emerge from the General Election of 2010 with an overall majority in the House of Commons. On the face of it, then, it might seem strange to suggest that David Cameron was one of the best Leaders of Her Majesty's Opposition in the post-war period. However, this is the precisely the claim that this chapter seeks to make. It is a claim founded on the fact that the Conservative Party, far from being poised to win what should have been an easy victory over Labour in 2010, had only just begun to make up for the time that it wasted between 1997 and 2005 (Seldon and Snowden, 2005a: 243–75). When Cameron won the leadership in the last month of that year, the Labour Government was well on the way to losing the affection of the British people (A. King, 2006: 153–4). But there was little to suggest that the Tories, who had gone from being one of the most unpopular Governments the country had ever seen to being one of its least impressive Opposition out-fits, were even close to being considered a realistic alternative (Norton, 2009: 31–43). Yet within a couple of years, most commentators were convinced they were on course for a clear victory at the next General Election. True, such predictions proved premature. But without Cameron's communication skills, his construction of a balanced policy platform, his ability to maintain party unity and, indeed, his personality, the Conservatives would almost certainly have performed more poorly in that election than they actually did. And without those selfsame qualities they may well have found it much more difficult to persuade the Liberal Democrats to enter into Britain's first peacetime coalition for seventy-five years.

Public communication

No-one who followed David Cameron during his successful bid for the Conservative Party leadership would have been in any doubt that, as a political communicator at least, he truly was 'the heir to Blair' (Denham and Dorey, 2006: 35–41). Whether one ascribes it to nature or nurture (a secure and loving family, a first-class education, working for the Major Government as a backroom boy, and a stint in public relations), Cameron quickly proved himself a polished performer in all the arenas in which a modern Opposition leader must make his case. Almost immediately upon taking over, the Tory leader was up against Tony Blair at Prime Minister's Questions in the House of Commons, and gave every bit as good as he got. Without the ability to do that, any leader of a British party is at a severe disadvantage, as one of Cameron's predecessors, Iain Duncan Smith, found to his cost. Cameron could match Blair and, on most days, he could wipe the floor with his successor, Gordon Brown (N. Jones, 2010: 107). He could also pretty much guarantee a standing ovation (and more often than not a genuine one) when addressing Tory supporters outside the House. But putting in a good performance at PMQs week after week or on the platform at Conservative Party Conferences, is, as another of Cameron's predecessors, William Hague, discovered, merely a necessary rather than a sufficient condition of success. To stand a real chance, an Opposition leader has to be able to handle television and radio, too. In the studio, the premium is not on the kind of debating points and oratorical flights that will impress political insiders. Instead, it is on coming over as authoritative yet ordinary – someone clearly in command but who can also convince millions of people who are largely uninterested in politics and often hostile to those involved in it that he is, at the very least, on the same planet (if not necessarily the same wavelength) that they are (Allen, Bara and Bartle, 2011: 184–5).

For an Old Etonian married to the daughter of a Baronet and with assets running into the millions, this could have presented a severe challenge, particularly because – unlike Tony Blair, who also had a pretty comfortable background – Cameron was in charge of a party associated in the public mind with the kind of privilege that renders it incapable of understanding how the other half lives (Bale and Webb, 2011: 40–1). Yet Cameron, even if he could never quite match Blair at his peak, ran him a respectable second. Indeed, in some respects, he might be said to have been ahead. Back in the mid-1990s, when Blair was sweeping all before him, the Web was, comparatively speaking, in its infancy. Ten years later, it was, for many people, simply a taken-for-granted part of their daily lives and, as a result, a communications opportunity that no Opposition leader could afford to pass up. Cameron had already shown himself adept as a blogger, writing occasional pieces for The *Guardian*'s online presence, first as a candidate in 2001 and then as an MP between 2001 and 2004 (http://politics.guardian.co.uk/Columnists/Archive/0,,649666,00.html). As he got closer to power within the Conservative Party and therefore increasingly constrained by collective responsibility, Cameron had to give up that gig. But his awareness and command of new as well as old media did not desert him, an obvious example being his web-chats on mumsnet.com and, perhaps most famously of all, his frequent appearances on something Conservative Campaign Headquarters (CCHQ) decided to call *Webcameron*. The webcast in which Cameron was seen tackling the washing-up as his cute kids and his yummy-mummy wife, Sam, ate breakfast around him may have made many old hands more than a little queasy (Bale and Webb, 2011: 42). But it also showed that Cameron, like Blair, not only understood but embraced the cliché that a picture is worth a thousand words – especially when it conveys an image that is counter-intuitive or purports to prove that the politician concerned is living in the real world. Almost as soon as Cameron took over, and as part of the 'shock and awe' campaign designed by his most influential adviser, Steve Hilton, to get disillusioned voters to take another look at the Tories, the electorate was treated to stills and footage of the party's new leader on his mountain bike, doing a spot of high-street shopping with his family, and – most iconically of all, perhaps – hugging a husky or two on a trip to the Arctic Circle taken to highlight his call on people to 'Vote Blue, Go Green' (see Carter, 2009: 233–42).

Of course, those who hated the Conservatives, and even neutral observers of a cynical disposition, mocked such efforts. The point, however, was to cut through to an audience that neither knew nor cared very much about Cameron or, indeed, politics in general, and to get over the message that he was very different from the Tory leaders who had gone before him. Cameron, in short, was determined and able to embody – to incarnate – the change he and his team were bent on conveying. If he sometimes came unstuck and risked committing what in contemporary political communication is the cardinal sin of inauthenticity – as he did when the media revealed that he was routinely followed on his bike-ride to work by a chauffeur-driven car carrying his stuff – then so be it. Think of Cameron in his designer eco-friendly trainers, his long shorts, his polo-shirts – or Sam, with her dolphin tattoo on her ankle, her art school past and her lovely children – and compare and contrast with, say, John Major and his wife Norma sitting down in Number 10 to another meal of grey garden peas, William Hague in his irredeemably naff cagoule and baseball cap combo, or Iain Duncan Smith warning his last Conference as leader that 'the Quiet Man is here to stay and he's turning up the volume'.

None of this is to say that Cameron got it right every time. There were a number of occasions where he misjudged the mood or failed to think through how what he was saying would be wilfully misinterpreted – often by those claiming to have the Conservative Party's best interests at heart. The 'party in the media' (the right-wing commentariat that, for the most part, remained convinced that any attempt to make for the centre ground of British politics was a counterproductive waste of time) were particularly outraged, for instance, by his claim in 2006 that society needed to understand, rather than demonise, young people who got into trouble – a claim caricatured by the tabloids (including the one edited by Andy Coulson, who was later recruited as the party's media supremo) as 'Hug a Hoodie'. And Cameron could sometimes let slip his irritation with those whose ideological commitment imposed limits on what they were prepared to swallow, most obviously when he allowed a little local difficulty over grammar schools to spin out of control by calling them 'completely delusional', and more interested in being 'a right-wing debating society muttering about what might have been' than 'a serious force for government and change'. The Tory leader was also guilty sometimes of allowing his enthusiasm for a pithy, alliterative phrase to trump his strategic sense: promising voters already reeling from the global economic and financial crisis 'an age of austerity' in April 2009 was almost certainly a soundbite too far. Finally, it is fair to say that, after his 'look-no-notes' performance at Blackpool during the leadership contest, not every platform speech Cameron made when in Opposition was an absolute humdinger – even if, as in Bournemouth the next year (when he celebrated marriage 'whether you are a man and a woman, a woman and a woman or a man and another man' and summed up his priority 'in three letters: NHS'), he got his message across very effectively (Bale, 2010: 314–15).

That said, the majority of Cameron's platform speeches between 2005 and 2010 hit the spot – especially when it really counted, as it did, for instance, at the 2007 Conference where his 'bring it on' bravado did enough (with the help of George Osborne's announcement of a cut in inheritance tax) to scare Gordon Brown off an early election (Bale, 2010: 353–6). And Cameron's straight-talking style sometimes had the advantage of reinforcing his relative normality, as well as distancing him from the past. This applied both to remarks that were genuinely off the cuff (a radio interview in July 2009 when he acknowledged that people were 'pissed off' with politicians and suggested that 'too many tweets might make a twat') and to supposedly spontaneous comments that were possibly more considered (another radio interview – this one during the leadership contest in 2005 – in which he dismissed UKIP as 'a bunch of fruitcakes and loonies and closet racists'). Such lapses were, however, fairly unusual. Indeed, one of Cameron's greatest strengths as a communicator while Leader of the Opposition was his message discipline: having decided on a line to take and a catchphrase to encapsulate it ('There is such a thing as society; it's just not the same as the state', for instance) he was prepared repeat it *ad nauseam*, knowing that only once those within the Westminster village, and political junkies outside it, were heartily sick of it was what he was saying likely to register with ordinary – and therefore ordinarily uninterested – voters.

Given all of the above, it more than a little ironic the Conservatives' failure to win an overall majority at the General Election in 2010 may have had something to do with the televised leader debates held during the campaign itself – debates that, as many people had warned they would, ended up providing an ideal platform for the Liberal Democrats and their über-personable leader, Nick Clegg (Allen, Bara and Bartle, 2011: 184–99). If that was indeed the case, then Cameron had no-one to blame but himself, both for allowing them to occur in the first place and for his surprisingly mediocre performance in the first, game-changing episode in what became something of a weekly soap opera. At the time Cameron had originally agreed to the debates he was clearly keen to secure the endorsement of Britain's biggest-selling daily newspaper, The *Sun* – something that was in the end forthcoming. Even then he should have avoided being bounced into the whole thing by Sky (owned, like The *Sun*, by Rupert Murdoch). He was also ultimately responsible for his failure in the first debate even to get the basics right – looking at the studio audience rather than straight to camera, for instance, and trying way too hard to bring into every answer some sort of human interest story from a voter he had apparently met and naturally empathised with. That said, Cameron clearly beat Brown, the only other potential Prime Minister, in all three debates and in the second and third debates either matched or came out on top of Clegg, too. And in any case, it is hard to believe that the debates cancelled out everything he did prior to the election campaign itself (Allen, Bara and Bartle, 2011: 195–9).

Public policy platform

It is sometimes tempting to think that politics – especially contemporary politics, existing as it does in an era of 24/7 media fuelled by opinion polling and fed by spin doctors – is all about mood-music, about symbols rather than substance. But a Leader of the Opposition has to convince voters that putting his party in power and getting rid of the Government will make some kind of difference, and that the difference made will benefit both them and the country in the long term. Doing that requires (not least in the eyes of the media) the construction of a policy platform – an offer to the electorate that not only enthuses partisan loyalists but does enough to overcome the inertia and the doubts of those who may not have bothered to vote at previous elections or else voted for another party. Now we live in age of 'valence politics', where competence and credibility are more important than appeals to great causes, these floating voters are rarely impressed by ideological zeal. Seeing themselves as centrists, they prefer what can be sold to them as common-sense initiatives – solutions that are distinctive from what is currently on offer but not so far away as to smack of extremism or to risk threatening their wherewithal and wellbeing. One of the Conservative Party's problems after 1997 was its failure to remember this, to realise that, whatever it wanted to do in office, it had to get there first – something it could never do without persuading the electorate that it was, before anything else, a safe choice.

David Cameron was acutely aware of this. He had played a key strategic role in the Conservatives' 2005 General Election campaign; as a result he had read (and just as importantly digested) the opinion polling and focus group reports that made it clear that the Conservative Party was a 'contaminated brand', seen as so out of touch and untrustworthy that many voters, even when they did like one or two of the policies it was offering, rejected them as soon as they were identified as suggestions being put forward by the Tories. From the moment he became leader, Cameron set out to 'decontaminate' the Conservative brand, but this involved more than simply the projection of a series of images and soundbites stressing that the party was changing and moving to the centre ground of British politics. It was also about dumping overboard any of his predecessors' policies that could be presented as either a threat or an irrelevance to the key public services on which the bulk of voters relied. In the crucial fields of health and education, Cameron unceremoniously ditched policies like the patient's and pupil's passports which, inasmuch as voters could understand them at all, suggested that the Conservative Party was more interested in helping the well-off to opt out of state provision than doing anything to improve such provision for the overwhelming majority who could not (McAnulla, 2010: 286–314).

Like most Leaders of the Opposition, David Cameron was wary about rushing into producing policies that might not stand the test of time, offer hostages to fortune or present easy targets for his opponents. He therefore announced the creation of six new policy groups covering social justice, quality of life, public services, security, overseas aid and economic competitiveness. These were chaired mainly by senior MPs who were no longer on the frontbench and came from both the right (Iain Duncan Smith and John Redwood) and the left (Steve Norris, Stephen Dorrell and John Gummer) of the party. Over the course of a year or so, the groups would consult non-party as well as party actors and interests, and come up with non-binding recommendations that would eventually feed into the Manifesto for the next election. As well as coming up with potentially usable suggestions, and allowing the party to deflect questions about when it was going to propose with some policy substance, it also gave the Tories the chance to show they were listening. It further helped them associate themselves with individuals who the public recognised and regarded as independent, the most obvious example being the ex-rock star and anti-poverty campaigner, Bob Geldof, who, it was announced, would be advising Peter Lilley who was chairing the overseas aid group (Kerr, 2007: 46–65).

While these groups were getting on with their work, Cameron also took steps to persuade people that any detailed policy would be underpinned with a framework of values into which the whole Conservative Party, via a vote at Conference, would be seen to buy. The draft of this framework, entitled *Built to Last*, was released in February but, perhaps because it was so anodyne, attracted little interest. The final version, which had doubled in size, was a little harder-edged – the declaration in the first draft that 'We are a modern, compassionate Conservative party' had been replaced by a commitment to 'a free society and a strong nation state' and to a 'responsibility revolution', which would create 'an opportunity society' in which 'everybody is a somebody, a doer not a done-for'; there was even a commitment to 'fairer, flatter and simpler taxes'. However it still gained little traction, either in the media or among members. The results of voting by the latter were announced on the eve of Cameron's first Conference as leader in October 2006. True, 93 per cent of members approved the document, but only 27 per cent of them had bothered to vote (Bale, 2010: 313). The fact that the whole exercise therefore proved something of a damp squib may have had negative consequences beyond a PR opportunity missed: one of the key criticisms that would be made about the Conservative's Election Manifesto in 2010 was that it lacked a convincing underlying theme that resonated with the electorate.

The policy groups began reporting in 2007, but their reports were only released after they had been seen, and some changes suggested, by the leadership in order to ensure that their recommendations were not so radical as to risk embarrassing the party – a policy that worked well, with the partial exception of the 'Quality of Life' group, co-chaired by the green campaigner, Zac Goldsmith. This no-surprises process was made all the easier by the fact that the groups were serviced by desk officers from the Conservative Research Department. The latter had been beefed up under Michael Howard and was further strengthened by David Cameron, especially after the appointment in 2007 of James O'Shaughnessy from the centre-right think-tank Policy Exchange as Head of Policy and Research. The other key figures on the policy front were Oliver Letwin, selected by Cameron to coordinate and pull together the work of the CRD and the policy groups into a Manifesto, and Francis Maude, a Thatcherite who had become a moderniser after a tough time serving in Hague's Shadow Cabinet. Maude was to head up an 'Implementation Unit', charged with talking to former (and eventually current) civil servants in order to ensure that Tory policies were both practicable and capable of being put into effect as soon as possible after an election victory.

That victory, Cameron and his team had decided even before he became leader, would be based on what was later christened by Tim Montgomerie, the founder of the high-profile website for Tory activists, ConservativeHome, 'the politics of and'. Once Cameron had obtained 'permission to be heard' by emphasising change and reassuring people on public services, he would gradually reintroduce policies on immigration, law and order and taxation, which were the Tories' traditionally strong suits. The point was to persuade the public that they could elect a Government that would crack down on crime and control Britain's borders at the same time as protecting health and education, caring for the environment and trying to extend help to developing countries. Likewise, there was no reason why the creation of a more dynamic, entrepreneurial economy should not go hand in hand with a desire to do something serious about social exclusion and entrenched poverty, albeit by moving on from supposedly simplistic top-down, state-centred solutions. In other words, there was no reason why the party, as long as it pitched its offer intelligently and avoided the tub-thumping populism of some Cameron's predecessors, could not simultaneously pass 'the dinner party test' (and please middle-class liberals) and appeal to 'white van man' (the iconic working-class bloke). The possibility of a snap election in 2007 slightly accelerated the process, ensuring that the rebalancing towards the right that Cameron had always intended took place rather earlier than he had planned (see Bale, 2010: 283–362).

In the end, however, 'the politics of and' was trumped by the politics of more or less. Conservative policy-making had always rested on the assumption – encapsulated in his soundbite 'sharing the proceeds of growth' and his suggestion that Britain had to think less about GDP than 'GWB' (General Well Being) – that the next Conservative Government would be operating in an essentially benign economic environment (Dorey, 2009: 315–31). This all changed as the result of the financial crisis that hit the UK, and the rest of the world, in the early autumn of 2007. In order to prevent banks collapsing and to mitigate the ensuing economic downturn, the Brown Government, which had already been borrowing relatively heavily in order to finance improvements in public services, began to run up the kind of deficit that would oblige whoever won the next election to reduce public spending and impose tax increases in order to balance the books. Since Cameron's strategy had been based on reassuring voters (and indeed public sector employees) that public services were safe in his hands, this represented a serious problem. On the other hand, making no attempt whatsoever to level with the public about how difficult things were going to be for the next few years – the approach arguably favoured by Gordon Brown – was not going to cut it either, not least because Cameron's critics were already prone to accusing him of being 'all spin and no substance' (Lee, 2009: 60–79).

After some confusion and delay, Cameron decided that his party, now with a healthy lead in the opinion polls and having to think seriously about what it would have to do after as well as before any election, would have to hope that it had done enough to convince the public of its good intentions and start softening people up for necessary spending cuts. Consequent warnings from Cameron of 'an age of austerity', however, possibly took things just a little too far. By the time the election eventually came around in May 2010, many of the other policies that the Conservatives had generated since he became leader (with the possible exception of Michael Gove's plans to allow parents to set up their own schools, Swedish-style) were forgotten: the focus was firmly on how much and how quickly public spending should be cut in order to balance the nation's books – not an issue that necessarily favoured the Tories given the potentially negative impact that precipitate action might have had on jobs and services. Certainly, Cameron's rather last-minute attempt to broaden out the debate by emphasising his party's belief in 'the Big Society' – the idea that welfare and other services might be better delivered by third-sector volunteers than government bureaucrats – went nowhere, meeting with a mixture of suspicion, incomprehension and even derision (Kavanagh and Cowley, 2010: 163–4).

Party management

David Cameron was elected to the leadership of the Conservative Party by a healthy margin of the 198,844 ordinary members who voted in the final run-off against David Davis, his more traditionally right-wing opponent. He was also elected on a change platform, which gave him something of a mandate for modernisation. On the other hand, although Cameron had beaten Davis and Liam Fox in the final round of voting in the Parliamentary Party by 90 to 57 and 51 votes respectively, and although he had gone into the contest in the country with the majority of Tory MPs declaring their support for him, it was nonetheless possible that a number of right-wing Members of Parliament could cause him problems (Denham and O'Hara, 2008: 151–60). Cameron was determined not to be constrained by them: after all, it was fairly obvious that the Thatcherite populism they favoured had been tested to destruction in 2001 and 2005, and that it was time to try something new. However, he was also sensible enough to employ all the means at his disposal to try to minimise any problems.

The most obvious way in which Cameron could head off trouble was to begin with a balanced Shadow Cabinet that included not only his right-wing opponents in the leadership contest but some of their most dedicated supporters. Hence the Home Affairs brief was offered to and accepted by David Davis and the Defence portfolio went to Liam Fox. Davis's campaign manager, Andrew Mitchell was given a job – quite a high-profile one in view of Cameron's attempt to boost the party's credentials on global poverty – shadowing International Development. Fox's campaign manager, Chris Grayling, became Transport spokesman. Younger right-wingers like Nick Herbert were also given their chance. While Cameron's closest ally, and fellow moderniser, George Osborne remained as Shadow Chancellor, Cameron balanced his appointment by persuading former leader William Hague to re-enter frontline politics as Shadow Foreign Secretary. This was designed to reassure Eurosceptics – a group that Cameron had bought off during the leadership election by matching Liam Fox's promise to pull Conservative MEPs out of the EPP–ED group in the European Parliament. In fact, as many commentators had predicted, this proved impossible to pull off in the short term, but Hague being there undoubtedly made it easier to defend the delay. Whether it facilitated acceptance of Cameron's decision taken in 2009 not to promise a posthumous referendum on the Lisbon Treaty is more of a moot point: it seems more likely that the party put up with it because to have kicked up a fuss so soon before a General Election risked inflicting severe damage on the Tories' new-found reputation for unity (Bale, 2010: 357).

While he and his circle may have admired the way Tony Blair helped turn around his party and steer it to electoral success, Cameron was also adamant, both in public and in private, that he was not looking for the proverbial 'Clause IV moment' (Bale, 2010: 333). He believed that, fundamentally, Tory values were not – as Labour's had been when it stood for socialism via public ownership – out of line with those held by most voters. It was enough, then, for Cameron (and Osborne) to insist that there would be no upfront, unfunded tax cuts and even, at one stage that the party would match Labour's spending plans for two years. Besides, the only obvious Tory totem with equivalent shock value would have been its hostility to European integration. For Cameron to have taken on his party on that issue made no sense: for one thing, neither he nor the public really had any problem with the Conservatives' Eurosceptic stance; for another, it would (unlike Blair's tearing up of a paper tiger) have risked reopening an argument that Cameron's predecessors, for all their other failures, had succeeded in completely closing down.

The only other issue that might have served as a Clause IV moment was the party's continued enthusiasm for grammar schools that selected by ability at the age of 11. In fact, one of Cameron's earliest policy announcements was that the Conservatives would not seek to build any more such schools, although nor would it seek to close existing provision – an announcement that had attracted relatively little attention either inside or outside the party. It therefore came as a surprise when the issue blew up again in May 2007 after Cameron's Education spokesman, David Willetts, not only reiterated the policy but backed it up with evidence that cast doubt on grammar schools' fabled contribution to social mobility – an article of faith for many Tory MPs and ordinary members. The row, as we have seen, was unnecessarily inflamed by Cameron's irritated reaction but was also something of a lightning rod for some of the unease that his brand decontamination measures had provoked, as well as a feeling among some that this privately educated son of a stockbroker had little understanding of the self-made men and women who supposedly made up the backbone of the party. Cameron's reaction, once he had calmed down, was instructive. Instead of staging a showdown with his critics, one of whom had resigned his frontbench seat, the Tory leader not only re-emphasised that he had no intention of getting rid of grammars but also agreed that more of them might be built in the case of population growth. A few months later, Willetts (who had committed the ultimate crime of not only telling his party it would have to play down its prejudices but that they were just plain wrong) was also effectively demoted: he was made responsible just for universities, with the rest of the education brief going to one of Cameron's closest allies, Michael Gove (Bale, 2010: 332–5).

This tendency on Cameron's part to push things only so far before allowing discretion to become the better part of valour was also evident in the way he handled another issue that provoked considerable disquiet within the party. This attempt to change the face the Tories presented to the outside world by encouraging constituency associations in target seats or whose MPs were retiring to adopt candidates from a 'Priority List' (or 'A-List') of people considered by the leadership to be especially able. Associations have long been wary of any interference in this aspect of their work, and that the fact that the list supposedly contained more than its fair share of celebrities, women and ethnic and sexual minorities went down very badly: what is the Conservative Party for, after all, if it doesn't take a stand against 'political correctness gone mad'? The grass-roots not only moaned – especially on increasingly influential websites like http://conservativehome. blogs.com/ and http://iaindale.blogspot.com/ – but also got around the rules by exercising their right to include local candidates and/or by holding primaries. Far from confronting this resistance, passive and otherwise, head on, Cameron let it be known in January 2007 that all associations, as long as they ensured that women would be present in every round of their selection process, would be allowed to choose from the much bigger 'approved list' rather than just the A-List – a change that effectively rendered the latter redundant. Even before then, Cameron could hardly have been said to have led the charge on the issue: for the most part he allowed his Party Chairman, Francis Maude, to take the flak. Indeed, when Maude was shifted sideways into a policy role in the summer of 2007, many saw it as at least in part a sop to activist opinion (Bale, 2010: 290–1, 301–2).

For all the grumbles, though, and leaving aside some of the complaints about him from the party in the media, David Cameron was virtually untroubled by vocal public dissent on the part of anyone who really mattered. Off-the-record criticism of his leadership was actually rather unusual – and on-the-record dissent was even rarer. Even, for example, when Cameron showed his ruthless side in March 2007 by peremptorily sacking one of his frontbench spokesman for remarks that could have been interpreted as racist, he earned, for the most part, not brickbats but at the very least grudging respect. True, there was some muttering about his leadership at the height of the 'Brown bounce' in the summer of 2007 (Bale, 2010: 352–5). But once Brown 'bottled' the election and the Tories roared into the lead in the opinion polls, it was obvious even to those MPs who were not his biggest fans that David Cameron was the only game in town and that the boat was best not rocked: hence the lack of outright opposition to their leader's decision in the run-up to the election not to re-litigate the Lisbon

Treaty or to promise the immediate reversal of Labour's increase in the top rate of taxation.

Like any Leader of the Opposition, Cameron's authority over his party rested not just on his willingness to gather around him people from all shades of party opinion but also on his ability to convince his supporters that he could win them the next General Election. He was also fortunate in his choice of Chief and Deputy Chief Whip, Patrick McLoughlin and Andrew Robathan respectively. But there was more to it than that: Cameron's 'politics of and', and in particular his professed support for measures that would support families getting and staying together, ensured that many of those on the right – especially those who thought of themselves as 'High Tories' rather than free-market fundamentalists – were prepared to discount some of the policies they were not so keen on in return for those that they were. Indeed, after 'grammarsgate' the only occasion on which he attracted serious and sustained grumbling from within his own ranks had nothing to do with ideology but with the way he handled the Parliamentary expenses scandal: his swift and supposedly tough response made the best of a bad job as far as the public were concerned, but it angered many of his own MPs, not least because it was felt that those Cameron considered close or important to him got off lightly compared to those for whom he seemed to care little or nothing. Unfortunately for Cameron – and perhaps surprisingly given the fact that an expensive education often endows people with the ability to appear well disposed to everyone they come across – there were a fair number of Tory MPs convinced that they were in the latter, less fortunate group. Their leader can be a charming man but not, apparently, if the person in question is of no use to him.

Emotional intelligence

Complaints that there seemed to be one rule for Cameron's friends and another for everyone else were, in fact, symptomatic of a more general feeling, namely, that Cameron was not connecting as much with his backbenchers as he should have been and that even the Shadow Cabinet was divided into those who were in the inner circle (like, say, Osborne and Gove) and those who were not (for example, Fox or Grayling). Allied to this was the widespread belief that Cameron was inclined to pay far too much attention to unelected advisers, and in particular Steve Hilton, an arch moderniser, as well as, later on, the more populist Andy Coulson, former editor of the *News of the World* and then the Tories' Media chief (Kavanagh and Cowley, 2010: 82). These accusations contained a grain of truth, perhaps, but it is difficult to think of a Conservative Leader of the Opposition who managed to avoid giving the impression of favouring a close-knit, even exclusive entourage. After all, the Tory Party is not, nor has it ever been, a democracy. It is a top-down organisation, whose leader is personally rather than collectively responsible for its strategic direction and ultimately for its success or failure. The only additional twist in Cameron's case was his supposed preference for fellow Old Etonians or, where they couldn't be found, others who had, like them, been expensively educated. Given the extraordinary over-representation of such people in the Conservative Party, however, its leader's discretion would be highly circumscribed if he or she were to go about trying to fill key posts according to some sort of quota system rather than on merit, real or perceived. In any case, Cameron showed himself willing, if circumstances seemed to demand it, to sacrifice the odd Old Etonian and old friend.

Cameron, then, did enough to suggest on a number of occasions – including the sacking of a frontbencher for apparently racist remarks referred to above – that he was more than capable of the kind of ruthlessness that Leadership of the Opposition demands. That leadership also demands decisiveness, another quality that those who have seen him operate at first hand insist that Cameron possesses. This does not mean that he does not listen; indeed, he apparently likes those around him to outline the arguments on all sides of any question. However, once he has heard them, he generally makes up his mind pretty quickly and tries where possible to stick to that decision. This, along with Cameron knowing (as an ex-PR professional) that anyone in trouble is best off apologising then explaining what they are doing to put things right, was why he was able to react so much more nimbly than Brown to the expenses scandal. Cameron is also good at adjusting and adapting any course of action on which he has decided: in fact, one of his key skills, shown in both policy-making and party management, is his ability to calibrate rather than lurch from full-on confrontation to embarrassing U-turn. He is helped in this by his ability – and those around him say this is one of the biggest differences between him and Tony Blair – to immerse himself in detail as well as thinking about the big picture. In short, Cameron, unlike his immediate predecessors as Leaders of the Opposition, combines tactical nous with strategic vision, which meant he was generally more concerned about repositioning his party in the long term than worrying too much about next day's headlines.

None of this is to say, of course, that David Cameron, as Leader of the Opposition, cared nothing for how his party was portrayed in the media. While some criticism from the usual suspects in the right-wing press was potentially useful because it suggested to sceptical progressives that he must be doing something right, he spent a great deal of time and energy trying to garner good publicity. But there is a big difference between aspiration and desperation, and Cameron almost always avoided the latter. Moreover, if things did go wrong, Cameron was resilient enough to bounce back. Whether this had anything to do with the experience of parenting a severely disabled child and having to come to terms with the death of that same child while Leader of the Opposition, only he, and those closest to him, can ever really know. Possibly, anyone who manages to cope in such circumstances, as Cameron clearly did, comes to see the trials and tribulations of politics as ultimately relatively trivial. This, as well as his natural disposition, may in part account for the fact that, according to those around him, David Cameron, although he is as bad-tempered and impatient as the next man when it comes to life's little irritations, almost always stays calm in what, in politics at least, passes for a crisis.

Conclusion

David Cameron's personal qualities – his strategic sense, his decisiveness, his calm and his charm – were clearly of immense importance in the last act of his time as Leader of the Opposition, namely, the wooing of the Liberal Democrats into a coalition with a Conservative Party with which, on the face of it, they had little in common. In fact, too much can be made of the importance of chemistry in the process. In Government formation, it is the mathematics that matters most: had it been Labour, rather than the Conservatives, who had been in a position to offer the Lib Dems (including those who, like Nick Clegg, turned out to be far more right-wing than many had realised) the chance to serve in a majority Government, then Britain would almost certainly been run after 2010 by a Lib/Lab rather than a Tory/Lib Dem administration. Yet, given the situation that actually pertained, Cameron undoubtedly played a difficult hand extremely well: he was the first to make an offer of coalition; he was able to work out quickly the kinds of compromises on policy that could seal a deal; he did not panic when Clegg began parallel negotiations with Labour but instead upped the offer on the table to include a referendum on the Alternative Vote; and he managed to sell the whole thing to his party, even though many of them were disappointed with the campaign he had fought and even though fewer of them would now get frontbench jobs as the result of having to govern together rather than alone.

Of course, it remains true that had Cameron, as Leader of the Opposition, been able to secure an overall majority for his party he would never have had to do any of the above. By the time of the Election in May 2010, Cameron had used his considerable skills as a communicator to construct a reasonably balanced and credible policy platform behind which his party could unite. But the brand decontamination he had undertaken was far from complete: many voters still didn't feel able to totally trust the Tories. This may not have mattered so much had the need to cut the deficit not raised so residual concerns about jobs and services or, indeed, if dislike of the Prime Minister and his tired Government had impacted more strongly on voters' feelings about the Labour Party more generally. A weaker showing by the Liberal Democrats would also have helped. But achieving a majority over both of these parties was always going to be difficult for the Conservatives.

By the time Tony Blair took over the Labour Party in 1994, it had been trying for the best part of a decade to convince people that it was a safe, centrist bet. But whereas Blair's predecessors had already done much of the heavy lifting required to put Labour back into power, Cameron's had done next to nothing to suggest that the Conservatives had moved on since their crushing defeat in 1997. For a man who had to do in just four or five years what it took three Labour leaders some thirteen years to accomplish, David Cameron did pretty well. More than that: he became Prime Minister.

Note

Much of this account is informed by my book *The Conservative Party from Thatcher to Cameron* published by Polity in 2010.

18
Conclusion

Timothy Heppell

The previous sixteen chapters have provided overviews of each Leader of the Opposition from Winston Churchill to David Cameron, with each of those leaders being assessed in terms of their proficiency as public communicators; the construction of their public policy platforms; their abilities at party management; and their emotional intelligence. Reading these chapters leaves us with two key questions to consider – how has the role of Leader of the Opposition changed in the post-war era; and what makes for an effective Leader of the Opposition?

The changing role of Leader of the Opposition

To assess the ways in which the role of Leader of the Opposition has evolved since the era of Churchill requires an appreciation of four issues: first, the decline of positional politics and the growth of valence politics and within this leadership effects; second, the changing dynamics of leaders in relation to their parties; third, the changing political characteristics of those becoming Leaders of the Opposition – that is, the decline in the importance attached to political experience; and, finally, the reduced tolerance of failure.

Valence politics and leadership effects

Many of the earlier Leaders of the Opposition profiled in this edited collection operated in an era of positional politics where class-driven political cleavages shaped electoral behaviour. The gradual decline of voting behaviour being orientated around stable class-based cleavages resulted in the growth of what Butler and Stokes defined as valance politics (Butler and Stokes, 1969; see also Stokes, 1992). Butler and Stokes differentiated between issues on which the electorate will differ – that is, positional politics, from issues in which there is general agreement on the ends if not the means – that is, valence politics. Positional politics referred to how voters located their positions on political issues and then voted for a party whose positions were closest to their own – that is, ends.

Valence politics referred to how voters evaluated the general political competence of parties in relation to the means by which they would aim to secure their political goals.

The increasing importance of valence-based politics was evident in the seminal work of Clarke, Sanders, Stewart and Whiteley on *Political Choice in Britain*. They argued that valence politics and judgements on the relative competence of the two main political parties was the most important factor underlying electoral choice. Within this the central determinant of party identification based on competence was leadership evaluations (Clarke et al., 2004: 9). Therefore, over time competition between the parties has become increasingly influenced by the personality and character traits of the respective party leaders, with electoral perceptions of *their* competence and charisma classified as having an influence on voter preferences (see, for example, Bean and Mughan, 1989; Crewe and King, 1992; Mughan, 2000). As a consequence electioneering has become increasingly more leadership-dominated, with party leaders playing the dominant role in campaigning and voters relating to parties and platforms through the images and messages transmitted to them through the party leader (Farrell and Webb, 2000: 135).

Therefore, the trend from Churchill to Cameron has been towards a growing focus on the leaders relative to parties (Denver, 2005: 292–9). In analysing the conduct of campaigns and electoral engagement with the democratic process and political parties, media commentators as well as academics have become increasingly focused on leadership effects (Evans and Anderson, 2005: 821). That trend intensified further in the 2010 General Election through the introduction of televised Prime Ministerial leadership debates. According to Wring and Ward, the effect of their introduction was to 'turn the focus of the campaign even more onto the characters of the leaders' (Wring and Ward, 2010: 804). The debates structured the campaign, and even though the format might change there is an expectation that they will feature in future General Election campaigns (Allen, Bara and Bartle, 2011: 195–9). Of their significance to the role of Leader of the Opposition, Allen, Bara and Bartle conclude that the introduction of the debates could redefine the terrain of leadership politics as 'parties may well *select* future leaders on the basis of how well they are expected to perform in this particular arena' (Allen, Bara and Bartle, 2011: 199).

We should note, however, that the shift to televised Prime Ministerial debates in 2010 represents an extension from the televising of Parliament, which was introduced in 1989. The personalisation of the politics of Opposition was intensified by this shift, and the spotlight on the Leader of the Opposition was increased by the media focus on the gladiatorial battles that are PMQs. This was previously the Leader's time to enhance morale among their Parliamentary Party. In the televised era of sound-bite politics it has become their opportunity to enhance their public profile and humiliate and embarrass the Prime Minister when highlights are shown on the evening news bulletins (Catterall, 2006: 6).

The increasing pervasiveness of the media has thereby contributed to altered expectations of how a Leader of the Opposition should behave. The detachment that Churchill displayed between 1945 and 1951 and to which Kevin Theakston referred to in Chapter 2 would be unacceptable in a Leader of the Opposition today. Similarly, the low profile that Wilson displayed in his second tenure as Leader of the Opposition (1970–4), which Peter Dorey noted in Chapter 5, would also not be acceptable nowadays. The shift away from positional politics premised on class-based cleavages towards valence-based politics, and its emphasis on competence, has intensified the importance of the role of Leader of the Opposition. Viewed as the Shadow Prime Minister by the 24/7 news media, they are now expected – by the media, by their Parliamentarians, activists and by voters – to be high-profile brand identifiers for their parties. Opinion pollsters track the relative suitability of party leaders in response to the question 'who would make the best Prime Minister?'; and tracking whether the attractiveness and appeal of the leader is greater or lesser than the party itself is another pressure Leaders of the Opposition are subjected to.

Given that intensification of pressure and expectation upon the individual political leader, so parties have adjusted their institutional arrangements in a way that aids their capacity to demonstrate strong and effective leadership. The mantra of democratisation and accountability has masked increasing party centralisation.

Party centralisation

In the era of Churchill to Callaghan debates on the organisation of the Conservative and Labour Parties were limited, and when change did occur it was often on an incremental and piecemeal basis. Labour possessed a federal structure, which shared power between the Parliamentary Labour Party (PLP), the National Executive Committee (NEC) and the Annual Conference, within which the latter two claimed to formulate policy, while the former implemented policy. As such Labour was defined as a bottom-up plural democracy, as compared to the Conservative Party, which was a top-down elitist oligarchy (Heffernan, 2000: 250–1). That the Labour movement did not subscribe to a hierarchical organisational mindset meant that Labour leaders were supposedly placed in a different context from their Conservative counterparts, who were responsible for formulating policy, for manifesto construction and for determining electoral strategy.

However, McKenzie questioned the validity of the pluralist democracy versus elitist oligarchy distinction, by implying that Labour leaders had the same *de facto* authority enjoyed by Conservative leaders (McKenzie, 1963: 635). While the extra-parliamentary party had on occasions acted as a restraint upon the leadership, if the Labour leader retained the support of key trade unions in possession of significant block votes, then control over Conference could be maintained (Minkin, 1980). Periods in office, such as 1945–51 and 1964–70, would demonstrate that Labour Prime Ministers did possess 'considerable strategic freedom' and were able to govern 'relatively unimpeded by the extra-parliamentary party' (Heffernan and Webb, 2009: 46). However, when he was Prime Minister James Callaghan (1976–9) faced particularly difficult circumstances. His ability to lead was impaired as the NEC fell under the control of the left, and the trade union block vote became 'detached' from his centre-right-wing leadership position on a range of issues, often leading to Conference being ignored (Heffernan, 2000: 252).

To many leftish activists the Callaghan administration had betrayed the wishes of the Labour movement. Redistributing power within the party became a dominant concern in order to guarantee the implementation of a left-wing agenda when Labour next entered Government (Minkin, 1991: 192). Placing control of the manifesto in the hands of the NEC and reforming the party leadership selection procedures became their objectives. That desire to decentralise power from the PLP to the extra-parliamentary party would contribute to bitter infighting and a realisation of the negatives of dispersing power. Empowering activists in policy formulation resulted in the unelectable platform of 1983, and the moves towards party centralisation that would characterise Labour modernisation over the next decade and a half (Kelly, 2003a: 110). Successive reforms were made to ensure the strengthening of the power of the leader at the expense of the NEC and Conference (Heffernan and Webb, 2009: 46). Through moves towards OMOV, a shift away from the principle of delegate-based democracy towards representative democracy occurred (Seyd, 1999: 385). Plebiscites were central. Party membership ballots were conducted on reforming Clause IV (1995) and endorsing the Draft Election Manifesto (1996). These allowed the leadership to legitimate their positions by securing the endorsement of moderates from within the inactive membership, thereby bypassing the resistance that would be evident from the traditional activist base (Heffernan and Webb, 2009: 47).

The Labour Party Annual Conference became a different institution. The divisive policy debates of the past were replaced by tightly managed and carefully choreographed events designed to emphasise unity of purpose and leadership strength (Seyd and Whiteley, 2001: 80). Heffernan and Webb concluded that the leadership had 'engineered a process' whereby they could set the 'agenda for policy debate from the outset'; they could maximise their 'opportunities for guiding the flow of debate'; they could stall the 'articulation of public opposition'; and they could interpret the 'outcome of consultation and the framing of proposals that Conference considered' (Heffernan and Webb, 2009: 47). This would mean that by the time he was Prime Minister, Tony Blair was able to provide the strongest and most centralised leadership that Labour had ever known – something his predecessors could 'only have dreamt of' (Heffernan, 2000: 254).

Shortly after their ejection from office in 1997 the Conservatives engaged in a far-reaching reform programme, which brought the three formerly separate elements of the party – that is, the Parliamentary Conservative Party (PCP), the voluntary and the professional wings – together as a single entity with a constitution. Built into the reforms was an emphasis on promoting membership participation to demonstrate democratisation, and like Labour the use of mass membership ballots to legitimate leadership positions (Seyd, 1999: 385). However, while 'ostensibly' democratic, the use of ballots on policy change was actually a tool of 'leadership manipulation' (Cowley and Quayle, 2001: 51).

Commenting on the parallels with the party reforms that characterised New Labour – that is, tightly managed consultations only considering proposals drawn up by the leadership, with ballots used to ratify or reject, not change – Kelly concluded: 'there too, a new party leader claimed democratic backing for a reform which arguably cheated party democracy' (Kelly, 2003b: 89). Of the reforms Heffernan and Webb concluded that the strategic autonomy of Conservative leaders, which had always been strong, remained intact (Heffernan and Webb, 2009: 46).

For both New Labour and the Conservatives the end product has been to enhance leadership autonomy, meaning that the central trend is for intra-party organisational transformation that boosts the profile and the power of the leadership vis-à-vis their parties when in office. That trend within both parties demonstrates the gap that exists between the rhetoric of democratisation and the reality of powerful leadership influence (Seyd, 1999: 386). As a consequence the power of leaders within their parties 'is probably as strong as it has ever been in peacetime' in terms of their dominance of their extra-parliamentary parties, which is to be expected from electorally professional organisations (Heffernan and Webb, 2009: 56).

Therefore on the first two issues about the changing nature of Opposition Leadership a clear picture emerges. First, there has been an evident intensification of the importance of the individual who is Leader of the Opposition as positional politics has been challenged by valance issues where leadership characteristics dominate. Second, parties have undergone processes of institutional change that have embedded or enhanced the dominance of the leader. This means that just as the importance of the individual leader has become more significant in terms of political choice, and just as parties have adapted to facilitate the ability of the leader to lead effectively, so the importance of experience as a qualification to lead has been dramatically eroded.

The decline in experience

David Cameron is the most recent Leader of the Opposition to have made that transition from Opposition to Government. Cameron had only just turned 39 when he was elected as the new Leader of the Conservative Party in December 2005 and thus became Leader of the Opposition. He had been a Member of Parliament for only four years, with two years' frontbench experience, and only one year in the Shadow Cabinet. His successor as Leader of the Opposition, Ed Miliband, was marginally older at 40 when he won the Labour Party leadership in September 2010. Like Cameron, he had been a Member of Parliament for only one term (2005–10), although he did have limited ministerial experience (2006–10), including two years in the Cabinet (2008–10).

Both Cameron and Miliband reaffirm a change that can be dated back to 1983 and the election of Kinnock as the new Labour Party Leader. Since then, with the exceptions of Smith (age 54; Parliamentary experience 22 years) and Howard (age 62; Parliamentary experience 20 years), the trend has been towards younger and less experienced Leaders of the Opposition – Kinnock (age 41; Parliamentary experience 13 years); Blair (age 41; Parliamentary experience 11 years); Hague (age 36; Parliamentary experience 8 years); Duncan Smith (age 47; Parliamentary experience 9 years). The average age of a new Leader of the Opposition from Kinnock to Cameron was 45, and the average years of Parliamentary experience was 12.

These figures compare dramatically with the period between 1945 and 1980. Churchill was 71 when he became Leader of the Opposition in 1945 and had been in Parliament since 1900, although he was absent from Parliament between 1922 and 1924. Attlee was 68 when he became Leader of the Opposition in 1951 and had been in Parliament for 29 years. When Gaitskell succeeded him as Labour Party Leader and Leader of the Opposition in late 1955 he was 49 years old and had been in Parliament for 10 years. Wilson was 47 years old when he replaced Gaitskell in both roles and had been in Parliament for 18 years.

The case of Douglas-Home (age 61 when he became Leader of the Opposition in 1964) is harder to clearly quantify in Parliamentary terms. He was a Member of Parliament in the years 1931–45 and 1950–1 before ceasing to be in the House of Commons as he inherited his father's seat in the House of Lords. Thereafter he was a constant member of the Conservative Governments from 1951 until his controversial selection as Conservative Party Leader and Prime Minister in October 1963. In House of Commons terms he had 15 years' experience, while in general Parliamentary terms he had 27 years' worth of experience. His successor, Heath, was 49 when he became Leader of the Opposition and had been in Parliament for 15 years, figures that corresponded exactly to those of Thatcher who succeeded Heath. Her successor (Callaghan) was 67 when he ceased to be Prime Minister after the General Election of 1979, and thus became Leader of the Opposition with 34 years' worth of Parliamentary experience. Foot was also 67 when becoming Leader of the Opposition after Callaghan resigned as Labour Party Leader in late 1980. By that time he had 30 years' worth of Parliamentary experience.

The period from 1983 has seen the average age when becoming Leader of the Opposition fall to 45, from an average of 58 in the 1945–80 period. The Parliamentary experience average since 1983 at 12 years represents a significant reduction from the 24 years' Parliamentary preparation that existed in the 1945–80 period. With that increased time period in office (and the more frequent swinging of the electoral pendulum), the pre-Kinnock Leaders of the Opposition had more substantive Ministerial and Cabinet experience. Since 1983 four of the Leaders of the Opposition have not had any Ministerial or Cabinet experience – Kinnock, Blair, Duncan Smith and Cameron. Smith served in the 1974–9 Labour Government and was in the Cabinet in the final year, while both Hague and Howard served in the long period of Conservative governance under Thatcher and Major – Hague between 1993 and 1997, including two years in the Cabinet, and Howard between 1985 and 1997, including seven years in the Cabinet. The average Ministerial tenure of just three years across seven Leaders of the Opposition from Kinnock to Cameron is a dramatic contrast to the pre-Kinnock era. The average Ministerial tenure from Churchill to Foot was 11 years.

The other dimension that is problematic for modern Leaders of the Opposition is the impact of defeat among party elites. Earlier Leaders of the Opposition could be buttressed in their position by the presence of experienced elites around which the burden of Opposition could be shared. For example, when defeated in 1970 Wilson still retained the services in his Shadow Cabinet of key elites such as James Callaghan, Denis Healey and Anthony Crosland. When Margaret Thatcher became Leader of the Opposition in February 1975 she benefited from the support of experienced former Cabinet elites such as William Whitelaw and Keith Joseph, albeit from differing wings of the party. In more recent times there has been a considerable increase in the number of elites opting out of frontbench responsibilities. Post-1997 the inexperienced William Hague was left leading a Shadow Cabinet devoid of political heavyweights as former Cabinet Ministers such as Kenneth Clarke, Stephen Dorrell (after 1998) and Michael Howard (after 1999) opted for the serenity of the backbenches to the futility of the opposition frontbenches. Clarke again chose not to serve under the inexperienced Duncan Smith post-2001, as did Michael Portillo. Ed Miliband has suffered in a similar way, losing the experience and gravitas provided by Jack Straw, Alastair Darling and most significantly his defeated leadership rival, David Miliband. Like Hague and Duncan Smith before him, he is an inexperienced leader devoid of high-profile experienced political heavyweights around him, thus intensifying the focus on him alone.

Tolerance of failure

That decline in experience when assessing who becomes Leader of the Opposition is clearly tied in to a reduced tolerance of electoral failure. Let us consider the period between 1945 and 1980 to highlight the point. In this thirty-five-year period the Leader of the Opposition happened to be a former Prime Minister for half of that time (seventeen years) – Churchill (1945–51); Attlee (1951–5); Douglas-Home (1964–5); Wilson (1970–4); Heath (1974–5); and Callaghan (1979–80). Of these, Churchill was defeated in 1945 but still led the Conservative Party into the 1950 and 1951 General Elections; Attlee was defeated in 1951 and was still leading Labour into the 1955 General Election; and Wilson was defeated in 1970 but was able to reclaim power for Labour in early 1974.

Although Douglas-Home (resigned), Heath (challenged) and Callaghan (calculated resignation) all ceased to be Leader of the Opposition within eighteen months of leaving Downing Street, their removals were not as immediate as in 1997 and 2010. John Major announced his resignation as Conservative Party Leader to the nation outside Downing Street en route to tendering his resignation as Prime Minister to the Queen on 2 May 1997. He did however briefly serve as Leader of the Opposition while the Conservative Party set about electing his replacement, a process that took seven weeks to complete. Gordon Brown resigned with immediate effect on 13 May 2010, meaning that the Labour Party Deputy Leader (Harriet Harman) had to act as Leader of the Opposition until a new Labour Party Leader could be elected (in September). In the thirty years since Callaghan resigned as Labour Party Leader in October 1980 we have had only seven weeks of a former Prime Minister serving as Leader of the Opposition.

This statistical comparison between 1945–80 (17 out of 35 years) and 1980–2010 (seven weeks out of 30 years) could be a reflection of the fact that we had regular changes of Government in the earlier era (especially in the 1960s and 1970s) and the long period of one-party government post-1979. While this argument might have some validity we also need to acknowledge the increasing susceptibility of party leaders to election outcomes – that is, a reduced tolerance of electoral failure (Andrews and Jackson, 2008: 660). The defeated parties in 1945 and 1950 (Churchill); 1951 (Attlee); 1959 (Gaitskell); 1966 (Heath); and 1970 (Wilson), retained the party leadership and thus remained as Leader of the Opposition for the next Parliament. Defeats in 1955 (Attlee); 1964 (Douglas-Home); 1974 (Heath); and 1979 (Callaghan) did result in leadership change but it took a number of months (six to eighteen) to formalise.

Since 1983 only one defeated party leader has survived to lead their party to the next General Election – Kinnock after 1987 (although in 1988 he suffered the first challenge to a Labour Party leader since 1961, which he easily overcame). Defeat led to immediate resignation announcements in 1983 (Foot); Kinnock (1992); Major (1997); Hague (2001); Howard (2005); and Brown (2010). All these resignations reflected the futility of their position and that an attempt to continue would lead to a direct challenge to forcibly evict them. The idea of resigning before being challenged reflects the idea that all of the above recognised that their continuance would be damaging to the wider interests of the party (Andrews and Jackson, 2008: 662).

One of the most significant developments in terms of Opposition politics in recent times was the decision of the Parliamentary Conservative Party to remove Duncan Smith from the leadership owing to the fear of electoral defeat, rather than the actuality. Prior to that all of the other Leaders of the Opposition in the post-war era had led their parties into General Election campaigns, even those who ultimately failed to become Prime Minister – that is, Gaitskell (1959); Foot (1983); Kinnock (1992); and Hague (2001). As Richard Hayton outlined in Chapter 15, it was clear that Duncan Smith had considerable limitations as a modern political leader, but it was still nonetheless a dramatic action on behalf of Conservative Parliamentarians to evict him via a confidence motion before facing the electorate (Denham and O'Hara, 2008: 95–6).

What makes for an effective Leader of the Opposition?

Having considered the changing demands of being Leader of the Opposition in the era since Churchill, we can conclude the book by offering an appraisal of what makes for an effective Leader of the Opposition. However, in seeking to make some assumptions of what Leaders of the Opposition should aim to do we must acknowledge context. Here it can be argued that two contextual factors need to recognised: first, the performance of the incumbent Government; and second, the timing and circumstances in which a Leader of the Opposition acquires that role.

First, the ability of any Leader of the Opposition to make an impact is dependent upon the incumbent Government experiencing difficulties – economic crisis, policy failings, internal divisions, scandals – which create a perception that a change of Government is necessary. All a Leader of the Opposition has to do is make sure that their party are seen as a credible alternative, and that they themselves are viewed as a credible alternative Prime Minister – that is, ensure that they are positioned to exploit any perception of incompetence attached to an incumbent administration (Norton, 2009: 31–3). Therefore, as Ball outlines, Opposition politics is shaped and conditioned by the performance of the Government, and 'the recovery of unity, support and morale in opposition flows from the difficulties of the government, rather than causing them in the first instance' (Ball, 2005: 4).

Second, the time when one becomes Leader of the Opposition is significant as it reflects the climate of expectation or the political mood. This will shape perceptions of the power of the Leader of the Opposition – both within and beyond the party – and will determine whether they are viewed as constrained or empowered by circumstances. Leaders of the Opposition can be constrained by acquiring the party leadership shortly after their party has been defeated at the polls. Defeat will be indicative of something fundamentally wrong with the party in terms of policy platform, party unity, organisational ability and electioneering. It will more often than not mean that the new party leader inherits the leadership with the party behind in the opinion polls, and thus they are immediately constrained. Such leaders will usually have fewer avenues of opportunity to exploit when facing a recently elected administration to whom the electorate are more willing to give the benefit of the doubt in the short term.

Leaders of the Opposition who were clearly constrained upon acquiring the role in recent times include Kinnock, Hague and Duncan Smith (all elected as party leader within months of their parties suffering crushing election defeats). On a slightly less severe end of constraint could be Thatcher, Smith and Cameron, as they had more reason for optimism than Kinnock, Hague or Duncan Smith. Thatcher faced a Labour administration that had virtually no Parliamentary majority and was internally divided. Smith faced a Conservative administration with a small Parliamentary majority that was badly divided over Europe, and within months of Smith becoming leader he had 'Black Wednesday' to exploit. Cameron and Smith both had the opportunity to make capital from the fact that the incumbent Government had been in power for a considerable amount of time. Multi-term administrations tend to suffer from degenerative tendencies, when, for example, their ability to avoid culpability for past mistakes and withstand the 'time for a change' argument is significantly reduced (Heppell, 2008b: 580–1).

The ideal time to be Leader of the Opposition is against a long-serving administration engulfed with economic difficulties and against an uncharismatic Prime Minister with question marks concerning their legitimacy – for example, Wilson against Douglas-Home (1963–4); Blair against Major (1994–7); and Cameron against Brown (2007–10). Few Leaders of the Opposition will face such favourable circumstances, so while recognising the importance of context, the book will close by outlining a few ideas of what a Leader of the Opposition can do to maximise their effectiveness. Or, as Ball states, what to do to ensure that 'the opposition puts itself in a position from which it can take advantage of the government's problems and weaknesses as they arise, and not let opportunities slip' (Ball, 2005: 4).

On the basis of analysing the previous sixteen chapters, while acknowledging the changing role of Leader of the Opposition, the following three areas need to be carefully considered in order to enhance effectiveness: strategic repositioning, political adaptability and leadership visibility.

Strategic repositioning

Leaders of the Opposition face a constant balancing act between the need to criticise the Government's policy and expose their failings, while dealing with media and electoral expectations that they should outline what they would do instead (Chorley, 2011). Here the Opposition does not necessarily need to provide fully laid-out policy solutions to every eventuality.

The advice of Nigel Fletcher and Peter Catterall in this context is worth noting. Fletcher comments that:

> It's sometimes difficult to keep that restraint but a party in opposition should be, as Churchill said, a lighthouse not a shop window. In the sense that you should offer a direction and a *narrative* of what sort of a government it would be without necessarily detailing every dot and comma of what it is going to do. Mainly because the government will steal all the best stuff.
>
> (quoted in Wheeler, 2011)

Catterall suggest that over-exposure of detailed policy is risky not just because the Government might try to expropriate aspects of them (to neutralise them if they are electorally appealing) but it also provides the Government with avenues of attack. Catterall suggests that if an Opposition outlines too much policy detail rather than an overarching narrative, then rather than the election being a referendum on whether or not a Government should be in office, the party of Government will 'seek to turn it instead into a referendum on whether or not the opposition is fit to govern' (Catterall, 2006: 10).

Policy selection, or what we define as the narrative, is clearly tied to political or electoral strategy. Effective opposition involves de-emphasising the policy areas where the party has ownership and dominance, and reaching out into policy territory that is traditionally defined as your opponents' (Bale, 2008: 273). This can be as much about the *symbolism* of party change so that it can appeal to the non-traditional voter or floating voters. Blair made this an aspect of his attempts at triangulating, and it was also evident in the positioning of Cameron (McAnulla, 2010: 286–314). The experiences of the Conservatives in 2001 and 2005, and indeed Labour in the 1980s, demonstrate the dangers of adopting core-vote strategies rather than reaching out. That tendency to construct policy positions that appeal to their own core, and indeed their own activist base, reflects the need in Opposition to listen to the reasons as to why they are still in Opposition (Catterall, 2006: 10) Effective Opposition politics requires that the party leadership reorientate the party towards the centre ground and the location of the median voter (Taylor, 2010: 490).

Political adaptability

That process of policy selection and strategic positioning demands that the party can show its adaptability. However, adaptation is an 'intensely political process', which is 'seldom smooth or unproblematic' because adaptation 'challenges' traditional party assumptions (Taylor, 2005: 133). Entering Opposition is a consequence of shifts in the policy mood. Here the central issue for the Leader of Opposition (usually new) is to acknowledge 'in the least damaging but still convincing way possible where [they] went wrong in the past and how it will make sure it does not make the same mistakes again' (Bale, 2008: 273).

However, this can be particularly challenging as parties can be reluctant to change. Norris and Lovenduski suggest that there can be a range of reasons why parties fail to learn in Opposition and make a rational adaptation to the altered policy mood. For example, adaptation can be impeded by long-standing principles and symbolic traditions – such as Clause IV, as Gaitskell found to his cost in 1959. Leaders of the Opposition might also feel that attempting to modify policy in an already factionalised party (parties often being divided in the aftermath of defeat) could trigger even deeper fissures. Alternatively, the party leadership might recognise the need for change but lack the internal party resources to initiate what they regard as the necessary change. The best illustration of the reluctance to adapt was the Conservatives after 1997, which Norris and Lovenduski attribute to selection perception, in that the attitudes of the Parliamentary Conservative Party at the time 'placed them the furthest away from the median voter' of all the parties, which was 'a puzzle for any rational vote calculating politician with ambitions for office' (Norris and Lovenduski, 2004: 86–90).

The ability of a Leader of the Opposition to face down internal opposition to adaptation is usually dependent on evidence that their strategic reorientation is creating benefits for the party. If adaptation results in improving opinion polling evidence or encouraging local, European or by-election results, then that resistance to adaptation will be more manageable. Blair and Cameron were able to sustain their strategic reorientations because the opinion polling data encouraged their parties to believe that adaptation would result in a return to Government. Gaitskell was stalled in his efforts towards reorientation and adaptation, while Kinnock was only able to engage in a slow, incremental process of repositioning. Hague and Duncan Smith were largely knocked off course through internal party objections to attempts to reposition the party that were clearly making no positive impact.

Fletcher is less than sympathetic to Leaders of the Opposition who fail to stand up to internal party opposition to adaptation. He implies that having identified the reasons for defeat and the necessary strategic adaptation to enhance voter mobilisation (reaching out beyond your own core vote), it is essential that the Leader of the Opposition 'sticks' to that their predetermined strategy (quoted in Wheeler, 2011). A Leader of the Opposition who is perceived to have backed down in the face of internal party opposition is individually weakened, while the process of backing down proves that the party is unwilling to adapt. It suggests that the party is still unable to accept the reasons for their removal from office. Backing down also leaves an impression of a party that is unsettled in its political outlook, and as such it will lose public trust (Norris and Lovenduski, 2004: 90).

Leadership visibility

It is odd that as the role of Leader of the Opposition has evolved there has been a shift towards a greater emphasis on the character and personality traits of individual leaders – their likeability – at the same time as shifting towards less experienced candidates for the leadership. That means that parties need their leaders to be highly visible and make a positive impact that benefits the party, yet such expectations come with less preparation time for such exposure. Recent Leaders of the Opposition have entered the role with lower public recognition than those from earlier generations, and the initial months can be critical in shaping electoral attitudes towards them. The case of Ed Miliband when he became Leader of the Opposition highlights this point. A surprise victor, he has been subject to some negative media portrayals, which Labour might fear could shape electoral perceptions of him. The media agenda has focused in on his disputed mandate to lead the Labour Party and the fact that the only tranche of the Electoral College in which he was first was the trade union tranche (Wickham-Jones and Jobson, 2010: 525–48).

They have utilised this to portray Miliband as 'Red Ed', and then they supplemented this with an unhealthy interest in his lifestyle choices. Tabloid editors have become fixated by the following: the fact that his name was not listed on the birth certificate of his eldest child; the fact that he and his long-time partner were not married; the suggestion that their subsequent marriage was an act of political calculation, not love; his weight and his need for nasal surgery to aid his sleep, or according to his critics to address his 'annoying' voice (Cannon, 2011; see also Heppell and Hill, 2012; Prince, 2010). Indeed, Miliband did show low visibility for a Leader of the Opposition in his first three months. In December 2010 Cameron exploited press speculation that Labour strategists were concerned about Miliband's low public profile, by ending a parliamentary confrontation with: 'three months and people are beginning to ask "When's he going to start?"' (Gimson) In this context Miliband might wish to reflect on the following warning from Greg Rosen: 'those who fail to define themselves early on their own terms are defined by their opponents' (Rosen, 2011: 160).

Given the probable importance of Prime Ministerial debates to future General Election campaigns, and the intensification of the focus on the party leaders, then performances at Prime Minister's Questions provide an indication to their debating skills. In this forum Miliband lacks the Parliamentary precision and forensic exposure of policy flaws that characterised the approach of Smith. Nor does he possess the quick-thinking wit and repartee of a Wilson. He has still to develop that method of constructing questions with an inbuilt and effective sound bite for the evening news – the technique that Blair mastered and Cameron then followed (Heppell and Hill, 2012).

Effective Opposition leadership therefore involves a complex interaction between the need to strategically reposition the party to broaden their appeal by demonstrating that the party is adaptable and ensuring that the Leader is visible, charismatic, likeable and competent. The demands on Leaders of the Opposition today are considerably greater than in the past, given the shift towards valence politics and the importance attached to leadership impacts, and with this a reduced tolerance of failure. Yet at a time when the expectations of Leaders of the Opposition to be the brand identifiers for their party have increased, the occupants are increasingly younger and in possession of lower public profiles prior to becoming Leader. Leader of the Opposition has been oft described as the hardest job in British politics, and on the basis of the preceding sixteen chapters it is easier to understand why. That combination of high levels of responsibility, expectation and exposure alongside limitations in terms of powers of influence makes it a frustrating role to occupy. As we have seen, a number have struggled to deal with those demands – will Miliband join the list of those who were Leader of the Opposition but never Prime Minister: Gaitskell, Foot, Kinnock, Smith, Hague, Duncan Smith and Howard?

Bibliography

Adams, J. (1992). *Tony Benn* (London: Macmillan).

Addison, P. (1975). *The Road to 1945: British Politics and the Second World War* (London: Cape).

Addison, P. (1992). *Churchill on the Home Front* (London: Cape).

Addison, P. (2005). *Churchill: The Unexpected Hero* (Oxford: Oxford University Press).

Ahmed, K. (2003). 'Tony's Big Adventure', *Observer*, 27 April.

Alderman, K. (1992). 'Harold Macmillan's Night of the Long Knives', *Contemporary British History*, 6 (2): 243–65.

Alderman, K. and Carter, N. (1994). 'The Labour Party and the Trade Unions: Loosening the Ties.' *Parliamentary Affairs*, 47 (3): 321–37.

Alderman, K. and Carter, N. (2002). 'The Conservative Party Leadership Election of 2001', *Parliamentary Affairs*, 55 (3): 569–85.

Allen, N., Bara, J. and Bartle, J. (2011). 'A Much Debated Campaign', in N. Allen and J. Bartle (eds). *Britain at the Polls 2010* (London: Sage).

Anderson, P. (1964). 'A Critique of Wilsonism', *New Left Review* 27.

Andrews, J. and Jackman, R. (2008). 'If Winning Isn't Everything, Why Do They Keep Score? Consequence of Electoral Performance for Party Leaders', *British Journal of Political Science*, 38 (4): 657–75.

Anon. (2004). 'Obituaries; Bernard Levin', *The Daily Telegraph*, 10 August.

Arnstein, W. L. (2000). *Britain Yesterday and Today: 1830 to the Present Day* (Boston: Houghton Mifflin Company).

Ashdown, P. (2001). *The Ashdown Diaries: 1988–1997* (London: Penguin).

Attlee, C. (1956). *As It Happened* (London: Odhams Press).

Baker, K. (1993). *The Turbulent Years* (London: Faber and Faber).

Bale, T. (2008). 'A Bit Less Bunny-Hugging and a Bit More Bunny-Boiling'? Qualifying Conservative Party Change under David Cameron' *British Politics*, 3 (3): 270–99.

Bale, T. (2010). *The Conservative Party from Thatcher to Cameron*, Cambridge: Polity.

Bale, T. and Webb, P. (2011). 'The Conservative Party', in N. Allen and J. Bartle (eds). *Britain at the Polls 2010* (London: Sage).

Ball, S. (ed.) (1999). *Parliament and Politics in the Age of Churchill and Attlee: The Headlam Diaries 1935–1951* (London: Royal Historical Society/Cambridge University Press).

Ball, S. (2001). 'Churchill and the Conservative Party', *Transactions of the Royal Historical Society*, 11: 307–30.

Ball, S. (2003). 'The Conservatives in Opposition 1906–1979: A Comparative Analysis', in M. Garnett and P. Lynch (eds). *The Conservatives in Crisis* (Manchester: Manchester University Press).

Ball, S. (2004). *The Guardsmen* (London: HarperCollins).

Ball, S. (2005). 'Factors in Opposition Performance: The Conservative Experience since 1867', in S. Ball and S. Seldon (eds). *Recovering Power: The Conservatives in Opposition since 1867* (Basingstoke: Palgrave Macmillan).

Ball, S. and Seldon, A. (eds) (1996). *The Heath Government, 1970–74* (London: Longman).

Baston, L. (2004). *Reggie: The Life of Reginald Maudling* (Stroud: Sutton Publishing).

BBC (1979). *Reputations: The Lost Prime Minister* (30 September, BBC2).

BBC (1999). *How to be Leader of the Opposition* (13 March, BBC2).

BBC (2009). *Yes We Can! The Lost Art of Oratory* (5 April, BBC4).

Bean, C. and Mughan, A. (1989). 'Leadership Effects in Parliamentary Elections in Australia and Britain', *American Political Science Review*, 83 (4): 1165–79.

Beckett, F. (2007). *Clem Attlee* (London: Politicos).

Beckett, A. (2009). *When the Lights Went Out: Britain in the Seventies* (London, Faber).

Beckett, F. (2010). Letters to the Editor, *The Guardian*, 16 March.

Beech, M. (2004). 'New Labour', in R. Plant, M. Beech and K. Hickson (ed.). *The Struggle for Labour's Soul: Understanding Labour's political thought since 1945* (London: Routledge).

Behrens, R. (1980). *The Conservative Party from Heath to Thatcher: Policies and Politics 1974–1979* (Farnborough: Saxon House).

Benn, T. (1987). *Out of the Wilderness: Diaries, 1963–1967* (London: Hutchinson).

Benn, T. (1988). *Office without Power: Diaries, 1968–1972* (London: Hutchinson).

Benn, T. (1990). *Conflicts of Interests* (London: Hutchinson).

Benn, T. (1994). *End of an Era: Diaries, 1980–1990* (London: Arrow).

Bevins, A. (1982a). 'Bennites Play Down Foot Attack on Left', *The Times*, 18 January.

Bevins, A. (1982b). 'Foot to Challenge Bank Takeover', *The Times*, 16 July.

Bevir, M. (2005). *New Labour: A Critique* (London: Routledge).

Black, L. (2001). 'The Bitterest Enemies of Communism: Labour Revisionists, Atlanticism and the Cold War', *Contemporary British History*, 15 (3): 26–62.

Black, L. and Pemberton, H. (eds) (2004). *An Affluent Society? Britain's Post War Golden Age Revisited* (London: Ashgate).

Blair, T. (1995a). Speech to NewsCorp Leadership Conference, Hayman Island, Australia, 17 July.

Blair, T. (1995b). Speech to Labour Party Conference, Brighton, 3 October.

Blair, T. (1996). Speech to Labour Party Conference, Blackpool, 1 October.

Blair, T. (2010). *A Journey* (London: Hutchinson).

Blake, R. (1998). *The Conservative Party from Peel to Major* (London: Arrow Books).

Blick, A. (2004). *People Who Live in the Dark: The History of the Special Adviser in British Politics* (London: Politicos).

Bogdanor, V. (1994). 'The Selection of the Party Leader', in A. Seldon and S. Ball (eds). *Conservative Century: The Conservative Party since 1900* (Oxford: Oxford University Press).

Bradley, I. (1982). 'Most Union Members Think Labour Will Lose' *The Times*, 19 January.

Brivati, B. (1996). 'Hugh Gaitskell' (London: Richard Cohen).

Brivati, B. (1999). 'Hugh Gaitskell', in K. Jefferys (ed.). *Leading Labour: From Keir Hardie to Tony Blair* (London: I. B. Tauris).

Brogan, B. and Helm, T. (2002). 'Unite or die, IDS warns Tories', *Daily Telegraph*, 6 November.

Brookshire, J. H. (1995). *Clement Attlee* (Manchester: Manchester University Press).

Brown, C. (1997). *Fighting Talk: The Biography of John Prescott* (London: Simon and Schuster).

Brown, G. (1971). *In My Way* (London: Book Club Associates).

Brown, P. and Sparks, R. (1989). 'Introduction', in P. Brown and R. Sparks, R. (eds). *Beyond Thatcherism* (Milton Keynes: Open University Press).

Burridge, T. (1985). *Clement Attlee: A Political Biography* (London: Jonathan Cape).

Butler, D. (1952). *The British General Election of 1951* (London: Macmillan).

Butler, R. A. (1971). *The Art of the Possible* (London: Hamish Hamilton).

Butler, D. and Butler, G. (2000). *British Political Facts 1900–2000* (London: Macmillan).

Butler, D. and Kavanagh, D. (1975). *The British General Election of October 1974* (London: Macmillan).

Butler, D. and Kavanagh, D. (1980). *The British General Election of 1979* (London: Macmillan).

Butler, D. and Kavanagh, D. (1984). *The British General Election of 1983* (London: Macmillan).

Butler, D. and Kavanagh, D. (1997). *The British General Election of 1997* (London: Macmillan).

Butler, D. and Kavanagh, D. (2002). *The British General Election of 2001* (Basingstoke: Palgrave Macmillan).

Butler, D. and Pinto-Duschinsky, M. (1971). *The British General Election of 1970* (London: Macmillan).

Butler, D. and Stokes, D. (1969). *Political Change in Britain* (London: Macmillan).

Callaghan, J. (1988). *Time and Chance* (London: Collins).

Cameron, D. (2009). 'Letter of Support on the Launch of the Opposition Studies Forum', March 2009. Available at http://oppositionstudies.webs.com/davidcameronsmessage. htm [accessed 23 February 2011].

Campbell, A. (1994). 'John Smith's Great Journey', *Today*, 13 May.

Campbell, A. and Hagerty, B. (eds) (2010). *The Alistair Campbell Diaries – Volume One: Prelude to Power* (London: Hutchinson).

Campbell, J. (1983). *Roy Jenkins* (London: Weidenfeld and Nicolson).

Campbell, J. (1993). *Edward Heath: A Biography* (London: Pimlico).

Campbell, J. (2000). *Margaret Thatcher, Volume One: The Grocer's Daughter* (London: Jonathan Cape).

Cannon, E. (2011). 'I'm Sorry Ed, but Nose Surgery May Not Solve Your Sleep Problems', *The Daily Mail*, 1 May.

Carlton, D. (1981). *Anthony Eden* (London: Allen and Unwin).

Carter, N. (2009). 'Vote Blue, Go Green? Cameron's Conservatives and the Environment', *Political Quarterly*, 80 (2): 233–42.

Catterall, P. (ed.) (2003). *The Macmillan Diaries: The Cabinet Years 1950–1957* (London: Macmillan).

Catterall, P. (2006). 'Making the Best of a Bad Job: The Role of the British Leader of the Opposition', Paper delivered to the American Political Science Association Annual Conference (Philadelphia) September.

Chorley, M. (2011). 'The Politics of Opposition: A Modern-Day Survival Guide', *The Independent*, 20 February.

Clarke, H., Sanders, D., Stewart, M. and Whiteley, P. (2004). *Political Choice in Britain* (Oxford: Oxford University Press).

Clarke, P. (1999). *A Question of Leadership: From Gladstone to Blair* (London: Penguin).

Coates, D. (2005). *Prolonged Labour: The Slow Birth of New Labour Britain* (Basingstoke: Palgrave Macmillan).

Coates, K. (1972). *The Crisis of British Socialism: Essays on the Rise of Harold Wilson and the Fall of the Labour Party* (Nottingham: Spokesman).

Cockerell, M. (1986). *Television and Number Ten: Part One, 'Into the Torture Chamber'*, BBC 2, 12 November.

Cocks, M. (1989). *Labour and the Benn Factor* (London: Macdonald).

Commission on Social Justice (1994). *Social Justice: Strategies for Renewal* (Vintage: London).

Conroy, H. (2006). *Callaghan* (London: Haus).

Corthorn, P. (2004). 'How "new" is New Labour?' *Modern History Review*, 16 (2): 30–2.

Cosgrave, P. (1973). 'Heath as Prime Minister', *Political Quarterly*, 44 (4): 435–46.

Cosgrave, P. (1978). *Margaret Thatcher: A Tory and Her Party* (London: Hutchison).

Cowley, P. and Bailey, M. (2000). 'Peasants' Uprising of Religious War: Re-examining the 1975 Conservative Leadership Contest', *British Journal of Political Science*, 30 (4): 599–629.

Cowley, P. and Green, J. (2005). 'New Leaders, Same Problems: The Conservatives', in A. Geddes and J. Tonge (eds). *Britain Decides: The UK General Election 2005* (Basingstoke: Palgrave Macmillan), pp. 46–69.

Cowley, P. and Quayle, S. (2001). 'The Conservatives: Running on the Spot', in A. Geddes and J. Tonge (eds). *Labour's Landslide II* (Manchester: Manchester University Press).

Cowley, P. and Stuart, M. (2004). 'Still Causing Trouble: The Parliamentary Conservative Party', *Political Quarterly*, 75 (4): 356–61.

Cowley, P. and Stuart, M. (2011). 'Ignored, Irresponsible and Irrelevant? Opposition MPs in the House of Commons', in N. Fletcher (ed.) (2011). *How to be in Opposition: Life in the Political Shadows* (London: Biteback).

Crewe, I. and King, A. (1992). 'Did Major Win? Did Kinnock Lose? Leadership Effects in the 1992 Election', in A. Heath, R. Jowell, J. Curtice and B. Taylor (eds). *Labour's Last Chance: The 1992 Election and Beyond* (London: Dartmouth).

Crewe, I. and King, A. (1995). *SDP: The Birth, Life and Death of the Social Democratic Party* (Oxford: Oxford University Press).

Crewe, I. and Searing, D. (1988). 'Ideological Change in the British Conservative Party', *American Political Science Review*, 82: 361–84.

Crick, M. (2005). *In Search of Michael Howard* (London: Simon and Schuster).

Critchley, J. (1973). 'Strains and Stresses in the Conservative Party', *Political Quarterly*, 44 (4): 401–10.

Critchley, J. (1986). *Westminster Blues* (London: Futura).

Cronin, J. E. (2004). *New Labour's Pasts: The Labour Party and its Discontents* (Edinburgh: Pearson).

Crosland, A. (1956). *The Future of Socialism* (London: Cape).

Crossman, R. (ed.) (1952). *New Fabian Essays* (London: Turnstile Press).

Crowcroft, R. (2008). 'The High Politics of Labour Party Factionalism 1950–1955', *Historical Research*, 81(214): 679–709.

Dalton, H. (1957). *The Fateful Years: Memoirs 1931–1945* (London: Frederick Muller).

Denham, A. (2009). 'From Grey Suits to Grass Roots: Choosing Conservative Leaders', *British Politics*, 4 (2): 217–35.

Denham, A. and Dorey, P. (2006). 'A Tale of Two Speeches? The Conservative Party Leadership Election of 2005', *Political Quarterly*, 77 (1): 35–42.

Denham, A. and Garnett, M. (2001). *Keith Joseph: A Life* (Chesham: Acumen).

Denham, A. and O'Hara, K. (2008). *Democratising Conservative Leadership Election: From Grey Suits to Grass Roots* (Manchester: Manchester University Press).

Denver, D. (2005). 'Valence Politics: How Britain Votes Now', *British Journal of Politics and International Relations*, 7 (2): 292–9.

Desai, R. (1994). *Intellectuals and Socialism: 'Social Democrats' and the Labour Party* (London: Lawrence and Wishart).

Donoughue, B. (2003). *In the Heat of the Kitchen* (London: Politicos).

Donoughue, B. (2009). *Downing Street Diary Volume Two: With James Callaghan in No. 10* (London: Pimlicos).

Donoughue, B. and Jones, G. W. (1973). *Herbert Morrison: Portrait of a Politician* (London: Weidenfeld and Nicolson).

Dorey, P. (1995). *British Politics since 1945* (Oxford: Blackwell).

Dorey, P. (2004). 'Attention to detail: The Conservative Policy Agenda', *Political Quarterly*, 75 (4): 373–7.

Dorey, P. (2009). 'Sharing the Proceeds of Growth: Conservative Economic Policy under David Cameron', *Political Quarterly*, 80 (2): 259–69.

Douglas, R. (2005). *The Liberals: A History of the Liberal and Liberal Democrat Parties* (London: Continuum).

Driver, S. and Martell, L. (2002). *Blair's Britain* (Cambridge: Polity).

Drower, G. M. F. (1984). *Kinnock* (London: Weidenfeld and Nicolson).

Dutton, D. (2006). *Douglas Home* (London: Haus).

Duncan Smith, I. (2002a). 'Defeating the Five Giants', First Anniversary Speech, 23rd September, Available at: http://www.totalpolitics.com/speeches/conservative/conservatism/34583/defeating-the-five-giants-thtml [accessed 5 December 2011].

Duncan Smith, I. (2002b). 'Full text: Iain Duncan Smith's statement', *The Guardian*, 5 November 2002. Available at: http://www.guardian.co.uk/politics/2002/nov/05/conservatives.uk3 [accessed 5 December 2011].

Elliot, A. (2011). 'The Younger Elder Statesman', *Total Politics*, 25 March.

Evans, B. and Taylor, A. (1996). *From Salisbury to Major: Continuity and Change in Conservative Politics* (Manchester: Manchester University Press).

Evans, E. (1997). *Thatcher and Thatcherism* (London: Routledge).

Evans, G. and Andersen, R. (2005). 'The Impact of Party Leaders: How Blair lost Labour Votes', *Parliamentary Affairs*, 58 (4): 818–36.

Evans, R. (1982). 'Labour Poll Pledge Hints at Year's Rent Freeze', *The Times*, 20 April.

Farrell, D., and Webb, P. (2000). 'Political Parties as Campaign Organizations', in R. Dalton and M. Wattenberg (eds). *Parties without Partisans: Political Change in Advanced Industrial Democracies* (Oxford: Oxford University Press).

Fielding, S. (1994). 'Neil Kinnock: An Overview of the Labour Party', *Contemporary Record*, 8 (3): 589–601.

Fielding, S. (2007). 'Rethinking Labour's 1964 Campaign', *Contemporary British History*, 21 (3): 309–24.

Finlayson, A. (2003). *Making Sense of New Labour* (London: Lawrence and Wishart).

Fisher, N. (1977). *The Tory Leaders: Their Struggle for Power* (London: Weidenfeld and Nicolson).

Fletcher, N. (2001). *The Organisation of the Conservative Party in Opposition 1997–2001* (Unpublished dissertation).

Fletcher, N. (ed.) (2011). How to be in Opposition: Life in the Political Shadows (London: Biteback).

Foley, M. (2000). *The British Presidency: Tony Blair and the Politics of Public Leadership* (Manchester: Manchester University Press).

Foley, M. (2002). *John Major, Tony Blair and a Conflict of Leadership* (Manchester: Manchester University Press).

Foot, M. Leadership Papers (a) Labour Party Archives, National Museum of Labour History Box L4.

Foot, M. Leadership Papers (b) Labour Party Archives, National Museum of Labour History Box L30/2.

Foot, M. (1960). *Tribune*, 24 October.

Foot, M. (1975). *Aneurin Bevan: Volume II 1945–1960* (St Albans: Paladin).

Foot, M. (1984). *Another Heart and Other Pulses. The Alternative to the Thatcher Society* (London: Collins).

Foot, P. (1968). *The Politics of Harold Wilson* (London: Penguin).

Fowler, N. (2008). *A Political Suicide: The Conservatives' Voyage into the Wilderness* (London: Politicos).

Gaitskell, H. *Hugh Gaitskell Papers* (University College London).

Gamble, A. (1988). *The Free Economy and the Strong State* (London: Macmillan).

Gamble, A. (1995). 'The Crisis of Conservatism', *New Left Review*, 214: 3–25.

Gardiner, G. (1975). *Margaret Thatcher* (London: William Kimber).

Garner, R. (1990). 'Labour's Policy Review: A Case of Historical Continuity?', *Politics*, 10 (1): 33–9.

Garner, R. and Kelly, R. (1998). *British Political Parties Today* (Manchester: Manchester University Press).

Garnett, M. (2004). 'The Free Economy and the Schizophrenic State: Ideology and the Conservatives', *Political Quarterly*, 75 (4): 367–72.

Garnett, M. (2005). 'Planning for Power 1964–1970', in S. Ball and A. Seldon (eds). *Recovering Power: The Conservatives in Opposition Since 1867* (Basingstoke: Palgrave Macmillan).

Garnett, M. (2007). 'Banality in Politics: Margaret Thatcher and the Biographers', *Political Studies Review*, 5 (2): 172–82.

Garnett, M. and Aitken, I. (2002). *Splendid! Splendid! The Authorized Biography of Willie Whitelaw* (London: Jonathan Cape).

Garton-Ash, T. (2009). *The File: A Personal History* (London: Atlantic Books).

Geddes, A. and Tonge, J. (eds) (2001). *Labour's Second Landslide: The British General Election 2001* (Manchester: Manchester University Press).

Gilbert, M. (1988). *Never Despair: Winston S. Churchill 1945–1965* (London: Heinemann).

Gilmour, I. (1992). *Dancing with Dogma* (London: Simon and Schuster).

Gilmour, I. and Garnett, M. (1997). *Whatever Happened to the Tories?* (London, Fourth Estate).

Gimson, A. (2010). 'David Cameron slaughtered Ed Miliband', *The Daily Telegraph*, 1 December.

Glover, J. (2003). 'Captain Oblivion's Last Stand', *The Guardian*, 10 October. Available at: http://www.guardian.co.uk/politics/2003/oct/10/society.policy [accessed 5 December 2011].

Goodhart, P. (1973). *The 1922* (London: Macmillan).

Gould, P. (1993). Memo from Philip Gould to Murray Elder, Assessment of Current Position, 20 May, Murray Elder papers, Box 2.

Gould, P. (1998). *The Unfinished Revolution. How the Modernisers Saved the Labour Party* (London: Little Brown).

Grainger, J. (2005). *Tony Blair and the Ideal Type* (Exeter: Imprint Academic).

Gray, J. (2003). 'Michael Howard Might Turn Out to be the Tory Leader Who Lays Thatcher's Ghost', *New Statesman*, 10 November.

Greenstein, F. (1967). 'The Impact of Personality on Politics An Attempt to Clear Away Underbrush', *American Political Science Review*, 61 (3): 629–41.

Greenstein, F. (2001). *The Presidential Difference: Leadership Style from FDR to Clinton* (Princeton: Princeton University Press).

Greenstein, F. (2009). *The Presidential Difference: Leadership Style from FDR to Barack Obama* (Princeton: Princeton University Press).

Hall, S. and Jacques, M. (eds) (1983). *The Politics of Thatcherism* (London: Lawrence and Wishart).

Hansard, House of Commons, 25 April 1995, vol. 258, col. 255–6.

Harris, K. (1988). *Thatcher* (Boston: Little, Brown and Company).

Harris, R. (1984). *The Making of Neil Kinnock* (London: Faber and Faber).

Haseler, S. (1969). *The Gaitskellites: Revisionism in the British Labour Party 1951–1964* (London: Macmillan).

Hatfield, M. (1978). *The House the Left Built: Inside Labour Policy Making, 1970–1975*, (London: Victor Gollancz).

Hattersley, R (1995). *Who Goes Home? Scenes from a Political Life* (London: Little Brown).

Hattersley, R. (1997). *Fifty Years On: A Prejudiced History of Britain since the War* (London: Little Brown).

Hayton, R. (2008). 'Conservative Party Leadership Strategy and the Legacy of Thatcherite Conservatism, 1997–2005' (Unpublished PhD thesis, University of Sheffield).

Hayton, R. (2012). *Reconstructing Conservatism? The Conservative Party in Opposition, 1997–2010* (Manchester: Manchester University Press).

Hayton, R., English, R. and Kenny, M. (2009). 'Englishness in Contemporary British Politics', in A. Gamble and T. Wright (eds). *Britishness: Perspectives on the British Question* (London: Wiley-Blackwell).

Hayton, R. and Heppell, T. (2010). 'The Quiet Man of British Politics: The Rise, Fall and Significance of Iain Duncan Smith', *Parliamentary Affairs*, 63 (4): 425–45.

Hay, C. (1999). *The Political Economy of New Labour: Labouring Under False Pretences?* (Manchester: Manchester University Press).

Healey, D. (1990). *The Time of My Life* (London: Penguin).

Heath, E. (1998). *The Course of My Life: My Autobiography* (London: Hodder and Stoughton).

Heffer, S. (1998). *Like the Roman: The Life of Enoch Powell* (London: Phoenix).

Heffernan, R. (2000). 'The Politics of the Parliamentary Labour Party', in B. Brivati and R. Heffernan (eds). *The Labour Party: A Centenary History* (Basingstoke: Macmillan).

Heffernan, R. (2001). *New Labour and Thatcherism* (Basingstoke: Palgrave Macmillan).

Heffernan, R. (2006). 'The Prime Minister and the News Media: Political Communication as a Leadership Resource', *Parliamentary Affairs*, 59 (4): 582–98.

Heffernan, R. and Marqusee. M. (1992). *Defeat from the Jaws of Victory: Inside Kinnock's Labour Party* (London: Verso).

Heffernan, R. and Webb, P. (2009). 'The British Prime Minister: Much More than First Amongst Equals', in T. Poguntke and P. Webb (eds). *The Presidentialisation of Politics: A Comparative Study of Modern Democracies* (Oxford: Oxford University Press).

Hegley, J. (1992). 'Happy Easter, Mr Kinnock', *The Guardian*, 18 April.

Helm, T. and Sylvester, R. (2002). 'Most Tories Do Not Want Duncan Smith as Leader', *Daily Telegraph*, 8 November.

Hennessy, P. (1992). *Never Again: Britain 1945–1951* (London: Jonathan Cape).

Hennessy, P. (1997). *Muddling Through: Power, Politics and the Quality of Government in Postwar Britain* (London: Indigo).

Hennessy, P. (2000). *The Prime Minister: The Office and its Holders since 1945* (London: Penguin).

Heppell, T (2006). *The Conservative Party Leadership of John Major 1992 to 1997* (Lewiston: Edwin Mellen Press).

Heppell, T. (2008a). *Choosing the Tory Leader: Conservative Party Leadership Elections from Heath to Cameron* (London: I. B. Tauris).

Heppell, T. (2008b). 'The Degenerative Tendencies of Long Serving Governments ... 1963 ... 1996 ... 2008? *Parliamentary Affairs*, 61 (4): 578–96.

Heppell, T. (2010a). *Choosing the Labour Leader: Labour Party Leadership Elections from Wilson to Brown* (London: I. B. Tauris).

Heppell, T. (2010b). 'The Labour Leadership Election of 1963: Explaining the Unexpected Election of Harold Wilson', *Contemporary British History*, 24 (2): 151–71.

Heppell, T. and Hill, M. (2010). 'The Voting Motivations of Conservative Parliamentarians in the Conservative Party Leadership Election of 2001', *Politics*, 30 (1): 36–51.

Heppell, T. and Hill, M. (2012). 'Labour in Opposition', in T. Heppell and D. Seawright (eds). *Cameron and the Conservatives: The Transition to Coalition Government* (Basingstoke: Palgrave Macmillan).

Hoffman, J. D. (1964). *The Conservative Party in Opposition 1945–51* (London: MacGibbon and Kee).

Hoggart, S. (1994). 'Sharp Wit with an Inner Fire', *The Guardian*, 13 May.

Hoggart, S. (2003). 'The Quiet Man Resorts to Road Rage Politics', *The Guardian*, 10 October.

Holland, S. (2004). 'Ownership, Planning and Markets', in R. Plant, M. Beech and K. Hickson (eds). *The Struggle for Labour's Soul. Understanding Labour's Political Thought since 1945* (London: Routledge).

Holmes, M. (1997). *The Failure of the Heath Government* (London: Macmillan).

Home, Lord (1976). *The Way the Wind Blows: An Autobiography* (London: Collins).

Hope, C. (2010). 'Michael Foot: Labour's 1983 General Election Manifesto and the 'Longest Suicide in History', *Daily Telegraph*, 3 March.

Horne, A. (1988). *Macmillan 1894–1956* (London: Macmillan).

House of Lords (2010). Constitution Committee – Fourth Report: The Cabinet Office and the Centre of Government (London: House of Lords), available at: http://www.publications.parliament.uk/pa/ld200910/ldselect/ldconst/30/3004.htm [accessed 1 October 2010].

Howard, A. (1987). *RAB: The Life of R.A. Butler* (London: Cape).

Howard, A. (1994). 'John Smith: the Lost Leader', *The Times*, 13 May.

Howard, A. and West, R. (1965). *The Making of the Prime Minister* (London: Jonathan Cape).

Howell, D. (1980). *British Social Democracy* (London: Croom Helm).

Howell, D. (2006). *Attlee* (London: Haus).

Howe, G. (1994). *Conflict of Loyalty* (London: Macmillan).

Hurd, D. (2003). *Memoirs* (London: Little Brown).

Hutton, W. (1995). *The State We're In* (London: Cape).

Illustrated London News (1965). Political Report, 7 August.

James, C. (1983). 'Campaign Down the Drain', *The Observer*, 29 May.

Jay, D. (1980). *Change and Fortune: A Political Record* (London: Hutchison).

Jefferys, K. (1992). *The Attlee Governments 1945–1951* (London: Longman).

Jefferys, K. (1993). *The Labour Party since 1945* (London: Macmillan).

Jefferys, K. (1997). *Retreat from New Jerusalem: British Politics 1951–1964* (London: Macmillan).

Jefferys, K. (2000). 'The Attlee Years 1935–55', in B. Brivati and R. Heffernan (eds). *The Labour Party: A Centenary History* (London: Macmillan).

Jefferys, K. (2004). 'The New Right', in R. Plant, M. Beech and K. Hickson (ed.). *The Struggle for Labour's Soul* (London: Routledge).

Jefferys, K. (2006). 'Labour in Opposition 1951–1964', in P. Dorey (ed.). *The Labour Governments 1964–1970* (London: Routledge).

Jenkins, R. (1948). *Mr Attlee: An Interim Biography* (London: Heinemann).

Jenkins, P. (1981). 'The Muddle that Ended in a Leap in the Dark', *The Guardian*, 26 January.

Jenkins, P. (1987). *Mrs Thatcher's Revolution* (London: Jonathan Cape).

Jenkins, R. (1982). 'Home Thoughts from Abroad: The 1979 Dimbleby Lecture', in W. Kennet (ed.). *The Rebirth of Britain* (London: Weidenfeld and Nicolson).

Jenkins, R. (1991). *A Life at the Centre* (London: Macmillan).

Jenkins, S. (2006). *Thatcher and Sons* (London: Allen Lane).

Jennings, I. (1961). *Cabinet Government* (Cambridge: Cambridge University Press).

Johnson, F. (1982). 'Minister for the Good News Fluffs his Brief' *The Times* 3 February.

Johnson, N. (1997). 'Opposition in the British Political System', *Government and Opposition*, 32 (4): 487–510.

Jones, E. (1994). *Neil Kinnock* (London: Hale).

Jones, M. (1994). *Michael Foot* (London: Victor Gollancz).

Jones, G., Brogan, B. and Peterkin, T. (2002). 'Duncan Smith Provoked Leadership Crisis, Says Clarke', *Daily Telegraph*, 7 November.

Jones, N. (2010). *Campaign 2010: The Making of the Prime Minister* (London: Biteback).

Jones, T. (1996). *Remaking the Labour Party: From Gaitskell to Blair* (London: Routledge).

Jones, T. (1997). 'Taking Genesis out of the Bible: Hugh Gaitskell, Clause IV and Labour's Socialist Myth', *Contemporary British History*, 11 (2): 1–23.

Jun, U. (1996). 'Inner-Party Reforms: the SPD and Labour Party in Comparative Perspective', *German Politics*, 5 (1): 58–80.

Kandiah, M. (1992). *Lord Woolton's Chairmanship of the Conservative Party 1946–1951* (Unpublished PhD thesis, University of Exeter).

Kavanagh, D. (1987). *Thatcherism and British Politics: The End of Consensus?* (Oxford: Oxford University Press).

Kavanagh, D. (1992). 'The Post-War Consensus', *Twentieth Century British History*, 3 (2): 175–90.

Kavanagh, D. (1996). '1970–1974', in A. Seldon (ed.). *How Tory Governments Fall: The Tory Party in Power Since 1783* (London: Fontana).

Kavanagh, D. (2005). 'The Making of Thatcherism: 1974–1979', in S. Ball and A. Seldon (eds). *Recovering Power: The Conservatives in Opposition since 1867* (Basingstoke: Palgrave Macmillan).

Kavanagh, D. and Butler, D. (2005). *The British General Election of 2005* (Basingstoke: Palgrave).

Kavanagh, D. and Cowley, P. (2010). *The British General Election of 2010* (Basingstoke: Palgrave Macmillan).

Kellner, P. (ed.) (1992). *Thorns and Roses – Neil Kinnock – Speeches, 1983–1991* (London, Hutchinson).

Kelly, R. (2003a). 'Renew and Reorganise: Party Structures and the Politics of Reinvention', *Political Quarterly*, 74 (1): 109–15.

Kelly, R. (2003b). 'Organisational Reform and the Extra-Parliamentary Party', in M. Garnett and P. Lynch (eds). *The Conservatives in Crisis* (Manchester: Manchester University Press).

Kenny, M. and Smith, M. (1997). 'Discourses of Modernisation: Gaitskell, Blair and the Reform of Clause IV', *Journal of Elections, Public Opinion and Parties*, 7 (1): 110–26.

Kerr, P. (2007). 'Cameron Chameleon and the Current State of Britain's Consensus', *Parliamentary Affairs*, 60 (1): 46–65.

Kilmuir, Earl of (1964). *Political Adventure* (London: Weidenfeld and Nicolson).

King, A. (1991). 'The British Prime Minister in the Age of the Career Politician', in G. W. Jones (ed.). *West European Prime Ministers* (London: Frank Cass).

King, A. (ed.) (2001). *British Political Opinion 1937–2000: The Gallup Polls* (London: Politicos).

King, A. (2006). 'Why Labour Won – Yet Again?', in J. Bartle and A. King (eds). *Britain at the Polls* (London: CQ Press).

King, C. (1975). *The Cecil King Diary, 1970–1974* (London: Jonathan Cape).

Kinnock, N. (1994). *Tomorrow's Socialism*, BBC 2, 5 February.

Kinnock, N. (2010). 'Learning the Lessons of Opposition' Launch event for the Opposition Studies Forum, January 2010. Available at: http://oppositionstudies. webs.com/news.htm [accessed 23 February 2011].

Kinnock, N. (2011). 'Interview with Author', House of Lords, 28 February.

Kitschelt, H. (1994). *The Transformation of European Social Democracy* (Cambridge: Cambridge University Press).

Koelble, T. A. (1991). *The Left Unravelled, Social Democracy and the New Left Challenge in Britain and West Germany* (London: Duke University Press).

Kominsky, P. (2002). *The Project*, Episode 1, BBC1, 10 November 2002 (transcript).

Labour Party (1976). *Report of the Annual Conference of the Labour Party* (London: Labour Party).

Labour Party (1980). *Report of the Annual Conference and Special Conference of the Labour Party* (London: Labour Party).

Labour Party (1983). *The New Hope for Britain* (London: Labour Party).

Labour Party (1992). *Ninety-First Annual Conference Report of the Labour Party* (London: The Labour Party).

Labour Party Manifesto Group Papers (Labour History Archive and Study Centre: Manchester).

Labour Party National Executive Committee (NEC) Minutes (Labour History Archive and Study Centre: Manchester).

Labour Party Parliamentary Labour Party Papers (Labour History Archive and Study Centre: Manchester).

Lawrence, J. (2009). *Electing our Masters: The Hustings in British Politics from Hogarth to Blair* (Oxford: Oxford University Press).

Lawson, N. (1992). *The View From Number 11* (London: Bantam Press).

Laybourn, K. (2000). *A Century of Labour: A History of the Labour Party* (Stroud: Sutton).

Lee, S. (2009). 'Convergence, Critique and Divergence: The Development of Economic Policy under David Cameron', in S. Lee and M. Beech (eds). *Built to Last? The Conservatives under David Cameron* (Basingstoke: Palgrave Macmillan).

Leonard, D. (2005). *A Century of Premiers: Salisbury to Blair* (Basingstoke: Palgrave Macmillan).

Letwin, O. (2003). *The Neighbourly Society: Collected Speeches, 2001–3* (London: Centre for Policy Studies).

Lewis, R. (1975). *Margaret Thatcher: A Personal and Political Biography* (London: Routledge and Kegan Paul).

Lindsay, T. F. and Harrington, M. (1974). *The Conservative Party 1918–1970* (London: Macmillan).

Macintyre, D. (1999). *Mandelson. The Biography* (London: HarperCollins).

Macmillan, H. (1972). *Pointing the Way 1959–1961* (London: Macmillan).

Macmillan, H. (1969). *Tides of Fortune 1945–1955* (London: Macmillan).

Macmillan, H. (1973). *At the End of the Day 1961–1963* (London: Macmillan).

Mandelson, P. (2010). *The Third Man: Life at the Heart of New Labour* (London: Harper Press).

Marquand, D. (1979). 'Inquest on a Movement: Labour's Defeat and its Consequences', *Encounter*, July: 8–18.

Marquand, D. (1999). *The Progressive Dilemma: From Lloyd George to Kinnock* (London: Phoenix).

Marshall, J. (2009). *Membership of the UK Political Parties*, House of Commons Library http://www.parliament.uk/documents/commons/lib/research/briefings/snsg-05125.pdf, accessed 25 July 2010.

Martineau, L. (2000). *Barbara Castle: A Biography* (London: Andre Deutsch).

Maudling, R. (1978). *Memoirs* (London: Sidgwick and Jackson).

Mayer, A. J. (1979). *Madam Prime Minister* (New York: Newsweek Books).

Mayer, F. A. (1992). *The Opposition Years: Winston S. Churchill and the Conservative Party 1945–1951* (New York: Peter Lang).

McAnulla, S. (2006). *British Politics: A Critical Introduction* (London: Continuum).

McAnulla, S. (2010). 'Heirs to Blair's Third Way: David Cameron's Triangulating Conservatism', *British Politics*, 5 (3): 286–314.

McDermott, G. (1972). *Leader Lost: A Biography of Hugh Gaitskell* (London: Leslie Frewin).

McKenzie, R. T. (1963). *British Political Parties: The Distribution of Power within the Conservative and Labour Parties* (London: Praeger).

McKibbin, R. (2002). 'The Luck of the Tories', *LRB*, 24 (5): 8–9.

McKie, D. (2005). 'Lord Callaghan', *The Guardian*, 28 March.

Meredith, S. (2007). 'Factionalism on the Parliamentary Right of the British Labour Party in the 1970s: A Reassessment', *Contemporary British History*, 21 (1): 55–85.

Meredith, S. (2008). *Labours Old and New: The Parliamentary Right of the British Labour Party 1970–79 and the Roots of New Labour* (Manchester: Manchester University Press).

Meredith, S. (2011). 'A Catalyst for Secession? European Divisions on the Parliamentary Right of the Labour Party 1962–72 and the Schism of British Social Democracy', *Historical Research*. DOI: 10.1111/j.1468-2281.2010.00567.x

Mikardo, I. (1988). *Back-Bencher* (London: Wiedenfeld and Nicolson).

Millar, R. (1993). *A View from the Wings* (London: Weidenfeld and Nicolson).

Minkin, L. (1980). *The Labour Party Conference* (Manchester: Manchester University Press).

Minkin, L. (1991). *The Contentious Alliance: Trade Unions and the Labour Party* (Manchester: Manchester University Press).

Moran, Lord (1968). *Winston Churchill and the Struggle for Survival 1940–1965* (London: Sphere Books).

Morgan, A. (1992). *Harold Wilson* (London: Pluto Press).

Morgan, J. (ed.) (1981). *The Backbench Diaries of Richard Crossman* (London: Hamish Hamilton and Cape).

Morgan, J. (ed.) (1983). *The Backbench Diaries of Richard Crossman* (London: Jonathan Cape).

Morgan, K. (1984). *Labour in Power 1945–1951* (Oxford: Oxford University Press).

Morgan, K. (1987). *Labour People: From Hardie to Kinnock* (Oxford: Oxford University Press).

Morgan, K. (1992). *Labour People: Leaders and Lieutenants, Hardie to Kinnock* (Oxford: Oxford University Press).

Morgan, K. (1997a). *Callaghan: A Life* (Oxford: Oxford University Press).

Morgan, K. (1997b). Interview with the Author, 17 October.

Morgan, K. (1999). 'James Callaghan 1976–80', in K. Jefferys (ed.). *Leading Labour: From Keir Hardie to Tony Blair* (London: I.B. Tauris)

Morgan, K. (2007). *Michael Foot: A Life* (London: Harper Press).

Mughan, A. (2000). *Media and the Presidentialization of Parliamentary Elections* (Basingstoke: Palgrave Macmillan).

Mullin, C. (2010). 'Short Cuts' *London Review of Books*, 32 (6): 26.

Murphy, J. (2002). 'Surprised and Delighted Clarke Praises Duncan Smith', *Daily Telegraph*, 7 April.

Nadler, J. (2000). *William Hague: In his Own Right* (London: Politicos).

Naughtie, J. (2001). *The Rivals. The Intimate Story of a Political Marriage* (London: Fourth Estate).

New Statesman (1960). Editorial, 24 October.

Nicholas, H. G. (1951). *The British General Election of 1950* (London: Macmillan).

Nicolson, N. (ed.) (1968). *Harold Nicolson: Diaries and Letters 1945–1962*, Volume 3 (London: Collins).

Norris, P. (1994). 'Labour Party Factionalism and Extremism', in A. Heath, R. Jowell, J. Curtice and B. Taylor (eds). *Labour's Last Chance? The 1992 Election and Beyond* (Aldershot: Dartmouth).

Norris, P. and Lovenduski, J. (2004). 'Why Parties Fail to Learn: Electoral Defeat, Selection Perception and British Party Politics', *Party Politics,* 10 (1): 85–104.

Norton, P. (1978). *Conservative Dissidents: Dissent within the Parliamentary Conservative Party 1970–74* (London: Temple Smith).

Norton, P. (1980). *Dissension in the House of Commons 1974–1979* (Oxford: Clarendon Press).

Norton, P. (1987). 'Mrs Thatcher and the Conservative Party: Another Institution "Handbagged"?' in K. Minogue and M. Biddiss (eds). *Thatcherism: Personality and Politics* (London: Macmillan).

Norton, P. (1990). 'The Lady's Not For Turning: But What About the Rest? Margaret Thatcher and the Conservative Party, 1979–1989', *Parliamentary Affairs*, 43 (1): 41–58.

Norton, P. (2006). 'The Conservative Party: The Politics of Panic', in J. Bartle and A. King (eds) *Britain at the Polls 2005* (London: CQ Press).

Norton, P. (2008). 'Making Sense of Opposition', *Journal of Legislative Studies*, 14 (1/2): 236–50.

Norton, P. (2009). 'David Cameron and Tory Success: Bystander or Architect?', in S. Lee and M. Beech (eds). *Built to Last? The Conservatives under David Cameron* (Basingstoke: Palgrave Macmillan).

Norton, P. and Aughey, A. (1982). *Conservatives and Conservatism* (London: Temple Smith).

Nott, J. (2002). *Here Today, Gone Tomorrow* (London: Politico's).

Owen, D. (1991). *Time to Declare* (London: Michael Joseph).

Owen, D. David Owen Papers (University of Liverpool).

Parkinson, C. (1992). *Right at the Centre* (London: Weidenfeld and Nicolson).

Parkinson, J. and Griffiths, E. (2010). Reactions and Tributes after Michael Foot's Death, *BBC News*, 3 March.

Patten, C. (1980). 'Policy Making in Opposition', in Z. Layton-Henry (ed.). *Conservative Party Politics* (London: Macmillan).

Patterson, W. and Thomas, A. (1986). *The Future of Social Democracy; Problems and Prospects of Social Democratic Parties in Western Europe* (Oxford: Clarendon).

Pearce, R. (1997). *Attlee* (London: Longman).

Pelling, H. (1984). *The Labour Governments 1945–1951* (London: Macmillan).

Pelling, H. (1997). *Churchill's Peacetime Ministry 1951–55* (London: Macmillan).

Perkins, A. (2003). *Red Queen: The Authorised Biography of Barbara Castle* (Basingstoke: Palgrave Macmillan).

Pimlott, B. (1986). *The Political Diaries of Hugh Dalton 1918–1940, 1945–1960* (London: Cape).

Pimlott, B. (1992). *Harold Wilson* (London: Harper Collins).

Ponting, C. (1994). *Churchill* (London: Sinclair-Stevenson).

Portillo, M. (2002). 'How Might the Right Right itself?', The Chatham Lecture, 15 November. Available from: http://www.michaelportillo.co.uk/speeches/speeches_pub/right.htm. [accessed 9 July 2010].

Powell, J. (2010). *The New Machiavelli: How to Wield Power in the Modern World* (London: The Bodley Head).

Prideaux, S. (2005). *Not so New Labour: A Sociological critique of New Labour's Policy and Practice* (Bristol: Policy Press).

Prior, J. (1986). *A Balance of Power* (London: Hamish Hamilton).

Prince, R. (2010). 'Ed Miliband "Too Busy" to Marry Pregnant Girlfriend', *The Daily Telegraph*, 27 September.

Pugh, M. (2010). *Speak for Britain! A New History of the Labour Party* (London: The Bodley Head).

Punnett, R. M. (1973). *Front Bench Opposition. The Role of the Leader of the Opposition, the Shadow Cabinet and Shadow government in British Politics* (London: Heinemann).

Punnett, R. M. (1992). *Selecting the Party Leader: Britain in Comparative Perspective* (Hemel Hempstead: Harvester Wheatsheaf).

Radice, G. (2002). *Friends and Rivals: Crosland, Jenkins and Healey* (London: Abacus).

Radice, G. (2008). *The Tortoise and the Hares: Attlee, Bevin, Cripps, Dalton and Morrison* (London: Politicos).

Ramsden, J. (1977). 'From Churchill to Heath', in Lord Butler (ed.). *The Conservatives: A History from their origins to 1965* (London: Allen and Unwin).

Ramsden, J. (1995a). *The Age of Churchill and Eden (History of the Conservative Party)* (London: Longman).

Ramsden, J. (1995b). 'Winston Churchill and the Leadership of the Conservative Party 1940–51', *Contemporary Record*, 9 (1): 99–119.

Ramsden, J. (1996). *Winds of Change: Macmillan to Heath 1957–1965* (London: Longman).

Ramsden, J. (1998). *An Appetite for Power: A History of the Conservative Party Since 1830* (London: Harper Collins).

Rawnsley, A. (2001). *Servants of the People: The Inside Story of New Labour* (London: Penguin).

Rees, M. (2001). 'James Callaghan', in G. Rosen (ed.), *Dictionary of Labour Biography* (London: Politicos).

Rentoul, J. (1995). *Tony Blair* (London: Little Brown).

Rentoul, J. (2001). *Tony Blair: Prime Minister* (London: Little Brown and Company).

Rhodes James, R. (1972). *Ambitions and Realities: British Politics 1964–1970* (London: Weidenfeld and Nicolson).

Rhodes James, R. (ed.) (1974). *Winston S. Churchill Complete Speeches 1897–1963* (London: Chelsea House Publishers).

Rhodes James, R. (1978). *The British Revolution: British Politics 1880–1939* (London: Methuen).

Rhodes James, R. (1986). *Anthony Eden* (London: Weidenfeld and Nicolson).

Richards, D. and Smith, M. J. (2002). *Governance and Public Policy in the UK* (Oxford: Oxford University Press).

Riddell, P. (2005). *The Unfulfilled Prime Minister* (London: Politicos).

Riddell, P. and Haddon C. (2009). *Transitions: Preparing for Changes of Government* (London: Institute for Government).

Ridley, N. (1991). *My Style of Government* (London: Hutchinson).

Robbins, K. (1992). *Churchill* (London: Longman).

Rodgers, W. (1979). 'Labour's Predicament: Decline or Recovery?', *Political Quarterly*, 50(4): 420–34.

Rodgers, W. (2000). *Fourth Among Equals* (London: Politicos).

Rose, R. (1964). 'Parties, Factions and Tendencies in Britain', *Political Studies*, 12 (1): 33–46.

Rose, R. (2001). *The Prime Minister in a Shrinking World* (Cambridge: Polity).

Rosen, G. (2011). 'Lessons for a Leader: Labour in Opposition' in N. Fletcher (ed.), *How to be in Opposition: Life in the Political Shadows* (London: Biteback).

Roth, A. (1972). *Heath and the Heathmen* (London: Routledge and Kegan Paul).

Roth, A. (1977). *Sir Harold Wilson: Yorkshire Walter Mitty* (London: Macdonald and Jane's Publishers).

Routledge, P. (1995). *Madam Speaker: The life of Betty Boothroyd* (London: Harper Collins).

Rubenstein, D. (2006). *The Labour Party and British Society* (Brighton: Sussex Academic Press).

Russell, A. and Fieldhouse, E. (2005). *Neither Left Nor Right: The Liberal Democrats and the Electorate* (Manchester: Manchester University Press).

Sandbrook, D. (2006). *White Heat: A History of Britain in the Swinging Sixties* (London: Little Brown).

Sandbrook, D. (2008). 'Crisis, What Crisis?', *New Statesman*, 2 October.

Sandbrook, D. (2010). *State of Emergency: The Way we Were: Britain 1970–1974* (London: Allen Lane).

Seawright, D. (2005). 'One-Nation', in K. Hickson (ed.). *The Political Thought of the Conservative Party since 1945* (Basingstoke: Palgrave Macmillan).

Seldon, A. (1981). *Churchill's Indian Summer: The Conservative Government 1951–55* (London: Hodder and Stoughton).

Seldon, A. (2004). *Blair* (London: Free Press).

Seldon, A. and Snowdon, P. (2005a). 'The Barren Years: 1997–2005', in S. Ball and A. Seldon (eds). *Recovering Power: The Conservatives in Opposition since 1867* (Basingstoke: Palgrave Macmillan).

Seldon, A. and Snowdon, P. (2005b). 'The Conservative Party', in A. Seldon and D. Kavanagh (eds). *The Blair Effect 2001–5* (Cambridge: Cambridge University Press).

Seyd, P. (1987). *The Rise and Fall of the Labour Left* (Basingstoke: Macmillan).

Seyd, P. (1999). 'New Parties/New Politics? A Case Study of the British Labour Party?' *Party Politics*, 5 (3): 383–405.

Seyd, P. and Whiteley, P. (2001). 'New Labour and the Party: Members and Organisation', in S. Ludlam and M. J. Smith (eds). *New Labour in Government* (Basingstoke: Macmillan).

Shaw, E. (1988). *Discipline and Discord in the Labour Party. The Politics of Managerial Control in the Labour Party, 1951–87* (Manchester: Manchester University Press).

Shaw, E. (1994). *The Labour Party Since 1979. Crisis and Transformation* (London: Routledge).

Shaw, E. (1996). *The Labour Party since 1945* (Oxford: Blackwell).

Shaw, E. (2004). 'The Control Freaks? New Labour and the Party', in S. Ludlam and M. J. Smith (eds). *Governing as New Labour: Policies and Politics under Blair* (Basingstoke: Palgrave Macmillan).

Shepherd, R. (1991). *The Power Brokers: The Tory Party and its Leaders* (London: Hutchinson).

Shepherd, R. (1995). *Iain Macleod: A Biography* (London: Politicos).

Shepherd, J. (2002). *George Lansbury: At the heart of Old Labour* (Oxford: Oxford University Press).

Shore, P. (1993). *Leading the Left* (London: Weidenfeld and Nicolson).

Sibley, J. R. (1978). 'Labour Party Committee Elections and the Labour Leadership', *European Journal of Political Research*, 6 (1): 71–104.

Smith, E. (1994). 'Introduction', in G. Brown and J. Naughtie (eds). *John Smith. Life and Soul of the Party* (Edinburgh: Mainstream).

Smith, J. (1992). Speech to the General Council Dinner at the Scottish Trades Union Congress, 23 April (David Ward papers).

Smith, M. J. (1992). 'The Labour Party in Opposition', in M. J. Smith and J. Spear (eds). *The Changing Labour Party* (London: Routledge).

Smith, M. J. (1999). *The Core Executive in British Politics* (Basingstoke: Macmillan).

Snowdon, P. (2010). *Back from the Brink: The Inside Story of the Tory Resurrection* (London: Harper Press).

Sopel, J. (1995). *Tony Blair: The Moderniser* (London: Michael Joseph).

Spectator (1965). 'The Conservatives' Dilemma', 14 January.

Stern, S. (2004). 'Labour's Lost Leader. How Smith Threw the Book at Straw', *New Statesman*, 19 April.

Straw, J. (1993). *Policy and Ideology* (Blackburn: Blackburn Labour Party).

Stokes, D. (1992). 'Valence Politics', in D. Kavanagh (ed.). *Electoral Politics* (Oxford: Clarendon Press).

Stuart, M. (2004). 'John Smith. His Battle for OMOV', *Labour History*, Issue 3, Autumn: 4–6.

Stuart, M. (2003). 'What if John Smith had lived?', in D. Brack and I. Dale (eds). *Prime Minister Portillo and Other Things That Never Happened. A Collection of Political Counterfactuals* (London: Politico's).

Stuart, M. (2005). *John Smith: A Life* (London: Politicos).

Stuart, M. (2006). 'Managing the Poor Bloody Infantry: The Parliamentary Labour Party under John Smith, 1992–94', *Parliamentary Affairs*, 59(3): 401–19.

Tatchell. P. (1983). *The Battle for Bermondsey* (London: Heretic).

Taylor, A. J. (2005). 'Economic Statecraft', in K. Hickson (ed.). *The Political Thought of the Conservative Party since 1945* (Basingstoke: Palgrave Macmillan).

Taylor, A. (2010). 'British Conservatives, David Cameron and the Politics of Adaptation', *Representation*, 46 (4): 489–96.

Tebbit, N. (1989). *Upwardly Mobile* (London: Futura).

Temple, M (2006). *Blair* (London: Haus).

Temple, W. (1942). *Christianity and Social Order* (London: Penguin).

Thatcher, M. (1995). *The Path to Power* (London: Harper Collins).

Theakston, K. (2007). 'What Makes for an Effective British Prime Minister', *Quaderni Di Scienza Politica*, 14 (2): 227–49.

Theakston, K. (2010). *After Number 10: Former Prime Ministers in British Politics* (Basingstoke: Palgrave Macmillan).

Theakston, K. (2011). 'Gordon Brown as Prime Minister: Political Skills and Leadership Style', *British Politics*, 6 (1): 78–100.

Theakston, K. and Gill, M. (2006). 'Rating 20th-Century British Prime Ministers', *British Journal of Politics and International Relations*, 8 (2): 193–213.

Theakston, K. and Gill, M. (2011). 'The Post-War Premiership League', *Political Quarterly*, 82 (1): 67–80.

The Guardian (1980). 'We are Not Prepared to Abandon Britain to Divisive and Often Cruel Tory Policies', 1 August.

The Times (1978). 'Mr Callaghan Renews Plea for 5% Pay Guideline', 5 September.

Thomas, J. (1997). '"Taffy was a Welshman, Taffy was a Thief": Anti-Welshness, The Press and Neil Kinnock' *Llafur: Journal of Welsh Labour History/Cylchgrawn Hanes Llafur Cymru*, 7 (2): 95–108.

Thomas, J. (1998). 'Labour, the Tabloids, and the 1992 General Election', *Contemporary British History*, 12 (2): 80–104.

Thomas-Symonds, N. (2005). 'A Reinterpretation of Michael Foot's Handling of the Militant Tendency', *Contemporary British History*, 19 (1): 27–51.

Thomas-Symonds, N. (2006). 'Oratory, Rhetoric and Politics: Neil Kinnock's "Thousand Generations" speech and the General Election of 1987', *Llafur: Journal of Welsh Labour History/Cylchgrawn Hanes Llafur Cymru*, 9 (3): 65–80.

Thomas-Symonds, N. (2010). *Attlee: A Life in Politics* (London: I. B. Tauris).

Thompson, N. (2006). 'The Fabian Political Economy of Harold Wilson', in P. Dorey (ed.). *The Labour Governments, 1964–1970* (London: Routledge).

Thorpe, A. (2001). *A History of the British Labour Party* (Basingstoke: Palgrave Macmillan).

Thorpe, D. R. (1996). *Alec Douglas-Home* (London: Sinclair-Stevenson).

Thorpe, D. R. (2003). *Eden* (London: Chatto and Windus).

Times (1965). '*Sir A. Home To Remain At The Helm Bid For Overthrow Fails*', 13 July.

TUC-Labour Party Liaison Committee (1973). *Economic Policy and the Cost of Living*.

Turner, J. (1996). '1951–64', in A. Seldon (ed.). *How Tory Governments Fall: The Tory Party in Power Since 1783* (London: Fontana).

Tyrie, A. (2001). *Back from the Brink* (London: Parliamentary Mainstream).

Walters, S. (2001). *Tory Wars: Conservatives in Crisis* (London: Politicos).

Warde, A. (1982). *Consensus and Beyond: The Development of Labour Party Strategy since the Second World War* (Manchester: Manchester University Press).

Watkins, A. (1998). *The Road to Number 10: From Bonar Law to Tony Blair* (London, Duckworth).

Watkins, A. (2008). 'This Sea-Change is a Gift for the Tories', *The Independent*, 25 May.

Watkins, A. (2010). 'Michael Foot: An Intellectual Prizefighter', *The Independent*, 7 March.

Weber, M. (1918). 'Politics as a Vocation'. Available at: http://www.ne.jp/asahi/moriyuki/abukuma/weber/lecture/politics_vocation.html [accessed 5 December 2011].

Webster, P. (1982). 'Foot Calls for New Social Contract', *The Times*, 16 March.

Wellings, B. (2007). 'Rump Britain: Englishness and Britishness, 1992–2001', *National Identities*, 9 (4): 395–412.

Westlake, M. (2001). *Kinnock: The Biography* (London: Little Brown).

Wheatcroft, G. (2005). *The Strange Death of Tory England* (London: Allen Lane).

Wheeler, B. (2011). 'The Secret to Being a Successful Opposition Leader', *BBC News*, 18 February.

Whiteley, P. (1983). *The Labour Party in Crisis* (London: Methuen).

Whitty, L. (1992). Letter from Larry Whitty to Murray Elder, 10 September, Murray Elder papers, Box 1.

Wickham-Jones, M. (1996). *Economic Strategy and the Labour Party. Politics and Policy Making, 1970–93* (Basingstoke: Macmillan).

Wickham-Jones, M. (2004). 'The New Left', in R. Plant, M. Beech and K. Hickson (eds). *The Struggle for Labour's Soul. Understanding Labour's political thought since 1945* (London: Routledge).

Wickham-Jones, M. and Jobson, R. (2010). 'Gripped by the Past: Nostalgia and the 2010 Labour Party Leadership Contest', *British Politics*, 5 (4): 525–48.

Willetts, D. (2005). 'The New Conservatism 1945–1951' in S. Ball and A. Seldon (eds). *Recovering Power: The Conservatives in Opposition since 1867* (Basingstoke: Palgrave Macmillan).

Williams, H. (1998). *Guilty Men: Conservative Decline and Fall, 1992–1997* (London: Aurum Press).

Williams, F. (1961). *A Prime Minister Remembers* (London: Heinemann).

Williams M. (1972). *Inside Number 10* (London: Coward, McCann and Geoghegan).

Williams, P. (1978). *Hugh Gaitskell: A Political Biography* (London: Jonathan Cape).

Williams, P. (ed.) (1981). *The Diary of Hugh Gaitskell* (London: Jonathan Cape).

Williams, S. (2009). *Climbing the Bookshelves* (London: Virago).

Wilson, H. (1964a). *Purpose in Politics: Selected Speeches* (London: Weidenfeld and Nicolson).

Wilson, H. (1964b). *The Relevance of British Socialism* (London: Weidenfeld and Nicolson).

Wilson, H. (1971). *The Labour Government, 1964–70: A Personal Record* (London: Michael Joseph).

Woolton, Lord (1959). *Memoirs of the Rt Hon The Earl of Woolton* (London: Cassell).

Wring, D. (2005). *The Politics of Marketing the Labour Party* (Basingstoke: Palgrave Macmillan).

Wring, D. and Ward, S. (2010). 'The Media and the 2010 Campaign: The Television Election?', *Parliamentary Affairs*, 63 (4): 802–17.

Young, H. (2001). 'Duncan Smith has Written the Tories Out of the Script', *The Guardian*, 11 October. Available at: http://www.guardian.co.uk/politics/2001/oct/11/conservatives2001.politicalcolumnists [accessed 5 December 2011].

Young, H. (2002). 'Where America has Elected to Go, No One Will Follow', *The Guardian*, 7 November.

Young, H. (2008). *The Hugo Young Papers: Thirty Years of British Politics – Off the Record* (London: Allen Lane).

Young, H. and Sloman, A. (1986). *The Thatcher Phenomenon* (London: BBC).

Young, K. (1970). *Sir Alec Douglas-Home* (London, J. M. Dent and Sons).

Ziegler, P. (1993). *Wilson: The Authorised Life of Lord Wilson of Rievaulx* (London: HarperCollins).

Ziegler, P. (2010). *Edward Heath: The Authorised Biography* (London: Harper Collins).

Zweiniger-Bargielowska, I. (1994). 'Rationing, Austerity and the Conservative Party Recovery after 1945', *Historical Journal*, 37 (1): 173–97.

Index

Acheson, Dean   89
Acland, Anthony   78
Akass, Jon   133
Allaun, Frank   127, 137–8
Armstrong, Hilary   158, 163–4, 166
Ashdown, Paddy   172
Asquith, H. H.   134
Assheton, Ralph   15
Atkinson, Norman   177
Attlee, Clement   2, 9, 20–32, 34–5, 44, 159, 242, 244

Baldwin, Stanley   15, 21, 132
Balfour, Arthur   15, 184
Balls, Ed   175
Beckett, Margaret   3–4, 68, 160, 162, 164, 166
Bell, Martin   196
Benn, Tony   40, 45, 60, 62–4, 112, 117–18, 120, 127, 129, 131, 136–9, 164–5
Bercow, John   198, 205, 218
Berkley, Humphrey   68, 74
Bevan, Nye   24–7, 30–2, 35, 37, 48, 124, 126, 137–8, 145
Biden, Joe   145
Bish, Geoff   130
Black, Guy   216
Blair, Tony   1–3, 34, 121–2, 142, 151, 153–5, 157–8, 161–3, 167–83, 191–2, 194, 199, 203, 210–13, 217, 221, 223–4, 231, 234, 236, 240, 242–3, 246–9
Block, Geoffrey   88
Blunkett, David   175
Bonham-Carter, Violet   9
Borrie, Gordon   161
Boyle, Edward   86
Bracken, Brendan   13, 17
Brittan, Leon   105
Brookway, Fenner   25
Brown, George   3, 50, 68, 73
Brown, Gordon   1–2, 4, 92, 161–4, 166, 170, 172–4, 176, 178, 190, 210,

217, 223, 225–6, 229, 232, 234, 244, 246
Buchannan-Smith, Alick   104
Butler, R. A.   11, 13, 16–9, 34, 68–9, 72–5

Callaghan James   1–2, 33, 50, 63, 98–100, 109–29, 131, 134–5, 138, 149, 159, 164, 167, 239, 240, 242–4
Cameron, David   2, 3, 6, 34, 97, 194, 205, 211, 217, 219, 221–38, 241–3, 246–9
Cameron, Samantha   224
Campbell, Alistair   160, 162, 171–2, 178–9, 181, 216
Carr, Robert   68
Carrington, Lord   76
Cartwright, John   135
Castle, Barbara   25, 57, 60, 62, 88, 132, 137, 139–40, 144
Chamberlain, Neville   21, 204
Cherwell, Lord   13
Churchill, Clementine   14, 17
Churchill, Randolph   10
Churchill, Winston   1, 3, 6–19, 21, 23, 27–8, 31, 107, 117, 199, 237–9, 242–5, 247
Clarke, Kenneth   185–6, 188, 191, 198, 202–7, 217, 243
Clegg, Nick   226, 235
Clinton, Bill   179
Coe, Sebastian   185, 187
Cocks, Michael   139
Coffman, Hilary   160
Cole, John   51
Collins, Tim   217
Commonwealth   22, 36, 43, 85–6
Consensus thesis   21, 23, 29, 34, 116, 123–4
Conservative Party Annual Conference
  (1946)   10
  (1947)   12
  (1950)   15
  (1965)   84
  (1977)   101